ABOUT THE AUTHORS

Peter D'Epiro received his Ph.D. in English from Yale University and works as an editor for *Patient Care* magazine. He has published a book and several articles on Ezra Pound's *Cantos*, a book of translations of African-American poetry into Italian, and rhymed verse translations from Dante's *Inferno*. He has a grown son, Dante, and lives with his wife, Nancy Walsh, in Ridgewood, New Jersey.

Mary Desmond Pinkowish received a B.A. from Trinity College in Hartford, Connecticut, where she studied biology and art history, and her master's degree from Yale University School of Medicine, Department of Epidemiology and Public Health. An editor and writer for *Patient Care* magazine, she lives with her husband, Peter, and their two children in Larchmont, New York.

Peter D'Epiro and Mary Desmond Pinkowish are coauthors of *What Are the Seven Wonders of the World? and 100 Other Great Cultural Lists—Fully Explicated* (Anchor Books, 1998).

ALSO BY PETER D'EPIRO AND MARY DESMOND PINKOWISH

*What Are the Seven Wonders of the World? and 100 Other
Great Cultural Lists—Fully Explicated*

Sprezzatura

50 WAYS
ITALIAN GENIUS
SHAPED THE WORLD

Sprezzatura

50 WAYS
ITALIAN GENIUS
SHAPED THE WORLD

Peter D'Epiro and Mary Desmond Pinkowish

ANCHOR BOOKS
A Division of Random House, Inc.
New York

FIRST ANCHOR BOOKS EDITION, OCTOBER 2001

Copyright © 2001 by Peter D'Epiro and Mary Desmond Pinkowish

Map by Joanne McCarthy

Grateful acknowledgment is made to the following to reprint previously published material:

Beard Books: An excerpt from *The Rise and Fall of the Medici Bank* by Raymond de Roover (1963). Reprinted by permission of Beard Books.

Rizzoli: An excerpt from *Ferrari 1947–1997* (1997). Reprinted by permission of Rizzoli.

Unless otherwise indicated, all verse translations from Latin and Italian sources and all prose translations from the works of Machiavelli, Della Casa, Leopardi, and Lampedusa are by Peter D'Epiro.

Library of Congress Cataloging-in-Publication Data
D'Epiro, Peter.
Sprezzatura : 50 ways Italian genius shaped the world / [Peter D'Epiro, Mary Desmond Pinkowish].— 1st Anchor Books ed.
p. cm.
ISBN 0-385-72019-X
1. Italy—Civilization. 2. Civilization, Modern—Italian influences. I. Pinkowish, Mary Desmond. II. Title.
DG442 .D46 2001
945—dc21
2001022765

Anchor ISBN: 0-385-72019-X

Book design by Oksana Kushnir

www.anchorbooks.com

Printed in the United States of America

10   9   8

Cover illustrations:
Giuliano de' Medici, Sandro Botticelli (1445–1510). National Gallery of Art, Washington, Samuel H. Kress Collection.
Violin: Courtesy of Culver Pictures.
Christopher Columbus: Courtesy of Culver Pictures.
Venus of Urbino, Titian (c. 1488–1576). Galleria degli Uffizi, Florence, Italy, Bridgeman Art Library, NY.
Ferrari: Copyright © AFB/Corbis.
Architectural Project for an Ideal City, Giuliano da Sangallo (1443–1516). Galleria Nazionale delle Marche, Urbino.
Julius Caesar: Copyright © Bettman/Corbis.
Leonardo da Vinci: Courtesy of Culver Pictures.

For our mothers

VIRGINIA CIAVOLELLA D'EPIRO, who first taught me
about her lovely native land, its mellifluous language,
and its warm and gifted people.

—P.D.

JEAN RIEPE DESMOND, who taught me that if
something is worth doing at all, it's worth doing right.

—M.D.P.

Everyone knows the difficulty of things that are exquisite and well done—so to have facility in such things gives rise to the greatest wonder.

—Baldassare Castiglione,
The Book of the Courtier (1528)

CONTENTS

FUNCTIONALITY AND BEAUTY ARE the very essence of Italian civilization. From the beginning, Italian genius has tended to be practical, down-to-earth, and concerned with getting things done, but it has also emphasized form, harmony, and radiance. A Roman aqueduct is not only durably functional but also lovely in its curves and proportions. The work of Dante, Giotto, Boccaccio, Donatello, and Masaccio brought a new realism into the arts—with incomparable grace.

The greatest achievements of the people who brought us the Renaissance have occurred mainly in the useful pursuits of life—law, political philosophy, business practices, anatomy and other applied sciences, exploration—and those that enhance life's beauty and pleasure—poetry (with a specialization in the amatory and erotic), the visual arts (ditto), music (especially in its most visually spectacular form, the opera), etiquette and comportment, film, fashion, and food. The ancient Roman and Venetian constitutions were marvels of their times; the institution of the Catholic Church, largely an Italian creation, has entered its third millennium; and universities, an Italian invention, seem here to stay, too.

When Castiglione (see Essay 27) advises his ideal courtier to do everything with a certain *sprezzatura,* he is providing suggestions on how to do things that are practical (even writing a love sonnet has a practical end in mind), and, most important, he is urging that they be done with a stylishness and panache that make them look easy. This "aesthetic pragmatism" has its roots in Italy's incomparable tradition of craftsmanship throughout the ages and is still evident in the country's flair for design, whether of clothes, furniture, utensils, buildings, railway tunnels, or custom-made automobiles.

The emphasis on the pragmatic and the lovely surface, at the expense of the ponderous, speculative, and metaphysical, has caused some to think of Italian civilization as somewhat superficial, but a moment's reflection on the life and thought of people like Francis of Assisi, Thomas Aquinas, Dante, Michelangelo, Galileo, and many of the other figures highlighted in this book must dispel that notion.

We here present fifty outstanding Italian contributions to world civilization out of a possible fifty thousand. Aside from our own biases and preferences, our selection criteria have generally been guided by the wish to focus on significant achievements that have been realized by Italians first, best, or most influentially over the past twenty-five centuries or so. (For the purposes of this book, Italians are people who were born in Italy and spent at least the formative part of their lives there—hence an inclusion like Frederick II Hohenstaufen in Essay 12.) Some of the essays focus on achievements that are entire cultural or geopolitical entities in themselves—like those on Venice and the unification of Italy—and a few deal with somewhat roguish figures, just for the sake of chiaroscuro (see Essays 22, 28, 43).

Our last book included a long essay on the most famous sons and daughters of Italy's twenty regions, and that work served as a springboard for the present volume. Here we have provided the general reader with a closer look at Italy's extraordinary cultural legacy, which is rivaled only by that of Greece, China, the British Isles, and France. Since Italy can also claim to have civilized the rest of Europe, and its contribution to the visual arts has never been surpassed, we were faced with a true embarrassment of riches in choosing our topics.

Flaubert said of writing his historical novel *Salammbô*, "Few would be able to guess how sad one had to be in order to resuscitate Carthage." Our experience in attempting to resurrect some of the outstanding personalities and achievements of the Italian people, from ancient Roman times to the present, has been a joyful one. We wish to thank some of the people who helped smooth our way, and first our contributors— Dante D'Epiro, Richard Jackson, Thomas Matrullo, and Nancy Walsh (see page 397)—who not only wrote essays but also provided invaluable guidance all along. Antonio Contestabile, Professor of Neurobiology, University of Bologna, helped clarify the issues in Essay 39; Tag Gallagher, Roberto Rossellini's biographer, made perceptive comments on Essay 47; Monica Green, Ph.D., Associate Professor of History, Duke University, sent suggestions and a prepublication version of a book chapter that helped with Essay 10; Robert Greenberg, Ph.D., Chair of the Department of Music History and Literature, the San Francisco

Conservatory of Music, and lecturer for the Teaching Company, Springfield, Virginia, provided a thoughtful commentary on Essays 32 and 35; Joanne McCarthy, our friend and colleague, designed our map of Italy, took a very lively interest in our book, and provided excellent advice on production-related matters; Ray Minichiello, P.E., Chairman of the G. Marconi Foundation, USA, Inc., and the U.S. National Marconi Museum, reviewed Essay 45 for us; Frank A. Rella, B.Litt. (Oxon.), shared his reminiscences of Venice and Rimini; the late Fabio Sampoli, Ph.D., *toscanissimo*, helped us decide on this book topic and supplied us with characteristically shrewd insights.

We are truly fortunate to have an agent like Raphael Sagalyn and editors like Tina Pohlman and Alice van Straalen. We thank Linda B. Desmond for her advice on Essay 36, and Joan Desmond, Mary Boone, Vicki Eng, and Rita Miller for their intelligent, informed commiseration throughout. We are profoundly grateful to Ned Desmond for his unstinting cheerleading, and to Nancy Walsh and Peter, Michael, and Caroline Pinkowish for their endless patience.

Peter D'Epiro
Mary Desmond Pinkowish

Sprezzatura

50 WAYS
ITALIAN GENIUS
SHAPED THE WORLD

One

Rome gives the world a calendar—twice

Caesar called in the best scholars and mathematicians of his time and, out of the systems he had before him, formed a new and more exact method of correcting the calendar, which the Romans use to this day, and seem to succeed better than any nation in avoiding the errors occasioned by the inequality of the solar and lunar years.
—Plutarch, *Lives*, "Life of Julius Caesar" (c. A.D. 100)

DESPITE CURRENT USE OF about forty traditional or religious calendars (such as the Jewish, Islamic, Hindu, and Chinese), it is the calendar of Julius Caesar, as slightly modified by Pope Gregory XIII, that functions as the worldwide civil norm. Yet it was a long, tortuous road that led to nearly universal adoption of this rational and elegant tool for measuring the length of the year.

In its earliest known form, the Roman calendar had only 10 months and 304 days, leaving 61 days in winter uncounted and unaccounted for. This peculiar method of reckoning time was attributed to Rome's legendary founder and first king, Romulus (traditionally reigned 753–717 B.C.). In those days, January and February didn't yet exist (at least in the calendar), since Roman farmers didn't have much fieldwork to do in that dead part of the year after the last crops had been harvested and stored. After a two-month hiatus, the new year began in March with preparation of the ground for the next season's crop.

Although Ovid, in his long poem on the Roman calendar, the *Fasti*, quips that Romulus was better at war than at astronomy, at least some of us might wish that "the year of Romulus" had prevailed, with all those discretionary days at the end. It was too good to last. The religious lawgiver Numa Pompilius, legendary second king of Rome, was credited with introducing, in about 700 B.C., the months of January and February at the end of the Roman year, lengthening it by 51 days. However, this

355-day year of what came to be called the Roman republican calendar was more probably brought to the city by the Etruscan Tarquinius Priscus (616–579 B.C.), traditionally Rome's fifth king.

The main purpose of this calendar was to ensure proper observance of forty-five religious festivals and to indicate on which days public business could or could not be conducted. Four months had 31 days, February had 28, and the rest had 29. In the attempt to rectify the discrepancy between this lunar 355-day year and the solar year, an extra month called Mercedonius, which had 27 and 28 days alternately, was intercalated every other year after February 23. (February 24 through 28 were apparently not observed in years with intercalations.) This meant that any four-year cycle contained 1,465 days, with the year averaging 366.25 days. First way too short, now a tad too long.

Compounding the problem, the intercalations were often haphazard, as a result of ignorance or political motives. (An artificially short year meant less time in office for magistrates who had made themselves unpopular with the pontiffs, the priests responsible for ordering the intercalations.)

Lunar calendars like early Rome's are notoriously troublesome. A year of 12 lunar months, or lunations, each averaging 29.5 days, consists of only 354 days. (The Roman republican calendar added an extra day to its year, since the even numbers were considered unlucky.) For a lunar calendar to remain in sync with the solar year of roughly 365.25 days and the turning of the seasons, a month of various lengths must be intercalated every few years.

By the time of Julius Caesar, the calendar was several months out of whack with the seasons. But while in Egypt in 48–47 B.C., Caesar discussed the Egyptian solar calendar with Alexandrian savants. As *pontifex maximus,* or chief priest, of the Roman religion, he was familiar with the responsibilities of the College of Pontiffs to regulate the calendar, including the insertion of intercalary months. But there had been only one intercalation since 58 B.C.

As dictator of Rome, Caesar was planning stupendous military campaigns in the East, and he wanted a single official calendar that would keep in step with the sun. Since January was now occurring in autumn, the harvest and vintage festivals and the proper times for planting and sailing were losing all correspondence with the seasons, and anarchic time-reckoning complicated the empire's legal and commercial transactions.

With his chief consultant, Sosigenes, an Alexandrian Greek astronomer and mathematician, Caesar devised a new calendar for the new Rome he was to rule, from Spain to the Middle East: a purely solar calendar of 12 months and 365 days with a leap year occurring every fourth year. Based on the calendar devised by the Alexandrian astronomer Aristarchus in 239 B.C., this Julian calendar was adapted by Caesar for the Roman world in 46 B.C. The extra day of leap years was worked in by repeating February 23 (which had once functioned as the last day of the Roman year). The length of most months was also changed.

Caesar ordered two intercalations in 46 B.C.: the first, which was normally due to be made that year under the old system, of 23 days in February; the second, the addition of 67 days in the fall to realign the calendar with the seasons. The 355-day year was thus bloated by 90 days, adding up to a truly epic 445 days—"the last year of confusion," as it was called.

The era of the Julian calendar formally began on New Year's Day, January 1, 45 B.C. A little more than a year after this epochal reform, Caesar was assassinated, but not before July was named in his honor (just as August was later named for his successor, Augustus). July was originally *Quintilis* ("fifth month") and August *Sextilis* ("sixth month"), harking back to when the Roman year began in March. The Latin names of our other months were handed down from very early Roman times.

The Julian calendar was adopted throughout the Roman Empire and later by the nascent Christian Church. For more than 1,600 years it served as the calendar for much of the Western world, and it's essentially the one we use today, but for the fine-tuning of a late-sixteenth-century pope.

After the Roman world was Christianized, the most significant calendrical developments in the West were the establishment of the modern week and the advent of the A.D. dating system. The ancient Romans originally had an eight-day week. By edict of Constantine the Great in A.D. 321, this was officially replaced by a seven-day week with Sunday (*dies solis*) as the first day, which was confirmed as the Christian day of worship. The account in Genesis of the first seven days of the world was clearly a major influence on this development.

The practice of dating events in years after the birth of Christ was devised in the early sixth century by the Roman abbot Dionysius Exiguus, although Jesus himself was probably born in 4 or 5 B.C. rather than in A.D. 1, as Dionysius had calculated. Dionysius also neglected to include a year 0, since the concept of zero had not yet been invented. This explains why 2001, and not 2000, actually marked the beginning of the current millennium.

The A.D. system is named for the Latin *anno Domini* ("in the year of our Lord"). Although the Roman scholar and monk Cassiodorus used A.D. dating in a published work as early as 562, it became widespread in Europe only in the tenth century. The use of B.C. ("before Christ") dating began in the seventeenth century. Before that, Western scholars counted years before the Christian era by using either the A.U.C. system (*ab urbe condita*, "from the founding of the city [of Rome]," which traditionally occurred in 753 B.C.) or the A.M. (*anno mundi*, "year of the world") reckoning of the Jewish calendar, which dates events from 3761 B.C., the supposed year of the Creation.

In the meantime, the average length of the Julian year, 365.25 days, kept right on varying from the true solar year of 365.242199 days. Caesar's year turned out to be 11 minutes, 14 seconds too long. About every 1⅓ centuries, the surfeit amounts to one day's additional deviation from the true progression of the seasons. By the sixteenth century the date of Easter, which is calculated with reference to the moon and the vernal equinox (then occurring on March 11), had drifted too far from the astronomical beginning of spring.

When the canon lawyer Ugo Boncompagni became Pope Gregory XIII (reigned 1572–85), he inherited a mandate from the Council of Trent to do something about the scandal of the dating of Easter, the most important Christian festival. In true modern style, Gregory appointed a committee to study the question. Among the proposals for revising the calendar was one from a physician and astronomer, Luigi Lilio (1510–76), who hailed from Calabria and later studied in Naples and taught at the University of Perugia.

In 1576 Lilio's manuscript was presented to the committee by his brother Antonio, also a physician, since Luigi had died earlier that year. Four years later, the pope's blue-ribbon panel welcomed Ignazio Danti (1536–86), a versatile Dominican friar who was a mathematician, astronomer, mapmaker, artist, and university professor. Danti had constructed a gnomon, a kind of gigantic sundial, in the church of San Petronio in Bologna, which confirmed the precise discrepancy of the Julian calendar from the true solar year.

The most prominent committee member was a Bavarian Jesuit astronomer and mathematician, Christopher Clavius (1537–1612), who became convinced of the soundness of Luigi Lilio's proposals and apparently wrote the bulky final draft of the panel's recommendations. To secure a more accurate length for the year over the long term, Lilio had suggested that century years not divisible by 400 should not be leap years. This would shave off 3 days of excess Julian-calendar accrual every 400 years, since Caesar's calendar had stipulated a leap year every four without exception. To correct the Julian calendar for its drift over more than sixteen centuries, Lilio had proposed either omitting the extra day from all the leap years slated for the next 40 years or just dropping 10 days from an upcoming year.

On February 24, 1582, the white-bearded octogenarian Gregory XIII issued the papal bull *Inter gravissimas*, which instituted the Gregorian calendar reforms. To catch up with the sun, that year was shorn of 10 days: The day after October 4 was declared to be October 15. This measure brought the date of the vernal equinox into conformity with what it had been in the days of the First Council of Nicaea, which in A.D. 325 had authoritatively ruled on how to use the beginning of spring to determine the movable feast of Easter.

Aside from the 10 days deleted from 1582, the major change of the Gregorian calendar was its requirement that years like 1700, 1800, 1900, and 2100 should not be considered leap years. In addition, New Year's Day was definitively established as January 1 (there had been many local variants), and the extra day of leap years was to be inserted after February 28.

The Gregorian calendar was soon adopted in the Catholic world but resoundingly rejected in all Protestant territories. Only more than a century later, between 1699 and 1701, did Denmark and the Protestant regions of the Netherlands, Germany, and Switzerland accede to the reasonableness of the "popish calendar." Great Britain and its colonies proved even more stubborn, retaining the Julian calendar until 1752. By that time 11 days had to be dropped to catch up, since 1700 had been a leap year in Britain but not according to the Gregorian calendar. Thus Parliament decreed that in 1752 the day after Wednesday, September 2, was to be Thursday, September 14. The beginning of the year was also moved from March 25 to January 1. To avoid all reference to Pope Gregory, the British had christened his calendar the New Style calendar (N.S.), while Julian reckoning was dubbed Old Style (O.S.).

Japan adopted the Gregorian calendar in 1873, Eastern Europe and Russia between 1912 and 1919, Greece in 1924, Turkey in 1927. China accepted Pope Gregory's calendar in 1912—but not throughout the entire country until 1949—and its traditional lunar calendar is also used. The Eastern Orthodox Churches still rely on the Julian calendar for determining Easter and thus celebrate it on a different day from Roman Catholics and Protestants.

But the average Gregorian year of 365.2422 days still runs almost 26 seconds faster than the true year. Since 1582, the surplus has amounted to about 3 hours. A further refinement—that of omitting a leap day from all years exactly divisible by 4000—will keep the Gregorian year accurate to within 1 day in 20,000 years.

Our official year is no longer measured in days, minutes, and seconds but in the number of atomic oscillations (290,091,200,500,000,000) of the rare metal cesium. Before humans were capable of feats like that, however, it was the determination of Julius Caesar and, much later, Luigi Lilio and Pope Gregory XIII that provided the world with a relatively uncomplicated and scientifically respectable method for keeping track of all-important time.

Two

The Roman Republic and our own

> My task from now on will be to trace the history in peace and war
> of a free nation, governed by annually elected officers of state and
> subject not to the caprice of individual men, but to the overriding
> authority of law.
>
> —Livy, *History of Rome*, Book 2 (c. 29 B.C.)

WITH ITS MIXED FORM of government and checks and balances, the
ancient Roman Republic served as a model for later constitutions, most
notably that of the United States. It's no accident that our system of
government—devised by men steeped in the classics—reflects the intricate countervailing forces of the Roman constitution, and that even our
words *republic, constitution, president, Congress, representative, executive,
legislature, assembly, judiciary, vote, veto, candidate, election, states,
plebiscite*, and so many others that figure in our political life are derived
from Latin. Congress, with our own version of the Senate, meets on
Capitol Hill, named for the citadel and spiritual center of Republican
Rome.

After the Roman patricians expelled the last of their kings, the hated
Etruscan Tarquin the Proud, in about 509 B.C., they established a republic. Originally a semipriestly caste, the patricians were aristocrats who
had served in the Senate (the king's council), and they now arrogated
all power in the new government to themselves, leaving the plebeians
with no political voice. Repeated clashes between the two orders led to
the development of an unwritten constitution that recognized three
sources of authority: the Senate, the magistrates, and the people.

The **Senate** was technically only an advisory body to the Roman
magistrates, but the wealth, social prestige, and political experience of
its three hundred members made it the most important arm of government in the Roman Republic, which has been described as an oligarchy
of senatorial landowners. Although its resolutions did not have the

force of law, the magistrates generally followed its advice. In addition to much of the legislative process, the Senate controlled state finances and domestic and foreign policy. It gradually became a body of ex-magistrates, and thus its members were indirectly elected by the people. Membership was for life, subject to good behavior.

Like most of the other **magistrates**, the second branch of the Roman government, the two consuls were elected yearly. They wielded supreme administrative and military power (the *imperium*), enforced the laws, and convened and presided over meetings of the Senate and the popular assembly. These magistrates were an impressive blend of chief executive, commander-in-chief, field general, legislator by edict, and priestly functionary. There were two of them, however, and each could overrule the other's acts.

After almost two centuries of sporadic political strife, plebeians won the right to stand for the consulship and the other magistracies, since there were now enough wealthy and powerful plebeian landowners to challenge the patricians' monopoly of office. Indeed, one of the consuls *had* to be a plebeian, though this stipulation was sometimes ignored. Thus, a new social and political ruling class took shape after about 300 B.C., that of the consular or senatorial nobility, encompassing all families, patrician or plebeian, that had produced a consul.

Ranking next below the consuls were the praetors, legal officers who controlled the Roman court system. Possessing the *imperium*, these magistrates could also command armies and govern provinces. Beginning in 197 B.C., the number of praetors elected annually was six. The four aediles were magistrates in charge of policing the streets and marketplace. They were also responsible for the elaborate games and festivals that were the delight of the Roman populace. The eight quaestors were treasury officials and financial officers.

Other Roman magistrates were the censor and dictator. Two censors held office for one and a half out of every four years (later five). They were often revered ex-consuls whose duties included conducting the census, supervising morals, removing from the Senate any members who didn't live up to standards, and overseeing taxation, state property and finance, and construction projects. The most famous censor was Cato the Elder, who held the office in 184 B.C. His austere old-style Roman virtue became legendary, and, much later, his hostility toward Rome's ancient enemy led him to end all of his speeches, on whatever topic, with the words, "In addition, I think Carthage should be destroyed."

In the early Republic, a dictator was a constitutional magistrate entrusted with supreme powers to deal with a military or political emergency. His term was six months, though he was expected to step down as soon as the crisis was over. The dictator was appointed by one of the consuls after debate in the Senate and confirmation by the popular assembly. The dictatorship was mainly resorted to in the fourth and third centuries B.C. The later form, that of Sulla and Julius Caesar, was an unconstitutional usurpation of power (see Essay 3).

Though technically not magistrates, the ten tribunes of the people, who served one-year terms, came to exercise vast political powers in Rome. These officials were first elected to protect the people against the excesses of magistrates in the early fifth century B.C. Their persons were sacrosanct (they couldn't be arrested or prosecuted, and violence against them was punishable by death), and each had the veto (literally, "I forbid!") over all consular edicts and senatorial or popular resolutions. Tribunes could introduce motions in the Senate and in one of the popular assemblies. They could also invoke a primitive kind of habeas corpus when any citizen was arrested.

The third branch of the Roman government was the **people** (consisting of patricians and plebeians), whose political power was embodied in several popular assemblies of male citizens over seventeen. The most important was the *comitia centuriata* (centuriate assembly), which voted on war and peace, judged citizens charged with capital crimes, and elected the higher magistrates, though only from candidates nominated by the Senate. This assembly could enact or defeat laws proposed to it by the consuls but lacked powers of deliberation or amendment. The voting system was stacked to favor the wealthy.

Although the people exercised theoretical sovereignty, the Senate's power remained foremost. Yet the rights and liberty of ordinary citizens were safeguarded in Rome as in no other state in antiquity, especially as the edifice of Roman law grew in scope and complexity (see Essay 8). There was no prouder formula for the power behind the decrees of any ancient state than that of *Senatus populusque Romanus—S.P.Q.R.—*the Senate and People of Rome.

Had it not been for the Greek historian Polybius, who lived in Rome in the mid-second century B.C., the American Constitution would read very differently. It was he who saw in the Roman republican constitution an ideal form of "mixed government," combining elements of monarchy in the consuls, aristocracy in the Senate, and democracy in the popular assemblies and the tribunes. Polybius had written his history to explain how the unparalleled imperial expansion of Rome in a mere half century (220–167 B.C.) was largely owing to its superior form of government. Statesmen of the new American nation pondered his words, since most of them believed that "the Roman republic attained to the utmost height of human greatness," as Alexander Hamilton wrote in *Federalist* No. 24.

According to Polybius, Rome benefited from its ability to incorporate the political wisdom and separate interests of the few and the many. Each branch of government—magistrates, Senate, and people—had to cultivate the support of the others if any state business was to be conducted. "The result is a union which is strong enough to withstand all emergencies," he concludes, "so that it is impossible to find a better form of constitution than this" (6.18).

In addition, only a mixed government, combining aspects of Aristotle's three ideal types (monarchies, aristocracies, and democracies), could avoid the degeneration over time that afflicted unmixed governments. Monarchies tended to degenerate into brutal tyrannies, aristocracies (rule by the best citizens) tended to become self-serving oligarchies (rule by the few), and democracies usually ended in ochlocracy (mob rule) or sheer anarchy. Constitutions that made room for all three main formulations of government "should remain for a long while in a state of equilibrium," Polybius claims, "thanks to the principle of reciprocity or counteraction" (6.10).

Despite certain exaggerations in Polybius's view (consuls were not really like monarchs), he correctly identifies a main strength of the Roman constitution. While the division of power among its various branches did not prevent the state from being controlled by the rich few, it allowed for enough popular features, especially in the tribunes' veto power, to keep the Senate on its toes.

Aside from Polybius and other ancient theorists such as Plato, Aristotle, and Cicero, Americans had a wealth of political tradition to draw on: the concepts of the English common law and the unwritten British constitution, the example of the English Puritan revolution of the 1640s, and the seminal writings of John Locke. American statesmen were also keen students of the Baron de Montesquieu, the French political thinker whose *Spirit of Laws* (1748) extolled the virtues of mixed government, which the colonists called "checks and balances."

Yet such was their distaste for the executive prerogatives of their former king and his governors that they established a unicameral Continental Congress during the Revolutionary War and carried over this "unmixed" form of government into the Articles of Confederation of 1781. The infant nation lacked an executive department and a permanent federal judiciary. The individual states were like feuding nations that had joined a loose "league of friendship" that couldn't tax its citizens, pay its debts, or compel individual Americans to abide by its decisions.

On the state level, however, all the new constitutions drawn up after the Declaration of Independence provided for the three main branches of government—executive, legislative, and judiciary—and tried to separate their powers. At the Constitutional Convention, summoned to create a viable instrument of state to replace the Articles of Confederation, the new Federal Constitution, drafted by James Madison in 1787, entrusted the central government with extensive powers over states and individuals alike. But it also incorporated the separation of powers and extensive checks and balances that ultimately derived from the Roman republican constitution.

As in ancient Rome, sovereignty was vested in the people. Two legislative houses were established. Members of the Senate, a more elite upper house with fewer members, were given six-year terms (versus the lifetime tenure of their Roman counterparts). They were originally elected not by the people but by their state legislatures. (Direct election of senators was introduced only by the Seventeenth Amendment in 1913.) The U.S. Senate was thus meant to foster the interests of stability, wealth, and property. Treaties made by the President, as well as the appointment of ambassadors, justices of the Supreme Court, other federal judges, Cabinet members, and other high-ranking federal officers, are subject to its approval, in a reflection of the foreign- and domestic-policy prerogatives of the ancient Roman Senate.

By contrast, the House of Representatives, with its rapid two-year turnover and popular election, was intended to keep its finger on the pulse of the people. Our lower House was seen as an analog of the college of tribunes, the representatives of the Roman populace. Hamilton was confident that the House would hold its own against the "aristocratic" tendencies of the U.S. Senate (*Federalist*, No. 63). This dichotomy of the Senate as the mouthpiece of wealth and the House as the voice of the masses was derived not only from similar bodies in

Roman history but also from the Lords and Commons of the British Parliament.

The Founding Fathers decided against "destroying the unity of the Executive," as Rome had done with its two coequal consuls (Hamilton, *Federalist*, No. 70). Like the consuls, the President is chief executive and commander-in-chief of the armed forces, but he is not a field general. Civilian control of the military in the U.S. Constitution avoids the later Roman Republic's fatal flaw of conferring immense political power on military leaders who proceeded to set up dictatorships or embroil the nation in civil wars. Again like the consuls, the President can issue decrees (executive orders). The Roman tribune's veto was given to the President, not the people, though his power to strike down legislation can be overridden by Congress.

Finally, the Framers were careful to create an independent U.S. judiciary. Although Supreme Court justices and other federal judges are appointed by the President, their lifetime tenure renders them impervious to executive control.

Despite the fact that the Roman and American constitutions were the most enlightened of their times, neither outlawed slavery or extended political rights to women. Yet the legal concept of inalienable rights for all began its slow, circuitous evolution twenty-five hundred years ago with the establishment of the Roman tribunes, the world's first public officials entrusted with protecting ordinary citizens from the arrogance of entrenched power.

Three

Julius Caesar and the imperial purple

If you must break the law, do it only for the sake of seizing power.
In all other cases, show respect for it.
—Julius Caesar, quoted by Cicero, *On Duties* (44 B.C.)

ON FEBRUARY 15, 44 B.C., during the fertility festival of the Lupercalia, Julius Caesar sat on the Rostra in the Forum, watching Roman magistrates and young nobles in goatskin loincloths running across the Palatine hill. Recently made dictator for life, he was appearing in public for the first time wearing the purple toga of the ancient Roman kings and seated on a gilded throne. One of the runners, Mark Antony, approached with a diadem and placed it on his head. When the mob groaned, the dictator ordered the crown taken to the Temple of Jupiter. This piece of political theater had probably been staged by Caesar to quell the rumors that he aspired to monarchy, though he was already king in all but name.

Ancient Rome, which gave the world the prototypical republic (see Essay 2), also transmitted to later Europe the antithetical model of absolute monarchic rule over an imperial state. If the first and greatest of the Caesars hadn't established his autocratic power in Rome, the corrupt and suicidally divisive oligarchic government might have succumbed much earlier to the onslaught of barbarians from the north and east, and Greco-Roman civilization might have perished. Instead, with Caesar pointing the way, the strong centralized rule of the Roman emperors, despite periodic disruption, rebellion, and even chaos, fended off the Germanic takeover for another five hundred years. By that time, the imperial territories, especially in the West, had become so thoroughly Romanized that the cultural heritage of the classical world was ensured of survival, even if for centuries it led only an attenuated existence in Christian monasteries (see Essay 9).

Gaius Julius Caesar was born in Rome on July 13, 100 B.C., into the Julian patrician clan, which claimed descent from Iulus, son of Aeneas, the Trojan ancestor of Romulus, founder and first king of Rome. Aeneas himself was son of the goddess Venus. More important than Caesar's impressive mythological pedigree was the fact that his father's sister Julia was wife to the fierce, vindictive general and statesman Gaius Marius. When Caesar was a boy, during the civil war that erupted in 88 B.C., Marius emerged as champion of the *populares,* the "Popular" political faction that seized control of Rome in the following year and inaugurated a reign of terror. Marius, who died in 86 B.C., had been opposed by Lucius Cornelius Sulla (leader of the *optimates,* or "best men"), who marched on Rome and used proscriptions (his invention) and the ensuing bloodbaths to reestablish the senatorial oligarchy's control of the state.

Caesar grew to be tall and gauntly handsome with dark, piercing eyes in this time of internecine strife and Sulla's dictatorship. Although he received a splendid education, he was also a wild young man, spending recklessly and cultivating numerous mistresses. Even decades later, when he celebrated his triumph over Gaul, his soldiers lustily sang out, "Men of Rome, guard your wives, we bring you the bald adulterer!" Never a heavy drinker, he was characterized by his enemy Cato the Younger as "the only sober man who ever tried to wreck the constitution."

Caesar was arguably the greatest Roman genius, but his first political decision was hardly shrewd. At age sixteen he had married Cornelia, a daughter of Cinna, the Popular consul and absolute despot of a few years earlier. Sulla ordered Caesar to divorce her. When the nineteen-year-old refused, the dictator confiscated his inheritance and his wife's dowry, and only the intercession of powerful friends persuaded him to spare his life. "There's many a Marius in this young fellow Caesar," Sulla warned.

Like his redoubtable uncle Marius, seven times consul of Rome who defeated the African king Jugurtha and cut to pieces the invading barbarian armies of the Cimbri and the Teutones, Caesar soon proved his mettle in battle. Removing himself from Sulla's Rome, he became an army officer and, at the capture of Mytilene, in Lesbos, won the oak-wreath civic crown for saving a fellow soldier's life.

Seeking to perfect his oratorical skills, he embarked for Rhodes at age twenty-five to study with Cicero's former teacher. On the way, he fell into the hands of Cilician pirates, the scourge of the Mediterranean, who held him hostage for about six weeks. While friends raised his huge ransom, he exercised with his captors, called them illiterate barbarians when they failed to appreciate recitations of his poems, and playfully threatened to have them executed someday. On his release, he immediately raised a naval force on his own authority, captured the pirates (recovering his ransom), and crucified them all. In the earliest instance of his touted clemency to vanquished enemies, he had their throats cut first.

After Cornelia's death in 69 B.C., he married Pompeia, a granddaughter of Sulla. This by no means signaled a shift in political orientation. His new wife was immensely wealthy, and Caesar's ambitions and extravagant spending—on political favors, women, dinner parties, houses, rare gems, statuary, and attractive slaves—required mountains of money in pricey Rome.

As aedile in 65 B.C., he courted the Roman mob with the most spectacular gladiatorial contests, wild-beast hunts, and circus games in the city's history, paid for by loans from multimillionaire Marcus Licinius Crassus, who had financed his candidacy. Caesar had also made overtures to Gaius Pompeius Magnus—Pompey the Great—by supporting a measure to give him unprecedented extraconstitutional powers in the protracted war against Mithridates, King of Pontus in Asia Minor.

In 63 B.C., Caesar's enormous bribes secured his election as *pontifex maximus,* high priest of Rome. At year's end, he found himself pitted against the entire Senate for the first time when, during the conspiracy of the disaffected patrician Catiline in the consulship of Cicero, he alone spoke against the death penalty for the five arrested ringleaders. His arguments had swayed the Senate to his view when his bête noire, Cato the Younger, stood up and carried the day for immediate execution. Cicero had the men strangled in prison.

After serving as praetor (head of the courts), Caesar was appointed governor of Farther Spain, and he left for his province without waiting for the Senate's formal confirmation (just as he later returned without waiting to be relieved). When his colleagues sneered at an Alpine village they were passing through, he said, "I'd rather be first man among these people than second at Rome."

In Spain he spared himself the tedium of provincial administration in favor of ruthlessly attacking independent tribes. Growing rich on plunder, he sent some of it back to the treasury at Rome and used the rest to buy political patronage and pay off some of his astronomical debts.

It was after his year as governor that the Senate made its first irreparable mistake in its dealings with him. Caesar expected to be awarded a triumph for his military victories in Spain and to stand for the consulship. There was a Catch-22, however: Roman law stipulated both that a conquering general could not enter the city before celebrating his triumph (unless he chose to forgo it) and that anyone seeking the consulship had to declare his candidacy in the city.

Despite ample precedent for waiving the latter requirement, Cato filibustered until the Senate denied Caesar permission to stand for the consulship in absentia. Forced to choose between a military parade and the highest state office, Caesar chose the reality of power rather than its mere trappings, but he soon made the Senate regret its attempt to trifle with him.

This retaliation took the form of persuading Rome's two most powerful men, Pompey and Crassus, whom the Senate had also slighted, to put aside their long-standing animosities and cooperate with him to achieve their designs. Thus arose the cabal that modern historians have called the First Triumvirate (group of three men), a private pact for shattering the senatorial oligarchy. Less kindly, the Roman polymath Marcus Varro dubbed it "The Beast with Three Heads."

Acting in concert, Pompey's veterans, Crassus's money, and Caesar's popularity could control the Senate, magistrates, and popular assemblies—in short, the Roman government. Each triumvir agreed not to support any measure that was opposed by one of the others and to place at their common disposal his network of henchmen and dependents to vote, bribe, and intimidate as needed.

The plan called for Caesar to be elected consul for 59 B.C. Once in office, Caesar acted more like a fire-eating tribune of the people—a Tiberius or Gaius Gracchus of the preceding century—than an austere Roman consul, ramming through his program of land-distributing legislation by taking his motions to the popular assemblies when the Senate balked at his proposals. To cement the new political alliance, Caesar married off his young daughter Julia to Pompey.

The audacity of Caesar's political gamble forced him to keep upping the ante. When the Senate tried to assign him supervision of Italy's cattle roads and forests as his proconsular duties after his one-year term of office, he got a tribune to secure him the governorships of Cisalpine Gaul (northern Italy) and Illyricum (the eastern Adriatic coastline) for an extraordinary five-year command instead of the usual single year. To these appointments was added the governorship of Transalpine Gaul (Provence and Languedoc) at Pompey's insistence when the governor-designate died suddenly.

During this time, not only would Caesar be immune from prosecution for his improprieties as consul, but he would also govern provinces close to Italy and have the right to raise armies. In an affront to the Senate, he refused its conciliatory offer to reenact all his "irregular" consular legislation in due and proper form, considering it an aspersion on his honor (and a tacit admission of guilt).

Having divorced Pompeia, Caesar married Calpurnia before embarking on his proconsulship, during which, by picking quarrels with friend and foe, he conquered barbarian Gaul. Though Roman governors were supposed to defend their frontiers, not engage in military adventures, he proceeded to carve out vast new territories for the Empire, including most of modern-day France, Switzerland, Belgium, southern Holland, and Germany west of the Rhine.

Caesar spent almost nine years in Gaul, shaping foreign policy, bribing cities and kings, warring at his own discretion, plundering on a cosmic scale, judging, condemning to death, and holding court while most of the Senate flocked to him at his winter quarters. He commanded as many as eleven legions and ten generals; amassed the wealth of a Croesus; captured eight hundred cities, towns, and forts; killed a million Gallic warriors; and enslaved another million. He forged a loyal, battle-hardened army that, in his words, "could storm the very heavens."

It was inevitable that Caesar's military glory would rankle Pompey and that Crassus, always resentful of Pompey for stealing his thunder, would grow restive again. In 56 B.C., Caesar met with his partners to patch up their agreement. The upshot was that Pompey and Crassus would share the consulship of 55 B.C., after which they would secure five-year governorships of Spain and Syria, respectively, and see to it that Caesar's Gallic command would be extended for another five years. With a little help from Caesar's soldiers (who were sent to Rome to vote) and Pompey's thugs (who administered beatings to the opposition), their program was achieved.

But after his beloved wife Julia died in childbirth in 54 B.C., Pompey began drifting closer to the Senate. The final unraveling of the triumvirate occurred in the following year, when Crassus, seeking to emulate his warrior partners, led a Roman army of 44,000 to a stunning defeat at the hands of the Parthians at Carrhae in Mesopotamia, where he lost his life.

As Caesar's term in Gaul drew to a close, the Optimates blundered catastrophically. Rome's outstanding general needed two things from them: retention of his command until the end of 49 B.C. and permission to stand for the consulship of 48 in absentia. These provisions would enable him to remain immune from prosecution for the foreseeable future, since he doubtlessly planned to secure another lengthy proconsulship after his year in office.

But the hardliners in Rome began agitating to recall Caesar prematurely. The moment he returned to Rome as a private citizen, stripped of his proconsular command (and his army) and lacking the *imperium* of a new consulship, he would pay the price for his notorious year as consul and his abuse of authority in Gaul. Even if the Senate judged him leniently, exile and political ruin were assured.

On January 7, 49 B.C., the Senate issued an ultimatum demanding that Caesar surrender his military command, and investing Pompey and the other magistrates with dictatorial powers. For the sake of his honor, which, he wrote, had always been dearer to him than life itself, Caesar took up the Senate's challenge. On the night of January 10–11, he crossed the bridge over the Rubicon, a small river near Rimini, the boundary between Cisalpine Gaul and Italy proper, with only his thirteenth legion—about five thousand men. *"Anerrhiphtho kubos,"* he said in Greek, quoting the playwright Menander: "Let the die be cast."

Caesar swept down the eastern coast of the peninsula as towns flung open their gates. Pompey, who had boasted that all he had to do was stamp his foot and soldiers would come flocking to his standards, was caught with his toga down. With both consuls and most of the Senate he abandoned Rome on January 17 and, on March 17, set sail for Epirus in northwestern Greece. In two months, using his time-tested strategies of blazing speed and surprise, Caesar had become master of Italy with almost no bloodshed.

The Republican plan was to crush Caesar in Italy with simultaneous advances by the Roman armies in the East and those in Spain. In a brilliant lightning campaign, Caesar knocked Spain out of the war in forty-four days. In the interim he seized the contents of the treasury in Rome, had himself appointed dictator to supervise the elections, and emerged as consul for 48 B.C.

After crossing the Adriatic, he outgeneraled Pompey at the Battle of Pharsalus in Thessaly, Greece, on August 9, 48 B.C., although his army was outnumbered by two to one. "They asked for this," the victor commented while surveying the 15,000 dead of the enemy forces. "I, Julius Caesar, despite all my achievements, was to be condemned, unless I called on my army for help."

Pompey fled to Alexandria, Egypt, where he was immediately murdered by order of young King Ptolemy. Caesar got there three days later and wept at the sight of Pompey's mummified head, but in true Roman fashion he mastered his grief and settled down to a prolonged affair with Cleopatra, the twenty-two-year-old queen, while he skirmished with her brother the king. When news of Caesar's definitive and lopsided victory at Pharsalus reached Rome, he was appointed dictator for an entire year.

He then moved against Pompey's ally, King Pharnaces II. At the Battle of Zela in Asia Minor, Caesar defeated this son of Mithridates four hours after catching sight of him. *"Veni, vidi, vici"* (came, saw, conquered) was his laconic report.

After a three-month stopover in Rome, he embarked for northern Africa, where the Republican forces had regrouped. At the Battle of Thapsus (in modern-day Tunisia), on April 6, 46 B.C., Caesar routed them. Cato committed suicide at Utica, not far from Thapsus, preferring death to Caesar's clemency.

Back in Rome, Caesar was made dictator for ten years and celebrated four phenomenally lavish triumphs: the Gallic, Alexandrian, Pontic (over Pharnaces), and African. He then set out for Spain again, where Pompey's two sons had mounted the last major resistance to his rule. On March 17, 45 B.C., at Munda (near Gibraltar), he fought his last and toughest battle, "where instead of fighting for victory, I was fighting for my life." In October he was back in Rome celebrating his fifth triumph and throwing a banquet for 22,000 guests.

As dictator, he resettled 80,000 veterans and urban proletarians in foreign colonies. He eased debt repayment, stiffened the penalties for corruption and extortion, extended Roman citizenship to northern Italy, and increased the membership of the Senate, even enrolling some loyal Gallic chieftains. He refounded Carthage and Corinth, mighty cities destroyed by the Romans a century earlier. He intended to codify Roman law (see Essay 8) and collect the entire corpus of Greek and Latin books in a magnificent library. His project for draining the Pontine marshes south of Rome was finally carried out by Mussolini two thousand years later.

In his day, Caesar was second only to Cicero as an orator and, besides being one of the greatest generals of all time, he was also a first-rate historian of his own campaigns. In his *Gallic War*, with its lucid third-person narrative and masterly descriptions of battle, he allows his deeds to speak for themselves. Reading it, we feel that Gaul practically asked to be conquered by Caesar. His *Civil War* is less objective, containing satiric sketches of the feckless Republican leaders and more passages of self-justification. All his other writings—speeches, poems, a tragedy on Oedipus, a diatribe against Cato, and treatises on literary style and astronomy—are lost.

At about the time this multifaceted man accepted the title of dictator for life, his aristocratic scorn for shamming became intolerable. He neglected to rise from his seat when the cringing Senate and magistrates came to shower him with new honors, and, at the other end of the political spectrum, he deposed two tribunes of the people for arresting a man in a crowd who had cheered him as king.

The word *rex* had remained anathema in Rome since the expulsion of its last king, Tarquin the Proud, almost half a millennium earlier. Yet Caesar had dared house his mistress Cleopatra in queenly state in a villa on the slopes of the Janiculan hill. Inside the temple he built for his ancestress Venus he placed a gold statue of his royal lover next to that of the goddess. The idea of a monarchy was repugnant to the Romans, but the prospect of also having an Egyptian queen was inconceivable.

For a group of about sixty senators headed by Marcus Junius Brutus and Gaius Cassius Longinus, Caesar had gone too far. On March 15, 44 B.C., the Senate met in an assembly hall of the Theater of Pompey. Caesar entered alone and unarmed. As he sat in his gilded chair, about twenty conspirators crowded around him and one of them presented him with a petition. When Caesar spurned it, Casca struck the first blow, grazing him beneath the throat. With Cicero watching among the other stunned senators, Caesar grabbed at Casca's knife and stabbed him in the arm with his metal pen. The rest then swooped in. When he saw Brutus draw his dagger, Caesar covered his head with his purple toga and fell to the floor. "*Kai su teknon,*" he said in Greek ("You, too, my child!"—and not Shakespeare's Latin "*Et tu, Brute?*") before being stabbed in the groin by the man whose mother, Servilia, had been his favorite mistress. The dictator died at the base of Pompey's statue, bleeding from twenty-three wounds. Cicero wrote that he had "feasted his eyes on the just death of a tyrant."

Caesar was gone, and Rome had outgrown her ancient constitution. Her sprawling empire was too unwieldy to be run by a clique of feuding millionaires. More civil wars followed. Caesar's murderers were overthrown by Octavian (his young grandnephew, adopted son, and chief heir, later known as Augustus) and Mark Antony. When Octavian subsequently defeated Antony and Cleopatra at Actium in 31 B.C., he became sole master of the Roman world.

Julius Caesar's autocratic rule had been the alternative to the factional violence, cynical exploitation, and government by bribery that had engulfed Rome and its empire. Although Augustus nominally restored the Republic in 27 B.C., he maintained control over the army and government by taking a page out of Caesar's book and concentrating the powers of several magistrates in his own person. Augustus's assumption of absolute power, in a "principate" that was actually a thinly disguised monarchy, inaugurated the *Pax Romana*—two hundred years of peace—the longest hiatus between major wars the Western world has ever known. This span included the period in which, according to Edward Gibbon, "the condition of the human race was most happy and prosperous."

Beginning with Augustus, the Roman emperors adopted *Caesar* as one of their names. *Caesar* was also the first Latin loanword in Teutonic, giving rise much later to the German title *Kaiser*. After the official fall of the Western Roman Empire in A.D. 476, the Byzantine emperors considered themselves the sole heirs of the Caesars. They were disconcerted when Charlemagne, harking back to ancient Rome, was crowned emperor by Pope Leo III in A.D. 800. What later became known as the Holy Roman Empire lasted a millennium, until 1806, when another emperor, Napoleon, abolished it. In Russia, *Caesar* became *Czar*, a title officially assumed by Ivan the Terrible in 1547. Even the Arabs had their corresponding term, *qaysar*. The dream of a powerful empire united under an absolute ruler died very hard—and relatively recently—in the Western world.

The German scholar Theodor Mommsen called Caesar "the complete and perfect man," and Italian historical novelist Giuseppe di Lampedusa (see Essay 48) considered him "without doubt the most alive of all the immortals," a masterfully complex personality who can mesmerize even at this remove. What Shakespeare has Caesar say about Cassius seems applicable to Julius himself, whose vulpine face, with its "lean and hungry look," still defies us from scores of portrait busts. "He thinks too much," Shakespeare continues, "such men are dangerous."

Four

Catullus revolutionizes love poetry

> *Your Catullus is depressed, Cornificius,*
> *depressed, goddammit, and fed up—*
> *and getting steadily worse by the hour and day.*
> —Catullus, Poem 38 (c. 59 B.C.)

IN ADDITION TO EXCELLING as warriors, builders, and lawgivers, the ancient Romans created one of the world's outstanding literatures. Though powerfully influenced by an even greater literature, that of the Greeks, Roman writers domesticated whatever they borrowed and managed to map out some novel literary terrain, especially in satire (see Essay 6). Gaius Valerius Catullus (c. 84–c. 54 B.C.) was, among other things, a particularly scathing Roman satirist, but his most important contribution to Western culture was his transformation of love poetry.

Here, too, the Greeks had been superb. Feverish Sappho, epicurean Alcaeus, and lusty Anacreon were the most influential masters of Greek erotic lyric. The best of them, Sappho, wrote of her passion for several young women of her coterie, such as Atthis and Anactoria. Although her work has a searing intensity, not enough has survived to indicate whether she developed a "lived story line" in verse about any of her crushes, but it seems unlikely. A multitude of other Greek poets occasionally named names in their evocations of the joys and tribulations of love. Yet the lovers of even a late Greek poet like Meleager of Gadara— Zenophile, Heliodora, and the boy Myiscus—are little more than names on the page, mere opportunities for witty lyrics.

It was Catullus who created the first extended body of verse describing the phases of a love affair from a subjective viewpoint and in considerable detail and complexity. For the first time in Western literature, love was depicted as a way of life in itself—and not an unworthy one— rather than as a fit of madness or a lighthearted discharge of lust.

When the wealthy young Catullus moved from his native Verona to Rome, he gravitated toward the brightest social and intellectual circles. He had also fallen in with a group of poets who derived their inspiration from the scholarly Greek poets of Alexandria in Egypt, where a highly sophisticated literary culture had flourished several hundred years earlier. Eventually the budding poet's path crossed that of a beautiful, smart, aristocratic, and eminently liberated woman—a heady potion for an impressionable genius a decade her junior, who would mistake her latest fling for a lifelong love.

To the woman he alternately celebrates and vilifies Catullus gave the pseudonym of Lesbia. She was almost certainly Clodia Metelli, a notorious member of the arrogant patrician family of the Claudians. When Catullus met her, she was married to her cousin, one of the consuls for 60 B.C. When her husband died in 59, she was suspected of having poisoned him.

Her brother was Publius Clodius Pulcher, a political gangster who manipulated the Roman mob, desecrated a women's religious ceremony (hosted by Pompeia, wife of Julius Caesar) by attending in drag, and finally died in a street brawl. Clodia was suspected of incest with this darling brother (but so were his other two sisters). In his *Pro Caelio*, Cicero undertook the legal defense of a young jet-setter, Caelius, whom Clodia prosecuted for supposedly attempting to poison her when their love affair turned sour. In this speech, Cicero refers to her as a depraved whore, the Medea of the Palatine hill, a socialite nymphomaniac, and her brother's wife. But Cicero was an implacable foe of both brother and sister and was known to exaggerate.

Catullus called this woman Lesbia in his poems because of associations with the island of Lesbos, where Sappho, "the tenth Muse," had loved and sung many centuries earlier. He recorded the story of his love affair with Lesbia in two dozen poems that span the emotional gamut from ecstatic fulfillment to savage disillusionment. Idealization, hope, pride, elation, suspicion, jealousy, anger, disgust, viciousness—all are conjured up with youthful ardor or brutal, heartrending bitterness.

What is often considered Catullus's earliest poem to Lesbia (Poem 51, "*Ille mi par esse deo videtur*"[1]) is a translation of a poem by Sappho. It

---

[1] The numbering of the poems is that of standard Latin editions (which bears no relation to the order in which the poems were written). Like most other ancient lyric poets, Catullus did not give his poems separate titles; the Latin phrase following the number is the poem's first line. All quotations from Catullus have been translated by Peter D'Epiro.

evokes the first awestruck phase of falling in love, when the beloved's presence acts like a stupefying drug. Yet the final stanza, which has no counterpart in Sappho, seems to undercut the breathless adoration of the first three, telegraphing the tragedy to come:

Far greater than Jove
the man who can sit
undaunted while watching and hearing you
laughing so sweetly—

while I on my part
am deprived of my senses
if only, Lesbia, I catch a glimpse of you:
voiceless and tongue-tied

I feel a faint fire
steal over my limbs;
blood pounds in my ears, the light in my eyes
is shrouded in midnight.

(Leisure, Catullus, leisure is your disease.
It's leisure that gives you leave to play the fool.
Rich cities have been pulled down by too much leisure,
kings have been ruined.)

Catullus's two sparrow poems, among his best known, belong to the same initial phase of flushed amatory enthusiasm. In the first (Poem 2, "*Passer, deliciae meae puellae*"), he wishes he were Lesbia's pet bird:

Lesbia's sparrow, apple of her eye,
she plays with you, presses you to her bosom,
lends you her fingertip to plant a peck on,
provoking you to give her bitter bird-bites—
my dear ravishing girl grants you the right
to share in all sorts of cute little games with her
(and she gets from this, I think, some very cold comfort
for desires raging like fierce fires inside her). . . .
Would that I, too, could play with her little sparrow
and ease my grieving heart of the pains of love.

When the sparrow dies, Catullus writes a mock-heroic eulogy (Poem 3) whose last two lines rebuke Death for the cosmetic changes it has caused in Lesbia: "Fine work you've done: now my girl's pretty eyes / are all puffy-puffy and red with her tears."

Another famous lyric of this period focuses on kisses. Catullus can't get enough of them, it seems. Here's his Poem 5 (*"Vivamus, mea Lesbia, atque amemus"*):

> *Let's live, my Lesbia, let's live and love!*
> *and let's not give two cents (or even one)*
> *for all the petty twaddle of uptight geezers.*
> *Suns can set, and suns can rise again;*
> *but we, when our brief candle has flickered out,*
> *we have no choice but to sleep an endless night.*
> *And so, give me a thousand kisses, then a hundred more,*
> *then another thousand, followed fast by another hundred—*
> *give me billions and billions of the damn things!*
> *And it's only then, when we've totally lost count,*
> *when we ourselves couldn't guesstimate the number,*
> *that we'll be safe from the evil eye of those nasty old buzzards*
> *who reckon up others' kisses on ten gouty fingers.*

There's no one like Lesbia. All other rivals are paltry things, hardly in the same league. This is Poem 43 (*"Salve, nec minimo puella naso"*):

> *Glad to meet you, Ameana of the hardly petite nose,*
> *the unlovely foot, the non-Maybelline eyes,*
> *the inelegant fingers, the never-dry mouth,*
> *and the tongue that is far from refinement.*
> *So you're the mistress of Mamurra the bankrupt,*
> *and they call you beautiful in the boonies—*
> *and even compare you with our Lesbia?*
> *Good God, what ignorant and boorish times we live in!*

In a similar lyric (Poem 86) about a charmless beauty, Catullus insists that Lesbia "combines in one woman the charms of all charming women." But a new note of diffidence sounds in Poem 70 (*"Nulli se dicit mulier mea nubere malle"*):

> My woman says she would rather marry me
> than anyone, though Jove himself came courting.
> So she says. But what a woman says to her eager lover
> should be written on the wind and in running water.

A temporary estrangement seems to have followed, after Catullus heard rumors about Lesbia. In Poem 8 (*"Miser Catulle, desinas ineptire"*), he resolves to stay away:

> Wretched Catullus, stop playing the fool:
> you're crying over milk spilt long ago.
> Once upon a time, bright suns shone upon you,
> when you followed your girl around wherever she led—
> she who was loved as no woman was ever loved.
> So many good times, so many joys were yours,
> and all of your desires meshed wholly with hers.
> Bright suns, indeed, shone upon you then.
> Now she wants out. Go and do likewise, weakling.
> Don't chase this will-o'-the-wisp and live in pain,
> but close up your heart, become as hard as a stone.
> Good-bye, my girl, Catullus has turned to stone.
> He will seek you out and ask for you no more.
> And you'll be sorry—a nobody nobody asks for.
> Miserable girl, what kind of life will be left you?
> Who'll visit you now? Who'll think you're beautiful?
> What man will you love? Whose girl will you call yourself?
> What man will you kiss? Whose lips will you bite in love?
> But you, Catullus, stay hard and still like a stone.

Then the rumors were confirmed. More than one jilted lover since the first century B.C. has fantasized about barging into his woman's seedy haunts and shouting out something like the first half of Poem 37 (*"Salax taberna, vosque contubernales"*):

> Hey, all you regulars of that pickup joint
> nine pillars down from the Temple of the Twins,
> do you actually think you're the only guys with pricks,
> with some sort of license to screw all the girls
> while the rest of us shmucks have b.o.?

Market Data

WORLD EQUITY MARKETS AT A GLANCE

Country	Index	Feb 8	Feb 7	Country
Argentina	Merval	1991.92	2011.07	**Ireland**
Australia	S&P/All Ordinaries	5723,9	5668.3	**Israel**
	S&P/ASX 200 Res	5555.3	5585.6.	
	S&P/ASX 200	5658.0	5596.7	**Ital**
Austria	ATX	3750.61	3764.53	
Belgium	BEL 20	3612.07	3652.59	
	BEL Mid	3637.93	3628.40	
Brazil	Bovespa	59190.62	58965.48	
Canada	S&P/TSX Met & Min	736.55	727.2	
	S&P/TSX 60	758.80	75	
	S&P/TSX Comp	12978.67	1292	
Chile	IGPA Gen ♥	12794.50	1	
China	Shanghai A	(c)		
	Shanghai B	(c)		
	Shanghai Comp	(c)		
	Shenzhen A	(c)		
	Shenzhen B	(c)		
	FTSE/Xinhua A200	(c)		
	FTSE/Xinhua B35			
Colombia	CSE Index	905		
Croatia	CROBEX			
Cyprus				

	52 week				Vol	Stock	Price	Chng	52 week		Yld	P/e	Vol
g	High	Low	Yld	P/e	'000s				High	Low			'000s
	£14	884.5	2.8	£11	10.4	Invista Re	59	-0.25	140	49.50	1.2	6.2	66
	743	454.3	–	701.7	5.8	Ishaan	113.50	–	119	89	–	129	-158
	273	157	1.6	205.1	14.2	JamesHal	525.50	+8.50	649.50	470	3.1	16.9	3
	237	167	–	197.1	3.6	Just Retir♣	98.50	+6.50	309	81	0.6	5.7	91
	?8.8	110.310.6		–	–	Kirkland Lake	545	+32.50	745	393.50	–	–	1
		76.5	5.3	120.4	29.4	KSK Pwr Vntr	483.50	-3	540	168	–	2.2	23
		£10.3	3.7	d11.2	4.2	Lamprell	365	+7	497.50	242	1.4	27.1	99
	303.5	3.3		301.5	-10	Lancashire	303	-4	384	281.75	20.8	3.9	245
	907	2.8		836.7	1.4	LMS Capital	69.75	-0.25	77.25	64.50	–	695	13
	0.2.9			d364.5	5.6	M.P. Evans	437.50	+12.50	487	290	1.5	25.6	23
	1.1			296.3	11.3	Majestic♣	233	–	405	229.25	3.9	13.1	15
	9			132.9	6.7	Max♣	53.25	+1.25	219	48.25	–	–	2,150
				372.4	14.6	MayGurney	261.50	–	345	260	1.4	14.7	28
				62.5	-1.7	Mears	260	+1	380	228.75	1.3	15.6	179
				8.2	2.2	Mecom Group	25.75	-1	97	22	–	–	3,805
					1.9	MirLand	492	–	710	440	–	15.4	0
					12.3	NEPR €	62.19	-0.03	94.22	46.89	4.8	–	1
					-1.4	Nikanor	410.50	+37.25	740	348.50	–	–	20
					2	Numis	231.50hd	+3	344	215	3	7.7	290
					5	Omega Ins	172.25	+4.25	174	138	2.6	19.1	198
						Oriel Res♣	60.75	-1.50	73.50	40.50	–	–	44
						Origin Enterp £	303.52	+1.03	303.52	215.87	–	22.5	2
						PeterHmbr	£13.89	+0.12	£16.86	850	–	54.4	149
						...tra	129	-0.50	167	119	–	–	82
							585.43	-0.87	744.40	539.21	2.6	–	2
									£37.25	£16.08	–	–	62
											–	–	25,152
													2,358

Or that if a few hundred of you assholes
sat there in a row, I couldn't go up and down
and shove it into all of you where the sun doesn't shine?
I'll fix your wagons—I'll scrawl huge hairy dicks
all over the door of your goddamn "Dew Drop Inn."

A brief reconciliation may have occurred, but the poet never recovered his enthusiasm: "I can't wish you well, even if you reform, / or put an end to my love, even if you get worse" (Poem 75). In a two-line lyric (Poem 85), of which the first three words, *odi et amo*, have become a Latin tag, Catullus enunciates a familiar paradox: "I hate her and love her. How can that be? / I haven't the vaguest—but it's killing me." Toward the end, Catullus learns that Lady Lesbia has been slumming (Poem 58, "*Caeli, Lesbia nostra, Lesbia illa*"):

Caelius, you're not going to believe this:
our Lesbia, the one and only Lesbia, the Lesbia
that Catullus loved more than himself and all that he owned,
now hangs around the highways and byways,
jerking off the lordly scions of Remus.

After beseeching the gods to rid him of his "deadly plague of love" (Poem 76), Catullus's bile erupts in a fierce valediction (Poem 11, "*Furi et Aureli, comites Catulli*"), in which he asks two of his friends to take a message to Lesbia. Here are the last seven lines:

Tell her to live and be happy with all of her lovers,
spreading it wide for all three hundred at once,
lovelessly pumping their guts out over and over.
Nor should she bother to look for my love, as before—
my love, which her faults have caused to fall
like a flower at the edge of a meadow
when a plough, passing through, has clipped it.

End of story. The poet must have died soon afterward, at age thirty. But Catullus's achievement—his sensitive personalizing of the get-them-in-the-sack ethos of much Greek erotic verse—profoundly influenced the Roman love poets of the next generation. Like Catullus, each of these wove elaborate verse tributes to his own (typically unfaithful) poetic mistress. Thus Gallus, whose works are lost, had his Lycoris, Tibullus his Delia and also his grasping Nemesis, Propertius his Cynthia, and Ovid his Corinna.

After the second century A.D., the complete oeuvre of Catullus, Rome's greatest lyric poet, was lost for a millennium. Only in about 1300 was a single surviving manuscript of more than one hundred of his poems found stopping up the hole of a wine barrel in his hometown of Verona. But through his impact on the work of the Roman love poets, especially Ovid (see Essay 7), Catullus indirectly fostered the astonishing revival of European love poetry in the Provençal language of southern France between 1100 and 1300. Troubadours like Bernart de Ventadorn, Bertran de Born, and Arnaut Daniel sang the praises of married noblewomen whose identities were concealed by a *senhal*, or pseudonym, much like those used by the Roman poets for their ladies.

From the troubadours, the great "triumvirate" of Italian writers learned to celebrate their own poetic mistresses (see Essays 14, 16, 17). Dante consecrated the divine virtue of his ineffably lovely Beatrice in the lyrics of the *Vita Nuova* and, much later, the narrative glories of the *Paradiso*. Petrarch wove the lyrics of his *Canzoniere* (Songbook) into a drama of his unrequited passion for Laura. Giovanni Boccaccio, author of the *Decameron*, compulsively chronicled his love for a flighty woman he calls Fiammetta in many sonnets and other works in verse and prose.

But the strategy of recounting a more or less unified story in individual poems detailing the varied stages of a love affair started with Catullus more than two thousand years ago. The raw power of his emotional roller-coaster ride still makes him a living literary presence instead of just another dead classic, like Callimachus and the other erudite Greek poets of Alexandria whom Catullus emulated. The innovating provincial from Verona, who believed that the story of his passion for fickle Clodia (his "radiant goddess") was worth commemorating in exquisite verse, bequeathed a legacy to untold numbers of poets who, writing from the heart (or convincingly faking it), vied with one another in immortalizing their lovers' virtues and vices.

Five

Master builders of the ancient world

Brosnath enta geweorc.
(*The buildings of giants crumble.*)
—"The Ruin" (c. tenth century)

THE REMAINS OF ROMAN ROADS, bridges, aqueducts, baths, theaters, forums, palaces, walls, and monuments, strewn from Scotland to Iraq across more than thirty modern nations, still bear the imprints of antiquity's greatest builders: massive scale, technical sophistication, extraordinary pragmatism, and meticulous attention to the surveyor's craft. The ancient Romans created a varied architecture that met the military and political requirements of the Empire and the social and civic needs of its people. To the anonymous Anglo-Saxon poet of "The Ruin" who described the Roman remains in Bath, England, these structures must indeed have seemed like the work of giants.

Mighty architectural feats of the ancient world included the pyramids, the Great Wall of China, and the 15,000-mile road system of the Incas, but Rome's achievement, in its extent, variety, and excellence, dwarfs them all. Indeed, it forms the basis of much of the civic and religious architecture of the Western world to this very day.

The engineers and architects of Rome were not strikingly original, at least initially, when they freely imitated their Etruscan and Greek forebears. Unencumbered by lofty artistic ideals, Roman builders were motivated by political, military, economic, and social concerns, rather than aesthetic theories. As befitted a warrior nation, soldiers did most of the building.

Several ancient civilizations were familiar with concrete and rudimentary arches. The success of the Roman engineers, however, was attributable to their mastery of the arch and a new formulation for concrete. The importance of the arch to architecture has been compared with that of the wheel to transportation. An arch gains strength as the load above it increases, and the Romans exploited this property in their monumental buildings. Arches can also accommodate mighty spans, as seen in extant Roman bridges and aqueducts (and our own modern structures). Triumphal arches, like the Arch of Titus (A.D. 81) and the Arch of Constantine (A.D. 315), ancestors of Napoleon's Arc de Triomphe in Paris, were raised as potent political symbols of the Empire.

Arches can be extended linearly to create a barrel vault, and two barrel vaults can be crossed at right angles to form a groin, or cross vault. Barrel vaults can also be made to curve or to incline, as when they are used over a staircase. The barrel vault and the cross vault were seminal components of Roman architecture, and the most highly evolved form of vault, the dome, as superbly exemplified in the Pantheon, became the Romans' architectural hallmark.

Roman builders also owed a debt to Italian geology. In Rome, they had a supply of easily manipulated buff volcanic tufa, which they began using in the sixth century B.C. Travertine marble, first used several hundred years later, was the jewel of building in the late Republic. But it was humble pozzolana that enabled the Romans to build like giants. As the architect and engineer Vitruvius wrote in the first century B.C., "There is a powder which from natural causes produces astonishing results."

By substituting the dark red volcanic ash called pozzolana for sand in the traditional sand, lime, and water recipe for concrete, the Romans created an extremely strong building material that was invaluable in bridges and port structures because it hardened on contact with water. When mixed with gravel, it took on the characteristics of rock. This Roman concrete made it possible to build massive walls and vaults over vast spaces, thus encouraging architectural daring. The use of this material also made it unnecessary to quarry, transport, and cut rock, since concrete could be manufactured and laid at a building site by unskilled manual laborers.

The Romans were the first ancient people to view interior space as an integral part of structures. Whereas in Egypt and Greece the exteriors of temples and monuments overpowered the spaces they enclosed, Roman walls and domes were used to shape interior space, not to intimidate the onlooker from the outside. Basilicas and temples were built as public spaces, and bland or staid exteriors often enclosed commodious, functional, and ornate interiors.

The way in which technical advances, especially concrete arches, were used to enclose soaring spaces was best exemplified during the so-called Roman architectural revolution (A.D. 50–130). Among the most artistically significant structures of this era was Nero's Domus Aurea (Golden House). Taking advantage of the large devastated area left by the great fire at Rome in A.D. 64, Nero engaged the architect Severus to construct a palace complex with baths, gardens, vineyards, pavilions, and an artificial lake on a hundred and twenty-five acres. "At last," he said, "I can finally live like a human being."

The Golden House marked a turning point in architecture. The builders now understood the artistic freedom conferred by concrete, and their expertise allowed them to construct within the Golden House a domed octagonal hall. Though probably not the first such room, the octagonal hall in the Domus Aurea served as a prototype for a great deal of imperial architecture to come, most notably the Pantheon.

When Vespasian seized power in A.D. 69, one of his most urgent political goals was to expunge Nero's infamous legacy. Three years later, he appropriated the Domus Aurea's vast garden, drained its man-made lake, and began building the Flavian Amphitheater, which is supported by a concrete raft and a bed of clay. Better known as the Colosseum, this structure exceeded all other amphitheaters in scale, with its lofty, four-band façade consisting mainly of more than three million cubic feet of travertine marble.

The first three bands of the façade feature eighty arcades, which on the ground level served as entrances numbered for ticket holders, as in a modern stadium. The arcades on the first level are flanked by Doric columns, the oldest of the Greek architectural orders, and these are surmounted by Ionic columns on the second level, and Corinthian on the third. The fourth level, decorated with Corinthian pilasters, served as anchorage for the *velarium*, an enormous awning supported on two-hundred-foot masts and operated by sailors of the imperial fleet. The inner structure, with its radial stairways and ringed passages, owed everything to the concrete barrel vault. The stadium could seat 50,000— a paltry crowd compared with the more than 200,000 that attended races at the nearby Circus Maximus.

The dismantling of the Domus Aurea continued, and only a portion survives today, including the octagonal hall. Palatial architecture progressed, however, with the building of Domitian's Palace on the Palatine hill (A.D. 81) and Hadrian's Villa at Tivoli (A.D. 125–34). The latter was a fascinating seven-square-mile complex of palaces, libraries, theaters, and baths that included reproductions of structures that the Hellenophile emperor Hadrian had admired on his travels throughout Rome's Greek and Grecianized dominions. A reflecting pool ringed by a colonnade with statues was a prominent feature.

Concrete vaults and domes were also essential components of Roman baths, which required high ceilings for dissipating the heat and humidity. Baths were integral amenities even in the smallest Roman towns, drawing men and women for exercise, relaxation, and conversation, as well as bathing. After disrobing, clients passed through a series of thermally graded chambers with tubs for washing. Temperature gradations in the chambers were maintained by ducts beneath the floors that distributed varying amounts of heat from furnaces. Patrons seeking refreshment on a hot day could proceed directly to a cool dip in the *frigidarium*.

The imperial baths, the *thermae*, are the establishments correctly associated with occasional orgies and general decadence. The prototypes were the Baths of Titus and of Trajan, and the best remaining examples are those built in Rome in A.D. 212–17 by Caracalla. These gargantuan baths were part of a twenty-eight-acre compound that featured a reservoir fed by an aqueduct, two gyms, a Latin and a Greek library, concert halls, and art galleries. The bath building itself had a capacity of 1,600. The Baths of Diocletian (c. A.D. 302) were even more massive, seating 3,200 within airy and elegant stucco and mosaic halls. By A.D. 354, there were nearly a thousand baths, large and tiny, just in the city of Rome.

In terms of their influence on subsequent architecture, basilicas— roofed rectangular halls often used as law courts—were among the most important Roman buildings. A basilica's interior was usually divided by colonnades into a wide central aisle (the nave) and narrower side aisles. An apse, a semicircular projection from the main structure, was situated at one or both ends of the nave. This basilica plan, which owed much to the central halls of imperial baths, later became the model for Christian churches such as the Lateran Basilica and Santa Maria Maggiore.

The Basilica Ulpia (A.D. 100–12), built by Emperor Trajan, was the largest Roman basilica and one of the city's most celebrated public buildings. Spanning the Forum of Trajan, this double-apsed structure was embellished with multicolored marble. The Basilica of Constantine and Maxentius, built in the fourth century A.D. to house law courts, is considered the last great pagan building in Rome. Variegated marble adorned the lofty interior, whose recesses, windowed walls, and high arches made it look almost medieval. Not for seven centuries, however, would European architects attempt a similar feat.

Rome was the first European superpower to build paved roads over its entire dominion, eventually weaving a network of 50,000 miles. The first of the mighty Roman roads was the Via Appia, constructed in 312 B.C. between Rome and Capua, and extended in the next century east to Benevento and across the peninsula to the port of Brindisi in Italy's heel. Portions can still be traveled starting at the Porta San Sebastiano, the best-preserved gate in the Aurelian Wall (a much later Roman feat—a 12.5-mile bulwark around the city completed in about A.D. 280).

Other famous roads included the Via Flaminia (220 B.C.), between Rome and Rimini, and the Via Aemilia, which ran from Rimini 176 miles northwest to Piacenza. The Via Appia was extended on the far side of the Adriatic in 145 B.C. as the Via Egnatia through Greece to Byzantium. By 133 B.C., a 1,000-mile road connected the Pyrenees with the Straits of Gibraltar.

By 40 B.C., all of Italy had been linked—and all roads led to Rome. As the Empire expanded, so did the highway system, which eventually ran from Britain to the Euphrates. It crisscrossed northern Africa for nearly 13,000 miles, traversed the Alps, formed a web in France with a hub in Lyon, and ringed Spain with a main road and secondary ones branching into the interior.

The roads were designed to accommodate the army's two- and four-wheeled vehicles, provide safe footing for the infantry, and require minimal upkeep. The surveyors maintained remarkably accurate alignments over long distances, avoiding valleys and indirect routes and often building steep-graded roads right over mountains. Tunnels were certainly not beyond their capacities, as when they linked Naples with nearby Pozzuoli by burrowing through a finger of the Apennines.

Hundreds of towns originated as trading outposts near Roman roads. After the surveyors chose a location with good drainage, soldiers and slaves dug a rectangular ditch and built a wall to enclose the area. The surveyors then plotted the two main streets—one running north and south (the *cardo*), the other, east and west (the *decumanus*). In a typical town, a forum was constructed just south of the intersection of the *cardo* and *decumanus,* a market placed across from the forum, and an amphitheater and theater in the northern corner. In addition to the main market, others were situated throughout the village, along with baths, tenements, and single-family dwellings.

The success of the urban planners may be gauged in part by the great European cities that arose on the sites of Roman towns, including London, Paris, Vienna, Cologne, and Milan. The tenor of Roman town planning is evident in various amenities and regulations. Living space was created for no more than 50,000 inhabitants. The height of buildings and the hours during which vehicular traffic was allowed on the streets were restricted, and property owners were required to construct shelters over their sidewalks. As for their urban drainage systems, the Romans excelled in this area from the time the Cloaca Maxima, or main sewer, was first constructed in Rome in the sixth century B.C.

Towns and cities need water, and Roman engineers devised an ingenious way to provide it, using gravity to transport it over aqueducts from springs and rivers. Surveyors calculated the precise slope at which the aqueduct should be built—steep enough to keep the water moving, yet not so steep that it flowed too fast and eroded the masonry channel. Because the slope had to be kept constant, at different points an aqueduct might run at ground level, underground, or high over ravines or rivers.

Mighty arched spans carried aqueducts across valleys and waterways. The most spectacular survivor is the three-tiered Pont du Gard, built without mortar in 19 B.C. near Nîmes, France, which carried water in its upper channel for nearly 300 yards across the Gard River at a height of 160 feet. Almost as awe-inspiring are the Roman aqueducts in Segovia and Alcántara (Spain) and Ephesus (Turkey).

Eleven main aqueducts eventually served Rome. The first, the eleven-mile Aqua Appia, was built in 312 B.C. The Aqua Claudia (A.D. 47), considered the most expertly constructed, brought water to Rome from forty-five miles away in Subiaco and featured more than ten miles of arched supports along its course. At the city limits, the water drained into a holding tank and was distributed to several water mains. An ancient Roman aqueduct still brings water from springs in Salone fourteen miles to the Trevi Fountain.

Most Roman temples followed the rectangular Greek prototype, like the massive Temple of Jupiter Capitolinus (509 B.C.). Of the elegant Roman temple now called the Maison Carrée, built in Nîmes in 20 B.C., Thomas Jefferson wrote to a friend, "Here I am, Madam, gazing whole hours at the Maison Carrée, like a lover at his mistress," and he later modeled the Virginia State Capitol after it. But the most illustrious of Rome's temples—the Pantheon—is not rectangular but round. "Size, surprise, and simplicity" is how art historian R. J. A. Wilson characterizes the impact of the loveliest antique structure to survive nearly intact.

Completely rebuilt by Hadrian between A.D. 118 and 128, the Pantheon may have been intended as a grand monument to all the Roman deities, as its name implies. From outside, the prosaic porch of Corinthian columns (which may date from the original Augustan structure) makes the building look like a conventional rectilinear temple, providing little hint of its sublime interior. But the massive dome establishes a breathtaking visual harmony inside the structure.

Perfectly proportioned, the Pantheon's dome has a span of 142 feet, and its summit stands exactly that high above the floor. Its inner surfaces meet in an oculus, a twenty-seven-foot circular "eye" that is the building's only source of natural light. Adding to the surreal airiness and upward movement are five rows of decorative coffers (each like picture frames enclosing several smaller ones) that diminish in size as they approach the oculus.

In a plaque placed there in 1632, Pope Urban VIII declared the Pantheon "the most celebrated edifice in the whole world." Although His Holiness was wrong about Galileo (see Essay 33), he was on the right track about what is arguably the most influential building ever constructed.

The Pantheon's great dome had already inspired Brunelleschi when, in designing the octagonal cupola of the cathedral of Florence, he inaugurated another age of stupendous Italian achievement in building (see Essay 19). It also profoundly influenced architects like Bramante, Michelangelo, Palladio (see Essay 30), Sir Christopher Wren, and Thomas Jefferson, who chose the Pantheon as the model for the University of Virginia's library. All the Roman gods must have been highly pleased, indeed, with Hadrian's offering, the epitome of Roman engineering and architectural panache, which, after almost two millennia, still dazzles the visitor who walks inside and cannot help gazing upward with awe and delight.

VI

Six

"Satire is wholly ours"

What's there to stop someone from telling the truth with a smile?
—Horace, *Satires*, Book 1, Poem 1 (c. 35 B.C.)

ALTHOUGH LATIN LITERATURE WAS almost entirely based on Greek models, in one literary domain the Romans pioneered. As the Roman rhetorician Quintilian proclaimed in the first century A.D., "Satire is wholly ours." Despite several Greek antecedents of distinction, including the excoriating poems of Archilochus (seventh century B.C.) and the scathing verse comedies of Aristophanes (fifth century B.C.), the Greeks had no specific name for satire and didn't perceive it as a discrete literary genre with its own conventions. From scattered Greek influences and a native tradition of obscene variety shows, indecent farces, and bantering competitions during festivals, the Romans created a literary form they called *satura* or *satira*—a farrago, medley, hodgepodge, or mélange.

The inventor of full-fledged literary satire was Gaius Lucilius (c. 180–102/101 B.C.), born of a noble and wealthy family in modern-day Sessa Aurunca on the Latium-Campania border. Settling in Rome at about age twenty, he started publishing his work only when he was close to fifty. Of his thirty books of satires, each containing one to six poems, fewer than 1,300 disjointed lines survive. After experimenting with other meters for his satires, he fixed on the dactylic hexameter, which was also the standard meter for epic verse.

The well-born Lucilius (great-uncle of Pompey the Great) was also well-connected, being an intimate of the greatest general of his day, Scipio Aemilianus, who destroyed Carthage in 146 B.C. and was the nucleus of a cultured Grecophile circle. Lucilius could thus afford to indulge in self-expression with impunity. His verse abounds in autobiographical incidents related in a colloquial tone and often in dialogue form—hence his name for his poems, *sermones* (conversations). Although he could be genial, he developed a reputation for flaying his enemies, and his outspokenness sometimes bordered on obscenity. He ridiculed high-ranking senators by name, indulging in caustic satire despite the strong penalties for slander and libel in Roman law.

"O the preoccupations of man! O the triviality in the world!" he laments in line 2 of his surviving fragments. In Lucilius, we already find most of the perennial targets of satire: gluttons, pederasts, cuckolds, whores, bores, misers, political crooks, and blowhard poets. He also had a sharp eye and nose for rustic images, such as pigs scratching their ribs against trees (356), cheese stinking of garlic (481), and rams with huge testicles (559–60). He scorns "beardless androgynes and bearded sodomite-adulterers" (1048) and paints an unflattering picture of contemporary politics, in which both nobles and commoners seek only "to swindle without getting caught, to fight treacherously, / To fall over one another with flattery, to act like good eggs, / To set traps as if all were the enemies of all" (1149–51). Roman morals are going downhill fast: "We're hard-to-please sourpusses, we grimace at the good things we have" (313).

Horace (Quintus Horatius Flaccus, 65–8 B.C.) harked back to Lucilius, whom he nonetheless considered a sloppy versifier for boasting he could improvise two hundred verses an hour standing on one foot. An Apulian from Venosa, Horace was proud of how his "best of fathers," though only an ex-slave, had him meticulously schooled in Rome, from about age ten, and then sent to Athens when he was twenty to round off his education.

After Virgil introduced him to Maecenas, the literary patron and counselor of Augustus, in 38 B.C., Horace became part of the charmed poetic circle that also came to include Propertius and that helped make the Augustan era in Rome one of the most magnificent of golden ages. We learn from a good-natured description by his friend Augustus that Horace was short with a potbelly, and the poet refers to himself as "a pig from Epicurus's herd" (*Epistles* 1.4.16).

His greatest achievements, fully justifying his boasts *non omnis moriar* ("not all of me shall die") and *exegi monumentum aere perennius* ("I have raised a monument more lasting than bronze"), are the first three of his four books of *Odes*. Besides celebrating wine, women, song, and handsome boys, these exquisitely crafted lyric poems sing the praises of Roman history and its stern heroes.

Horace's fame also rests on two books of *Satires* in dactylic hexameter verse, eighteen poems in all (35–29 B.C.). Inspired by Lucilius's conversational approach and autobiographical focus, Horace avoids the earlier poet's acerbity. Instead, he adopts an urbane persona, smiling at the follies and foibles of the world rather than lambasting its vices, trying to reason good-naturedly with the reader to shun self-punishing traits such as avarice and to live more humanely. His satirical targets were either types or people who were dead, unimportant, or, like Porcius the glutton, disguised under descriptive pseudonyms.

Horace is the polished poet of the golden mean, *aurea mediocritas,* which he appropriated from Aristotle's *Ethics,* in which virtue is a mean between opposite vices—liberality, for example, involving a proper balance between miserliness and prodigality. The poet illustrates his abstract moral ideas with vivid images: "Rufillus the Dandy smells like candy, Gargonius like a goat. / No middle ground" (*Satires* 1.2.27–28). Later in the same poem, Horace shows us the genitals—severed with a sword—of an adulterer caught in the act. In his influential *Art of Poetry,* written in verse, he mocks pretentious poetasters with lines like this: "Mountains are in labor—and out pops a ridiculous mouse" (139).

Although a few of his early *Epodes* are fiercely obscene, his forte in satire was poking mild fun at absurd or irrational behavior, including his own. In Satire 2.7, for example, Horace's slave Davus, taking advantage of the traditional license of the Saturnalia, reproaches his master for being a "slave" to his passions.

According to Davus, Horace is a hypocrite who is always praising the past but would actually hate to live in those bad old days. When in rat-race Rome, Horace praises the simple country life; in the boring country, he longs to be back in sophisticated Rome. Furthermore, he is a puppet of the powerful, always praising his frugal lifestyle but jumping with glee at any invitation from the rich and famous. He's also the slave of a married woman, and is gluttonous, bibulous, and incapable of being alone for even an hour, seeking oblivion in wine or sleep. The impertinent slave's Stoic lecture ends abruptly with Horace's threatening to stone him, shoot him with an arrow, or demote him to field hand on his Sabine farm.

Titus Petronius Niger was the mystery man of Nero's Rome—we don't even know with certainty whether Petronius the writer was the one Tacitus mentions as a victim of Nero's tyranny who was forced to commit suicide in A.D. 66: "His days he spent sleeping, his nights working and having a good time" (*Annals* 16.18). In any event, this *arbiter elegantiae,* the arbiter of taste at Nero's debauched court, has traditionally been identified as the author of the novel or mock-epic *Satyrica* (Adventures of Satyrs), commonly called the *Satyricon*, the earliest surviving Latin novel and the first realistic novel in European literature.

The book relates the picaresque adventures of three cultured but shiftless young men in the dives and other low-life haunts of southern Italian port cities: the narrator Encolpius (Greek for "Crotch"); his pretty serving boy, the curly-haired sixteen-year-old catamite Giton (Neighbor); and Ascyltus (Unperturbed), Encolpius's rival for Giton's favors. Of what must have been a vast work, we have major fragments of Books 14, 15, and 16. Book 15, which survives nearly intact, features the *Cena Trimalchionis* (Trimalchio's Dinner Party), the epic feast hosted by an ex-slave merchant who has amassed vast wealth in lands and money while remaining a vulgarian on a truly cosmic scale.

At table, while the three main characters and half a dozen other guests are served by singing waiters, bald old Trimalchio (Semitic for "Thrice-Blessed") makes his grand entry, borne in by his slaves to the sound of music. The host immediately establishes himself as undisputed lord of the feast, ordering a serving boy's ears boxed for a faux pas. A cooked sow is served wearing an ex-slave's liberty cap and with pastry piglets sucking at her teats. When Trimalchio stabs the sow's side with a knife, out flies a flock of thrushes.

After the host regales the assembled company with the recent vagaries of his bowel movements, he has three pigs sent into the dining room and asks his guests which one they'd like slaughtered for the next course. In a display of erudition, he refers to how the Cyclops put out Ulysses' eye and how Hannibal captured Troy. When the unfortunate pig reappears, cooked this time, Trimalchio complains it hasn't been gutted, orders the chef to be brought out and flogged, but then shows mercy and merely tells him to disembowel it. When the man cuts into it, piles of sausages and blood puddings spill out. Just a little joke!

During dinner, Trimalchio's accountant begins reading aloud an update on his business transactions. The host has his wife Fortunata's gold jewelry brought to him so that he can show it off, adding that his own gold bracelet weighs ten pounds—and he has a scale passed around to prove it. He then reads his will out loud, including the inscription for his monumental tomb, which mentions how much money he's leaving. At this, he and the beneficiaries burst into tears.

The party then moves to the baths, where an appallingly drunk Trimalchio starts slobbering over a handsome slave boy. When Fortunata calls her husband some nasty names, he flings a wine cup in her face, reminding her that she was just a common slut before he made an honest woman of her. This sets him weeping again, but, soon remembering his manners, he cheers up his guests by revealing that he was once just like them, before his abilities made him what he is today. These abilities included letting his former master use him in bed for fourteen years, but—he doesn't want to brag—he also serviced the lady of the house, and that's how he earned his freedom and inherited a monstrous fortune.

Now it's time for the funeral rehearsal, and his burial clothes are fetched so that the fabric can be admired. Ordering his horn players to strike up a funeral march, he urges his guests "to pretend I'm dead and say something nice about me." Mercifully, an especially loud horn blast alerts the local fire brigade, which breaks the door down and rushes in with buckets and axes to put a frenzied end to the festivities.

Trimalchio was F. Scott Fitzgerald's original title for the novel that became *The Great Gatsby* (both characters being nouveaux riches who throw grotesquely extravagant parties for guests who ridicule them). The 1969 film *Fellini Satyricon*, complete with copulations, amputations, and an albino hermaphrodite, was the great Italian director's dazzling attempt to capture Petronius's decadently surreal atmospherics (see Essay 47).

The verse satirist Martial (Marcus Valerius Martialis, c. A.D. 40–c. 104) was born in Bilbilis, Spain (near Saragossa), but as a freeborn Roman citizen who spent thirty-four years in the metropolis, he can be considered an honorary Italian for the purposes of this book. Migrating to Rome at age twenty-four, he lived in a third-floor garret on the Quirinal, tormented by the noisy city at night. (Some things never change.)

The miseries of being a client, a retainer of rich but stingy patrons, figure prominently in his verse. He laments having to cadge dinners from tightwads and live on doles and pittances, wasting his time, losing sleep, and having no time to write. His checkered reputation rests on twelve books of *Epigrams* (about 1,200 poems) published between A.D. 86 and 102, most of them written in elegiac meter (alternating hexameter and pentameter lines).

Martial transformed the epigram from an innocuous occasional poem on a variety of subjects—often an epitaph, dedication, or elaborate compliment—into a toxic little verbal tarantula with its sting in its tail (a venomous, ironic, or surprising last word or few words). A noted example of the pointed epigram he perfected is a poem on a typical legacy-hunter of his day (1.10):

Gemellus wants to marry Maronilla:
He begs and pleads, implores and sends her presents.
Is she some great beauty? No, nothing could be more disgusting.
What is it about her, then, that he treasures and loves? Her cough.

Using invented names, Martial could afford to vent his spleen with impunity: "I don't like you, Sabidius, and I can't even say why. / This much, though, I *can* say: I don't like you, Sabidius" (1.32). Or "If you think you smell yesterday's wine on Acerra, / You're wrong: Acerra *always* drinks until dawn" (1.28).

Martial loves to poke fun at women who are past their prime but still try to be chic, as in 2.41, where he counsels Maximina never to laugh. Yes, he admits, Ovid had advised girls to laugh—but Maximina is not a girl anymore, and her three teeth are black. Adopting the doleful mien of a Hecuba or Andromache, she should studiously avoid farces, lively parties, and other occasions of mirth, making sure to attend only funerals and tragic plays. Downright cheerfully, the poet tells of men who prostitute their wives (1.73) and women who try to cover up fetid drunken belches with mints (1.87). He's also entirely at home with the crudest obscenity: "You want to know why I won't marry you, Galla? You're educated. / My dick, on the other hand, is often guilty of boners" (11.19).

For these qualities, Martial has been reviled and avidly read through the ages. The Renaissance Italian poet Andrea Navagero hated Martial so much that he burned a copy of the satirist's works every year. Lord Byron asks in *Don Juan* (1.43.343–44), "And then what proper person can be partial / To all those nauseous epigrams of Martial?" To such critics and carpers, Martial had already responded, claiming that "my book is dirty, but my life is clean" (1.4). Despite a wealth of obscene, pederastic, and scatological poems, he has some touching verses on his little slave girl Erotion, who died just short of her sixth birthday (5.34 and 10.61). His line "I can't live with you—or without you" (12.46) has become a proverbial statement of love's paradox.

But the greatest satirist of ancient Rome—and certainly the angriest— was Decimus Iunius Iuvenalis. Hailing from Aquinum (Aquino) in Latium, Juvenal (c. A.D. 55–c. 130) inveighed like a Jeremiah against the degeneracy of his time (mainly the reigns of Domitian, Nerva, Trajan, and Hadrian). Like his friend Martial, he was poor and fulminated against the degradations of the Roman client system.

In his sixteen dactylic hexameter satires, Juvenal delights in skewering his victims, hating both the sin and the sinner. His First Satire lays out his program. Given the infuriating conditions of contemporary Rome, when "every vice is at its height" (1.149), Juvenal claims that "it's impossible *not* to write satire" (1.30). Although he'd like to follow in the path blazed by Lucilius, there's a great danger that anyone who maligns an emperor's favorite will end up as a human torch, so he'll satirize the famous dead instead (like the tyrannical Domitian, who was murdered in A.D. 96).

But Juvenal also rails against nouveaux riches ex-slaves and the upstart "Greeklings," Jews, Syrians, and other Easterners who poured into the city with their alien languages, foods, religions, prostitutes, music, and mores. The Rome of his Third Satire is a nightmarish collocation of fires, poverty, collapsing tenements, and poets reciting their works in brutal August. Like Martial, Juvenal can't stand the nocturnal din—the clanking wagons carting in goods, their drivers cursing at each other. People fling urinals and pails of garbage out the window. Muggers, drunken brawlers, and burglars prowl the streets.

Much of Juvenal's apparent hysteria results from his extensive training in rhetoric and reflects a poetic strategy to say the worst things possible about any topic he sets his sights on, heaping together loathsome images of the vice he's castigating in a cinematic montage. Above all, he attacks the sexual license of Rome, spouting a sewer of vituperation at his victims. Confronted with the arrogance of rich studs and tramps, Martial laughed, but Juvenal screamed.

His most astounding performance in this vein is Satire Six, a tirade of almost 700 lines against the corrupt ways of Roman women. The occasion of the rant is the decision of his friend Postumus to get married. Advising Postumus to hang himself, jump out a window, or drown himself instead, Juvenal tries to dissuade his friend from his insane resolution by presenting him with a torrential catalog of female faults.

Things were different in the Golden Age, when "women suckled huge infants with their functional breasts / And were often shaggier than their acorn-belching husbands" (6.9–10). Modern wives, on the other hand, have orgasms while watching homosexual dancers at the theater and become the groupies of musicians and gladiators. Nowadays a chaste wife is "a rare bird [*rara avis*] on this earth, sort of like a black swan" (6.165).

Juvenal has a particular animus against women athletes, all decked out in their exercise suits, and their trainers, who are only seemingly gay. One of his messier tableaux is of a wife who works out at the gym, gets her erotic massage, comes home late to her starving dinner guests, gorges herself on wine, and throws it up all over the floor. Even worse are the wives who, on their way home from midnight oyster suppers, stagger out of their litters to urinate and engage in some casual sex with one another. It's also a known fact that women smuggle men into their secret religious rites, which are really just excuses for unspeakable orgies. Of course, some husbands try to appoint guardians over their wives—but who will guard the guardians? (6.347–48).

Then there's the female meddler in men's business, like war and foreign affairs. There's the female intellectual who kills the dinner conversation with a monologue of literary babble. There's the woman who always looks awful for her husband but stunning for her lover. Some women have their slaves flogged mercilessly if they're sexually frustrated; others poison their husbands, their wards, even their own children. What else is there to say on the subject?

Only somewhat more generous is Juvenal's Tenth Satire, the basis of Samuel Johnson's "The Vanity of Human Wishes" (1749). The poem is a Stoic demolition of everything humans pray for: wealth, power, fame, good looks, longevity. Caesar, Pompey, and Crassus were all killed: "Few tyrants die in their beds" (10.113). Many famous beauties have been destroyed by the lust of others or their own. If your prayers for a long life are answered, think how ugly you'll become. If you're lucky enough not to become demented, you'll at least have to see all your loved ones die. If you have to pray for something, pray for a sound mind in a sound body, mens sana in corpore sano (10.356), and a valiant heart uncowed by death. Ask the gods for virtue, the only guarantor of a peaceful life.

During the Restoration and the eighteenth century, the greatest age of satire in English literature, Juvenal's influence was particularly strong. John Dryden translated five of his satires, and Jonathan Swift imbued his satiric masterpiece Gulliver's Travels with Juvenalian misanthropy. Swift's scatological poems, such as "The Lady's Dressing Room" and "A Beautiful Young Nymph Going to Bed," are steeped in Juvenal's misogyny. Though Alexander Pope imitated various satires and epistles of Horace, the spirit of Juvenalian sarcasm pervades his mock-epic Dunciad. Better known as a literary critic and lexicographer, Samuel Johnson also wrote modern-dress versions of the Third and Tenth Satires of Juvenal, transposing to London and his own times the timeless insights of ancient Rome's most uncompromising satirist.

Seven

Ovid's treasure hoard of myth and fable

The sweete wittie soule of Ovid lives in mellifluous and hony-tongued Shakespeare.
—Francis Meres, *Palladis Tamia: Wit's Treasury* (1598)

ROME MAY HAVE PRODUCED a handful of poets greater than Ovid, but none was more influential on subsequent European literature, painting, and sculpture. In his *Metamorphoses* (Transformations), he recounts all the major Greek myths (including many that, but for him, would have been lost), preserves much Roman lore, and includes a few stories from the Near East—two hundred and fifty tales in all, about fifty told in detail and the rest more briefly. Since knowledge of Greek was almost entirely lost in Western Europe during the Middle Ages, the fact that his works were in Latin and widely available made him the prime authority on the Greek myths (and the art of love) for Christian Europe when its vernacular literatures were forming. As classical scholar Moses Hadas has written, "European literature and art would be poorer for the loss of the *Metamorphoses* than for the loss of Homer."

Born into a wealthy family in Sulmo (Sulmona) high in the mountains of the Abruzzi, Publius Ovidius Naso (43 B.C.–A.D. 17) early manifested an irrepressible love of poetry, though his father had destined him for a legal career. Coming to Rome, he studied rhetoric and law and then went on the grand tour to Athens, Asia Minor, and Sicily. On his return, he held a few political offices but soon turned to verse. Though he was acquainted with Horace and knew Virgil by sight, he emulated his friends Propertius and Tibullus, and the long-dead Catullus (see Essay 4), in their cultivation of love poetry. The man who styled himself "The Professor of Love" eventually married three times.

Like Homer's, the gods of Ovid's masterpiece, the *Metamorphoses*, are basically humans with larger sexual appetites who live forever, while the mortal victims of their intrigues are just their messy detritus. Only his oldsters, like the hospitable Baucis and Philemon, or the pious survivors of the Greek deluge myth, Deucalion and Pyrrha, see their virtue rewarded.

The epitome of witty sophistication, Ovid believed in none of the old stories he retold, focusing instead on the passions they embodied. He was fascinated by the relations between the sexes, the irresistible nature of desire, and the rationalizations people use. Camille Paglia, who dubs Ovid "the first psychoanalyst of sex," claims his "encyclopedic attentiveness to erotic perversity will not recur until Spenser's *Faerie Queene*, directly influenced by him."[1] His tales of all-consuming sexual love end tragically but without any sermonizing.

Divided somewhat arbitrarily into fifteen books, Ovid's massive poem weighs in at almost 12,000 smoothly flowing hexameter lines. Its theme is the instability of all natural things, and its unifying principle is the miraculous transformation of humans and other beings into plants, animals, birds, stones, and streams. From widely heterogeneous materials Ovid constructed a continuous narrative, in more or less chronological order, from the Creation (when Chaos was transformed into Cosmos) to the apotheosis of the slain Julius Caesar, a new god and blazing star in the heavens.

All of Ovid's poems are mother lodes of mythological lore, even his urbanely scandalous handbook of seduction, the *Ars amatoria* (The Art of Love). This work was viewed with distaste by Augustus, who was trying to revamp Roman morality, and its author became persona non grata after being implicated in a vague offense probably involving the emperor's promiscuous granddaughter Julia. Ovid was thus exiled to semi-barbarous Tomis (modern Constanţsa, Romania) on the Black Sea, near the mouth of the Danube, just after completing the *Metamorphoses*.

This personal tragedy hardly diminished Ovid's impact over the next two millennia. He and Virgil became the favorite poets of the Middle Ages, and the genius-rich twelfth century has been called the Age of Ovid. His influence was foremost in France and Provence, where he helped shape the verse of the troubadours, the Arthurian romances of Chrétien de Troyes, and the courtly love tradition of *The Romance of the Rose*. France also witnessed the strange allegorizations of the *Ovide*

---

[1]Camille Paglia, *Sexual Personae: Art and Decadence from Nefertiti to Emily Dickinson* (New York: Vintage Books, 1991), p. 132.

moralisé, whose anonymous fourteenth-century author interpreted Ovidian myths in terms of Christ, Mary, and the Church.

In Italy, Dante embellished his *Divine Comedy* with Ovidian lore and enrolled Ovid in his *"bella scola"* (beautiful school) of the greatest poets of all time whom he meets in the *Inferno*—with Homer, Virgil, Horace, and Lucan (and Dante himself as sixth). Later in the fourteenth century, the multiple narrators of the *Metamorphoses* influenced the framed-story device of Boccaccio's *Decameron* (see Essay 17). The Latin poem was also a major source of Boccaccio's *On Famous Women*, with its 104 capsule biographies, and of his Latin prose encyclopedia of ancient myths, *Genealogy of the Pagan Gods*.

In medieval England, Geoffrey Chaucer singled out the *Metamorphoses* as his favorite book in the *House of Fame* (712). Ovid's poem not only provided Chaucer with several tragic love stories for *The Legend of Good Women* but also served as the source of "The Manciple's Tale" (on how the raven was changed from white to black for tattling) and influenced the linking devices of the disparate stories told by the Canterbury pilgrims.

In 1567 Arthur Golding published an English translation of the *Metamorphoses* in heptameter couplets, or fourteeners, which Ezra Pound (who adapted numerous Ovidian myths for his *Cantos*) called "the most beautiful book in the language," "from which Shakespeare learned so much of his trade." By far the greatest number of mythological allusions in Shakespeare are derived from Ovid, whose cognomen Naso (Nose) gives rise to a remark in *Love's Labor's Lost* by the pedantic Holofernes, "And why, indeed, Naso, but for smelling out the odoriferous flowers of fancy, the jerks of invention?" (4.2.128–30)

Puritan poet John Milton, who wrote reams of Ovidian Latin verse in his youth, plundered the *Metamorphoses* for details for his *Paradise Lost*. He endowed his Eve, for example, with love for her own reflection, like Ovid's Narcissus, and with vulnerability to the ruler of Hell, like Ovid's Proserpina. Neoclassical authors of the caliber of Dryden, Swift, Congreve, Addison, and Pope all tried their hands at verse translations from the *Metamorphoses*.

In later literary history, the title characters of Shelley's "Arethusa," Swinburne's *Atalanta in Calydon*, and Rilke's *Sonnets to Orpheus* owe a debt to Ovid's magnum opus, and Pushkin's "To Ovid" is a verse tribute by the Russian poet, who found himself temporarily exiled not far from Tomis. Franz Kafka's fiercely ironic story, *The Metamorphosis*, tells how the unloved schlimazel Gregor Samsa is transformed, not into a bird or flower, but into a gigantic insect. Ted Hughes, that modern poetic master of feral and natural violence, translated two dozen of Ovid's tales shortly before his death.

At least part of the reason for Ovid's perennial appeal is his unerring ability to home in on the magic moment, the intersection of the quotidian with the uncanny, as in his tale of Apollo and Daphne (1.452–567). When the god of poetry belittles the powers of Cupid, the latter makes him fall in love with a nymph dedicated to virginity. As Apollo pursues Daphne (whose Greek name means "laurel"), she prays to her river-god father to transform the beauty that has so inflamed the god. There follows a description of how her sides harden with bark, her hair turns into leaves, her arms become branches, and her feet take root. Apollo feels her heart still beating inside the trunk of the laurel, kisses the wood, and makes it his sacred tree, its evergreen leaves woven into wreaths as an emblem of the undying fame conferred by poetry. Bernini's marble *Apollo and Daphne* (1622–25) portrays the girl's finely filigreed twig/fingers and root/feet in a statuary group of breathtaking virtuosity (see Essay 36).

The tragic love of a divinity for a mortal also figures in Ovid's story of Venus and Adonis (10.503–739). A painting of Titian shows the seated goddess (her nude back and ample buttocks facing us) clinging to her headstrong young lover in an attempt to prevent his going off to hunt the wild boar that will slay him. The best-known literary treatment of the myth is Shakespeare's brief epic in six-line stanzas, *Venus and Adonis* (1593). The poem features a comically aggressive Venus who commences her wooing by knocking Adonis off his horse and pouncing on him. On learning of his fatal plans to go hunting, the goddess swoons: "She sinketh down, still hanging by his neck, / He on her belly falls, she on her back." When she finds his gored body, she supposes the sharp-tusked boar had only meant to *kiss* Adonis, "nuzzling in his flank."

Ovid's story of another goddess and hunter, Diana and Actaeon (3.138–252), inspired a wealth of Renaissance paintings. In a Titian canvas of 1556–59, Actaeon is shocked to stumble on the plumply naked goddess of chastity and of the hunt as she's being dried off after bathing in a pool with her nymphs. Though the young man is innocent of any attempt to desecrate, Diana is incredulously indignant as she tries with the help of an attendant to cover herself while her little spaniel snarls at the intruder. In Titian's *The Death of Actaeon*, Diana, in the foreground of a stormy landscape, resumes her hunting while Actaeon, whom she has changed into a stag as punishment, is attacked and killed by his own hounds.

The tale of Pyramus and Thisbe is set in Babylon (4.55–166). With its young lovers kept apart by their parents and its tragedy-of-errors ending, it resembles the story of Romeo and Juliet. Living next door to each other, their houses separated by a common wall, Pyramus and Thisbe whisper through a chink and indulge in some very mediated kissing. Their plan to escape together goes awry when Pyramus, seeing a lion's tracks and Thisbe's torn bloody cloak at their meeting place beneath a mulberry tree near Ninus's tomb, assumes his beloved has been slain. In despair, he stabs himself beneath the tree, whose fruit was white in those far-off days but is now dyed red with his blood.

Thisbe, however, had dropped her cloak while fleeing the beast's approach, and the lion, which had just dined on some cattle, ripped the garment apart with its bloody jaws. On her return, Thisbe finds the dying Pyramus, who opens his eyes one last time to gaze on her before she kills herself with his sword.

Here, too, Shakespeare perceived the bathos always lurking beneath the surface of pathos. In A *Midsummer Night's Dream* some Athenian half-wits decide to put on a play, *The most lamentable comedy, and most cruel death of Pyramus and Thisby*, for Theseus and his court. With the carpenter Peter Quince as the unflappable director, Flute the bellows-mender as Thisby, and formerly ass-headed Bottom the weaver as the hero (with roles for the Wall and the Moonshine), their play within a play contains touches like "Ninny's tomb" and "with bloody blameful blade, / He bravely broached his boiling bloody breast" (5.1.147–48).

A notoriously violent Ovidian myth involves the sisters Philomela and Procne, and the latter's husband, Tereus (6.401–674). After Tereus rapes his sister-in-law and cuts out her tongue, Philomela weaves the story into a tapestry she sends to Procne. Tereus's infuriated wife slaughters their young son Itys and cooks him up for the unsuspecting rapist. In the chase that ensues when Tereus discovers the nature of his meal, the gods transform Philomela into a nightingale, Procne into a swallow, and Tereus into a hoopoe.

This gruesome tale contributes several details to Shakespeare's *Titus Andronicus*. Titus's daughter Lavinia, who has had her tongue cut out and her hands chopped off, uses her stumps to point to the story in a copy of the *Metamorphoses* to indicate that she was also raped. She then uses a stick guided by her mouth and feet to scrawl in the dirt the Latin word for *rape* and the names of the two brothers who did it. After killing the rapists, Titus serves their heads baked in a pie to their wicked mother, and then kills her and Lavinia before being killed himself. Even here, Shakespeare's use of Ovid (and Seneca) borders on parody.

Ovid's repertoire includes a delicate depiction of paternal love in the adventure of Daedalus and Icarus (8.152–235), but the background is one of bestial lust. Daedalus, whose name means "cunning artificer," builds the Labyrinth to hide the Minotaur, the half-man, half-bull offspring of Pasiphaë, wife of King Minos of Crete, and a beautiful white bull with which she had mated.

The king, reluctant to have the architect spread the story of the queen's shameful lust, has forbidden him and his young son Icarus to leave the island. Daedalus, who is also a brilliant sculptor and inventor, makes wings for himself and the boy out of feathers and wax, and off they fly. In his exultation Icarus forgets his father's warnings about soaring too high, and the sun melts the wax in his wings. He falls into the sea, named Icarian after him, while Daedalus brokenheartedly makes good his escape to Sicily. In Pieter Brueghel the Elder's *The Fall of Icarus* (which itself inspired W. H. Auden's poem *"Musée des Beaux Arts"*), the boy is just a tiny pair of legs at the center of a background splash while a plowman plows, a shepherd leans on his staff facing away from the water, a fisherman fishes, and a stately ship sails on, all of them indifferent to human suffering that is not their own.

James Joyce was so taken with this myth that he gave the autobiographical protagonist of *A Portrait of the Artist as a Young Man* (1916) the name Stephen Dedalus and used a line from Ovid (8.188) as the book's epigraph: *"Et ignotas animum dimittit in artes"* ("He [Daedalus] sets his mind to work on unknown arts," that is, his invention of flying). In the climactic scene by the seashore, a vision of the "hawklike man" Daedalus in flight inspires young Stephen to embrace his artistic vocation: "Yes! Yes! Yes! He would create proudly out of the freedom and power of his soul, as the great artificer whose name he bore, a living thing, new and soaring and beautiful, impalpable, imperishable."

The similar tale of Phaëthon, the boy who tried to drive his father Phoebus's chariot of the sun through the sky, is one of Ovid's best (1.747–79; 2.1–400). As with Daedalus and Icarus, the theme is the danger of hubris: "You'll be safest taking a middle path," Phoebus warns his son. Soon after setting out, the boy loses control of the chariot with its fiery steeds and begins scorching the earth, prompting Jupiter to blast him out of the sky with a thunderbolt.

• • •

Stricken by the thunderbolt hurled by Augustus, the fifty-one-year-old cunning artificer and bon vivant arrived in cold, bleak Tomis in A.D. 9. He wept the rest of his life away, writing the *Tristia* (Songs of Sadness) and the *Epistulae ex Ponto* (Letters from the Black Sea), in which he bemoaned his fate, begged the emperor to forgive him, and pled with his wife and friends to help him.

All in vain. Even after Augustus's death in A.D. 14, Ovid's sentence was not lifted, and the last great poet of Rome's golden age died in Tomis three years later. The exile, who had won the admiration of the locals, had even composed a poem in their Getic language. Delacroix's Romantic painting *Ovid among the Scythians* shows the refined, sorrowful poet reclining outdoors in a wild landscape and being offered a basket of mare's milk by reverential barbarians.

But Ovid always knew his work and reputation would endure. In the final metamorphosis of his great epic, he envisions himself, too, transformed after death: "The better part of me shall be borne immortal / Beyond the lofty stars—my name indelible."

Eight

The Roman legacy of law

The commandments of the law are as follows: to live honorably,
not to harm one's fellow men, and to render to all that which is right-
fully theirs.

—Ulpian (c. A.D. 200)

IT WAS THE ULTIMATE paper chase: Byzantine Emperor Justinian
(reigned 527–65), who built the splendid cathedral of Hagia Sophia and
reconquered Italy, North Africa, and other parts of the Western Roman
Empire from the barbarians, authorized a commission to codify the laws,
statutes, legal opinions, and imperial decrees accumulated over the thirteen hundred years of Rome's existence. For only one part of the epic
task, the *Digest*, members of the commission read approximately 3 million lines of text in 2,000 treatises and distilled them into 150,000 lines,
which make up a book half again as long as the Bible. The entire project,
the *Corpus Iuris Civilis* (Body of Civil Law), completed in A.D. 534, is a
monument to the Roman passions for order, systematization, and due
process (not to mention litigiousness).

With its magisterial comprehensiveness, precision, clarity, and perva-
sive influence, the legal system of the ancient Romans has often been
considered the greatest ever devised. As adapted to local medieval traditions, it was the ancestor of the legal systems of Western nations in
which English common law did not exert the predominant influence,
including nearly all the nations on the European continent. In addition,
it was appropriated by the medieval Church as a basis for its canon law.

The first codification of Roman law, the Twelve Tables (c. 450 B.C.),
resulted from an attempt to mitigate the fierce power struggles between
the patricians, who adhered to ancient unwritten codes of social conduct completely understood only by their priests, and the plebeians, who
were usually the ill-informed casualties of these codes. A committee
known as the *decemviri* (ten men) transcribed these customary Roman

laws onto twelve bronze or wooden tablets for display in the Forum. Although the Twelve Tables broke no new legal ground, they removed the law from the arbitrary realm of religion and disseminated it to all who could read. The orator and statesman Cicero (106–43 B.C.) recalled that "when we were boys, we learned the *Twelve* as a ditty," but he lamented, "no one learns them now."

The Twelve Tables provide a glimpse of life in a still-agrarian society. A father was prohibited from regaining rights over his son after selling him three times. A woman could avoid some of the legal strictures of marriage by absenting herself from her husband's house on three consecutive nights each year. The "enchanting-away" of a neighbor's crops was forbidden. Professional female mourners were not allowed to tear out their hair, and funeral expenditures were limited to "three veils, one small purple tunic, and ten flute-players." The penalty for physical assault that resulted in fractured bones depended on the victim's social status—three hundred copper coins for a freeman, half that number for a slave. Pragmatism was also in evidence. Four-footed animals that caused property damage were to be surrendered to the offended party unless other restitution was made. If a watercourse directed through a public place damaged private property, the state pledged to repair it. Annual interest rates exceeding 8⅓ percent were prohibited.

Although capital punishment was on the books for diverse offenses, a death sentence could be appealed to a citizen assembly, which usually commuted it to exile from Rome. The execution of a citizen who had not been convicted of a capital crime was strictly forbidden. Since capital offenses included libelous speech and political lampoonery, the later art of satire tended to make use of pseudonyms (see Essay 6). The concept of intent, central to modern criminal and civil law, also began to emerge in the Twelve Tables. If a death resulted when "a missile has sped from the hand and the holder has not aimed it," the perpetrator was required only to present the decedent's family with a ram.

The body of Roman law grew to keep in step with an increasingly complex society. The early Roman *ius civile* (civil law), with its source in the Twelve Tables, was considered authoritative because it was either rooted in custom or had been duly enacted by popular assemblies. But eventually magistrates found the scope of the *ius civile* too narrow for contemporary economic and social conditions. For situations the *ius civile* did not address, the unwritten Roman constitution gave the higher magistrates the jurisdiction and authority—the *imperium*—to issue their own edicts.

The shortcomings of the *ius civile* were exemplified by the plight of foreigners, or *peregrini*, who had no protection under Roman law unless a citizen agreed to act as a legal patron. This situation became especially troublesome during the First Punic War (264–241 B.C.), when Rome, already a regional power, was thronged by foreign traders. To facilitate transactions between citizens and *peregrini*, the Romans appointed a *praetor peregrinus*, a law officer in charge of cases involving foreigners. With increasing commercialization and the expansion of Rome's empire, the rulings of this and other magistrates merged with a body of law called the *ius gentium* (law of the nations). Based on existing laws in the Mediterranean governing trade and other matters, the *ius gentium* developed from the enactments of Roman officials administering provinces. With time, it was applied more broadly regardless of the citizenship status of the parties involved.

The main divisions of Roman law applied to persons, property, or procedure. According to the law of persons, full citizens had the right to vote, marry other freeborn persons, enter binding contracts, and hold public office. Others had only the right to marry or enter contracts, and freed slaves could vote and enter contracts but could not marry freeborn persons or hold office. Slaves, also called "impersonal men," had no rights. All children of a slave were condemned to servitude, even if the other parent was freeborn. Female slaves who were raped had no legal redress in older Roman law, but Justinian's Code made the rape of any woman punishable by death. Until A.D. 410, women were kept in perpetual legal guardianship, "because of their levity of disposition," but already, hundreds of years earlier, this law had become a mere technicality.

The bulk of Roman laws, however, concerned property, and these were the most complex, specifying the myriad types of crime against property and the possible ways by which citizens could acquire land and other goods. Inheritance laws, for example, stipulated that a man must leave a certain percentage of his estate to his offspring, another amount to his wife (but only if she had borne him at least three children), and the remainder to other relatives. In contracts between individuals, uttering *spondeo* (I promise) in front of a witness was considered to be as binding as any written contract. "Lemon laws" were on the books in the form of *caveat emptor* and *caveat venditor,* and anyone selling property was obliged to disclose its defects before the sale was completed.

From earliest times, the law of procedure was tortuously detailed and highly formalistic, and it tended to remain so. Court cases might involve a magistrate and a judge, attorneys, jurists, consultants, clerks, and evidence specialists. Modern trial lawyers have nothing on some of their ancient Roman counterparts, who browbeat witnesses, played to the jury's emotions and prejudices, hired claques to applaud their speeches, charged outrageous fees, and did their utmost to circumvent the law at every turn.

Magistrates were constrained by the law regarding the sentences they could impose, and punishments still depended on the social class of the offender. Slaves, but not citizens, could be crucified. In imperial times, Roman citizens who were sentenced to death had the right of appeal to a higher court, then the Senate, and eventually the emperor (as St. Paul vainly attempted with Nero).

When Rome became a world power, the *ius gentium* proved a practical means of resolving disputes among parties from different provinces, and the idea that a "natural" law applied universally to all free men gained a foothold in legal thought. Natural law received an impetus from Roman thinkers influenced by Greek Stoic philosophy, especially Cicero and Seneca (4 B.C.–A.D. 65). Stoics believed that all humans were born with a divine spark of right reason (Greek, *logos*) that impelled them to strive for moral excellence. Though not all men acted in accordance with the *logos*, the very fact that they possessed it made them worthy of protection by natural law and its derivative, *aequitas* (fairness).

With a wider acceptance of natural law, the latter part of the first and the second century A.D. ushered in a golden age of legal thought and reform, including more humane treatment of women, children, slaves, and those at society's fringes. In the first century, Vespasian accorded some legal protections to prostitutes, and Domitian forbade the castration of slaves, but it was during the reign of Hadrian (117–138) that Roman law shed many of its archaic, barbarous features. This peripatetic emperor, who had observed the local governments of Greek cities and ordered the variable yearly edicts of the praetors codified into an *edictum perpetuum* (perpetual edict), deprived slave owners of their right to put slaves to death without court sanction. During this period, fathers and husbands lost many privileges long associated with the Roman paterfamilias, including the power of life and death over household members, the prerogative of selling a child into slavery, and the right to kill an adulterous wife.

The work of five outstanding jurists illuminates the annals of Roman law in the second and third centuries. Julian (Salvius Julianus,

c. 100–169), a North African who was primarily responsible for compiling the Perpetual Edict, wrote legal opinions renowned for their clarity and acumen. The jurist known only as Gaius (c. 110–180) wrote the standard introductory law text that became the chief source of Justinian's *Institutes*. Papinian (Aemilius Papinianus) was considered by the Romans their preeminent jurisconsult. He was murdered by Caracalla for criticizing the latter's murder of his brother, Geta, in the same year (212) that Caracalla extended Roman citizenship to all the city dwellers of the empire.

Both Ulpian (Domitius Ulpianus, d. A.D. 223) and his colleague Paul (Julius Paulus) produced detailed commentaries that became the most authoritative pronouncements on Roman law in the postclassical period. It was Ulpian's opinion that "it is better to leave the crime of the guilty unpunished than to condemn the innocent." He also claimed that class distinctions were social artifacts that should not be recognized under the law because "according to the law of nature, all men are equal." With his random murder in 223—just one of many indications of the growing chaos of the Roman world—the era of the great jurists came to an end.

Before Justinian, several attempts had been made to codify imperial enactments, most notably the Code of Theodosius II in 438. But with the *Corpus Iuris Civilis* of 534, Justinian achieved his ambitious goals of compiling an authoritative, uniform, legally binding statement of all Roman law—not just imperial edicts—and of providing schools of law with a single text. The *Corpus Iuris* is divided into the *Code*, or *Codex Justinianus*, a collection of about 5,000 enactments of the emperors from Hadrian onward, which were corrected and updated; the *Digest*, or *Pandects*, the core of the *Corpus Iuris*; the *Institutes*, an introductory handbook for law students; and the *Novels*, containing Justinian's own imperial edicts in the years after 534.

For the *Digest*, sixteen eminent lawyers under the presidency of Justinian's minister Tribonian were ordered to collect extracts from the *responsa prudentium*, or "opinions of the learned lawyers," that is, the great jurisconsults whose legal opinions were considered to be legally binding precedents. The lawyers were not to quote the jurists verbatim, but to rephrase the excerpts for concision and currency, pruning away obsolete, redundant, or contradictory materials. Of the more than nine thousand extracts from the writings of thirty-nine jurists, the vast majority date from A.D. 100 to 250, half of the total number being supplied by Ulpian and Paul. The compilation of the *Digest* and the rest of the

Corpus Iuris Civilis marked the last great manifestation of the ancient Greco-Roman mind.

But as Edward Gibbon wrote, "The public reason of the Romans has been silently or studiously transfused into the domestic institutions of Europe, and the laws of Justinian still command the respect or obedience of independent nations." The persistent influence of Roman law is due in large part to the rediscovery of a complete manuscript of the *Digest* at Pisa in the late eleventh century, a time of rapid change in Western Europe. In the wake of that discovery a group of scholars, who formed the nucleus of the world's first university at Bologna, soon began the scientific study of Justinian's masterpiece of jurisprudence (see Essay 10).

In all its various incarnations throughout the ages, Roman law always retained its pellucid quality as *ratio scripta*, or "written reason." When the legal philosopher A. P. d'Entrèves singled out the world's greatest debt to the Roman legacy, he chose "the notion that law is the common patrimony of men, a bond that can overcome their differences and enhance their unity."

Nine

St. Benedict: Father of Western monasticism, preserver of the Roman heritage

We are about to open a school for God's service, in which we hope nothing harsh or oppressive will be directed. For preserving charity or correcting faults, it may be necessary at times, by reason of justice, to be slightly more severe. Do not fear this and retreat, for the path to salvation is long and the entrance is narrow.[1]

—St. Benedict, *The Rule* (c. A.D. 535)

IN HIS BIOGRAPHY OF the father of Western monasticism, Pope St. Gregory the Great describes how St. Benedict, calling to mind a woman he once knew, was sorely tempted to "abandon the lonely wilderness" and return to her. "Just then," Gregory writes, "he noticed a thick patch of nettles and briars next to him. Throwing his garments aside, he flung himself naked into the sharp thorns and stinging nettles. There he rolled and tossed until his whole body was in pain and covered with blood. Yet once he had conquered pleasure through suffering, his torn and bleeding skin served to drain off the poison of temptation. . . . Benedict's soul, like a field cleared of briars, soon yielded a rich harvest of virtues."

In addition to this harvest, Benedict's pursuit of a holy life helped save the heritage of the ancient world during a bleak, tumultuous period of European history. He also left *The Rule of St. Benedict,* his practical guide for monastic living that inspired thousands of monasteries of various orders that eventually arose in Europe, serving as a blueprint for religious communities down to this day.

The scion of an aristocratic Roman family, Benedict was born in Nursia (Norcia), near Spoleto in Umbria, in about A.D. 480, shortly after the

---

[1] St. Benedict, *The Rule of St. Benedict,* trans. by Anthony C. Meisel and M. L. del Mastro (Garden City, N.Y.: Image Books, 1975), p. 45. This and sebsequent quotations from *The Rule* are from this edition.

last emperor of the Western Roman Empire was deposed. Like many other adolescent boys of his class, he traveled with his nurse to Rome to study rhetoric and law. According to St. Gregory, who was born about seven years before Benedict died, and who spoke with people who had known him, "Even while he was still living in the world, free to enjoy all it had to offer, Benedict saw how empty it was and turned from it without regret."

Perhaps it was the students' "abandoning themselves to vice," or maybe it was the religious strife in Rome between the papacy and the Eastern Church that drove Benedict, accompanied by his devoted nurse, to Affile, a small town about thirty-five miles east of Rome. Here, encountering a group of similarly disaffected Christians, he was afforded solitude for prayer and the study of Scripture and the writings of the early Church Fathers, as well as those of hermits like John Cassian (360–435), who was an important link between Eastern monasticism and Western Europe.

Benedict left Affile abruptly several years later in the aftermath of his first miracle. His nurse had broken a piece of borrowed earthenware, and, seeing her extreme distress over the accident, Benedict knelt to pick up the pieces, praying as he did so. By the time he rose to his feet, the dish was supposedly whole again. Dismayed by the instant celebrity the incident brought him, Benedict departed, alone this time, for Subiaco, an area about five miles to the north. With the aid of a local monk who helped him settle in a cliffside cave, gave him a sheepskin robe to wear, and brought him food occasionally, Benedict lived as a hermit for three years.

He was eventually discovered by shepherds, and word of his holiness spread. A group of monks whose abbot had recently died asked him to become their new spiritual father. Benedict warned them that they would find his rule too severe. When they persisted, he went to live with them. But just as he had predicted, the monks considered him too harsh, and they tried to poison his wine. His thwarting of their attempt constituted his second recorded miracle, and he immediately returned to his cave in the cliff.

But Benedict's days of solitude were over. Besieged by men who wished to live in a community with him as abbot, he relented again, this time with a better outcome. Soon the area around Subiaco had twelve small monasteries, each housing twelve men and a superior. Benedict served as abbot of all the houses and lived in a thirteenth with the monks whom he judged most likely to benefit by his own teaching. In his *Rule,* Benedict later wrote that an abbot "should recognize the difficulty of his position—to care for and guide the spiritual development of many different characters. One must be led by friendliness, another by sharp rebukes, another by persuasion. The abbot must adapt himself to cope with individuality."

The monks under Benedict's rule in Subiaco lived quite differently from their contemporaries. Early Christian monks, such as those in the Egyptian desert, where Christian asceticism was developed by St. Anthony of Egypt more than two hundred years earlier, were hermits (also known as eremites or anchorites). Each lived in isolation, eschewing all social contact at a time when Christians were still widely persecuted, especially in the cities.

Benedict's varied experiences led him to a different model for monastic life because he felt that only a few saintly people could live apart from the world. It was too easy for a hermit to fall prey to unwholesome ways, becoming self-satisfied and arrogant, willfully ignorant of his own spiritual errors. Most people, he believed, were refined by their social instincts, especially when they were banded together in a community with the goal of leading holy lives.

"Idleness is an enemy of the soul," wrote Benedict, and *"Laborare est orare"* (to work is to pray) later became the motto of the Benedictines. The *Rule* clearly outlined a daily schedule consisting primarily of either manual labor or study, according to the monks' individual skills and the needs of the community. Regardless of whether they spent most of their time in the fields or in the library, however, the monks were urged to read and study Scripture or the Church Fathers for three to five hours daily, depending on the season. Those who did not know how to read were taught, since Benedict believed that edifying reading and work were nearly as important to the pursuit of holiness as prayer.

The physical labors of the monks were directed toward achieving self-sufficiency for the monastery. The monks built their simple dwellings, hauled water, and worked in the fields to grow their own food. Some attended to the needs of travelers and other visitors, since, according to the *Rule,* "All guests should be welcomed as Christ."

Despite requiring the monks to spend much of their time in prayer and in chanting psalms during the eight liturgical "hours" of the Divine Office, such as Matins, Lauds, and Vespers, Benedict's rule was notable for its moderation. Monks were allowed to have a glass of wine at meals and to get about eight hours of sleep daily. When it was time to rise for prayers, they were to encourage each other, "for the sleepy make many excuses."

Although ample provision was made for corporal punishment, Benedict's compassion for human weakness is apparent throughout the *Rule*. A brother being punished by isolation was to be visited by a wise older monk "who will console him as if by stealth . . . to keep him from being overwhelmed by sorrow." Special care was taken of the sick, who, unlike the others, were allowed to eat meat until they recovered. Benedict admonished the sick, though, "not to distress the brothers who care for them with unreasonable demands."

Much more than a guide to harmonious communal living, the *Rule* was intended to provide a framework for the attainment of spiritual perfection, to which the keys were obedience and humility. "They do not live as they please, nor as their desires and will dictate," writes Benedict of the monks, "but rather they live under the direction and judgment of an abbot in a monastery. Undoubtedly, they find their inspiration in the Lord's saying: 'I come not to do my own will, but the will of Him who sent me.'" Benedict describes how true humility, attained by ascending a spiritual twelve-step ladder, leads to "that perfect love of God which casts out fear. . . . The monk will no longer act out of the fear of hell, but for the love of Christ."

Among the monks at Subiaco, as in Benedictine communities down to this day, all property was held in common. Individual ownership of even the most insignificant item was forbidden. Furthermore, men who joined the community lost their worldly rank: "Unless there is good cause, the freeman should not be considered superior to the serf. . . . Only if we are found to excel in good works and humility are we preferred in the eyes of God as individuals."

After several years, a local priest who had become jealous of the growing reputation of the monasteries in Subiaco tried to scandalize Benedict by paying a group of young women to dance naked outside the abbot's residence. Wishing to spare his monks further harassment and temptation, Benedict relocated them.

The monks found a new home in A.D. 529 atop Monte Cassino, on the site of a temple to Apollo that Benedict ordered destroyed. He then decided to house all the monks under one roof and establish a governing system that included a prior and several deans. It was here that Benedict wrote the *Rule*. The abbey at Monte Cassino was established within months of another event that marked the symbolic transition from the ancient to the medieval world: the Byzantine Emperor Justinian's closing of the age-old schools of pagan philosophy in Athens.

Perched above the town of Cassino, halfway between Naples and Rome, the abbey of Monte Cassino rapidly made a name for itself as a center of learning and sanctity. The period from its founding until the mid-twelfth century has been called "The Golden Age of Monasticism" and "The Benedictine Centuries" because of the accomplishments of the monks at Monte Cassino and the other Benedictine monasteries that arose in Italy, France, Britain, and elsewhere in Europe. From these monasteries, missionaries were sent to convert much of northern and central Europe to Christianity.

The monasteries' preeminent contribution was the transmission of the literature and lore of the past, both Christian and pagan. Benedictine monks collected, copied, illustrated, summarized, taught, and wrote commentaries on the ancient classics, preserving the heritage of Greece, Rome, and Christianity through all the vicissitudes of the Dark Ages. Their scholarly and pedagogical activities—epitomized in the work of Bede and the monks of the Carolingian Renaissance—kept learning alive in Europe between the fall of Rome and the rise of the universities many centuries later (see Essay 10), despite the ravages of Goths, Franks, Byzantines, Vikings, Magyars, and Muslims.

The Roman statesman and monk Cassiodorus, a contemporary of Benedict's, almost surely used Monte Cassino as a model when he founded the monastery of Vivarium at Squillace in Calabria with the goal of preserving Roman and early Christian culture by copying and distributing ancient texts. Cassiodorus referred to these educational activities as "fighting the Devil by pen and ink." His exemplary methods, in turn, greatly influenced the workings of the Benedictine scriptoria.

Benedict died at Monte Cassino in 547. He was buried beside his twin sister, St. Scholastica, who had founded a convent nearby. After being devastated through the centuries by Lombards, Saracens, earthquakes, and Napoleon's French, Monte Cassino was obliterated by Allied bombers in 1944 to drive out the Germans who were using the abbey as a stronghold. The monastery was rebuilt over the next decade, and it remains the mother church, and hub, of the Benedictine religious order. When Pope Paul VI visited Monte Cassino in 1964, he proclaimed Benedict the main patron saint of Europe, honoring him as a "messenger of peace."

X

Ten

Salerno and Bologna: The earliest medical school and university

Civitas Hippocratica (City of Hippocrates)
—Nickname of Salerno (eleventh century)

In many respects the [legal] work of the School of Bologna represents the most brilliant achievement of the intellect of mediaeval Europe.
—Hastings Rashdall, *The Universities of Europe in the Middle Ages* (1895)

THE SOUTHERN ITALIAN coastal city of Salerno and the northern mercantile center of Bologna were responsible for Italy's European supremacy in medicine and law during the later Middle Ages. It was at Salerno, a wealthy, culturally diverse center of trade on the warm Gulf of Naples and the site of a health resort since ancient Roman times, that Europe's first school of medicine and secular institution of higher learning arose. At Bologna, a crossroads of northern Italy, the merchant aristocracy who had grown rich on international trade encouraged law studies, which became the nucleus of the world's first university.

Different as they were, both Salerno and Bologna fostered the development of institutions for propagating the transmission of newly recovered Greek and Roman texts and expanding the boundaries of knowledge. The university, with its prescribed courses of study, curricula, faculties, colleges, examinations, graduation ceremonies, and awarding of degrees, was unknown in the ancient world. It made its first appearance in Italy only during the Middle Ages.

Before the rise of Salerno, medical instruction centered on monastic infirmaries that served as hospices for old or sick monks and travelers. The monks' armamentarium included bloodletting, cupping, and bathing, and the emetics, purgatives, and diuretics from medieval herbals and folk medicine, but it also relied heavily on prayer, penitence, relics, and scapulars.

At Salerno, however, some scholars gradually realized that diseases arose from natural causes rather than from divine wrath, and healers were no longer specialized forms of monks but professionals with diplomas who charged fees. Influenced by the medical learning of earlier rulers of the area—the Byzantine Greeks and the Arabs—and by the presence of the largest Jewish community in southern Italy, the school at Salerno, staffed mostly by lay practitioners from the twelfth century onward, based its instruction on the best available contemporary sources. This coalescence of Greek, Arabian, and Jewish medical traditions with the native Latin one gave rise to the legend of the school's founding by four physicians, one from each culture, allegedly as early as the tenth century.

Although no formally constituted university arose at Salerno until 1280, the *civitas Hippocratica* was, by the eleventh century, with practitioner/writers like Gariopontus and Archbishop Alfanus, already attracting students of medicine from northern Europe and even Asia and Africa. One of these, Constantine the African, a Tunisian, greatly augmented the school's resources when he came to Salerno in about 1070 bearing the gifts of Arabic medical manuscripts acquired on his travels in the Islamic Middle East. After a brief stay at Salerno, he entered the Benedictine Abbey of Monte Cassino to become a monk (see Essay 9).

There, in the last decades of the eleventh century, Constantine used his native knowledge of Arabic to translate into Latin at least twenty medical works by Greek, Arabic, Jewish, and Persian writers from Arabic originals or translations. The texts he thus made available to Salerno (only seventy-five miles southeast of Monte Cassino) included versions of Hippocrates, the fifth-century B.C. Greek "Father of Medicine"; several treatises of the Greco-Roman physician Galen (second century A.D.); and works of the tenth-century Jewish physician Isaac Judaeus. Constantine's *Pantegni* (The Universal Art), an abbreviated translation of a vastly influential work by the tenth-century Persian physician Haly Abbas, incorporated the main tenets of ancient Greek anatomy, physiology, and pathology. These translations were the first rational books on medicine to enter the West in half a millennium.

Shortly after 1100 there developed at Salerno an extremely influential core curriculum that came to be called the Articella (The Little Art), based on Latin translations of a ninth-century Arabic medical handbook and several Hippocratic and other Greek texts including, later in the century, Galen. The *Antidotary* (c. 1150), a collection of compound medical prescriptions by Nicholaus of Salerno, became a highly popular medieval formulary or pharmacopoeia.

At Salerno, anatomy was taught based on the texts of Galen and Haly Abbas, but dissection was also practiced for the first time since antiquity. Pigs were used for this purpose, as described in the *Anatomia porci* of Copho (written in the second quarter of the twelfth century). Progress was made in surgery because of homecoming Crusaders who stopped at Salerno to be treated for their wounds.

Roger Frugardi, who practiced in Parma, wrote by far the most influential twelfth-century work on surgery in the Christian West, *Practica Chirurgiae* (c. 1170), which became a standard text at Salerno. Roger showed how to suture torn intestines, taught the management of skull fractures, and prescribed seaweed ashes, which contain iodine, to be taken orally for goiter—a precursor of modern iodine therapy for various thyroid disorders.

Although women are known to have practiced medicine at Salerno, only one, Trota, lent her name to a body of twelfth-century medical treatises subsumed under the rubric of *Trotula*. This document is a patchwork collation of at least three different texts. The sections *On the Conditions of Women* (later called *Trotula major*) and *On Women's Cosmetics* were, according to the most recent scholarship,[1] written by men, whereas the part called *On Treatments for Women* (or *Trotula minor*), attributed to Trota, seems to reflect a woman's empiric perspective on a broad range of gynecologic problems. In its totality, the *Trotula* became the preeminent medieval textbook on women's health, dealing mostly with conception, pregnancy, embryonic development, and childbirth.

Of the hundred medical texts produced at Salerno, none was more influential than the *Regimen sanitatis Salernitanum* (The Salernitan Regimen of Health, 1260), a rhymed Latin poem by various hands providing rules of health for daily living. It recommended light meals, exercise, hygiene, herbs, drugs, rest, recreation, enemas, laxatives, and various other preventive measures, such as avoiding too much sex or bathing. A similar product of the Salerno school, *De flore dietarum* (The Flower of Diets), offers the following observations:

---

[1] Monica H. Green, *The "Trotula": A Medieval Compendium of Women's Medicine* (Philadelphia: University of Pennsylvania Press, 2001).

Pork . . . is more nutritious than other meats and produces better blood. . . . Cheese that is old and dry or too salty . . . causes thirst, headache, liver constriction, and kidney stones. . . . Clear wine with an elegant bouquet produces clear blood, comforts the heart, lightens the spirit, banishes sadness and cares, and is suitable for every age and temperament.

In 1231 Emperor Frederick II (see Essay 12) decreed that physicians in his kingdom of southern Italy and Sicily were to be licensed only at Salerno. Requirements were stringent: three years of logic and five of medical study, including surgery; a public examination by the medical masters of Salerno; and a year's internship with an experienced doctor.

Salerno remained solely a medical school. Bologna, the earliest true university, known as *la Dotta* ("the Learned"), first achieved worldwide fame as a law school and later developed a high-powered medical faculty. Luminaries as diverse as Thomas à Becket, Albertus Magnus, Petrarch, Copernicus, and Erasmus studied at Bologna; and Vesalius, Marcello Malpighi, Luigi Galvani, and Umberto Eco taught there (see Essays 16, 37, 39).

In the eleventh and twelfth centuries, according to John Addington Symonds, Italians "became a race of statesmen and jurists." In about 1076, when Constantine the African was revivifying medical studies at Salerno, a scholar named Pepo began lecturing in Bologna on parts of the *Corpus Iuris Civilis*, the sixth-century law code of Emperor Justinian (see Essay 8). This new focus on Roman law intensified after a complete manuscript of the *Digest* (the chief text of the *Corpus Iuris Civilis*) was found in Pisa in the late eleventh century.

The man who capitalized on this discovery, Irnerius, was a teacher of grammar at Bologna who had studied law in Rome and now undertook a painstaking analysis of the entire *Corpus Iuris Civilis*, bringing a new complexity to European conceptions of legal principles and establishing law as an autonomous discipline. Later called *Lucerna Iuris* (Lamp of the Law), Irnerius (c. 1055–c. 1125) is thought to have delivered his first lectures on law in 1088, the traditional date of the founding of the university. He became the first great legal "Glossator" of Bologna by glossing the text in the margins, where he explained technical terms, cited parallel passages, and harmonized discordant statements. This rebirth of the study of Roman law spread from Italy to the rest of Europe, profoundly influencing the development of subsequent legal and political theory.

The first so-called "universities" at Bologna were actually guilds formed by lay students (who as noncitizens lacked legal rights) to protect themselves against abuses of the law and the extortionate prices for food, shelter, and books that were demanded by the townies. By banding together into groups according to nations of origin, the students of Bologna used the power of the purse to strictly regulate the educational process and their teachers' prerogatives, schedules, and diligence. The school was thus effectively ruled by the students, many of whom were already civil or canon lawyers rather than callow undergraduates.

The guilds of the teachers at Bologna were known as *collegia*, formed chiefly for conferring degrees, which were basically licenses to teach and thus to join the guild of masters. Tuition took the form of modest fees that the students paid directly to the professors whose courses they took. Only in the mid-fourteenth century did the city of Bologna begin to pay some of its most renowned professors a regular salary.

There were no permanent buildings at first; the masters' lodgings or halls of convents were used as classrooms. Instruction assumed various forms: lectures (the professor's reading aloud of the assigned texts with his comments), interactive sessions with a dialectical method of examining a text or problem, and elaborate disputations. All students needed to be able to read, write, and speak Latin, the language of instruction.

Medieval universities offered training in the seven liberal arts, which consisted of the trivium (grammar, rhetoric, and logic) and the quadrivium (arithmetic, geometry, astronomy, and music). These were the usual prerequisites to advanced study in the professional fields of law, medicine, or theology. The degrees awarded included the familiar baccalaureate, master's, and doctorate (*magister* and *doctor* both meaning "teacher").

At Bologna, the successors of Irnerius as glossators were "the four doctors," Bulgarus, Martinus Gosia, Hugo da Porta of Ravenna, and Jacobus de Voragine. All of them were also counselors of Frederick I Barbarossa. As Holy Roman Emperor, Frederick benefited from the four doctors' expertise in Roman imperial law, which he cited to justify his pretensions to hegemony over free Italian communes and the papacy. A contemporary of these four, the Italian monk Gratian (Franciscus Gratianus) lectured at Bologna on canon (Church) law. His systematic codification of canon law, the *Decretum* (c. 1140), is a vast collection of 3,800 texts with his commentary. This work established canon law as a science distinct from theology and became the standard textbook of the new discipline.

The greatest of the Bolognese Glossators was Accursius (Francesco Accursio), a Florentine whose monumental *Glossa ordinaria* (c. 1250) summarized the results attained by the school. After one and a half centuries, the Glossators had meticulously explicated the entire body of Roman law. Their method was soon eclipsed by that of the legal scholars of the fourteenth century, the Postglossators or Commentators, concentrated in Perugia, who founded the disciplines of commercial law and criminal law.

The University of Bologna had some women students and professors as far back as the Middle Ages. Accursius's daughter may have lectured on law, and noted fourteenth-century canon law scholar Joannes Andrea sometimes had his daughter Novella lecture in his place. She was so attractive she had to wear a veil while teaching so as not to distract her ardent students.

The medical faculty of Bologna, which is still producing physicians, arose in the thirteenth century. It first provided university training for surgeons, who elsewhere in Europe long remained primarily barbers, executioners, or hog gelders. Ugo Borgognoni of Lucca, surgeon of the Crusades and of the commune of Bologna (1214), was the first to use an inhaled (instead of oral) soporific anesthesia via a sponge drenched with opium, henbane, hemlock, and mandrake applied to the patient's nostrils. His surgeon son or disciple, Teodorico Borgognoni (1205–98), was far ahead of his time in his attention to the control of bleeding, the removal of necrotic tissue, and the use of wound dressings bathed in wine, the first tentative step toward the aseptic treatment of wounds.

In his *Chirurgia* (1276), Guglielmo (or William) of Saliceto, professor of medicine at Bologna, advocated the use of the knife for surgical incision, which yielded better wound healing and less scar formation than the use of red-hot cautery, which was favored by Arabian physicians. He sutured severed nerves and taught students how to diagnose arterial bleeding by the spurting of blood. He also recognized that the cerebrum governs voluntary motion and the cerebellum presides over involuntary function.

At the turn of the fourteenth century, Guido Lanfranchi was the foremost cranial surgeon in Europe. He brought the medical knowledge of Bologna to northern France, where he wrote a textbook of surgery that became standard at the University of Paris. He trepanned the skull to treat wounds, gave the first surgical description of concussion, and stressed the need for surgeons to have a knowledge of medicine and for physicians to have a knowledge of surgery.

Bologna's innovative response to the increased educational needs of the day soon influenced the rise of other centers of learning at Paris, Oxford, Padua, and Cambridge. By 1404, twenty-nine universities had been founded in Europe (ten of them in Italy), and they now span the world. Among their goals is the training of students in the logical thinking and precise analysis that the Glossators of Bologna strenuously emphasized and that Cardinal Newman, in *The Idea of a University*, praised as the ability "to see things as they are, to go right to the point, to disentangle a skein of thought, to detect what is sophistical, and to discard what is irrelevant."

Eleven

St. Francis of Assisi, *"alter Christus"*

I advise, warn, and exhort my brothers in the Lord Jesus Christ, that
when they go out into the world, they shall not quarrel, nor contend
with words, nor judge others. But they shall be gentle, peaceable,
and modest, merciful and humble, honestly speaking with all.
                                    —Francis of Assisi, *The Rule of St. Francis* (1223)

GIOTTO'S FRESCO OF the crowded scene shows a man being restrained
from striking a bare-chested younger man—his son—whose joined
hands are supplicating heaven while a bishop covers the haloed figure's
nakedness with a cloth. The immortal depiction of St. Francis's *Renunci-*
ation of Worldly Goods in the Upper Church of San Francesco at Assisi
belies popular images of him as a mere friend of animals or garden-statue
saint. The man known as the *alter Christus*, or second Christ, was in fact
a complex visionary who helped save the Church from its obsession
with wealth, land, tithes, titles, and all the other trappings of the
worldly institution it had become during the later Middle Ages.

To begin with, Francis wasn't even his original name. His mother,
Pica, had him christened Giovanni after his birth in Assisi in 1181 or
1182. When his father, the wool merchant Pietro di Bernardone,
returned from a business trip in France, he renamed the boy Francesco—
"Frenchman"—after the beloved country in which he may have met
his wife.

Little Francesco's poor health contrasted sharply with his warm, exu-
berant personality. His mother taught him to speak and sing in French,
and he learned to read and write Latin at a nearby school. By the time he
reached his teens, however, the future saint was the ringleader of a group
of spoiled, spirited boys who lived for good times, and Francis could be
observed "acting even more stupidly than the rest," according to his first
biographer, the Franciscan friar Thomas of Celano. In 1202 Francis

joined the military forces of Assisi against neighboring Perugia. What started as a giddy adventure ended with his being held prisoner for nearly a year until his father ransomed him.

In 1205, again with romantic and chivalrous ideals in mind, Francis attempted to join the papal forces in Apulia, but he fell ill on the way. While resting at an inn, he had a dream or vision in which he received a message to return to Assisi and wait for a nonmilitary assignment, so he left his friends and went home. Although the source of the message remained unclear even to those closest to Francis, it was from this point that his conversion proceeded, albeit slowly and fitfully.

At first he prayed and waited for the promised sign. Since childhood, Francis had loved the songs of the troubadour poets. Their courtly verses expressed a deferential, highly idealized, and often chaste love for an unattainable woman whose identity the poet disguised with a pseudonym, or *senhal*. When Francis began speaking of his love for Lady Poverty, his friends assumed that, with his flair for dramatic gestures, he was emulating the troubadours and referring to an earthly lover.

Another turning point occurred when the fashionable and fastidious young man was accosted by a leprous beggar on the road outside town one day. Rather than averting his eyes and riding on as he had done many times before, Francis dismounted, gave the man alms, and kissed his hand. Shortly afterward, while praying in the tiny, dilapidated chapel of San Damiano, he heard the figure of Christ on the crucifix over the altar say, "Go, Francis, and repair my house, which you see is in ruins."

Interpreting the injunction literally, Francis hurried home, took some of his father's finest cloth and a horse, sold both in an adjacent town, and tried to give the money to the old priest at San Damiano. The priest, who knew Francis only as the local playboy, assumed the money was stolen and refused it. Pietro was enraged and pressed charges against his son. When Francis refused to appear before the civil authorities, his father appealed to the Bishop of Assisi, and this time Francis answered the summons. At a public gathering, he listened quietly as his father presented his case before the prelate.

When Pietro finished, Francis startled the assemblage by removing his clothing and returning it to his furious father, along with the money. The naked young man told the bishop that he now had only a heavenly father. According to Thomas of Celano, the bishop "saw clearly that Francis was divinely inspired and that his action contained a mystery."

Covering Francis in his own cloak, the bishop blessed him and sent him on his way. Francis then set off for a new life at Mt. Subasio, which overlooks Assisi. After someone gave him a rough brown robe and a rope sash like those of the poorest Umbrian beggars, Francis's friends began to guess the identity of Lady Poverty.

In the following months, Francis repaired San Damiano and several other nearby chapels, including St. Mary of the Angels (known as the Porziuncola, "little portion of land"). He nursed lepers in an infirmary and began preaching to the locals, most of whom called him *pazzo*— "crazyman." Their ridicule turned to awe when a town magnate, Bernard of Quintavalle, and a local canon, Peter of Cattaneo, became disciples of Francis, along with a poor man named Egidio (Blessed Giles). Traveling and preaching in pairs, the four were soon joined by others.

Then at Mass one morning in February of 1208, Francis heard a familiar Gospel passage that suddenly reverberated in his soul as a revelation of God's will for him: "Take no gold, nor silver, nor money in your belts, no bag for your journey, nor two tunics, nor sandals, nor a staff; for the laborer deserves his food. And whatever town or village you enter, find out who in it is worthy, and stay with him until you depart" (Matthew 10:9–11).

Francis felt called to "walk in Christ's footsteps" and embrace evangelical poverty. As Dante later imagined it in Canto 11 of the *Paradiso*, Christ had been Lady Poverty's first spouse. After his crucifixion, the world and the worldly Church had scorned the widow until Francis of Assisi took her as his bride. For his disciples, whom he called Friars Minor to emphasize the importance of humility, Francis wrote an informal *Rule* to help them live in imitation of Christ.

The official founding of the Franciscan Order dates from 1209, when Francis and his mendicant friars ("begging brothers"), now numbering twelve, walked to Rome to obtain Pope Innocent III's approval for the *Rule*. The barefoot men, dressed in scruffy brown cloaks, made a poor impression on the regal pontiff, and he initially rebuffed them, supported by Church officials who considered the *Rule* impracticable if not downright revolutionary.

In the early thirteenth century, the Church owned a vast amount of the land of Europe and commanded enormous revenues. No Christian religious order had ever enjoined radical poverty, rejecting all forms of property and ownership, in as thoroughgoing a fashion as was proposed in Francis's *Rule*. Some prelates couldn't help associating it with heretical reformers like the Waldenses and Cathari of France. In reaction against the worldliness of the Church, these groups espoused poverty and emphasized spiritual values, but they also rejected tenets of the faith on the nature of the sacraments or the divinity of Christ.

According to legend, however, Innocent dreamed that night of a ragged man in a brown cloak struggling to balance the tottering Roman basilica of St. John Lateran on his shoulders. The very next day, the pope gave his oral approval of Francis's *Rule,* and the friars returned to Assisi.

With their numbers growing, the brothers soon needed a new shelter, and the Benedictine monks of Mt. Subasio gave them the Porziuncola, the chapel Francis had repaired several years earlier. The friars now built some small huts around it. Francis's disciples continued to wander through the countryside and towns, preaching in pairs, uttering their familiar greeting, *"pace e bene!"* (peace and love), and referring to themselves as *les jongleurs de Dieu* (jesters of the Lord). On meeting a ragged beggar, a friar might give him a sleeve from his garment or a portion of his own scanty meal. Often sleeping in the open, these peripatetic preachers worked to obtain food or shelter but did not accept any money for their labors.

Francis jocularly referred to his own body as "Brother Ass" because of its stubborn inborn cravings. A true ascetic, he took a harsh stance against sexual sins and for years refused the requests of St. Clare of Assisi, his protégée and founder of the second Franciscan order, the Poor Clare nuns, to share a meal. When he finally relented, he insisted that others be in attendance.

In 1217 the first general meeting of the friars was held at the Porziuncola. Despite Francis's notorious lack of organizational skills, the ranks of the order had swollen, and it was necessary to divide it into provinces, including Tuscany, Lombardy, Provence, Spain, and Germany. Shortly afterward, Francis embarked on an outdoor preaching tour of Italy, during which thousands heard him speak. Moved by his pithy sermons in the vernacular and his personal charisma, entire crowds in Italian cities asked to be admitted to the order. Since many were married or otherwise unable to lead a life of poverty, Francis later created a Third Order, consisting of lay Franciscans, which is still active throughout the world.

Frail and tubercular, Francis even traveled to Egypt in 1219 to preach to the Muslims. The sultan, whose city of Damietta was being attacked by Crusaders, was nonetheless impressed by Francis and pronounced his religion "a beautiful one," but the quixotic mission accomplished little. On his return, Francis found the Order in chaos. During his absence, several leaders had tried to make the fasting regulations even more rigorous, another had attempted to start an order of leprous monks, and the Benedictine *Rule* had been imposed on Clare's nuns against her wishes. Clearly, the friars needed a leader with administrative capabilities, so Francis made Elias of Cortona vicar in 1221.

When Francis decided to compose a more formal version of the *Rule*, he reiterated his belief that extreme poverty was the best way to imitate Christ: "The brothers shall appropriate nothing to themselves, neither a house, nor a place, nor anything. . . . Nor need they be ashamed, for the Lord made Himself poor for us in this world." Pope Honorius III gave his written approval to the Franciscan *Rule* in November of 1223. In the following month, Francis inaugurated the tradition of the crèche, or Nativity scene, complete with manger, hay, and a real ox and donkey, according to St. Bonaventure, the Italian theologian and head of the Franciscan order who completed his authorized life of Francis in 1263.

The best-known element of the Francis legend, abundantly treated in the *Fioretti*, or *Little Flowers of St. Francis*, a fourteenth-century compilation of pious tales, is the saint's reverence for all of God's creatures. Thomas of Celano reports how Francis urged the birds to love "your creator deeply. . . . He has given you feathers to wear, wings to fly with, and whatever else you need. He has made you noble among his creatures and given you a dwelling in the pure air." To fish, Francis explained how to avoid nets. He asked a hapless creature that had been caught in a trap, "Brother Hare, why did you let yourself be fooled in this way?"

After the gargantuan Wolf of Gubbio had slain several people in addition to the usual livestock, Francis marched out to meet the malefactor, with the townsmen following far behind. As feared, the wolf leaped at Francis, but the saint stood his ground, blessed the wolf, and enjoined him not to eat Brother Ass. With the wolf meekly curled up at his feet, *Il Poverello* reproached him for his crimes but also made him an offer he couldn't refuse: If the wolf stopped his killing, the townspeople would feed him. From that day forth, the wolf lived inside the gates of Gubbio, well fed and impeccably behaved.

During the summer of 1224, while Francis prayed on the Apennine peak of La Verna, he had a vision of a seraph with three pairs of wings who was affixed to a cross and bore the stigmata, the wounds of the

crucified Christ. When the vision cleared, Francis, too, had the stigmata, which he was the first to receive.

This mystical event coincided with the start of a physical decline. In
addition to tuberculosis, Francis suffered from an eye infection that
eventually blinded him. Despite his pain, after a vision of eternal bliss
he composed the first immortal Italian poem, "The Canticle of the
Creatures":

> *Most powerful, most high, most gentle Lord,*
> *yours be the praise, the honor, and the glory—*
> *all these and every blessing that is made.*
> *To you alone, Most High, do they belong,*
> *and no one else is worthy to speak your name.*
>
> *Be praised, my Lord, be praised with all your creatures,*
> *especially our brother, Master Sun,*
> *through whom you bring us day and give us light.*
> *He is, Most High, a living sign of you,*
> *so beautifully he shines with splendor bright.*
>
> *Be praised, my Lord, for Sister Moon and stars:*
> *in heaven you formed them—lovely, precious, clear.*
>
> *Be praised, my Lord, for Brother Wind and air,*
> *and every kind of weather, cloudy and fair,*
> *by which you give your creatures what they need.*
>
> *Be praised, my Lord, be praised for Sister Water—*
> *she is so useful, precious, chaste, and humble.*
>
> *Be praised, my Lord, be praised for Brother Fire,*
> *by whom you help illuminate the night—*
> *such a lively, strong, robust, and lovely sight.*
>
> *Be praised, my Lord, for Mother Earth, our sister,*
> *who supports us all and takes good care of us,*
> *producing fruits and grass and painted flowers.*
>
> *Be praised when men forgive for love of you,*
> *and bear with tribulations and infirmities:*

blessèd be those who suffer all in peace,
for they, Most High, shall all be crowned by you.

Praise and bless my Lord, you creatures, render thanks,
and serve him with profound humility.

In the summer of 1226, Francis returned to Assisi to die at the Porziuncola. He spent his last days consoling the brothers and urging them to bear patiently with evils, love poverty, have faith in the Church, and follow the discipline of the Order. On October 3, he asked to be undressed and placed on the floor of his cell so that he could be closer to his Lady Poverty as he died. Those who witnessed his death the next day said his soul rose to heaven like a shining star. Shortly before dying, he had inserted this stanza into the Canticle:

Be praised, my Lord, for Sister Bodily Death,
from whom no living person can escape.
Woe to all those who die in mortal sin;
blessèd be those she finds in your holy will:
the second death will do no harm to them.

Francis was buried at the church of San Giorgio in Assisi and was canonized there less than two years later, on July 16, 1228, by Pope Gregory IX, who laid the cornerstone of the Basilica of St. Francis during the same journey. In 1230 the saint's remains were interred in the Basilica, which features works of Cimabue and Simone Martini, and where Giotto (though the attribution is hotly contested) created a magnificent cycle of twenty-eight frescoes, *The Life of St. Francis* (c. 1290–95), at the request of the first Franciscan pope, Nicholas IV. In September 1997, earthquakes severely damaged the Basilica, shattering several thousand square feet of works by Giotto and Cimabue that are now undergoing restoration.

When he heard the voice of Christ in San Damiano asking him to repair his "house," Francis thought of the ramshackle chapel, not the Church of Rome. Although he has been called the least aggressive reformer who ever lived, he reinvigorated the Church with his own example and initiated one of the most extensive, popular, and fastest-growing reform movements in its history. Franciscan missionaries eventually traversed the globe, preaching the Gospel and ministering to the poor and sick. Many eminent scholars of the later Middle Ages were Franciscans, notably the English scientist Roger Bacon and the theologians and philosophers St. Bonaventure, Duns Scotus, and William of Occam.

Without Francis and his Spanish contemporary St. Dominic, whose Dominican Order was founded in 1215 to teach, preach, and combat heresy, the late-medieval Church might have succumbed to a massive Protestant-like revolt three centuries before it actually struck. Between them, the first two mendicant orders helped redirect the burgeoning spiritual energies of Christian Europe into orthodox channels, preserving it from schism until its maturing humanistic culture was capable of thriving without a unified and all-encompassing religious creed.

Twelve

"*Stupor mundi*": Emperor Frederick II, King of Sicily and Jerusalem

Manifestare ea quae sunt, sicut sunt. (To show those things that are, as they are.)
— Frederick II, *The Art of Hunting with Birds* (c. 1247)

WHEN THE DEATH OF Frederick Hohenstaufen was announced in December of 1250, Pope Innocent IV intoned, "Let us rejoice and be glad!" to which the congregation replied, "Down to Hell he went!" This seems an incongruous liturgical send-off for a man who had asked for absolution of his sins and died in the habit of a Cistercian monk, cradled in the arms of his son and attended by a devoted assemblage, including his friend, the Archbishop of Palermo.

In life, Frederick II had alternately been vilified as the Antichrist and lionized as *stupor mundi*, "Wonder of the World." In Sicily, peasants believed that devils had conveyed his soul through Mount Etna into Hell. In Germany, he was said to reside in a mountain, awaiting a propitious time to return and restore the glory of the Holy Roman Empire. Like other illustrious revenants, he was sighted in widely scattered locations.

Historians continue to debate his role in the creation of the modern centralized state, but few dispute the impetus that he and his Sicilian court gave to Italian poetry, the visual arts, the recovery of Greco-Arabic learning in the West, and the rudiments of tolerance toward non-Christian cultures. The son of a Norman princess and a German Hohenstaufen king, Frederick was regarded by some as an interloper in Italy, but he was Italian both by birth and by choice. Heir to two domains, he chose to live in Italy; a polyglot, he chose to write his poetry in Italian.

Frederick was born as he died—surrounded by a crowd. His mother, Constance, gave birth to him on December 26, 1194, in Jesi, near Ancona, while traveling to meet her husband, Holy Roman Emperor Henry VI, who only the day before had been crowned King of Sicily. Constance knew that unless she garnered many witnesses, the relative rarity of a forty-year-old woman giving birth would cast doubt on whether she was the child's mother. At her request, a tent was set up in the town square, where a score of bishops and other clerics were among the spectators at her royal son's debut.

His Sicilian subjects greeted the birth of red-haired Frederick Roger with their customary wariness. His paternal grandfather, Frederick I, whom the Italians dubbed *Barbarossa* (Redbeard), was King of Germany and Holy Roman Emperor for four decades (1152–90) and dedicated himself to German unification and the restoration of the Empire. Barbarossa undertook six expeditions to Italy in pursuit of his expansionist policy, but it was his son, Henry VI, who married the reigning Norman princess and secured the crown of Sicily and southern Italy.

Constance was the last of her Norman line, which arrived in the peninsula in the mid-eleventh century, when freebooter Robert Guiscard and his brother, later Count Roger I of Sicily, began wresting southern Italy from the Saracens. Although Frederick II is often lauded for his cosmopolitanism, the Normans practiced administrative and cultural eclecticism from at least the time of Constance's father, Roger II, who ruled over Sicily and the mainland regions of Calabria and Apulia until his death in 1154.

King Roger II, who dressed in Persian silks and maintained a harem, built the cathedral at Cefalù, with its noted Byzantine mosaics, and the Palatine Chapel in Palermo, which exhibits Byzantine Greek and Arabic architectural features. Roger also evinced an interest in science, which was whetted by his Muslim subjects and passed down to his grandson, Frederick.

After Henry VI died suddenly in 1197, Constance ruled Sicily with the goal of perpetuating the Norman line. Disregarding her son's claims in Germany, she focused instead on his Italian inheritance, appointing Pope Innocent III as Frederick's guardian in her will. Fourteen months later, she, too, was dead, but the little King of Sicily and southern Italy had been duly crowned in 1198, at age three, and the redoubtable pontiff became his regent and protector.

Neglected by his caretakers, Frederick had few emotional attachments during childhood, and at times he did not even have enough to eat. Free to roam the streets of Palermo, he came into contact with his capital's Jews and Arabs, synagogues and mosques, fine silks and exotic imported animals. He enjoyed fencing, riding, and hunting, but he also received an excellent education, learning Latin, Italian, French, and some German. Like very few Westerners in his time, he went on to acquire Greek and Arabic. Wherever he journeyed in later life, a long line of mules bore chests brimful with his precious books.

In 1209 Pope Innocent arranged the first of Frederick's four marriages, to Constance of Aragon, who brought her adolescent husband an infusion of cash and much-needed troops. Frederick's goal was to join his southern Italian kingdom to Tuscany and Lombardy within the Holy Roman Empire. Innocent's objective was to loosen the bonds between Sicily and Germany so that the central Italian Papal States would not be caught between Hohenstaufen pincers.

But in 1212, when the German nobles chose Frederick as their king, he had his one-year-old son, Henry, crowned King of Sicily and departed for his ancestral land. He ended up spending the next eight years there, consolidating his power among warring factions and taking an oath to go on crusade to the Holy Land. He sent for Henry and had him elected King of Germany in his own stead in 1220 before returning to Sicily, where Innocent's more malleable successor, Pope Honorius III, crowned Frederick Holy Roman Emperor later that same year.

While stalling on his crusade pledge, Frederick indulged his omnivorous intellectual pursuits. He maintained a lavish menagerie that he used for conducting experiments in animal breeding. From his Muslim physicians, he learned human anatomy. He sent for a noted Egyptian mathematician, al-Hanifi, and befriended the outstanding mathematician of his time, Leonardo Fibonacci, who, among other achievements, was instrumental in introducing Arabic numerals (originally Indian) into Europe. Frederick imported translators, scholars, philosophers, and falconers from Spain, Baghdad, Syria—wherever the most learned men could be found, whether Christian, Muslim, or Jewish. In 1224 he founded at Naples the first state-funded university, endowing it with a large collection of his Arabic philosophical and scientific manuscripts.

Although his harem and Eastern dancing girls convinced his more orthodox contemporaries otherwise, Frederick believed in God, but he was less certain about the afterlife. Thirteenth-century Provençal poet Uc de Saint-Circ wrote of Frederick: "Believing neither in Paradise nor life after death, / He said a man is nothing after drawing his last breath." Dante, who admired Frederick ("a logician and great scholar") as a munificent patron of poets, nonetheless consigned the emperor to his *Inferno* (Canto 10), where Frederick inhabits a fiery tomb with other Epicurean heretics who denied the afterlife.

There is also a story that Frederick paid one of his dancing girls to seduce St. Francis of Assisi, who had lodged at his court at Bari. When the seduction failed (Francis held the girl at bay with burning coals), Frederick begged the holy man's forgiveness (see Essay 11).

Frederick's attempt on St. Francis's virtue may have been more of an experiment than a practical joke. Other nastier experiments attributed to Frederick, although almost certainly apocryphal, attest to his contemporaries' fascinated dread of a man who was accustomed to investigating Nature on his own. Frederick is said, for example, to have ordered several infants to be deprived of all exposure to speech to determine whether they would begin speaking Hebrew, Greek, Latin, Arabic, or their parents' language on their own, thus ascertaining whether indeed there was a "natural" language of mankind spoken in Eden. (The infants died.) He reportedly had a man suffocated in a sealed barrel to see whether his soul could be observed leaving the container. He is said to have fed two condemned convicts a hearty meal and sent one to bed and the other out hunting. After several hours, he had both disemboweled to determine which one had digested his food more thoroughly. (It was the one who slept.)

"How is it," Frederick is said to have asked Michael Scot, the court astrologer who was also a mathematician, alchemist, and translator, "that the soul of a living man which has passed away to another life than ours cannot be induced to return?" All his metaphysical questions demanded precise answers: "Where are Hell, Purgatory, and Heaven?" "What is God's precise location in the heavenly spheres, and exactly how does he sit on his throne?" "What do the angels and saints do in his presence?" More strictly scientific were his questions about volcanoes, geysers, salt water, and the Earth itself—"Does it have hollow spaces, or is it solid throughout?"

The versatile Michael Scot also compiled a Latin summary of Aristotle's works on biology and zoology from Arabic translations. From these, and his menagerie, Frederick became an expert in scientific observation, especially applying his skill to his great passion for falconry. The father of modern ornithology, he avidly corresponded with falconers and other bird-watchers as far away as Greenland. His Latin treatise on falconry, *De arte venandi cum avibus* (*The Art of Hunting with Birds*), a seminal work in the field, is still read and admired by falconers.

The book provides detailed information on the nesting habits of falcons, their most common diseases, their prey, and the fine points of training and hunting with them. Its author had no compunction about correcting Aristotle's errors, saying that he merely wished "to show those things that are, as they are," thus situating himself, a slightly older contemporary of Roger Bacon, right at the cradle of early modern science, and anticipating the objective and empirical orientation of Italian thinkers as different as Machiavelli and Galileo. "This ability to apply the philosopher's rules and yet not be in awe of Aristotle," according to Frederick's recent biographer, David Abulafia, "is one of the main reasons why the *De arte* must be seen as a considerable intellectual and scientific achievement."

Frederick's was an age when translations were opening up broad new intellectual vistas. *Guide for the Perplexed,* the masterpiece of the greatest Jewish medieval philosopher, Moses Maimonides, attempted to reconcile Aristotelian science with Jewish revelation. Originally written in Arabic, the book was soon translated into Hebrew, and this version was translated into Latin under Frederick's aegis. It thus became accessible to Thomas Aquinas, who, in attempting to reconcile Aristotelian science with Christian revelation, incorporated Maimonides' insights into his own magisterial *Summa theologica* (see Essay 13).

Il Novellino, a late-thirteenth-century Italian collection of anecdotes, portrays Frederick as a generous patron whose court attracted talent from everywhere: "musicians, troubadours, and eloquent speakers, artists, jousters, swordsmen—all kinds of people." Dante exalts the "nobility and righteousness" of Frederick and his son Manfred, who "followed what is human and disdained what is bestial," claiming that "in their time, whatever the best Italians attempted, first appeared at the court of these mighty sovereigns" (*De vulgari eloquentia,* 1.12).

Indeed, Frederick's court became the first center, or "school," of poetry in the Italian language, and, like his illegitimate sons Manfred and Enzo (or Enzio), Frederick himself was a poet. Among the works sometimes attributed to him is an allegorical piece entitled "On His Captive Lady," in which the distressed woman has been interpreted as a symbol of the Empire or the Church under the domination of the papacy. The most influential poet at his court, however, was Giacomo da Lentini, who first developed the sonnet, a form that was to enjoy an astounding literary afterlife. Here's a snippet from one of Giacomo's sonnets in which he claims he'd rather forgo the joys of Paradise than be without his love:

> *Without my lady, I'd not want to go there—*
> *The one with the blond head and the bright face—*
> *Because, without her, I could not rejoice,*
> *Separated from my lady in that place.*

The emperor's circle of poets also included Guido delle Colonne, Jacopo Mostacci, and Rinaldo d'Aquino, a member of the noble family of St. Thomas Aquinas. Some of Rinaldo's poems have female speakers, one of them lamenting her lover's going on crusade, another describing the rebirth of spring and of love. This is part of a poem by Giacomino Pugliese ("Jimmy from Apulia"):

> I then sought out her fragrant mouth
> And both those breasts of hers,
> Clasping her tightly in my arms.
> And while she kissed, she told me:
> "Sir, if this is a one-night stand,
> You'd better be on your way.
> I think it's pretty bad manners
> To leave a love and get a move-on."

These poets were primarily judges, counselors, and magistrates for whom verse was an elegant pastime, to be dashed off with *sprezzatura*. For the most part, they were anemic imitators of the courtly love conventions of Provençal poetry (which had already seen its best days), but within a half century they were to have a glorious progeny. The Sicilian school influenced the Bolognese school, led by Guido Guinizzelli, and both, in turn, influenced the Tuscan school of Guido Cavalcanti and Dante (see Essay 14). Frederick also encouraged a revival of sculpture, and his efforts paved the way for Nicola Pisano (flourished 1258–78), a native of Apulia whose classically inspired work—such as the carved pulpit in the baptistery of Pisa—antedates by more than a century the heightened realism of early Italian Renaissance sculptors.

But Pope Honorius had not forgotten that crusade. Hoping to make the prospect more appealing, he arranged for the widowed Frederick to be married to Isabella of Brienne, heiress to the Latin Kingdom of Jerusalem. After Honorius's death, Frederick finally set out in 1227, having assumed the title "King of Jerusalem" by virtue of his marriage, but he returned sick within days when the plague broke out aboard his ships. The new pope, the irascible Gregory IX, excommunicated him for imperial malingering.

No harm done, thought Frederick, who embarked again the following year. But since this Sixth Crusade was undertaken by an excommunicate, the pope seized the opportunity to declare a crusade against Frederick himself, invading his Sicilian kingdom and instigating a rebellion among his barons. On his part, Frederick used the arts of diplomacy (which may have included flaunting his ability to discourse on the Koran in Arabic) to obtain Jerusalem, Bethlehem, and Nazareth from the Egyptian sultan, Malik al-Kamil. When Frederick crowned himself King of Jerusalem in the Church of the Holy Sepulcher in 1229, some of his followers compared his entrance into the city with that of Jesus Christ himself on Palm Sunday. Frederick was not overly impressed with his new kingdom, however, remarking that if the God of the Jews had seen his southern Italian domains, he wouldn't have singled out the Holy Land for special commendation.

Frederick returned home and drove the papal troops from Sicily. After concluding an uneasy truce with the pope, who rescinded the excommunication, Frederick ordered his chancellor, the jurist and poet Pier della Vigna, to draw up the Constitutions of Melfi in 1231. The Constitutions were the first important codification of European statutory law since the days of Justinian in the sixth century (see Essay 8) and the most remarkable body of legislation since Charlemagne's enactments in the ninth century.

Benefiting from the revival of Roman law studies at the University of Bologna (see Essay 10), the Constitutions empowered the emperor to make laws in accordance with his sense of *justitia,* or "righteousness." Often seen as a harbinger of European absolutism and divine-right sovereignty, Frederick's code contributed to the gradual shift away from the Church and toward the monarch and the state as the primary authority in human affairs. The Constitutions of Melfi also diminished the autonomy of Frederick's restless nobles, transferred some of their lands to him, abolished trial by combat, and centralized his judicial and political power by establishing the right of appeal from feudal courts to imperial judges.

The Constitutions provided for the adjudication of inheritance disputes, regulated the training of physicians, and even, in a series of pioneering public health measures, attempted to improve the air quality around Palermo. Minority groups were given the right to bring legal suits because, as Frederick explained, "we do not wish them to be persecuted in their innocence simply because they are Jews or Saracens." Although denied full participation in civic life, minorities fared better in Frederick's dominions than elsewhere in Christendom and were accorded broad religious freedoms.

The rest of Frederick's life was marked by the fierce ongoing struggle between his imperial party of the Ghibellines and the papal party of the Guelfs. It was with the Guelf Lombard League that Frederick's son Henry, still on the throne in Germany, conspired against him. Quashing the rebellion, the emperor imprisoned his disloyal son, who later apparently committed suicide.

Placing his son Enzo on the throne of Sardinia, which the pope claimed as a fief, earned Frederick yet another excommunication in 1239. Just as the emperor was about to besiege Rome in 1241, however, Gregory IX died, leaving Frederick unable to press home his victory against a city mourning its sovereign.

Frederick continued his struggle for survival against Pope Innocent IV, who declared him deposed from the imperial throne in 1245 and later tried to have him poisoned. After a series of military successes by the Lombard League in the mid-1240s, Frederick's army was destroyed during the siege of rebellious Parma in 1248, and his son Enzo was captured by the Bolognese in the following year. Frederick's chief minister, Pier della Vigna, accused of treason and blinded by Frederick, apparently committed suicide in prison in 1249 by dashing out his brains, a story told in a dazzling episode of Dante's *Inferno* (Canto 13).

After heavily taxing his Sicilian subjects for years to finance his wars, Frederick died of dysentery at Fiorentino, in Apulia, on December 13, 1250, and was buried in the cathedral of Palermo just as his troops were beginning to reverse their fortunes in northern Italy. An anonymous Latin chronicler (no doubt a Ghibelline) mourned him with these words: "The sun of the world has set, which illuminated all the people. The sun of justice has set, and so has the love of peace."

Within twenty-two years, the Hohenstaufens would be eradicated. Frederick's son and successor Conrad IV died in 1254, his son Manfred was killed at the Battle of Benevento in 1266, and Frederick's grandson Conradin was publicly beheaded in a square in Naples in 1268 at age fifteen. In 1272, after more than twenty years of captivity, Enzo of Sardinia died in a Bolognese prison. The next rulers of Sicily marched in— French this time—led by Charles of Anjou, whose cruelties provoked the savage revolt known as the Sicilian Vespers of 1282, which brought the Aragonese trooping in. And so it went, until the arrival of Giuseppe Garibaldi and his Redshirts in May of 1860 (see Essay 42). For good or ill, however, Sicily and southern Italy, with Frederick's marvelous castles still looming over the landscape, were never again ruled by a "Wonder of the World."

Thirteen

St. Thomas Aquinas: Titan of theology

The ultimate beatitude of man consists in the use of his highest function, which is the operation of the intellect.
—Thomas Aquinas, *Summa theologica* (c. 1270)

IMAGINE AN INTELLECTUAL WHO graduated from college in 1900 and lived into the mid-twentieth century. Toward the end of his or her life, how tame the turn-of-the-century world of ideas must have seemed in comparison with the turmoil generated by the thought of Freud, Einstein, Wittgenstein, Heidegger, Heisenberg, and Watson and Crick.

That's roughly what it was like for European scholars in the time of Thomas Aquinas (1225–74) when, for the first time, the entire corpus of Aristotle's works became available in accurate Latin translations, accompanied by commentaries written by Muslim scholars like Alfarabi, Avicenna, and the brilliantly disturbing Averroës. The encyclopedic scope of Aristotle's achievement—in logic, physics, ethics, metaphysics, cosmology, politics, biology, ontology, rhetoric, and psychology—revolutionized European intellectual life of the thirteenth century to much the same extent as the thinkers mentioned in the preceding paragraph did in the twentieth.

No wonder the thirteenth century was marked by philosophical chaos and rabid theological controversy. The stakes were enormous—infinite, in fact. Aristotle's Gibraltar-like canon, composed more than fifteen centuries earlier, seemed to represent the ultimate that human reason could attain without the benefit of revelation. His orderly treatises evinced such prodigious erudition that he was known simply as "the Philosopher," while Dante called him "the master of those who know." But a millennium earlier, the Church Father Tertullian had already asked, "What has Jerusalem to do with Athens?" Could the sacred truths of religion survive a head-on collision with antiquity's most learned pagan?

Thomas Aquinas, the man who made the most ambitious attempt to accommodate the old faith to the newly recovered learning, was born in 1225 in the castle of Roccasecca, near Aquino, about halfway between Rome and Naples. His father, Count Landulf of Aquino, was, as a member of the Lombard nobility, a German by descent. Thomas's mother, Countess Theodora of Teano, traced her lineage to the Norman princes of Sicily. At age five, Thomas was sent to study at the nearby Benedictine monastery of Monte Cassino, where he often asked the monks, "What is God?" When he was fourteen, he attended the recently established University of Naples.

Though fellow students dubbed him the "Dumb Ox" because of his slow, deliberate manner and his strict avoidance of showing off in school, he later became known as the "Angelic Doctor" for his penetrating intellect. Since he remembered perfectly everything he read, a contemporary likened his mind to "a huge library."

At Naples, Aquinas was impressed by the Dominicans, whose order of preaching friars had been founded only three decades earlier. Despite the opposition of his family, who wanted him to enter the venerable (and powerful and wealthy) Benedictine monastic order (see Essay 9), Thomas joined the order of barefoot begging friars in 1244. His brothers promptly abducted him, and his family put him under house arrest at a fortress to persuade him to reconsider. In the words of the *Catholic Encyclopedia*, "The brothers even laid snares for his virtue, but the pure-minded novice drove the temptress from his room with a brand which he snatched from the fire." After more than a year, the stubborn young man, virtue intact, was allowed to return to his order. The legend that he escaped by being lowered in a basket from a window is amusing in light of his noted portliness, which gave rise to the story that his fellow friars had to carve a semicircular hole out of the dining table so that Thomas could tuck up to his bowl.

Aquinas soon became the disciple of the German Dominican St. Albert the Great (Albertus Magnus), one of the most learned and prolific authors of the Middle Ages, who wrote commentaries on most of Aristotle's works. Under Albert's tutelage, Aquinas studied at the University of Paris, the epicenter of European theological speculation. After accompanying Albert to Cologne, where he continued his studies and was ordained a priest, Thomas returned to Paris, started teaching, and received his master's degree in theology.

While attending to various teaching duties in Italy, Aquinas composed his *Summa contra gentiles* (1258–64), a long philosophical explanation of Christianity for use in missionary attempts to convert the Muslims and Jews of Spain. Word of his learning and polemical skills spread. In 1268 he was summoned back to Paris to combat a clutch of secular Aristotelians who were wreaking havoc with the orderly worldview of medieval Christianity.

Intrepid Jewish and Islamic thinkers had already tried to assimilate Aristotle into the body of their faiths, but the forces of orthodoxy had spewed him out again. Several decades after the death of the twelfth-century Jewish physician and philosopher Moses Maimonides, his *Guide for the Perplexed* and other works, saturated with Aristotle, were publicly burned by the Inquisition at the instigation of his Jewish opponents. His Muslim contemporary and fellow Cordovan Averroës, building on the work of Avicenna and other Muslim Aristotelians, wrote such authoritative commentaries on Aristotle that he was known as "the Commentator." Before his death in 1198, Averroës's teachings were condemned by Muslim religious leaders, marking the end of a glorious era of Islamic science and scholarship.

The Commentator's works, which accompanied the texts of Aristotle that were being newly translated from the Arabic, bore poisoned fruit in the West, exacerbating the intellectual battles of the thirteenth century. This heyday of Scholasticism (the rationalistic philosophizing of the universities) saw a proliferation of teachings the Church considered suspect, among them the works of the secular Aristotelians, or Latin Averroists, led by Siger de Brabant at the University of Paris.

The most notorious of the Christian heresies associated with Siger and the Averroists was that of the "double truth," which held that reason and revelation sometimes led to different conclusions. The Averroists also denied divine Providence and free will, claiming that the laws of Nature and the influence of the stars determined all events. The world existed from all eternity, and there was only a single collective soul for all men, not an afterlife of individual immortality.

Many of the central tenets of Christianity were being challenged in Paris when Aquinas arrived on the scene and began refuting the Averroists. Thomas stoutly rejected the double truth argument: The laws of God and of reason both proceed from the same divine source and lead to the same conclusions. Reason is not enough, however; revelation is also needed to gain access to higher truths (like those of the Trinity, Incarnation, Redemption, and Last Judgment) to which reason alone cannot attain. "It was necessary for man's salvation," he wrote in the *Summa theologica,* "that there should be a knowledge revealed by God, besides the philosophical sciences investigated by human reason."

Against the Averroists' determinism, Aquinas championed human free will in the choice of good or evil, thus justifying the system of cosmic rewards or punishments. He argued that time, matter, and the universe were not eternal, as Aristotle and Averroës claimed, but were created by God out of nothing, although Aquinas admitted that the truth of this assertion could not be shown by rational proofs. Besides refuting the collective soul thesis in a brief work of 1270, Aquinas also taught in the *Summa theologica* that each individual human body has a separate soul infused into it.

After four exhausting years at Paris, he returned to Naples in 1272 and continued working on his masterpiece, the *Summa theologica* (more properly, *Summa theologiae*), which he had begun in 1265. With his precise definitions and the subtlety of his distinctions and deductions from accepted premises (sometimes shading over into sophistry), Aquinas proceeded to enshrine Christian dogma in an Aristotelian framework, placing the best available logical, scientific, and philosophical thought at the service of theology, "queen of the sciences." Though he earmarked the multivolume work for "the instruction of beginners," it was actually a complete exposition of the Christian belief of his day.

His work was structured according to the formal method of disputation then followed in the universities. The book is divided into three main parts, each of which is subdivided into treatises, these into questions, and the questions into articles. Each article introduces the topic to be discussed using the Latin *utrum* (whether)—as in *"Utrum Deus sit?"* (Whether God exists?). Several numbered objections against the correct formulation are then stated.

Aquinas's solution, introduced by "On the contrary," confutes the gist of the objections, often by citing a relevant authority. With the words "I answer, saying. . . ," he sets forth his full explanation of the correct view. Finally, the objections are individually refuted before Aquinas moves on inexorably to the next topic—through 38 treatises, 612 questions, and 3,120 articles, in the course of which about 10,000 objections are answered and many thousands of illustrative passages are quoted from hundreds of authors.

The first part of the epic work is on God and his Creation. Aquinas offers five proofs for God's existence, three of them from Aristotle via St. Albert: God is the unmoved Prime Mover of all movement, the First Cause of all causes, and the Designer of all the design seen in the world.

Among God's qualities are goodness, infinity, omnipresence, immutability, eternity, and unity in trinity. Aquinas also expatiates on the nature of angels, whose number surpasses all reckoning though each is a separate species unto himself, and on the works of the six days of Creation. Following Aristotle, Aquinas teaches that the rational soul is the substantial form (vital principle) of the human body, and thus man is a composite being, not merely a soul trapped in the prison of the body's matter, as in earlier Neoplatonizing Christianity and the Franciscan thought of Thomas's time. As pure immaterial form, the soul is not subject to destruction.

The second part (in two parts) deals with ethics. Since humankind's ultimate goal, or Aristotelian telos, is the beatific vision of God in heaven, Aquinas expounds the role of human acts, passions, habits, laws (divine, natural, and human), and grace in attaining it. The various virtues and vices are incorporated into a moral system derived from Aristotle's *Ethics*, especially in its consideration of virtues as means between vicious extremes. Evil acts are those against reason and God's laws. The guilt of Adam and Eve's sin devolves on everyone, maiming human nature with malice, ignorance, weakness, lusts, and desires that confuse our moral choices. The punishment for this original sin, as for the sin of Satan and his demons, is eternal damnation in hell.

But Christ, the second Person of the Trinity, and the major theme of the third part of the *Summa*, became flesh and suffered and died for the sins of the world in the mystery of the Redemption or Atonement. In his infinite mercy, God accepted the sacrifice of his only begotten Son as satisfaction for the guilt of mankind. The gates of heaven were thus thrown open to humans once again, provided that they followed the commands of God and his Church and availed themselves of the grace offered through the seven sacraments instituted by Christ. Aquinas broke off his work while discussing the fourth sacrament, but a follower later compiled a lengthy supplement based on Thomas's other works. After having composed or dictated, in a life of less than fifty years, more than sixty works, including thirteen commentaries on Aristotle alone, this scholar who frequently experienced ecstatic visions laid down his pen forever on December 6, 1273, saying, "I can do no more. Such secrets have been revealed to me that all I have written seems but straw."

A few months later, setting out for the Council of Lyon, Aquinas collapsed on the way and was taken to his niece's nearby castle and then to the Cistercian abbey of Fossanuova, where (after dictating a brief commentary on the Song of Songs) he died on March 7, 1274, not far from where he was born.

With the aid of an omnivorous mind brimming with Scripture, the Church Fathers (especially St. Augustine), Plato, Aristotle, Cicero, Boethius, the Arabic and Jewish philosophers, and a hundred other venerable texts, and with his faith in the ability of human reason to pluck Truth out of a congeries of discordant texts, dogmas, ideas, and authorities, Aquinas erected a cathedral of lofty thought whose foundations were suspended over the chasm of the hubris of his age. As Francesco De Sanctis wrote in the nineteenth century, "At the time of St. Thomas, reason was barely entering its youth. It woke from a long rest—curious, credulous, sharp-witted, and all the more confident the less aware it was of its own true measure and that of things in general. Everything was asked of it, and it promised everything."

Neither the Averroists (who criticized his logic) nor the orthodox (who disliked putting so many Christian truths in the fragile hands of human reason) nor the mystical Neoplatonic/Augustinians like his friend and philosophical opponent St. Bonaventure (the general of the Franciscan order and "Seraphic Doctor") were happy with Thomas's solution to the thirteenth-century crisis of Christianity. In 1277, a few years after Thomas's death, the Bishop of Paris condemned 219 philosophical propositions, most of them associated with the Latin Averroists, but more than a dozen of them Aquinas's.

Nevertheless, a generation after his death, Thomas was recognized by the Church as its best defense against secularizing rationalists. By the time Aquinas was officially canonized in 1323, Dante had already cast him as one of the most eminent saints in his *Paradiso*.

Living in a more worldly-wise age, the Renaissance humanists ridiculed the Scholastics for their substances and accidents, universals and particulars, potentialities and actualities, necessities and contingencies, quiddities and quodlibets, which seemed to them just so much quibbling claptrap. Luther fulminated against them, Rabelais compiled scores of titles for imaginary monkish tomes, such as "*On the Serving of Mustard after Meals* (14 books)." Francis Bacon called the Schoolmen "*cymini sectores*" (cutters of cumin seed—hairsplitters) and their works "cobwebs of learning." Yet, like the Bolognese jurists (see Essay 10), Aquinas and his peers furthered habits of precise verbal analysis, intellectual discipline, and veneration of reason—sowing excellent seeds for the growth of a hairsplitting scientific culture like that of later Europe.

Despite all its critics, the *Summa theologica* exerted a profound influence at the reforming Council of Trent (1545–63). Aquinas was declared a Doctor of the Church in 1567, the Jesuits officially made his philosophy, Thomism, their own in the seventeenth century, and Leo XIII, in his encyclical *Aeterni Patris* (1879), declared Thomism the official philosophy of the Roman Catholic Church.

In the twentieth century, Aquinas inspired the Neo-Thomist movement, whose most prominent exponents were Jacques Maritain and Etienne Gilson, as well as the aesthetic theory propounded in James Joyce's *A Portrait of the Artist as a Young Man*. In Joyce's *Ulysses*, the young poet Stephen Dedalus makes much of Aquinas, "whose gorbellied [corpulent] works I enjoy reading in the original," much as the young Joyce himself did, savoring a page a day.

Anyone who could furnish Dante with the main dogmas for the *Divine Comedy*, supply a philosophy to the Catholic Church, and captivate freethinking James Joyce (who boasted of being "steeled in the school of old Aquinas") had to be a man of extraordinary genius. Yet this stolidly humorless Italo-Teutonic friar, who did little besides pray, study, write, preach, and teach, would seem to have the least claim to *sprezzatura* of any major figure in this book.

But those of us who sang it will always remember his *"Pange lingua"* (and especially its two concluding stanzas, the *"Tantum ergo"*), perhaps the crowning glory of the Catholic hymnal. In thirty-six supple Latin verses, Aquinas touches on the Incarnation, Christ as the Logos, the Virgin Birth, the institution of the Eucharist at the Last Supper, Transubstantiation, the supremacy of faith to the evidence of the senses, the superseding of the Old Law by the New, the Trinity, and the procession of the Holy Spirit from both the Father and the Son. Indeed the hymn is practically a microcosm of the *Summa*. Who would ever have thought this hulking and forbidding master theologian was also a gifted and sensitive Latin poet?

Fourteen

Dante's incomporable *Comedy*

> *And if I prove a timid friend to truth,*
> *I am afraid that I will not survive*
> *To be read by those to whom these times are ancient.*
> —Dante Alighieri, *Paradiso* 17.118–20 (c. 1318)

OF HOMER, DANTE, AND SHAKESPEARE, the three giants of world literature, Dante can lay claim to being the creator of the single greatest work of
art. His *Divine Comedy* is more varied, complex, and all-encompassing
than Homer's *Iliad* or *Odyssey* or any of Shakespeare's plays. Harold Bloom
has written that Dante and Shakespeare "excel all other Western writers
in cognitive acuity, linguistic energy, and power of invention."[1] T. S. Eliot
said the *Divine Comedy* could be compared with "nothing but the *entire*
dramatic work of Shakespeare."

The stature of Dante Alighieri (1265–1321) can be discerned from
that of his admirers. Boccaccio and Michelangelo idolized him.
Petrarch, Chaucer, Milton, and Shelley were strongly influenced by
him. Botticelli made drawings for the *Divine Comedy*, and another of its
illustrators, William Blake, learned Italian so that he could read the
poem in the original. In the twentieth century, Dante was the favorite
author and literary master of W. B. Yeats, James Joyce, Ezra Pound, and
T. S. Eliot. Henry James pronounced him "greatest of literary artists."

Dante was born in Florence in 1265 of an ancient Florentine family
of the minor nobility. Despite artistic depictions of him in middle age
with jutting jaw, menacing nose, and stern brow, the young Dante was
the most romantic of poets. The woman he immortalized as Beatrice
(she who makes blessed) was probably the Florentine Bice Portinari,

---

[1] Harold Bloom, *The Western Canon: The Books and School of the Ages* (New York: Harcourt
Brace and Company, 1994), p. 46.

with whom Dante fell in love when she was eight and he was a little shaver of not quite nine. The next time they met and she first greeted him, he was eighteen, according to *La Vita Nuova* (*The New Life*, c. 1293), a collection of thirty-one lyrics, mostly sonnets, interspersed with prose narratives, in what Dante later called the *"dolce stil nuovo"* (sweet new style).

The *Vita Nuova* tells how Beatrice directed the thoughts of her admirers to God (who had sent this angelic miracle of beauty and virtue to mankind) rather than to physical love. As a result, Dante worshiped Beatrice very much from afar: He ended up married to Gemma Donati (with whom he had at least four children), and Beatrice wed the banker Simone de' Bardi. But the woman Dante called "the glorious lady of my mind" died on June 8, 1290, at age twenty-five, and at the end of the *Vita Nuova* he vows to study as hard as he can to prepare himself "to write of her what has never before been written of any woman."

And he succeeded. His *Divine Comedy* is a Christian version of Orpheus's quest through the world of the dead to repossess a lost love. But besides being an apotheosis of Beatrice, the poem is also an encyclopedia of medieval thought, a prophetic work clamoring for a new world order of justice, and a tremendously engrossing narrative. About six hundred characters swarm through Dante's poem and, according to the Hungarian critic Georg Lukács, "the remembered earthly life of each . . . is as present to their souls as is Dante, to whom they are speaking, or as is the actual place of their punishment or reward."[2]

Arthur Schopenhauer had earlier pointed to this main source of Dante's enduring appeal, asking, "For where did Dante get the material for his Hell, if not from this actual world of ours?" The poem that Dante entitled *Commedia* because of its happy ending, and that was only dubbed "Divine" in a Venetian edition of 1555, sprang from many causes in "this actual world of ours": the turmoil in Dante's own emotions that resulted from Beatrice's early death, the political chaos of Italy, the degeneracy of the papacy and the Church hierarchy, the replacement of the chivalric ideal by an avaricious mercantile society, and his own undeserved banishment.

A main political axis of the poem dates from 1300, when Dante was elected a prior, one of the six chief magistrates of Florence, for a standard two-month term beginning June 15. Indeed, the poet later set the

---

[2]Georg Lukács, *The Theory of the Novel: A Historico-philosophical Essay on the Forms of Great Epic Literature*, trans. by Anna Bostock (Cambridge, Mass.: MIT Press, 1973; 1920), p. 127.

action of the *Divine Comedy* during Holy Week of 1300, just two months before he entered on this disastrous political office. At a time of internal strife—and external threat in the person of Pope Boniface VIII—Dante and his fellow priors banished the leaders of the warring Black and White factions of Guelfs, the ruling party of the city-state of Florence.

When the Black Guelfs seized power, there was a terror and purge. On January 27, 1302, Dante, who as a White Guelf opposed the grasping policy of Boniface, was accused of graft during his term of office. He was heavily fined and sentenced to banishment for two years. After prudently declining to return from an embassy to the pope to answer the trumped-up charges, Dante was banished for life on March 10 and condemned to be burned at the stake if apprehended. He never saw his native city—or his wife—again.

While the injustice of his punishment rankled, he conceived of the long poem that would absorb him until his death. Instead of using Latin, the language of learned works, he decided to write his epic in Italian, whose fitness for lofty poetic matters he had expounded in his unfinished Latin tract *De vulgari eloquentia* (*On Writing in the Vernacular*). He invented his own braidlike rhyme scheme for the poem, terza rima, or triple rhyme—*aba, bcb, cdc,* and so forth—the rhyme of the middle line of one tercet, or three-line stanza, giving rise to the first and third rhymes of the next. This emphasis on the number 3, in honor of the Trinity, is also reflected in the *Divine Comedy*'s main divisions (called *cantiche,* "songs"): *Inferno, Purgatorio,* and *Paradiso.*

The medieval rage for order is nowhere better exemplified than in Dante's vast poem of one hundred cantos, with its three *cantiche* of thirty-three cantos each (and an introductory canto to the whole, prefixed to the *Inferno*). The perfect number ten finds structural underpinning in the nine circles of Hell plus an Ante-Hell or vestibule, the seven terraces of Purgatory plus two cornices of an Ante-Purgatory and the Earthly Paradise, and the ten spheres of Heaven. In addition, each of the three *cantiche* ends with the word *stelle,* as in the last line of the *Inferno:* "And thus we emerged to see again the stars." The studied symmetry of the 14,233-line *Comedy* is apparent even in the number of lines of its constituent parts: 4,720, 4,755, and 4,758. The three *cantiche,* though almost identical in length, follow an ascending order from the pit of Hell to the heavens of Paradise.

Dante's first encounter with the forces of evil in the *Inferno* occurs in the opening lines: "Midway along this life we journey through, / I found myself in a dark wood, astray, / For the right path was wholly lost to view" (*Inf.* 1.1–3). We are immediately involved in a dramatic situation that's familiar enough on the literal level (someone gets lost in a forest at night) but that also begs for an allegorical interpretation: At a crucial point in his life—at age thirty-five, in 1300—Dante realizes he has lapsed into sin, error, and spiritual confusion.

He tries to escape the moral bewilderment symbolized by the dark forest, but three mysterious beasts appear in succession—a restless leopard, a fierce lion, and, most threatening of all, a famished she-wolf—preventing him from climbing a sunlit hill (symbol of God). The beasts may be seen as various obstacles to salvation: our own human propensities to incontinence, violence, and malice (or fraud). These three Aristotelian categories of vice that assail us correspond to the major divisions of Dante's Hell.

As Dante turns to flee, a ghost appears—the spirit of his literary idol, the long-dead Roman poet Virgil (70–19 B.C.), who convinces him that the only way to escape the beasts is to undertake an epic journey through the afterlife—the realms of Hell, Purgatory, and Paradise. Virgil, who will guide Dante through the first two, will show him the true nature of evil in Hell so that he can learn to despise it for how it twists the human soul and character; he will then point out to Dante the way of repentance in Purgatory. There Beatrice will descend from Heaven to guide him through the heavenly spheres so that he can learn the true goal of humankind by witnessing the bliss of the saints in Paradise.

The quest motif permeates epic from *Gilgamesh* and the *Odyssey* to the *Cantos* of Ezra Pound, but Dante is both singer and hero of his epic, and his two great loves, Virgil and Beatrice, guide him on his journey to illumination. Virgil, greatest of Roman poets, represents for Dante the highest that human reason, without the benefit of revelation, can accomplish in the quest for self-fulfillment in the here and now. As author of the *Aeneid*, which describes the descent of Aeneas to the Underworld, Virgil was a natural choice to serve as guide in a poem about a journey to the afterlife. The *Aeneid* also celebrates the founding of the Roman state, which Dante believed was divinely ordained for man's earthly happiness, as set forth in his Latin tract *De Monarchia*.

Virgil, who as a virtuous pagan dwells in Limbo, has been sent to Dante's aid by the soul of Beatrice, who is grievously distressed about "her friend's" salvation. Much later in the poem, Beatrice (symbol of the truths of Divine Revelation) takes over Dante's instruction from Virgil—the revealed truths of Scripture coming to the aid of reason when reason reaches its limits.

On Good Friday evening, Virgil and Dante (who is always himself in the poem, but also an Everyman) set out for Hell. After a vestibule in which fence-sitting nonentities are punished, the two poets travel down nine increasingly awful infernal circles of sinners: (1) the Limbo of innocent souls and virtuous heathens; (2) the lustful; (3) the gluttonous; (4) the avaricious and prodigal; (5) the wrathful and sullen; (6) the heretics; (7) the violent (in three rings—murderers and tyrants in the first, suicides and squanderers in the second, and blasphemers, sodomites, and usurers in the last); (8) the fraudulent (in ten concentric trenches); (9) the treacherous (in four zones).

Circles 2–5 punish sins of incontinence (the leopard); circle 7, the violent sins of the lion; and circles 8 and 9, the malicious sins of the she-wolf. (Circles 1 and 6, dealing with Christian belief, are outside the threefold Aristotelian schema.) For the purposes of his poem, Dante imagined Hell as a huge narrowing funnel beneath the ground with its vertex at the center of the earth.

The inscription over the gates of Hell opens Canto 3, "THROUGH ME THE WAY INTO THE CITY OF WOE, / THROUGH ME THE WAY TO ENDLESS AGONY, / THROUGH ME THE WAY AMONG THE LOST BELOW," ending with the most famous line in the poem: "ALL HOPE ABANDON, YOU WHO ENTER HERE" (*Inf*. 3.1–3, 9). Since all the punishments of Hell and Purgatory are made to fit the crime, when Dante depicts the abode of the lustful, for example, he wants us to understand that their sufferings are only a concretization of their own inner turbulence and helplessness vis-à-vis their unbridled sexual passion:

> I came to a region mute of any light,
> > That bellows like a storm upon a sea
> > Which warring winds attack, and toss, and smite.
> That hellish tempest roars incessantly;
> > It grasps and draws the spirits in its train,
> > Spinning and thrashing souls in agony (Inf. 5.28–33).

Dante speaks with Paolo and Francesca, two adulterous lovers condemned to suffer together for all eternity. Francesca da Rimini was married to handsome Paolo Malatesta's lame, ugly brother, who, in about 1285, killed them after catching them in the act. This is Francesca explaining to Dante how she and Paolo began their affair in a life-imitating-art parody of the illicit passion of two literary characters, Lancelot and Guinevere:

> *One day, to charm the time away, we read*
>   *Of Lancelot, whom love had so constrained;*
>   *We were alone, without suspicious dread.*
> *Though time and time again our reading drained*
>   *Our cheeks of blood and drew our eyes aside,*
>   *Yet at one point alone were we enchained:*
> *When we read how her smile, so long denied,*
>   *A kiss from such a noble lover took,*
>   *This man, who now shall never leave my side,*
> *Then kissed me on the mouth and, kissing, shook.*
>   *A pander was that work and he who wrote it.*
>   *That day we read no farther in that book* (Inf. 5.127–38).

Dante finds in Hell a number of damned souls whose heroic nobility resonates within his own proud spirit, such as the Florentine aristocrat and heretic Farinata, who rises arrogantly from his fiery tomb "as if he held all Hell in great disdain" (*Inf.* 10.36). The poet's most famous portrait of flawed grandeur is that of Ulysses, whose sins as a false counselor have caused him to be enveloped in flames like a human torch (*Inf.* 26). The Greek hero tells the story of his catastrophic last voyage, when his eloquent speech persuaded his men to join him on a mad quest beyond the Straits of Gibraltar and into the unexplored reaches of the Southern Hemisphere, ending in their utter destruction. Dante the proto-humanist puts into Ulysses' mouth the lines, "You were not made to live your lives like beasts, / But to follow paths of virtue and of knowledge."

A man of ardent loves and searing hates, Dante admires some grandiose sinners but despises the wishy-washy, "who lived their lives without disgrace or praise" (*Inf.* 3.36), and abominates the treacherous. Falsely accused of treason against Florence, he makes his alter ego in the poem yank tufts of hair from the head of one traitor and refuse to open the frozen eyes of another after promising to do so, claiming "it was courtesy to be a boor to him." The soul of yet another traitor, who was still alive in 1300, is put into Hell anyway, with the explanation that what appears to be the man on earth is actually a kind of zombie inhabited by a devil (*Inf.* 32 and 33).

Where else but in the *Inferno* can you find corrupt popes planted upside down with just their writhing legs exposed and the soles of their feet on fire (*Inf.* 19)? Dante's enemy, Pope Boniface VIII, is exposed as a crafty fraud who tricks his enemies and helps an unwary penitent damn his own soul (*Inf.* 27). And no one has ever accused Dante of prissiness. The thief Vanni Fucci, still in fine fettle even in Hell, "raised his hands with both the figs" (the equivalent of the finger), screaming, "Take them, God, it's you I'm aiming them at!" Thaïs, an ancient Greek prostitute, now has "shitty fingernails" and, like the other flatterers, must dwell in the excrement that once flowed so copiously from her mouth. A famous devil's fart ends Canto 21—"And he had made a trumpet of his ass"—in a long episode involving some of the most comically energetic and blundering demons in all of literature. In this section dealing with political graft, for which he was condemned, Dante lets flatulent Malacoda (Bad-Tail) issue the poet's resounding rebuttal to his Florentine foes.

Near the bottom of Hell we meet Count Ugolino, the Pisan traitor who was starved to death in 1289 with two sons and two grandsons by being locked up in a tower (*Inf.* 33). To heighten the pathos, Dante imagines Ugolino's fellow victims as four young sons, and indeed the count's horrific tale of starvation as he watched his children die before him, one by one, is, in Goethe's words, "among the supreme productions of poetry." Ugolino speaks while taking a break from gnawing on the head of his enemy, Archbishop Ruggieri. Since both were traitors, the two are trapped forever in the frozen ice of the River Cocytus. But Ugolino, starved to death by Ruggieri, is the gnawer, and the worse traitor the gnawee.

The anarchy of Italian city-state politics, with its interminable feuds, made Dante dream of a universal monarchy like that of the old Roman emperors. As a result, Brutus and Cassius, the betrayers of Julius Caesar, are placed, along with Judas, in the three mouths of Lucifer to be chomped on in endless torture as the worst of all human sinners—traitors against lords and benefactors (*Inf.* 34).

Lucifer himself, whose three faces are a parody of the Trinity, weeps from six eyes for the revolt against God that damned him. Like a towering windmill at the very center of the earth (and of the universe)—the farthest point from God—he flaps his enormous bat wings to freeze the Cocytus and increase the torment of the souls stuck in the ice. Dante and Virgil climb down on Lucifer's gigantic body past the center of the

Earth and then follow a subterranean path to emerge into the light of day on Mount Purgatory on Easter Sunday morning.

Dante's Purgatory is an enormous island-mountain rising out of the ocean in the uninhabited Southern Hemisphere, at the antipodes of Jerusalem, with the Garden of Eden at its summit. After an Ante-Purgatory in two levels, where excommunicates, late repenters, and negligent princes must linger before beginning their purgation, the seven deadly sins provide the main structuring principle: Terraces 1–7 imaginatively punish pride, envy, wrath, sloth, avarice, gluttony, and lust (in descending order of seriousness). The repentant sinners spend as much time on each terrace as they deserve—Dante himself doing a little extra work on pride, wrath, and lust. After terrace 7, Dante and Virgil climb to the Earthly Paradise of Eden.

Despite its punishments, the *Purgatorio* is an abode of calm and reflection. It sparkles with artists: the Italian troubadour Sordello, who looks like a crouching lion in his haughtiness; the ancient Roman poet Statius, whose freedom from purgation after more than 1,200 years is announced with a terrific earthquake; the Bolognese poet Guido Guinizzelli, who initiated the "sweet new style" that Dante perfected; the troubadour Arnaut Daniel, whom Guinizzelli calls "the greater craftsman," and who has the unique privilege in the poem of speaking eight lines of Provençal; as well as miniaturists, musicians, and singers (one of whom sings a poem of Dante's). Giotto, said to have been Dante's friend, is praised as the greatest living painter. This *cantica* also abounds in liturgical rituals (prayers, hymns, scriptural passages, and beatitudes), and many of the penitents ask Dante to pray for them.

When Virgil tells Dante that only a wall of flames (the punishment for lust) separates him from his beloved muse Beatrice, he consents to go through fire to see her again. Before ascending to Heaven, the souls of the redeemed sojourn briefly in the Eden that was lost through the sin of Adam and Eve, and here, amid a spectacular processional scene representing the history of the Church, Beatrice makes a triumphal entry in a chariot (*Purg.* 30).

Virgil disappears just when Dante needs his comfort most, since Beatrice, who speaks his name for the only time in the entire poem, bitterly reproves him for unfaithfulness to her memory after her death. Among other worldly distractions that had imperiled his soul, Dante's admiration had strayed to a certain "compassionate woman" whom he had tried to allegorize as "Lady Philosophy" in his unfinished encyclopedic treatise

Il Convivio (*The Banquet*, 1304–7). We also know of a woman he calls Pietra (stone), about whom he wrote some of his most virtuosic (and vitriolic) poems, calling her in one of them "that hardest stone / that speaks and hears as if it were a woman."

But after a display of deep remorse, all is forgiven, and Dante, who has been absolved of his sins in climbing Mount Purgatory, and is now "pure and all ready to rise to the stars," gazes fixedly into Beatrice's eyes and begins to ascend to Heaven with her. Her lovely eyes, radiant like suns, and her inexpressibly beautiful smile will continue to raise him from heaven to heaven of the *Paradiso*.

The last *cantica* is a light-and-sound show orchestrated by God for Dante's spiritual edification. Although all the saints actually dwell in the Empyrean with God, myriads of them descend to the various spheres of the universe to welcome and instruct the questing human pilgrim. In the Ptolemaic astronomy of Dante's time, ten heavens, or spheres, encircled the stationary earth. In sphere 1, that of the Moon, Dante places faithful but weak souls whom others forced to break their vows. The rest are as follows: sphere 2 (Mercury): lawmakers and other officials whose service was marred by ambition or thirst for fame; 3 (Venus): lovers tainted by lust; 4 (the Sun): the wise, mostly theologians; 5 (Mars): martyrs and warriors; 6 (Jupiter): just rulers; 7 (Saturn): contemplatives; 8 (the Fixed Stars): the Church Triumphant; 9 (the Crystalline, or Primum Mobile): the angelic orders and chorus; 10 (the Empyrean): the Holy Trinity and the Blessed Virgin in the true abode of all the angels and saints.

The greatest human interest in the third *cantica* arises from Dante's meeting with his great-great-grandfather Cacciaguida, who died while on the Second Crusade (1147–49) and was thus a martyr for the Faith. Dante's pride in his knightly ancestor is attested by the episode's length, content, and central position (*Para.* 15–17). Here Dante the character learns the details of his exile, which Cacciaguida prophesies to him. (Of course, the events had already occurred when Dante was writing.) After leaving behind everything most dear, "You'll learn firsthand how salty is the bread / Of others, and how difficult his path / Who up and down another's stairs must tread" (*Para.* 17.58–60). As for the wrath of the family and friends of all the well-connected souls he's seen in Hell, Cacciaguida urges his descendant to unflinchingly set down the truth—"and let them scratch wherever it itches."

In Canto 30, Dante and Beatrice ascend to the Empyrean, the immaterial heaven of pure intellectual light and love, outside of all time and space, the tenth and last heaven, that of God's immediate presence, where the choirs of angels and the souls of the blessed glorify the Deity and partake of his ineffable joy. The staggering effulgence blinds Dante at first, but then he dazedly sees a river of light with flowers on both banks, and living sparks flitting among the flowers like bees, bringing them God's joy and love from the river. When Dante's vision strengthens, he sees the sparks as angels and the flowers as the saints who dwell in the fragrant, snow-white rose of Paradise, consisting of more than a thousand tiers—and Dante can see all of them face-to-face in that unimaginably vast region where distance is meaningless.

After Beatrice disappears from Dante's side to take her place among the petals of the rose, St. Bernard, the great twelfth-century mystic, assumes the task of preparing Dante for the final mysteries he will witness (*Para.* 31). Bernard becomes Dante's guide to where even Revelation cannot lead—the Beatific Vision. When Dante looks for his beloved, he sees her in her proper seat next to Rachel, symbol of the contemplative life. He thanks her for saving him, and she smiles at him one last time before turning to the "eternal fountain" of light.

T. S. Eliot called the last canto, *Paradiso* 33, "the highest point that poetry has ever reached or ever can reach." Bernard, most ardently devoted to Mary, implores her to intercede with her Son that Dante may be vouchsafed the vision of God. Lifting his eyes to her who is blazing with light and whose beauty is beyond description, he addresses her in an exquisite prayer structured on a series of paradoxes and antitheses, beginning "O Virgin Mother, daughter of your Son, / Humblest and most exalted of all creatures."

Acceding to Bernard's prayer, Mary raises her eyes toward the Sun that warms the Celestial Rose. In one hundred sublime verses, Dante describes the joy of a direct vision of the Trinity, and of Christ as God and man, in a radiant beam of simple light. That divine ray gathers in itself, as in a book, all the forms of things scattered like loose pages throughout the universe, and appears in the last line of the poem as "the Love that moves the sun and the other stars."

During the many years he worked on his *Comedy*, Dante wandered to Forlì, Bologna, Arezzo, Padua, Lucca, staying twice with the Scaligeri in Verona and, from about 1318, settling with Guido Novello da Polenta, the ruler of Ravenna who was a nephew of the Francesca immortalized by the poet. When Dante refused an offer of amnesty from Florence in 1315 because it involved a ceremony of penitence, the Florentines renewed their death sentence. What Dante had in mind was a triumphant return to his native city, where he would be crowned poet laureate at the font in the Baptistery of Florence where he had been christened (*Para.* 25.1–12).

At age fifty-six, the man who has been called the greatest of all Europeans fell ill while returning through malarial swamplands from an embassy to Venice, and died in Ravenna on September 13 or 14 of 1321. He became a classic overnight, his masterpiece immediately attracting learned commentaries and exegeses. Today, with scores of existing translations—in English alone, not to mention other languages—and with others proliferating at an accelerating pace with no end in sight, the reputation of what Longfellow (himself one of its translators) called a "mediaeval miracle of song" is more than assured.

Fifteen

Banks, bookkeeping, and the rise of commercial capitalism

Modern capitalism . . . has its roots in Italy during the Middle Ages and the Renaissance. From the Crusades to the Great Discoveries, Italy was the dominant economic power in the western world, and its merchants were the leading businessmen. . . . This hegemony of the Italians rested largely upon superior business organization. As a matter of fact, they laid the foundations for most of the business institutions of today.
  —Raymond de Roover, *The Rise and Decline of the Medici Bank* (1963)

IN THE WINTER OF 1290–91 the brothers Ugolino and Guido Vivaldi, members of a prominent Genoese family, were busy with plans for a bold undertaking: finding a sea route to the Indies. Over the next few months, they raised funds from investors, small and large. In May Ugolino and Guido set out with two well-armed galleys, sailed through the Straits of Gibraltar, and never returned.

The voyage of the Vivaldi brothers had no immediate sequel, except perhaps to inspire their contemporary Dante Alighieri's account of Ulysses' last voyage in Canto 26 of the *Inferno*. Two centuries would pass before another Genoese named Christopher Columbus followed in their wake (see Essay 24). Yet in 1291, if only for a moment, the New World seemed within reach of the Italian maritime republics—the next logical step in their long history of market expansion.

During the late eleventh and twelfth centuries, Genoa and its rivals Pisa and Venice wrested control of Mediterranean commerce from the Arabs and Byzantine Greeks, exacting lucrative trading privileges and establishing overseas colonies. When business acumen didn't suffice, they resorted to force, sacking Caesarea on the First Crusade and Constantinople on the Fourth. During the thirteenth century, the maritime republics expanded their commercial horizons beyond the Mediterranean. In 1277 the Genoese began sending galleys to Flanders and

England, and by the end of the century, even as the Vivaldi brothers were sailing, scores of their compatriots were following the caravan routes eastward to Persia, India, and ultimately China. Marco Polo of Venice is famous not because he was the only Italian to visit the court of Kublai Khan, but because the romance-writer Rustichello of Pisa, with whom he later shared a Genoese jail cell, turned Marco's travels into a medieval bestseller.

At the same time, the inland cities of Lombardy and Tuscany became the uncontested masters of international finance in Europe. As bankers to kings, the Italians financed both sides in the Hundred Years' War between France and England. As bankers to the popes, they collected tithes as far away as Greenland, where the tribute was paid in sealskins and whalebone. The most famous of these financial powerhouses was the Medici Bank of Florence, which at its height maintained branches in Rome, Venice, Naples, Milan, Pisa, Geneva, Lyon, Avignon, Bruges, and London. Under Cosimo de' Medici and his grandson Lorenzo (a.k.a. "the Magnificent") the bank's enormous profits helped underwrite the rebirth of art and learning known as the Renaissance (see Essay 21).

At the turn of the twentieth century, German sociologist Max Weber published an influential essay in which he argued that commercial capitalism grew out of the Protestant work ethic and that its origins are to be sought among the Dutch and the English during the sixteenth and seventeenth centuries. In fact, all of the foundations of capitalism were already in place in Italy during the later Middle Ages and Renaissance, including a nascent bourgeois ideology that justified the pursuit of profit as the engine of secular progress. As Benedetto Cortugli of Ragusa (a Venetian protectorate now called Dubrovnik) put it in his 1458 handbook *On Commerce and the Perfect Merchant*, "The advancement, the comfort, and the health of republics to a large extent proceed from merchants." Cortugli goes on to explain that merchants enable sterile countries to prosper, that they encourage industry, and that, through their activity, they "allow the poor to live."

It may seem odd that this thoroughly modern appreciation of entrepreneurship was penned in a society that high school textbooks call "feudal." But feudalism was a dead letter in northern Italy long before Cortugli's time. Beginning in the eleventh century, Europe, led by the Italians, entered a long period of demographic and economic expansion known as the medieval commercial revolution. At the same time, the cities of northern Italy fought off, or bought off, their feudal overlords to become independent communes—city-states ruled as business concerns by merchant oligarchies. The old order made its last stand at Legnano in 1176, when the feudal cavalry of German Emperor Frederick Barbarossa was crushed by the citizen soldiers of the Lombard League. North of the Alps, the center of economic and political life remained the castle and the cathedral. In northern Italy, it became the urban marketplace.

Italy's economic ascendancy rested on its mastery of flexible and sophisticated methods for raising capital, distributing risk, and gathering market intelligence. The principles behind the methods, and in some cases the methods themselves, continue to shape business practice to this day.

The usual means of raising capital in the maritime republics, at least until the fourteenth century, was the *commenda*—the contract the Vivaldi brothers used to outfit their ships, buy trading goods, and pay their sailors' advances. The *commenda* brought into association a stay-at-home capitalist and a traveling merchant for the duration of a voyage. If the voyage was successful, the stay-at-home party generally received three-quarters of the profits, the traveling party one quarter. If it was a failure, the former lost his capital, the latter his labor.

The *commenda* had many advantages. Because it was not a loan, it did not violate the ecclesiastical prohibition against usury, which in the Middle Ages meant not only excessive interest, but any interest at all. The *commenda* allowed for diversification, thus minimizing risks: A stay-at-home capitalist could divide his investment funds among as many merchants and routes as he pleased—so much for the spice trade with the Levant, so much for the wool trade with England. It also left room for the traveling party to take entrepreneurial initiative, because he might raise funds from many different investors and because he usually retained the discretion to trade and traffic "wherever the ship might go." Finally, by allowing investments of any size, the *commenda* maximized the amount of capital put to productive uses: Thousands of contracts in the Genoese notarial archives attest that members of all social classes routinely acted as "capitalists" in *commenda* contracts—not just magnates like Benedetto Zaccaria (the Genoese tycoon and admiral who in 1284 helped annihilate the Pisan navy at the battle of Meloria) but ordinary artisans and sailors, too.

In the overland trade between Italy and northern Europe, merchants relied on another type of credit instrument, the letter of exchange. In the exchange contract, a first party advanced money to a second party, who agreed to repay the sum at a later date in another place and in another currency. Actually, the transaction involved four parties, since the principals ordinarily depended on "correspondents" to execute the exchange. Letters of exchange served more than one function. They were loans in which the interest charge could be concealed in the exchange rate. They were speculative investments whose value rose and fell along with the value of the currency in which they were denominated. And they were even a kind of paper money whose use enabled merchants to avoid the danger and expense of transporting coin. By the fourteenth century, transactions at the famous Champagne Fairs, where merchants from northern Italy met those from Flanders and England, were often settled via letters of exchange without a single florin changing hands.

Money changers, pawnbrokers, and loan sharks have existed in most societies from time immemorial. It was Italy, however, that seems to have invented the first "full-service" banks. By the thirteenth century, banks in most of the northern Italian cities took deposits on time or demand, transferred funds to other institutions, and extended credit by allowing overdrafts. Originally, transfers had to be ordered in person by the depositor or his agent, but eventually checks came into use. By the early fourteenth century, there were eighty such banks in Florence alone, three of which—the Bardi, the Peruzzi, and the Acciauoli—presided over vast financial empires based on international trade and credit.

Medieval and Renaissance banks were usually set up as partnerships called *compagnie*, or "companies." In some banks, branches were run by salaried employees. In other, less centralized banks, the branches were autonomous partnerships that reported to the parent partnership. The Medici Bank, whose organization resembled that of a modern holding company, was such an institution. The partnership model, with its joint and unlimited liability, meant that a series of bad trade deals or the default of a large debtor could bring the whole financial edifice crashing down. The history of high finance during the later Middle Ages and Renaissance is studded with spectacular bank failures. Siena never recovered from the collapse of its Bonsignori Company in 1298. The triple failure of the Bardi, Peruzzi, and Acciauoli in the mid-1340s—all three had overextended credit to Europe's crowned heads—triggered an international financial crisis. Giovanni Villani, an agent of the Peruzzi Company and the author of a famous Florentine chronicle, explains that when Edward III of England defaulted on his loans in 1343, he owed his bankers "the value of a realm."

Monarchies weren't the only governments to borrow prodigiously. So did the Italian communes, whose citizens preferred lending the government money to paying it taxes. In most communes, such loans came to constitute a permanent and accumulating public debt, the shares of which were negotiable—that is, they could be bought, sold, and bequeathed just like any other asset. Governments guaranteed the payment of interest on the shares through dedicated tariffs and excise taxes, whose collection was often handed over to private corporations of the state's creditors. At Genoa, this development went a step further. During the fourteenth century, the commune began granting creditor organizations not just the right to collect taxes but to administer colonies. In 1407 these organizations united as the Bank of Saint George, which Niccolò Machiavelli admiringly described as a state within the state. The Bank was to all intents and purposes a joint stock company—the precursor of the more famous East and West India Companies founded by the Dutch and English.

Along with flexible and efficient methods of raising capital, the Italians laid another foundation of capitalism: insurance. True insurance was unknown in antiquity and the early Middle Ages, although a credit instrument called the sea loan functioned much like it. In the sea loan, repayment of principal and interest was contingent on the safe arrival of the ship at its destination. When the Church condemned this contract as usurious in the thirteenth century, the Italians set about developing substitutes. By the early fourteenth century, clear examples of maritime insurance involving third-party underwriters appeared at Genoa. It's no accident that many of the early instances are for the Flanders trade, where regular galley convoys helped reduce risks and made it easier to determine premiums. Italians also pioneered other types of insurance, including life insurance.

Timely and accurate information is as important to capitalism as credit and insurance. During the early stages of the commercial revolution, entrepreneurs stayed abreast of market developments by traveling with their wares. But by the late thirteenth century, at least along established trade routes, a growing number of them managed to administer far-flung business empires without ever leaving their desks. These "sedentary" merchants and bankers entrusted their affairs abroad to resident agents or factors, sometimes employees and sometimes partners, who received their instructions (and sent back reports) by courier. A surprising number of letters survive. The invaluable Datini Company archives, which are located in Prato, a town near Florence, alone contain more than 100,000 letters dating from the late fourteenth and early fifteenth centuries. The letters deal with business opportunities, market developments, management issues, political news, and even personal matters.

Meanwhile, advances in accounting made managing complex business concerns easier. The basic method of business accounting still in use today—double-entry bookkeeping, in which every transaction gives rise to both a credit and a debit—was in widespread use in Italy by the end of the Middle Ages. In larger enterprises, separate ledgers were kept for each account, including God's, where charitable contributions were recorded like any other business expense. The invention of double-entry bookkeeping is often attributed to Luca Pacioli, a Venetian monk who published a treatise on the subject in 1494. In fact, its development dates back to the late thirteenth or early fourteenth century and seems to have occurred contemporaneously at Genoa and Florence.

Merchants could also consult business manuals like Benedetto Cortugli's. Along with the occasional foray into political economy, these how-to books contained a wealth of practical details on almost every subject of interest to merchants: the goods traded along different routes, weights and measures, formulas for converting currency and calculating interest, tariffs, calendars, and itineraries. The best-known medieval business manual is the mid-fourteenth-century *Practice of Commerce* by Francesco Pegolotti, an agent of the Bardi Company. Pegolotti devotes considerable space to describing the road to China, which he calls "perfectly safe, whether by day or by night." Among his tidbits of advice: Let your beard grow long and take along a woman, preferably one who speaks the Tartar language.

It's difficult to overstate the contribution Italians made to modern capitalism—or their dominance of the later-medieval and Renaissance economy. They enjoyed a near monopoly over long-distance trade in the Mediterranean, the only question being which of the maritime republics would emerge the final victor in their fratricidal wars. (The answer: Venice—see Essay 40.) Their business organization was centuries ahead of the Hanseatic League, Europe's other major commercial power. And until the late-fifteenth-century rise of the Fuggers, the fabulously wealthy southern German financiers, Italy was synonymous with banking—an identification so close that the financial district in London was called Lombard Street.

The rest of Europe complained, perhaps with some justification, that the Italians were using financial trickery to rob them. Commenting on Venice's favorable balance of trade, Doge Tommaso Mocenigo boasted in the early 1420s that the Venetians would soon become "masters of all the gold in Christendom." A century later the tables turned in favor of the Genoese, who had reinvented themselves as bankers after losing the disastrous War of Chioggia (1378–81) to the Venetians and their eastern colonies to the Turks. Christopher Columbus never cashed in on his discoveries, but Genoa's great families—the Spinola, Doria, Grimaldi, and Centurione—did. During the sixteenth century, they financed the Spanish conquest of the New World, siphoning off its silver as payment for the enormous loans they made. A sixteenth-century Spanish saying had it that wealth was born in the Indies, died in Spain, and was buried in Genoa. The Baroque palaces that line the city's New Street (now Via Garibaldi) were built with Aztec and Inca treasure.

Even so, Italy was destined to lose its commercial and financial hegemony. Already during the sixteenth century the voyages of discovery and the emergence of nation states north of the Alps were shifting the center of gravity of the European economy. Although Genoa enriched itself in the service of Spain, and Venice continued to profit for a while from the Eastern luxury trade, Italy was progressively overshadowed by the new "Atlantic economies." By the seventeenth century the Dutch and the English were clearly in the lead, founding their East and West India Companies and setting up the first stock exchanges.

In the end, it is not the scale of the commercial and financial activity of the Italian communes that is most impressive. Amsterdam and London would preside over larger and wealthier business empires. Rather it is the precocious modernity of the communes' business institutions and attitudes. In an age better known for trials by ordeal than letters of exchange, the Italians created the first modern economies. In the mid-fourteenth century, Giovanni Villani relates how a plan to establish a seasonal fair in his native city flopped because "there always is a market in Florence." For the same reason, there was never any need for a merchant's guild in Genoa. To quote a contemporary proverb that says it all, *"Januensis ergo mercator"*—A Genoese, and thus a merchant.

—Richard Jackson

Sixteen

Petrarch: Creator of the modern lyric

> As there is none among earthly delights more noble than literature,
> so there is none so lasting, none gentler, or more faithful; there is
> none which accompanies its possessor through the vicissitudes of life
> at so small a cost of effort or anxiety.
> —Petrarch, Letter to Boccaccio (April 28, 1373)

FRANCESCO PETRARCA (1304–74) didn't invent the sonnet—that distinction belongs to Giacomo da Lentini, a Sicilian poet of the preceding century—but he did tune this "small sound" of fourteen lines to a pitch of melodious artistry that has seldom been equaled. More important, Petrarch crafted in himself a sensibility that made his sonnets and other lyrics the first modern poems.

The introductory sonnet of his *Canzoniere* (Songbook) sets forth Petrarch's recurrent themes of pain at his fruitless love, shame at its folly, and the fame (here disguised as ridicule) that it garnered him. He ends this recantation with a melancholic observation that sounds the keynote of his entire literary career:

> O you who in these poems hear the sound
> of all the sighs on which I fed my heart
> in days of youthful folly when, in part,
> I was a different man—if there be found
> among yourselves a lover, he is bound
> some pity and forgiveness to impart
> on me who weep as I rehearse the smart
> of empty hopes that empty woes confound.
>
> But now I clearly see how I became
> the talk of everyone for many years—
> and often this the greatest shame I deem.

The fruit of all my folly has been shame,
regret, and knowledge that whatever appears
alluring in this world is but a dream.

The emotional life of the poet, in all its conflicted complexity, here announces itself as subject matter for poetry. Though worldly pleasures are proclaimed to be deceptive, Petrarch would weave out of them an enormous garland of verse tributes to a beautiful young woman who wrenched his heart into song.

Or that, at least, is the fiction. *Il Canzoniere* is a collection of 366 lyrics (one for each day of a leap year), most of them sonnets and other poems about a woman named Laura. At age twenty-two, Petrarch first saw and fell in love with her in the Church of St. Clare in Avignon on April 6 (Good Friday) of 1327. She is traditionally identified as Laure de Noves, who bore eleven children to her husband, an ancestor of the Marquis de Sade, before dying in the Black Death in 1348, exactly twenty-one years after the poet set eyes on her.

Some say Laura was just a lyric motif that the poet used to ring his endless punning changes on *"lauro"* (the undying laurel tree and crown, sacred to Apollo, god of poetry), *"l'aura"* (the breeze of poetic inspiration), and *"l'auro"* (the gold—of her hair and her worth). Whether or not she was a fiction, Petrarch uses Laura as a peg on which to hang the most exquisite torments of unrequited love. While taking many a page from the troubadours' books, Petrarch went far beyond them in forging a poetic drama out of his emotional turmoil and in bringing Dante's sonneteering about his divine Beatrice back down to earth. Before such a poetic project could suggest itself to him, however, Petrarch had to shift the scale of values of the world he inhabited and to elevate the status of the human personality into a fit subject for extensive analysis.

In Italy's wealthy mercantile centers, a new spirit of humanism was sprouting alongside the Scholasticism of the theologians, drawing its inspiration from ancient Roman literature, history, and philosophy. After the predominantly otherworldly concerns of the ten medieval centuries since the Christianization of the Roman Empire, man and the world were moving back into sharper focus, and there was a keener emphasis on the dignity, rationality, beauty, and enjoyment of life, as glimpsed through the secular literary monuments of Roman civilization.

The man who became the first great Renaissance humanist was born in exile, and his later cosmopolitanism may owe something to this fact. His father, Petracco, was a government lawyer who was banished from

Florence in 1302, the same year as Dante. The infant destined to be (in the words of French historian Ernest Renan) "the first modern man" first saw the light of day in Arezzo on July 20, 1304. "I was, in truth, a poor mortal like yourself," Petrarch reassures us in his *Epistle to Posterity*, the first modern autobiography, "neither very exalted in my origin, nor, on the other hand, of the most humble birth, but belonging, as Augustus Caesar says of himself, to an ancient family."

In quest of employment at the papal court, which took up residence in Avignon in 1309, Petrarch's father moved his family to southern France when Petrarch was a young boy, settling them in Carpentras. Petracco forced his son to study law at the universities of Montpellier and Bologna, but as soon as he died, in 1326, the headstrong twenty-one-year-old Petrarch left school and returned to Provence.

A bit of a fop in his youth, Petrarch later indulgently recalled curling and perfuming his reddish-brown hair. But he had already devoted himself to the literary life, seeking fulfillment through study and poetic achievement, which he saw as portals of self-discovery, self-expression, and self-perfection. The man who would go on to make a myth of himself and his love life nonetheless took minor orders in the Church, qualifying him to receive benefices that would enable him to pursue his literary career without the vexation of having to earn a living.

The ancient world and the Latin language became fetishes for Petrarch. On his early travels—which took him to Paris, Flanders, Germany, and Rome, not on business, but for sight-seeing and edification—he scavenged for old Latin manuscripts that had been buried in oblivion. In Liège in 1333 he discovered Cicero's speech *Pro Archia* (on the importance of poetry) and, in the Cathedral Library of Verona in 1345, Cicero's letters to Atticus, Quintus, and Brutus. Petrarch not only searched out, collected, and studied ancient manuscripts, but he also had them copied or copied them out himself, compared variant readings, and suggested emendations, thus anticipating modern textual criticism.

Prizing ancient literature both for its moral instruction and its formal excellence, Petrarch modeled his Latin prose style on Cicero's philosophical treatises, Seneca's epistles, and the writings of St. Augustine. All of his prose works—including his numerous letters—were written in a Latin that, though far from Ciceronian perfection, represents a decided advance over the ecclesiastical Latin of his day. At age thirty-three he took a cottage with two gardens in Vaucluse, twenty miles east of Avignon, to write and pursue his Latin studies.

The author of *De vita solitaria* (1346) always stressed the importance of periodic solitary retreats ("with only two servants") in order to commune with nature. Taking his cue from the Roman ideal of studious leisure (*otium*) praised by writers like Cicero, Horace, and Pliny the Younger, Petrarch initiated the humanist mania for villa life as a scholarly and meditative haven away from the distracting bustle and corruption of city or court life.

In 1336, inspired by a passage in the Roman historian Livy, Petrarch took his brother with him on the ascent of Mount Ventoux in Provence. If not the first to climb a mountain merely to enjoy the view, Petrarch wrote about the experience more thoughtfully than anyone had before. What did he do at the top? He opened his copy of St. Augustine's *Confessions* at random to a passage berating those who marvel at the height of mountains and at other natural wonders but neglect their own selves.

For Petrarch, the patterns for how that "self" was to think, feel, and act were already at hand—the Bible, of course, but also the lives of the great ancients. In *De viris illustribus* (*Lives of Famous Men*, begun c. 1338) he composed biographies of the mighty Romans. One life in particular, that of the magnificent general of Republican Rome, Publius Cornelius Scipio, so fired his imagination that, also in about 1338, he began an epic in Latin hexameters, his unfinished *Africa*. Virgil's *Aeneid* provided the model for this account of the titanic struggle between Scipio and Hannibal in the Second Punic War, culminating in the Battle of Zama (202 B.C.), the decisive defeat of the Carthaginians in Africa.

Petrarch's circulation of this poem—the earliest attempt in postclassical Europe to write a Latin epic—led to the most spectacular public event of his life. On April 8, 1341, he was crowned with the poet's laurel wreath on the Capitoline hill by a member of Rome's Senate in an honor that historians have suspected the poet of soliciting. With his customary straddling of two worlds, he immediately laid his laureate's crown on the tomb of St. Peter. At age thirty-six, he became not merely an Italian but a European celebrity.

In between scholarly activities, this lax churchman found time to father two children out of wedlock—the scapegrace Giovanni, who died as a young man, and his beloved Francesca. It's not known who their mother was, but Petrarch later implied that he had treated her shabbily.

Profoundly religious, even ascetic in many of his impulses, Petrarch was also a sensualist with a neurotic ambivalence toward the things most important to him: "I would be glad to be able to say that I had always been entirely free of lustful desires, but I would be lying if I did," he wrote in his autobiography. Laura or God? His thirst for fame or St. Augustine? The *Secretum*, his most important work after the *Canzoniere*, consists of three Latin dialogues between Petrarch and St. Augustine in which the entice-ments of a life of love and poetic glory are set off against Christian Stoical self-denial and preparation for death. The dialectic is left unresolved.

At this time, Petrarch met Cola (Niccolò) di Rienzo, an Italian lawyer of humble birth who, like Petrarch, was obsessed with the virtu-ous heroes he had read about in Livy. Cola's wild scheme of restoring the Roman Republic earned the poet's enthusiastic support. A fiery speaker, Cola managed to wrench control of popeless Rome from the feuding nobility and proclaim a republic with himself as dictatorial tribune. For seven months in 1347 Cola ruled Rome with stern justice before being driven out. On his return to power seven years later, he was killed by the Roman mob after only two months. Petrarch's bold canzone "*Italia mia*" (*Canzoniere* 128), written in 1344–45, after he met Cola, is one of the earliest expressions of a peninsular, rather than a local, Italian patriotism.

When his periodic wanderlust seized him, the world's first modern lit-erary celebrity roamed over northern Italy, leaving disciples everywhere, including his greatest, Giovanni Boccaccio, whom he met on his first visit to Florence in 1350 (see Essay 17). As a result of Petrarch's influ-ence, Boccaccio dedicated the rest of his literary career to producing Latin scholarly works.

Just as in earlier life Petrarch had celebrated the Roman Republican hero Scipio and cheered on Cola, in later life he wrote a laudatory life of Julius Caesar, the dictator who put an end to the Republic (see Essay 3). In 1353 Petrarch scandalized his politically correct Florentine friends by accepting the offer of the belligerent Milanese tyrant and archbishop Giovanni Visconti to live at his court. For nine years, the poet served as a celebrity diplomat for Visconti and his ruthless successors.

Driven from Milan by the plague, he settled in Venice in 1362 and lived there with his daughter and her young family for five years. The Republic gave him a house in return for a pledge to bequeath his per-sonal library to the state. The aging poet left in a huff in 1367 when four young Venetian Scholastic thinkers insulted him as an ignoramus. What happened to his library is unknown.

In later life Petrarch disparaged his Italian poems as "*nugellas meas vulgares*" ("my popular trifles") and "*juveniles ineptias*" ("adolescent botches")—confident that he would win eternal fame from his largely forgotten Latin works, such as the *Lives of Famous Men* and his epic *Africa*. Yet something kept him hard at work polishing and rearranging the lyrics of the *Canzoniere* till the very end.

This collection, mostly written over a span of about twenty years, is a portrait of the artist as a young and middle-aged man in which the idealized, aloof, shadowy Laura is more the artist's model than his lover. The work is an extended self-analysis of psychological states, moods, and aperçus on the part of the poet/lover, an artistic mother lode of introspection.

Love, the most joyous human emotion, becomes the most tormenting—or conflicted—when unrequited. The tension between reason and desire, combined with the vicissitudes of frustrated love, gives rise to daydreams, fantasies, and an almost masochistic dwelling on the speaker's pain in many of these 317 sonnets, 29 canzoni, 9 sestinas, 7 *ballate*, and 4 madrigals.

The *Canzoniere* follows a roughly chronological order in two groupings: *Poems in Life of Laura* (the first 266) and *Poems in Death of Laura* (the last 100). In the first part, the most famous canzone—a long, elaborate poem—is *"Chiare fresche e dolci acque"* ("Clear, fresh, and sweet waters"; 126). The speaker describes a lovely spot by a lake where he once saw Laura under a tree that showered blossoms on her lap, hair, and dress. Others fell on the grass and in the water—and one, twirling in the air, seemed to say, "Here Love reigns." He hopes that since he must soon die of his love, it will happen here. Perhaps someday Laura will return, see his tomb, sigh, and win his soul mercy in heaven.

In the following unrhymed translation of a sonnet (164) that was set to music by Claudio Monteverdi (see Essay 35), note the typically Petrarchan poetic conceits (clever comparisons and other figures of speech):

> Now that the sky and earth and wind are silent,
> and sleep binds up the wild beasts and the birds,
> Night goes the rounds in her starry chariot,
> and the sea lies becalmed in its waveborn bed.
> I wake, and think, and burn, and weep—and she who
> consumes me is always there in my sweet anguish;
> my state is one of war, full of anger and pain,
> and only the thought of her brings some peace.
>
> Thus only from a single living fountain
> flows all the sweet and bitter I feed upon;

only one hand heals my wound and wounds me.
And to make sure my suffering has no end,
a thousand times a day I die, I'm born—
so far am I from the death that would save me!

Here, after the first four exquisite lines, are all the antitheses, oxy-morons, and paradoxes that mirror the contradictions of love but that soon became poetic clichés: "sweet anguish," "all the sweet and bitter I feed upon," "a thousand times a day I die, I'm born." The assertion "only one hand heals my wound and wounds me" works in an allusion to the spear of Achilles, which could cure the wounds it inflicted. Petrarch's verse, always musical, polished, and elegant, has often been faulted for its rhetoric and ornamentation, which were seized upon by his myriad imitators.

Through all the hyperbole—he can't speak in her presence, he's pale, can't sleep, takes no pleasure in anything, contemplates suicide—shine innumerable felicities of thought and expression in his incomparably fluent Tuscan idiom. Though her beauty is not what it was, Laura was once so inexpressibly lovely that he is now no less smitten with her than ever (90). Like the Phoenix, she is unique and uniquely beautiful (185). She's ill, and he fears for her life (184). He dreams she tells him he'll never see her again (250). In one of his most audacious comparisons, an old man going off to Rome to see the Holy Shroud, on which Christ's features were thought to have been impressed, is likened to the poet's seeking Laura's face in all the other women he sees (16).

In Poem 267, Petrarch laments the loss of Laura, who died in Avi-gnon while he was in Verona. After this point, the fripperies tend to drop away from the poems. Like Dante's Beatrice, Laura becomes more "alive" after her death. Scorning all thought of another love, the poet now believes she was right to spurn his unchaste suit. He refuses to praise her beauty, which is now dust (292), but he will keep writing to immortalize her name. The return of spring, the season in which she died, gladdens nature but brings him sorrow (310). The lament of the nightingale—"mourning perhaps her young ones or her mate"—reminds him of his own grief (311). He regrets that Laura was taken from him just as his passion was turning into serene affection (315). She appears to him in all his dreams, and all he desires now is to join her as soon as possible in heaven. The collection ends with a sublime canzone addressed to the Virgin Mary, beseeching her aid during the rest of his life and at the hour of his death.

Laura also figures in Petrarch's last poems in Italian, the *Trionfi* (*Triumphs*), a series of six allegorical works in terza rima (the meter of Dante's *Divine Comedy*) in which Chastity, represented by Laura, triumphs over Love, Death triumphs over Chastity, Fame over Death, and Time over Fame, until Eternity conquers Time—and Laura reappears in heaven.

In 1370 Petrarch bought a modest villa in Arquà, outside of Padua, in the Euganean hills. Open to visitors today, it still houses his chair, desk, and mummified cat. Always the scholar, Petrarch managed to die at his desk bent over a book on the night of July 18–19, 1374, one day shy of his seventieth birthday. In his will he left his dear friend Boccaccio fifty florins to buy himself a warm mantle "for winter study and lucubrations by night."

German literary scholar Ernst Robert Curtius said that Petrarch's invention of the sonnet cycle "spread almost like an epidemic disease and made the sixteenth century sonnet-mad." Of the legions of Petrarchists in Italy, Spain, Portugal, and France, the last nation produced two master sonneteers in Pierre Ronsard and Joachim du Bellay. Sir Thomas Wyatt and Henry Howard, Earl of Surrey, introduced the form into England early in the sixteenth century.

Sir Philip Sidney's *Astrophel and Stella* and Edmund Spenser's *Amoretti* are outstanding English sonnet cycles, but the culmination of the genre is Shakespeare's 154-poem bravura performance, mostly addressed to a beautiful young man, although it includes twenty-six sonnets on the vampish, unnamed "Dark Lady." Other adept English practitioners of the sonnet include John Donne, John Milton (who also wrote five in Italian), William Wordsworth, John Keats, and Dante Gabriel Rossetti. The twentieth century's most remarkable sonnet sequence is German poet Rainer Maria Rilke's *Sonnets to Orpheus*.

In the introductory poem to his sonnet cycle *The House of Life* (1876), Rossetti writes, "A Sonnet is a moment's monument." Ever in search of immortalizing his perceptions, Petrarch would surely have agreed. But what would Laura's Platonic lover have made of the nineteenth-century French master of the form, Charles Baudelaire, whose sonnet on the bodily splendors of a friendly young giantess ends like this?

And sometimes in summer, when tropical heats
Made her stretch herself out, all tired and still,
I'd sleep without cares in the shade of her teats,
Like a peaceful town at the foot of a hill.

Seventeen

Boccaccio and the development
of Western literary realism

At no epoch have the Italians been sternly and austerely pious. . . .
Their true nature is critical, susceptible to beauty, quick at seizing
the ridiculous and exposing shams, suspicious of mysticism, realistic,
pleasure-loving, practical.

—John Addington Symonds, *Renaissance in Italy* (1881)

GIOVANNI BOCCACCIO (1313–75) CREATED the preeminent prose work of Italian literature while establishing a new European standard for the depiction of everyday reality. Nothing as elegant as his *Decameron*, with its Ciceronian periods and rhythmical cadences, had been written in prose in the Western world since the days of the Roman Empire. Along with Dante and Petrarch, Boccaccio takes his place in that triumvirate of Italian writers of whom Symonds wrote, "That one city should have produced three such men, and that one half-century should have witnessed their successive triumphs, forms the great glory of Florence, and is one of the most notable facts in the history of genius."

Boccaccio was born in Florence, or nearby Certaldo, in 1313, the illegitimate son of Boccaccino di Chellino, a wealthy Florentine merchant for the powerful Bardi Bank. (The legend of Giovanni's birth in Paris, of a Jeanne de la Roche of noble blood, was his own fabrication.) At fourteen, the boy was sent to Naples to learn business, and then to study canon law at the university, but he couldn't keep his mind off poetry and women, especially the women he met at the splendid and decadent court of King Robert the Wise of Anjou. The more or less disguised story of his unhappy love affair with a young married woman is woven into most of his early works. For years she was identified with an apparently fictitious Maria d'Aquino, illegitimate daughter of King Robert. Boccaccio calls her Fiammetta (Little Flame).

Besides sonnets and other short poems, Boccaccio's first literary efforts included the massive prose work *Filocolo* (*The Love-Afflicted,*

c. 1336); the *Filostrato* (*The Man Prostrated by Love*, c. 1338), a long narrative poem in ottava rima on the tragic amour of Troilus and Cressida, the source of Chaucer's poem and the inspiration for Shakespeare's play on the same theme; and the *Teseide* (*The Book of Theseus*, 1340–41), also in ottava rima, an epic about a love triangle at Theseus's court and the source of Chaucer's "Knight's Tale." In 1340 the ambitious young author returned to Florence, recalled by his father's financial ruin.

More works followed, each evincing a growing sophistication. The *Elegia di Madonna Fiammetta* (1343–44), often called the first European psychological novel, presents a jilted woman's thoughts and emotions in her own voice. The lovely long poem *Ninfale fiesolano* (*The Nymph of Fiesole*, 1344–45) is the first Italian pastoral romance. And then Boccaccio struck gold with the *Decameron* (1349–51).

While working on his masterpiece in Florence in 1350, Boccaccio first met the living author he most revered, Francesco Petrarca (Petrarch). Their friendship later resulted in the first Latin translations of Homer to be made in the postclassical world, with Petrarch supplying the Greek manuscripts of the *Iliad* and *Odyssey* (which he could not read) to a slovenly and ill-tempered self-styled Greek named Leontius Pilatus. Boccaccio let this unsavory scholar live in his own home while he learned some Greek from him and kept him at his crude translation, which nonetheless provided an impetus to Greek literary studies in Italy.

Aside from his *Life of Dante* (1351), the first ever, and the *Corbaccio* (*The Nasty Old Crow*, c. 1355), a misogynistic work of prose fiction Boccaccio supposedly wrote to avenge himself on a beautiful widow who had betrayed him, he stopped writing in Italian and, under the influence of Petrarch, devoted himself to producing works of scholarship in Latin. His most significant achievement in this vein was a huge, groundbreaking encyclopedia of ancient myth, the *Genealogia deorum gentilium* (*Genealogy of the Pagan Gods*, 1350–75). *De claris mulieribus* (*Famous Women*, 1360–74), with its 104 capsule biographies, was the first collection of lives exclusively of women. These and other Latin tomes of Boccaccio, which fed the flame of nascent Humanism, were vastly influential during the Renaissance, often eclipsing the fame of the one book, composed in Italian, that immortalized him.

In choosing as his title the Greek *Decameron* (Ten Days), the author alluded to St. Ambrose's *Hexameron*, on the six days of God's creation, and implied that his book heralded a whole new world. This was not a vain boast, since there had never been so realistic and artistic a recreation of contemporary society. The *Decameron* is a literary cornucopia that fostered the birth of the Italian Renaissance in a new secular spirit after the devastation of the Black Death.

There are two frame stories in the book. In the outermost, the author, who had derived much solace from friends during the travails of his miserable love affair, offers to repay that kindness by providing diversion to lovesick women who are kept housebound by their fathers or husbands. In the more important frame, a group of wealthy and cultivated young Florentines (seven women, aged eighteen to twenty-eight, and three men, none younger than twenty-five) meet in the church of Santa Maria Novella in Florence on a warm Tuesday morning in 1348 and decide to flee the plague that is devastating their city. Their destination is one of their luxurious villas on the slopes beneath Fiesole, a few miles outside Florence.

Boccaccio's introduction includes a riveting description of the bubonic plague, which arose in Asia and was brought back by Genoese and Venetian ships to the ports of Europe, killing one third of the population. Those who survived suffered the loss of the bonds of family, community, morality, and religion. Many thought the pestilence, in the course of which at least half of Florence's 100,000 people died, foreshadowed the end of the world.

For each day of their idyll in the country, Boccaccio's young Florentines agree to appoint a different king or queen to direct their entertainment and other activities. Each member of the group will tell a story per day over ten days, on a topic to be set by the day's monarch. This plan, in juxtaposition with the frame story of the Black Death, reinforces a major theme of the book: how art helps us escape from, or at least cope with, the pain and sorrow of life.

Although the young men's sweethearts are among the seven women, the living arrangements of the group are all very proper. Nonetheless, some of the tales the young ladies tell, listen to, or laugh at (with a blush here and there) were repeatedly censored and bowdlerized until after the mid-twentieth century. One of the men, Dioneo, obtains the right to always tell his story on any subject he pleases, no matter what the day's theme, and to be the last to tell a story every day. He's the loose cannon who tells the saltiest tales, a kind of Saturnalian lord of misrule.

Boccaccio's hundred stories have sources and analogues in Greek and Roman literature, troubadour legends, local Italian tales, and the folklore of Persia, India, and China. Many of the bawdiest are based on fabliaux—brief comic narratives that originally developed in France, were usually written in verse, and were often crude and obscene, with earthy dialogue and a plot involving the ridicule of a victim of a practical joke.

Boccaccio was the first to endow these coarse popular anecdotes with literary form, but his claim to originality stems not from his plots but from the telling. He established, for example, a sophisticated interplay among three levels of voices: that of the author, those of his ten narrators, and those of the myriad characters within the stories, who represent all the social strata and prominent types in contemporary Italy. Vividly sketched and supplied with brilliantly appropriate dialogue, these characters still live. As Luigi Barzini observed, "There are real people in the Italian stories, merchants, monks, artisans, shopkeepers, and princes, human beings of solid flesh and sound appetites, who speak the quick and colorful dialects of the market place and the wine shop."[1]

Boccaccio's word for the kind of story he tells is *novella* (news, a novelty), a term stressing topicality and currency rather than any venerable tradition. Even when the plots of his stories are ancient, he eschews the aims and methods of the old chivalric or religious allegorical tales, the legends of Arthur and the knights of his Round Table in quest of the Holy Grail, or of Charlemagne and his Paladins, which take place in a never-never land. Nor do Boccaccio's anticipations of the modern short story treat of human love in the mode of the troubadours, the courtly love romances of France, the *dolce stil nuovo* of Dante, or Boccaccio's friend Petrarch (see Essays 14 and 16). Instead, we get tales like one of Dioneo's (2.10: second day, tenth story), in which a young Pisan woman, captured and seduced by the dashing young pirate Paganino of Monaco, refuses to go back to her husband, an old doddering judge.

Boccaccio's unabashed recognition that lust, greed, and self-serving cleverness are basic instincts of life marked a radical departure from the medieval Christian ethical ideal of ascetic innocence and purity. His world is one of humans shifting for themselves, without the aid of grace or Providence. The *Decameron* is thus the apotheosis of the values of the haute bourgeoisie, the worldly-wise businessmen of the educated class and their ladies, who break into delighted laughter at the naïveté of their ignorant fellow humans and the impudent chicanery of the shrewd, or *furbi*, who prey on them.

Then, as now, the clash between fools and scoundrels provided entertainment for the sophisticated—and that, rather than any edifying moral purpose, is Boccaccio's goal. Indeed, one of his surrogates is the

[1]Luigi Barzini, *The Italians* (New York: Bantam Books, 1964), p. 179.

haughty Florentine aristocrat, poet, philosopher, and friend of Dante, Guido Cavalcanti (6.9). To a hostile question by a group of Florentines who had cornered him in a cemetery, Guido's riposte is, "Gentlemen, in your own house, you can say whatever you like to me." After his escape, only one of the group is able to puzzle out the insult: "He means to say that we, and other ignorant and uneducated men like us, are, compared with him and other learned men, worse than dead."

Another of Boccaccio's major themes is the futility of trying to suppress sexual desire, as in the story of Filippa (6.7), who is caught by her husband with a lover in Prato, where adultery was punishable by burning at the stake. At her trial she claims that laws must be made with the consent of the governed—and no woman ever participated in framing *that* law. She then asks her husband whether she has ever denied him sex. On his replying in the negative, she says, "Well then, what should I have done with the extra—thrown it to the dogs? Isn't it better that a noble gentleman who loves me more than himself should have it, instead of its being lost or wasted?" Bursting into laughter at this sally, her townsmen in the courtroom decide to repeal their harsh statute. The laws of nature, the author implies, should take precedence over those of society, the Church, and even God. "Free action," a French literary theorist has said of the *Decameron,* "is the most appreciated in this universe."[2]

With Dioneo as king of the seventh day, the theme is, somewhat inevitably, the tricks wives have played on their husbands. The plot of one story (7.7) involves a husband who is not only cuckolded but whose wife arranges for her lover to beat him with a club. In another (7.9), similar to Chaucer's "Merchant's Tale," a young wife whose old husband sees her copulating with her lover up in a pear tree makes him believe he's been "enchanted" and has thus witnessed a mirage.

The theme of the eighth day is the tricks women play on men, men on women, or men on one another. Simpleminded Calandrino's friends make him think "heliotrope" can make people invisible (8.3). This allows them to nonchalantly shag many stones at the spot that the "invisible" Calandrino, who is testing the heliotrope's effects, is occupying. Another story (8.7) tells of the revenge exacted on a lovely widow by a scholar whom she had bamboozled into staying out in the snow all night in the vain hope of sleeping with her. He in turn tricks her into getting stranded, naked, on the top of a tower for an entire hot July day

---

[2]Tzvetan Todorov, *Grammaire du Décaméron* (The Hague: Mouton, 1969), p. 82.

while insects cover her with stings. In a hoary fabliau (8.8), a man who had seduced his friend's wife is locked in a chest and made to hear overhead the sounds of his wife's vigorous copulation with his friend.

The ninth day is a free-for-all with no set theme for the tales. In one (9.3), when Calandrino's friends convince him he's pregnant, he blames it on his wife, who always demands to be on top when they have sex. In yet another Calandrino adventure (9.5), his sadistic friends trick him into falling in love with a prostitute and then bring his wife to the scene of the crime so that she can bury her nails in his face. In an analogue of Chaucer's "Reeve's Tale" (9.6), the host of an inn gets both his wife and his young daughter debauched in one night in a comedy-of-beds routine. Of course, the wife manages to talk her way out of it.

Thoroughly earning its place on the Church's now defunct Index of Prohibited Books, the *Decameron* exposed the Christian pieties of the previous thousand years to utter ridicule. Its very first story is an ironic tale about the gullibility of the Church in not recognizing pious frauds. Cepparello, the worst scoundrel who ever lived, dupes a simple old confessor into thinking he's led a spotless life and, after his death, is revered by the common people as St. Ciappelletto.

Dioneo's story (6.10) of Frate Cipolla ("Brother Onion") mocks friars, relics, miracles, and the credulity of the ignorant. When Frate Cipolla promises the yokels he's preaching to that in return for their offerings he will show them a feather of the angel Gabriel that was left behind in Mary's room at the Annunciation, two young wags in the audience steal his prop (plucked from a parrot's tail) and leave some coals in his relic box instead. Opening the case, Cipolla sees the coals but, far from being dismayed, delivers an impromptu double-talking sermon in which he claims to have been shown by the Patriarch of Jerusalem, in the Holy City itself, such precious relics as the Holy Ghost's finger, the forelock of the seraph who appeared to St. Francis, a fingernail of the cherubim, some rays of the star of the Magi, and a vial of the sweat perspired by St. Michael the Archangel while he was battling the Devil.

Among the gifts Cipolla received from the good Patriarch were the sound of the bells of Solomon's Temple trapped in a little jar, Gabriel's feather, and some of the coal with which St. Lawrence was roasted to death. Instead of bringing the case containing the feather today, he mistakenly took the one with the coal in it. But God must have made him do it, because the feast of St. Lawrence was fast approaching. He promises his hearers that whichever of them he signs with a cross from that soot will, for an entire year, not have fire burn him but he'll feel it. So they all come up and get huge black crosses made all over their clothes. The two fellows who had tried to trick Brother Onion almost dislocate their jaws with laughter at his irrepressible rascality. They give him back the parrot feather, which he uses to gull the same group of simpletons the following year.

In another tale involving Gabriel (4.2), Frate Alberto convinces a vain and foolish married woman, Lisetta, whose husband is away, that the meek angel, captivated by her beauty, wants to have sex with her. When she seems quite flattered by this prospect of a new Annunciation, Frate Alberto asks whether he can lend the immaterial angel the use of his own body for the assignation, so that his soul can spend those few hours in Gabriel's place experiencing the joys of Paradise. That the friar is eventually caught and punished does not lessen our delight in Alberto's outrageous deception and Boccaccio's masterly style, salted with a deliciously nasty irony. "Of such artistry," says German critic Erich Auerbach in analyzing this story, "there is no trace in earlier narrative literature."

Nuns in Boccaccio's world are no chaster than friars or monks. Masetto the convent gardener, who is said to have cuckolded Christ himself, almost perishes in trying to satisfy the desires of nine young nuns (3.1). In another story set in a convent (9.2), the abbess catches a nun in bed with her lover, but when the peccant sister points out that, in her rush to get dressed, the abbess has mistakenly thrown her priest-lover's pants over her head instead of her veils, she is allowed to stay with her own lover. In Dioneo's most notorious tale (3.10), the hermit Rustico teaches Alibech, an aspiring young virgin hermitess, how to put the Devil (Rustico's penis) back into hell (Alibech's vagina).

But only about a quarter of Boccaccio's stories are at all bawdy, and quite a few are characterized by a tender pathos. Of these, the most famous is the tale of Federigo and his falcon (5.9). Federigo, a Florentine, spends all his money trying to win the love of the beautiful but virtuous married woman Monna Giovanna. After her husband's death, Giovanna's young son falls grievously ill and tells his mother he would recover if only he could have Federigo's wonderful falcon. Giovanna drops in on Federigo at lunchtime and plans to beg the bird from him. Chagrined at not having anything to offer her, Federigo kills the falcon (his last and most prized possession), roasts it on a spit, and serves it to her. The boy dies, but Giovanna has a change of heart after learning of Federigo's generous deed. "Better a man in need of riches than riches in

need of a man," she reasons. The two are wed, and she makes him wealthy again.

The tenth day's theme is liberality or magnificence regarding love or another subject, and here we meet with a few bloated, tedious, rhetorical tales (10.8, 10.9) told in an orotund and unrealistic medieval manner—examples of what Boccaccio rescued the Western narrative tradition from. In the book's very last story, Dioneo, against all odds, tells a tale that so captivated the aged Petrarch (who was otherwise underwhelmed by the *Decameron*) that he adapted it in Latin to endow it with a proper dignity and make it more widely accessible. (This translation was Chaucer's source for his "Clerk's Tale.")

Although Dioneo presents this story of patient Griselda and her lordly husband's testing of her as one of ineffable cruelty, it lends itself to allegorization as a model of the soul's ideal, Job-like relationship toward a God who sorely tries humans before rewarding them with eternal life. Given that his ten young narrators plan to return to plague-ravaged Florence on the following day, it was a stroke of genius on Boccaccio's part to end his book with a story that could be interpreted as a harrowing version of the actions of an inscrutable God.

Aside from inspiring a host of storytellers in Italy—Sacchetti, Cinthio, Firenzuola, Straparola, Bandello, and so many more—the *Decameron* also influenced *Les cents nouvelles nouvelles* (c. 1460) and Marguerite de Navarre's *Heptaméron* (c. 1549) in France, not to mention Rabelais's zany irreverence and Molière's mordant wit. Chaucer's poetic verisimilitude was crucially molded by Boccaccio's heightened realism, though he never mentions the Italian author by name and may not have known his *Decameron*.

Other English authors who came under Boccaccio's spell include Shakespeare, Dryden, and Keats, whose verse tale *Isabella* (1820), about a woman who keeps her murdered lover's head in a pot of basil that she waters daily with her tears, is derived from the *Decameron* (4.5). Boccaccio's magnum opus was the fourteenth-century equivalent of James Joyce's *Ulysses*, not only in its naturalism but also in its immensely sophisticated literary polish and its new (or newly reclaimed) narrative and rhetorical strategies. After it, storytelling in the Western world would never be the same.

In 1362 Boccaccio, who had been nicknamed Giovanni della Tranquillità for his easygoing ways, met a monk who tried to turn him against literature with prophecies of his impending death and damnation.

Petrarch had to persuade his terrified friend not to renounce his scholarly vocation and sell his library. Just as Petrarch mistakenly considered his Italian poems to be mere juvenilia and his Latin poems and prose works to constitute his undying legacy, so Boccaccio now saw his epic Italian prose masterpiece as frivolous and indecent.

Poverty dogged Boccaccio in old age, as did ill health—obesity, skin diseases, fevers, dropsy. He had always idolized Dante, and now he copied out the entire *Divine Comedy* as a gift for Petrarch. In 1373–74, he was the first to give public lectures on Dante's great poem, and he penned a commentary on the first half of the *Inferno*.

On December 21, 1375, Italy's premier raconteur died at Certaldo at age sixty-two, only seventeen months after Petrarch, whose death he had memorialized in a sonnet. In that work Boccaccio's delicacy and refinement—so different from his reputation—shine through as he pictures his "dear master" in the company of Dante and other poets, "where my lovely Fiammetta / sits beside Laura in the sight of God," and he asks Petrarch's spirit to "draw me after you that I may see, / joyous, the one who kindled me with love."

Eighteen

The mystic as activist: St. Catherine of Siena

He would have liked to see in me another Catherine of Siena who would boldly confront bishops and Wall Street magnates.
—Dorothy Day, speaking of Peter Maurin, her cofounder
in the Catholic Worker movement (1973)

HAD SHE LIVED IN OUR TIME, Catherine of Siena would probably have confronted many a bishop, magnate, or head of state. Here's what she wrote in 1376 to Pope Gregory XI, who had dragged his feet about moving the papacy from its so-called Babylonian Captivity in Avignon back to Rome: "[God's] will . . . demands that you execute justice on the abundance of iniquities committed by those who are fed and pastured in the garden of the Holy Church. Since he has given you authority and you have assumed it, you should use your virtue and power; and if you are not willing to use it, it would be better for you to resign."

A woman not yet thirty years old who held no official position was telling the Supreme Pontiff to do his job or step down. She concluded the letter with this backhanded compliment: "Do not make it necessary for me to complain about you to Christ crucified. (There is no one else I can complain to, since there is no one greater than you on earth.)"

Partly as a result of Catherine's exhortations, Gregory eventually did move the Church's hierarchy back to Rome. But for some clergymen, the high life continued as in Avignon. Catherine wrote of them: "They have abandoned the care of souls and made a god of their belly, eating and drinking in disorderly feast; they fall into filth, living in lasciviousness, feeding their children with the substance of the poor." Even sharper was her reproach to a group of dissident cardinals: "You are flowers who shed a stench that makes the whole world reek."

This political pugnaciousness is all the more remarkable because of its coexistence with a deeply mystical, contemplative nature in a woman who experienced frequent visions of Christ and conversations with God. Catherine was also renowned for her charitable works among the poor and imprisoned. On one occasion she caught with her own hands the severed head of a young convict who had asked her to serve as his spiritual advisor. "I said to him, 'Get down, . . . for soon you will be in the eternal life.' I reminded him of the blood of the Lamb. And so saying, I received his head in my hands."

Caterina di Benincasa was born in 1347, the twenty-third child of a wool dyer and his wife. At age seven, Catherine had her first vision of Christ. By her mid-teens, she had pledged her life to him, cut her long blond hair, and begun to wear a veil to discourage prospective husbands. Although her mother berated her for refusing to marry, her father gave her a room of her own so that she could pray in solitude. She became a member of the *mantellate* (cloaked ones), female tertiaries, or lay members, of the Dominican order who lived outside the confines of a religious community. Without either the responsibilities of marriage and children or the restrictions of the convent, Catherine enjoyed an extraordinary degree of freedom for a woman of the fourteenth century.

The defining spiritual moment of her life occurred in 1366, when she was nineteen. While Siena celebrated the pre-Lenten *carnevale*, she had a vision in which she became the bride of Christ. Amid an assemblage including the Virgin Mary and King David, Christ put a pearl- and diamond-encrusted gold band on her finger. During this rapturous scene, Catherine felt her heart stop. In response, Christ opened her side and replaced her heart with his own. In his hands, her heart was revitalized, and he then placed it in his own side. Catherine later explained, "with all due humility," to her spiritual advisor and biographer Raymond of Capua that although others could not see her wedding ring, it was always visible to her and a constant reminder of her mystical marriage.

Afterward Catherine emerged from the solitude of her room and began to work tirelessly among the sick and destitute of Siena. Stories circulated that she cured many of the ill, and contemporary accounts describe a preternaturally happy woman with exceptional charisma, whose relatives sometimes called her Euphrosyna, Greek for "child of mirth." Noted for dispensing pragmatic advice on everyday matters, as well as providing spiritual counsel, Catherine soon became revered as the focus of a group whose lay and clerical members she referred to as "my family." Several of them, including Raymond of Capua, went on to become reforming heads of religious orders.

In 1370, during a four-hour vision of hell, purgatory, and heaven, Catherine received a call from God to embark on a public life. Initially her response was prodigious letter writing. Since she was illiterate, members of her circle took dictation, although some sources attest that she eventually learned to read and write. She wrote to everyone—from simple people who had requested her spiritual guidance to warring princes and kings. She implored ecclesiastical authorities to reform the dissolute clergy. The nineteenth-century literary historian Francesco De Sanctis called her 382 extant letters, all written in limpid Tuscan, "a love manual of Christianity."

During the 1370 vision, God also instructed Catherine to urge Gregory XI to return the papacy to Rome from Avignon. The Babylonian Captivity of the Church (named for the exile of the Jews in Babylon in the sixth century B.C.) had its origins in an acrimonious conflict between King Philip IV of France and Pope Boniface VIII in the mid-1290s. The pope challenged the authority of the king to tax clerics, while the king questioned the pope's authority to govern the French Church. Boniface died in 1303, a month after being briefly imprisoned by Philip's agents on trumped-up charges of heresy and immorality. In 1307 the craven French Pope Clement V transplanted the Roman Curia to Avignon, where it functioned as a tool of the French monarchy for the next seventy years.

Although several earnest, well-intentioned pontiffs ruled the Church from Avignon, the papal court, housed at the extravagant Palace of the Popes, became notorious for its nepotism, greed, and sexual profligacy. In addition, the papacy lost control over much of its vast Italian territories. Petty tyrants assumed power in many areas, and the French popes were unable to reestablish their authority or impose peace in Italy. Since the pope is also the Bishop of Rome, his continued residence in Avignon was seen as a grave dereliction of duty, and pressure mounted to reestablish the seat of the Church in the ancient Holy See.

It was only natural that Catherine widened her circle of correspondents to include Gregory XI, who was to be the last French pope. In admonitory letters that often began "Pardon me, *Babbo* (Daddy)," she went so far as to urge him to be more "manly" in his efforts to restore the papacy to Rome and moral order to the Church hierarchy. "Up, father! No more irresponsibility!" she wrote in her earliest surviving missive to him (Letter 54).

In 1374 Catherine was called to Florence to account for herself before the Dominican authorities. Some of the Sienese, resentful of her presumption in writing to Church and civil officials on the thorniest religious and political issues of the day, began to whisper that she was a hypocrite, a fanatic, or possibly a tool of Satan. Even some fellow Dominicans grew exasperated with her.

It was a close call, but in the end her superiors found nothing heretical, seditious, or objectionable in her letters or speech and saw no evidence of demonic possession. Had it not been for the intervention of some members of her circle, Catherine might have shared the fate of many other mystics and reformers—a fiery death at the stake like that of Joan of Arc in the following century.

Returning to Siena just as the plague descended, this woman who subsisted on bread, water, and bitter herbs (sometimes only on water and the communion wafer) distinguished herself by caring for the sick and dying. Nor did she neglect her remarkable prayer life. Raymond of Capua reports that Catherine was occasionally observed levitating during her prayers or visions. His descriptions of her ecstatic states suggest that she may have suffered from a form of epilepsy. According to Raymond, her visions began when she suddenly "fell senseless," her eyes tightly shut, limbs rigid, and hands clenched for many minutes. When she awoke, she sometimes told Raymond that she would surely die if the Lord failed to cure her soon.

In 1376, at the request of Florence, Catherine traveled to Avignon to mediate in a war between the excommunicated city and Gregory XI over the control of papal territories. The mission was unsuccessful, but while in France Catherine spoke persuasively to Gregory about returning to Rome. Raymond of Capua, who served as interpreter between Gregory's Latin and Catherine's Tuscan, recorded that "the Pope was speechless, and I . . . wondered how such words came to be spoken with such authority in front of such a high Pontiff."

On January 17, 1377, Gregory transferred the Curia back to Rome. After his death in the following year, Catherine became a strong supporter of his successor, the Neapolitan Urban VI, who called her to Rome late in 1378. Her elation at the release of the Church from its Avignon captivity was short-lived, however. Urban had barely ascended the papal throne when the powerful French faction of the College of Cardinals elected a rival, the antipope known as Clement VII, who was of royal French blood. For the next thirty-nine years, the Church was riven by the Great Schism, in which two—and sometimes three—competing popes strove for recognition, excommunicated one another's followers, and sharply divided Europe along national lines.

Catherine was distraught, although Raymond says that in 1375 she had predicted such a schism—and the eventual reunification of the Church. During the last two years of her life, she worked diligently to muster support for Urban. She died in Rome in 1380 after a three-month illness, apparently a result of a series of strokes that may have been induced by severe emaciation. Catherine was canonized in 1461, and in 1939 she and Francis of Assisi were named the chief patron saints of Italy by Pius XII.

Despite her involvement in temporal affairs, Catherine was politically unsophisticated, and some historians doubt she played a pivotal role in restoring the papacy to Rome. Be that as it may, she is still revered as one of the greatest Christian mystics. Besides her letters, she dictated to her assistants the *Dialogues*, her conversations with God during her ecstatic states.

Based on this work and her letters, in 1970 Catherine was declared a Doctor of the Church, a title conferred on writers who make notable intellectual or doctrinal contributions to the life of that institution. Only two other women, Teresa of Ávila and Thérèse of Lisieux, have had this honor bestowed on them. Many of Catherine's dialogues concern the unfathomable divine grace, as when she hears God say

> This is that sin which is never forgiven, now or ever; the refusal, the scorning of my mercy. The despair of Judas displeased me more and was a greater insult to my Son than his betrayal had been. Therefore, such as these are reproved for this false judgment of considering their sin to be greater than my mercy.

Catherine, whose reputation as a reformer and mystic was unparalleled for a laywoman in her time, remains a source of inspiration for many devout Catholics six hundred years later in a world very far removed from her own. Hundreds of American parishes and schools are named for her, dozens of Web sites are dedicated to her and her writings, and her family home in Siena is still a popular stop for the faithful and curious. Even Catherine, whose letters exude such confidence and purposefulness, would be surprised. A century and a half ago, De Sanctis wrote of her, "She lives beyond life and this world in a realm of spirit," and perhaps that explains her mystique in an age of relentless materialism and sensory overload.

Nineteen

Inventors of the visual language of the Renaissance: Brunelleschi, Donatello, Masaccio

I recognized in many, but above all in you, Filippo [Brunelleschi], and in our great friend the sculptor Donatello and in the others, Nencio [Ghiberti], Luca [della Robbia], and Masaccio, a genius for every laudable enterprise in no way inferior to any of the ancients who gained fame in these arts.

—Leon Battista Alberti, On Painting (1436)

In his *Lives of the Artists*, Giorgio Vasari describes how the sculptor Donatello, awash in success and adulation in Padua, abruptly returned home to Florence, "saying that if he stayed where he was any longer he would forget all he knew because of their flattery, and that he was only too anxious to return to his own land, where he would be constantly criticized and so would have an incentive for studying and winning even greater glory."

At the turn of the fifteenth century, Florence was the flash point of the Renaissance, arguably the most significant artistic revolution in history. It was a wealthy and boisterous city where artists vied aggressively for commissions. The five men that Alberti singled out in the dedication of his groundbreaking treatise *On Painting* were at various times bitter competitors, as well as fruitful collaborators. Brunelleschi (1377–1446), Donatello (1386–1466), and Masaccio (1401–28), an architect, sculptor, and painter, respectively, rediscovered Italy's classical artistic heritage and appropriated it to create the new visual language of the Renaissance.

This story begins with a contest. In 1402 Filippo Brunelleschi, a twenty-five-year-old Florentine goldsmith, learned that Lorenzo Ghiberti, and not he, had won the competition to craft new bronze doors for the Baptistery in Florence (see Essay 20). Haughty Brunelleschi, refusing the judges' offer of a collaborative venture with Ghiberti on the doors, never again attempted sculpture. He left for Rome almost immediately with Donato di Niccolò di Betto Bardi, known as Donatello, on an antiquarian foray that forever changed the course of Western art.

In Rome, dilapidated and depopulated as it then was, Brunelleschi and Donatello were able to immerse themselves in the principles of ancient Roman art and construction, especially of the Pantheon, whose enormous second-century dome so stupefied medieval Romans that many assumed it was the work of demons (see Essay 5). The two Florentines, whom the locals took for treasure hunters, also scavenged for Roman coins and other artifacts. Brunelleschi drew numerous ground plans and elevations based on his surveys of ancient buildings, and, at some point, he began to think seriously about the problems of two-dimensional representations of three-dimensional reality.

When he returned to Florence he was equipped with technical skills that had been lost since the fall of Rome. One of them was the use of linear perspective and a single vanishing point, by which objects in the distance of a painting appear smaller than closer ones, and parallel lines are seen to converge at a single point in the background, creating the illusion of spatial depth.

For a celebrated experiment, Brunelleschi painted a geometrically correct view of Florence's Baptistery with a pinhole at the vanishing point. The viewer, standing on precisely the spot where Brunelleschi's easel had stood, was instructed to hold the canvas so that the painted side faced the Baptistery and to peer through the pinhole at the painting's reflection in a mirror of the same size held with the other hand. The viewer could then confirm that the mirrored painted scene corresponded meticulously with the actual one. It was for this momentous accomplishment that Alberti lauded Brunelleschi in *On Painting*, a codification of theories on visual perspective that profoundly influenced Renaissance artists.

In August 1418 the building commission of Florence's Santa Maria del Fiore cathedral announced a competition for the design of a cupola for the central crossing of the immense marble-faced building that had been under construction since 1296. Although the cathedral defied stylistic categorization, the dome was destined to represent the pinnacle of Renaissance engineering.

The contestants faced numerous challenges, including the octagonal shape mandated by the building's design, a prohibition against the use of flying buttresses to support the dome, and the enormous expanse to be enclosed—the largest since the construction of the Pantheon. When Brunelleschi made the outrageous proposal that the dome be constructed without the support of a wooden framework, or centering, several members of the committee questioned his sanity and expelled him from meetings. In fact, the dimensions involved—the opening for the dome was 143 feet across and 180 feet above the cathedral floor— made it almost impossible to find timber massive enough for the framework. Brunelleschi eventually managed to convince the commission of the feasibility of his design and was appointed *capomaestro*, chief architect, in 1420.

He reduced the cupola's weight by building it as two shells, an inner one capable of sustaining the lighter outer one, in the first such construction of its kind. The individual shells were thick enough for a circle to be inscribed within the octagon, thereby conferring the self-supporting characteristics of a circular dome, with inward and outward forces counterbalanced. The design also included eight exposed ribs, sixteen minor, hidden ribs, transverse sandstone chains and a wooden chain to strengthen the dome's eight faces, and more than seventy porthole-type windows in the outer dome to reduce wind stresses. In addition to admitting light, the massive lantern atop the cupola acted as a weighted cap, preventing the dome's ribs from buckling outward. (A staircase, open to the public, spirals between the two shells, emerging at the lantern.) Only in the twentieth century were larger domes built, made possible by the availability of ultralightweight materials.

In 1419, while planning his work at the cathedral, Brunelleschi began designing the Ospedale degli Innocenti, the world's first foundling hospital. His ability to adapt and interpret the classical architectural vocabulary is manifest in the building's elegant loggia, composed of Corinthian columns bearing arches surmounted by a long entablature, or horizontal band. His signature elements are all present in the façade of the Ospedale, including simple, unfluted columns topped by Corinthian capitals, a design based on squares and circles, the multiple repetition of a single design unit to create a feeling of order and stability, and decorative roundels above the spots where adjoining arches meet. The effect is spacious, symmetrical, clean, and classical, prompting art historian Ludwig H. Heydenreich to call the building an "austere purification of . . . medieval forms."

When Brunelleschi accepted a commission from the Medici family in about 1421 to design the church of San Lorenzo and add the so-called Old Sacristy, another re-creation of ancient forms was in the offing. In building the sacristy, he capped a plain cube with the prototype of all hemispheric Renaissance domes by creating a transition zone of semicircles and pendentives that provided a round base. His reintroduction of this technique, which he had observed in ancient Roman buildings, was another watershed in Renaissance architecture.

In the main church of San Lorenzo, Brunelleschi imitated the ancient basilica, framing the center aisle with a column-arch-pendentive motif to create a spacious and classically lucid interior. The church of Santo Spirito, which he began in 1436 (the year of the great dome's completion), has a similar quality but more massive and sculptural. The sublime Pazzi Chapel, the chapter house of Florence's Santa Croce, on which he started working in 1433, is a more geometrically complex version of the Old Sacristy. Here the cube topped by a dome forms the center of a rectangle, and gray stone accentuates the cream-colored walls in harmonious, proportional patterns.

Many of Brunelleschi's works were completed by associates after his death on April 15, 1446. Famed throughout Italy, he was accorded the honor of burial in Santa Maria del Fiore, the cathedral he helped make into a worldwide landmark.

Donatello, the hot-tempered, rough-hewn, and unaffected son of a wool carder, was renowned for his knowledge of ancient sculpture, most of it acquired in Rome with Brunelleschi. Shabby and unpresentable as he was, his patrons, especially Cosimo de' Medici (see Essay 21), spoke to him as an intellectual equal, and Vasari says that under Donatello's influence, Cosimo "grew ambitious to introduce to Florence the antiquities which are still in the house of the Medici."

During his life of eighty years, in which he crafted numerous statues and low reliefs in bronze, marble, terracotta, wood, and stucco, he single-handedly fathered Renaissance sculpture. Medieval sculpture was concerned primarily with religious subjects—stylized, symbolic, hieratic, formalized—but Donatello shifted the focus to the realistic human form: wizened Old Testament prophets and New Testament saints, noble generals on horseback, and heroic women. He also broke new ground by considering how particular works would be viewed, whether from below, at great distance, or up close, much as Brunelleschi did in his experiments on perspective.

Donatello first made his reputation working in marble. In 1410 he carved *St. John the Evangelist* for Florence's cathedral. The statue, which appears oddly proportioned when viewed from straight ahead, was meant to be seen from below, from which viewpoint it assumes a powerful triangular shape. The artist's *St. Mark* (1411–13) at Orsanmichele was the first modern work sculpted in the ancient *contrapposto* pose, with one knee bent and one hip higher than the other. (Medieval sculptors had sometimes imposed an S shape on a figure to simulate *contrapposto* but—without any sense of shifted weight—unconvincingly.)

In the 1430s Donatello won a commission to sculpt generic prophets for niches on Florence's campanile. Although they lack specific identifications, each is a highly individualized portrait, as exemplified by the prominently bald one nicknamed *Zuccone*, "Pumpkin-Head," which may represent Habakkuk or Elisha. Like Bernini's "talking statues" of two centuries later, Zuccone is caught in the act of speaking or prophesying. Knowing the figure would be viewed from far below, Donatello finished it with rough, broad strokes, and the mouth is more of a slash than an orifice. From a distance, however, the effect of the stern, angry prophet is striking. Donatello's assistants claim to have heard him barking at his creation, "Speak, speak, or may dysentery seize you!"

Donatello is credited with inventing *rilievo schiacciato*, "squashed relief," which he first used in *St. George and the Dragon* in 1417. In this technique, likened to painting with a chisel, none of the surfaces in a *schiacciato* extends more than fractions of an inch above the background. The most famous of his low reliefs is the *Pazzi Madonna*. With her forehead and nose set playfully against those of her chubby son, the Virgin Mary, looking very Greek and classical, seems to gaze right through him as if anticipating his death. Dispensing with conventions like halos and distancing from the viewer, Donatello achieves a palpable intimacy.

His mastery of *schiacciato* is exemplified in *The Feast of Herod* (1425), created for the Baptistery of Siena. In the foreground the sculptor conveys agitated bustle as Herod and the other guests, again of classical appearance, recoil chaotically from the sight of John the Baptist's head on a platter. Other groups of figures reside within several different architectural planes that recede into the background in a tribute to Brunelleschi's linear perspective.

The most famous and historically important of Donatello's works is the first freestanding, life-size nude since antiquity, his silky-black *David*, a bronze cast in the mid-1440s. It is one of the first examples of Renaissance sculpture not associated with an architectural framework. The curiously young, almost prepubescent David—dressed only in high boots and with the body of a Dionysus—stands in marked *contrapposto* with his left foot atop the severed head of Goliath, left hand on his hip, and right hand poised on his sword. A feather from Goliath's helmet rests suggestively against the boy's inner thigh. With *David*, Donatello exceeded the ancients with his informal, naturalistic (indeed, seductive) depiction of a young hero smiling dreamily over his vanquished enemy. So astounded were his contemporaries by the statue's realism that, according to Vasari, "artists believe it must have been formed over a living body."

Donatello clearly aimed for emotional immediacy from the 1430s onward, when he began to carve gilded wood, as in his *John the Baptist* and the hard-to-date *Mary Magdalen*. Far from any medieval saintly abstraction, his Magdalen appeared as never before, in decrepitude and raggedly dressed. Her once lustrous hair, with which she had washed Christ's feet, is now tangled and sparse, and her realistically rendered body is that of an emaciated old woman. Her hands folded in prayer, she turns toward the viewer in an arresting, almost monitory, fashion, her eyes lit by intelligent penitence and faith.

Sometime between 1446 and 1460 Donatello crafted an emotionally intense gilded bronze depicting the biblical story of Judith's beheading of the lustful Assyrian conqueror Holofernes. Having already wounded the drunken warrior in the neck, the avenging Jewish heroine raises her blade to strike the final, decapitating blow, one foot firmly planted on the Assyrian's genitals. After the *David*, this was the second Renaissance sculpture intended to stand independently in the round—and the first of his works that Donatello signed.

During his stay in Padua in the 1440s, Donatello was commissioned to create a bronze memorial for the Venetian condottiere Erasmo da Narni, known as Gattamelata (The Honeyed Cat). The result was the first life-size equestrian monument since antiquity. Again drawing on ancient models, especially the equestrian statue of Emperor Marcus Aurelius he had seen in Rome, Donatello cast his subject as a stern Roman general astride a massive steed and wearing components of an idealized ancient military uniform.

Vasari relates that when Donatello grew old, Piero de' Medici gave him a farm, but the sculptor soon complained that he'd rather starve than worry about his grapes, cattle, taxes, and peasants. Piero, taking Donatello's decision with good humor, bought the farm back from the aging artist and gave him an allowance from the proceeds. Donatello's death on December 13, 1466, was deeply mourned in Florence. He was interred near his patron, Cosimo, in the Medici Chapel in San Lorenzo.

• • •

Tommaso di Giovanni di Simone Cassai, nicknamed Masaccio, "Big Bad Tom," is one of the most enigmatic—and perhaps also the most influential—of European painters. Painfully little is known about him or his six-year career, from which only six documented paintings survive. Born in a village in Florentine territory on December 21, 1401, he developed a painting style with no strong ties to prevalent Florentine modes or the popular International Gothic. His bulky, emotive figures are clearly the direct descendants of those painted by the great Florentine Giotto (1267–1337). Renowned for his scenes from the life of St. Francis in Assisi and Florence's Santa Croce, Giotto unmoored European painting from its idealized medieval style, steering it toward more realistic expressiveness that inspired not only Masaccio but also Michelangelo.

Masaccio entered the public arena on being accepted into the Florentine painters' guild in January 1422, just after his twentieth birthday. He was already an accomplished artist with a reputation for absentmindedness. Like Donatello, he soon became a favorite of Cosimo de' Medici. Vasari refers to Masaccio's "endless studies," for which he apparently traveled to Rome. The painter also spent considerable time analyzing the science of perspective with Brunelleschi.

Masaccio's earliest extant painting is the San Giovenale triptych of 1422, featuring a Madonna and angels in the centerpiece and two saints in both the right and left panels. It already demonstrates the artist's mastery of single-point perspective and his ability to model figures convincingly with chiaroscuro.

Between 1424 and 1428, Masaccio painted approximately half of the twelve frescoes on the life of St. Peter in the Brancacci Chapel in Florence's Santa Maria del Carmine in conjunction with an older artist, Masolino ("Little Tom") da Panicale (1383–1447). Stylistic similarities between the two artists have made it difficult to attribute specific frescoes, although Masaccio is currently credited with *The Expulsion of Adam and Eve*, *The Baptism of the Neophytes*, *The Tribute Money*, *St. Peter Enthroned*, *St. Peter Healing the Sick with his Shadow*, *St. Peter Distributing Alms*, and *The Resurrection of the Son of Theophilus*. He may also have provided architectural backgrounds for several scenes by Masolino. In the 1480s Filippino Lippi completed some scenes that had been left unfinished.

The Brancacci Chapel became the school of European painting for the next five centuries. Vasari notes the "endless stream" of painters who later studied there, including Fra Angelico, Fra Filippo Lippi,

Andrea del Castagno, Verrocchio, Ghirlandaio, Botticelli, Leonardo da Vinci, Perugino, Fra Bartolommeo, and Michelangelo, not to mention Raphael, Andrea del Sarto, Pontormo, and countless others. There, these masters imbibed Masaccio's reordering of artistic priorities, from the medieval concentration on the relationship between God and the human soul to a modern preoccupation with man and his solid physical presence in nature depicted in a realistic, logical fashion. The cycle is introduced by *The Expulsion*, and a more emotionally harrowing depiction of this event, as registered on the distraught faces of Adam and Eve, is difficult to imagine.

Masaccio's figures are striking, monumental, and powerful, the painted equivalents of Donatello's prophets or *Judith and Holofernes*, but with greater warmth and no hint of the slightly frenzied or neurotic. St. Peter is a majestic, dignified, graceful, unquestionably three-dimensional human whose furrowed brow and distant gaze suggest his preoccupation with some more pressing spiritual concern, even as his shadow heals the sick lining his path.

The streets and classical architectural elements in the Brancacci frescoes are as convincing as the figures themselves. In *The Tribute Money*, distant landscapes and atmospheric conditions are depicted naturalistically. All the scenes in the chapel appear to be set in fifteenth-century Tuscany.

In 1426 Masaccio completed a polyptych (multipaneled painting on wood) for the church of Santa Maria del Carmine in Pisa. The subjects, which include St. Augustine reading, the martyrdoms of St. Peter and John the Baptist, St. Julian murdering his parents, and a sublime adoration of the Magi, are evoked by exceptionally strong modeling with light and shadow and vibrant colors in the clothing and drapery.

Like Donatello's statues, Masaccio's people—and skittish horses—stand independently and move with sureness and ease. Very few are handsome or beautiful, but each is real, with no trace of the Gothic insistence on the glittering, regal, and lovely. Speaking of unlovely, in a corner of the Brancacci frescoes inhabited by four men, the burly and surly plain-looking one with thick, curly black hair who stares eerily out of the frame at the viewer is believed to be a self-portrait. His companions are thought to be Alberti, Brunelleschi, and—the shortest one—Masolino.

Masaccio's last known work is *The Trinity*, a fresco at Florence's Santa Maria Novella that is believed to have been completed in early 1428, only months before the artist's death. Crafted with engineering-like precision, a coffered barrel vault flanked by Corinthian pilasters forms an elaborately painted architectural frame for Christ crucified, God the Father supporting the lateral beam of the cross, and the dove of the Holy Spirit hovering between them. The work is characterized by a meticulously rendered single-point perspective that imparts massive depth and volume, an alternating red (passion) and black (death) color scheme far removed from the delicate pastels of the Gothic, and individualized human figures.

After completing *The Trinity*, Masaccio left for Rome, where he died, probably in the summer of 1428. Rumors circulated that he had been poisoned, perhaps by a jealous associate or a Vatican official who objected to the political message he inferred in the Brancacci frescoes. Perhaps Masaccio came to a more mundane end from malaria. He left no students, only admirers and friends. Brunelleschi is said to have mourned him for months after his death.

Art historians have long debated the precise nature of the relationships and influences among the three artists who created the visual language of the Renaissance. Creighton Gilbert tried to sum up the discussion by stating that "Masaccio's people stand at the center of always ordered space, Donatellian creatures in a Brunelleschian cosmos." No facet of the visual arts—buildings, statues, reliefs, portraits, still lifes, or landscapes—was unaffected by the vast scope and revolutionary nature of their work. Although Alberti hailed them for their mastery of the arts of the ancient past, subsequent generations have revered them for their heightened portrayal of reality, which remains vital many centuries later.

Twenty

Lorenzo Ghiberti and the "Gates of Paradise"

The scene which Lorenzo offered [to the judges] . . . was finished so carefully that it seemed to have been breathed into shape rather than cast and then polished by iron tools.
—Giorgio Vasari, *Lives of the Artists*, 2d ed. (1568)

PROSPERITY REIGNED IN FLORENCE in 1400, prompting civic leaders to continue a project started seventy years earlier—replacing the humble wooden doors on the town's octagonal Baptistery, already one of Florence's oldest buildings, with grander ones. The first of the Baptistery's three portals had been hung in 1330 with divided doors faced by gilded bronze reliefs depicting scenes from the life of St. John the Baptist and crafted by the sculptor Andrea Pisano (1290–1348).

Who would create the new doors? Members of the Arte dei Mercanti di Calimala, the merchants' guild that was responsible for the Baptistery's maintenance, decided to sponsor an artistic competition, with the winner to be awarded the commission. In Pesaro, a town on the Adriatic north of Ancona, lived a twenty-two-year-old painter's assistant, Lorenzo Ghiberti (1378–1455), who had abandoned Florence several years earlier because of a double threat: the plague and Gian Galeazzo Visconti, the ferocious ruler of Milan who was rapidly engulfing northern Italy. Ghiberti was given leave by his Malatesta patrons to return to his hometown and participate in the competition.

Seven artists were declared finalists, including Ghiberti, Jacopo della Quercia (the greatest Sienese sculptor), and Filippo Brunelleschi, a seminal figure in Renaissance architecture (see Essay 19). We know little about how the finalists were chosen, but young Ghiberti, beloved stepson of a noted goldsmith, must have already demonstrated considerable talent in that medium.

With one year to complete his task, each artist received four pieces of bronze and instructions to portray the Old Testament story of Abraham's sacrifice of Isaac within a thirteen-by-seventeen-inch quatrefoil (the four-lobed, flowerlike frame used by Pisano on the first set of doors), while demonstrating his ability to depict nude and clothed humans, vegetation, landscape, and animals. It took two years for the judges to reach a verdict, in part because of the high stakes involved: To complete the project, the winner would be given an amount of money equivalent to Florence's defense budget. The world was treated to a contest that historians generally view as the beginning of the Renaissance in the visual arts.

Details of the judges' decision are sketchy. According to some sources, the deadlocked panel asked Ghiberti and Brunelleschi to collaborate on the doors, but Brunelleschi refused. In contrast, Ghiberti reported in his autobiography that Brunelleschi removed himself from the competition after seeing Ghiberti's entry. In any case, Ghiberti won the commission.

The bronze reliefs by Brunelleschi and Ghiberti, now housed in Florence's Bargello and the only ones from the contest to survive, betray the artistic origins of the two men. Brunelleschi was primarily an architect, and his composition, with Abraham and Isaac in the center, is fairly static, despite Abraham's swirling robes. Even the nick-of-time angel who rushes in to grab Abraham's wrist, thereby preventing the boy's slaying, appears to have been grafted onto the scene. Brunelleschi fulfilled the requirement for animals, landscape, and vegetation, but at the cost of producing a cramped, out-of-scale composition and a sense that the people, animals, rocks, and plants reside in the same plane.

In the jeweler Ghiberti's more sophisticated depiction of the awful scene, Abraham and Isaac are placed slightly to the right of center, defining a more energetic, diagonal compositional line. Foreshadowing his later work, Ghiberti created an illusion of depth by flattening figures that appear in the background and creating more rounded ones to protrude from the foreground. As a result of his success in suggesting spatial relationships, the frame appears less crowded than Brunelleschi's while still containing the requisite figures.

The emotional impact of Ghiberti's relief is enhanced by the boy's observation of the angel barreling headlong into the frame before his father notices it. In the instant that Abraham is poised to stab his son, Isaac's facial expression thus already registers gratitude for his rescue. Most important, young Isaac is depicted as a nude in the classical Greek style, the first such male figure in Renaissance art.

Among the more mundane factors that might have influenced the judges was the fact that Ghiberti's relief, hollow-cast by the lost-wax (cire-perdue) method, was seven kilograms lighter than Brunelleschi's, which represented a considerable cost savings for a door that would eventually contain twenty-eight such panels. Ghiberti's relief was cast primarily in one piece except for a few elements that were attached after the casting. In contrast, Brunelleschi's relief was fabricated by mounting figures on a base plate, a more labor-intensive process.

Ghiberti's initial contract of 1403 called for him to create the east doors of the Baptistery, which, because they faced the cathedral, were to depict the life of Christ in twenty-eight panels, fourteen each on the right and left sides of the divided doors. He was scheduled to finish in nine years, but the doors were gilded only in 1423 and finally hung in 1424—twenty-one years after they were started. The delay could not be ascribed to a lack of talent in the workshop. Ghiberti's assistants at various times during this project included some of the most eminent artists of the early Renaissance, including Benozzo Gozzoli, Paolo Uccello, Antonio del Pollaiuolo, Luca della Robbia, and a sculptor who would soon astound Italy with his genius, Donatello (see Essay 19). Brunelleschi, whose contest panel was acquired by Cosimo de' Medici, was now immersed in building the magnificent dome for Florence's cathedral.

Because Ghiberti's panels were fabricated over such a long period, certain stylistic differences are apparent in them, which, like those on Pisano's first set of doors, were framed by quatrefoils. The panels made before 1415 reflect the influence of the International Gothic style, with curvilinear poses and scant suggestion that the billowing clothing covers real human bodies. In later years, as his technique matured, Ghiberti used more substantial classical figures, like that of Isaac in the contest panel, and more geometric and architectural forms.

Despite the delay in finishing his first set of doors, the commission for his second pair (the third for the Baptistery) came within a year. By that time, Ghiberti was no longer a mere craftsman but an architect. The wool and cloth merchants' guild had appointed him to help oversee the building of the cathedral's dome, making him akin to an academic or scholar, a change of status that gave him considerable independence in his sculptural work. The unprecedented freedom of content and execution he was granted set Ghiberti and many of the artists who came after him apart from the medieval craftsmen of centuries past. This last set of doors was designed and modeled in wax between 1429 and 1437, and finally hung in 1452, after the arduous processes of casting, finishing, and gilding.

Exercising his new artistic license, Ghiberti fashioned ten large rectangular panels—five on each side of the divided doors—instead of twenty-eight old-fashioned quatrefoil panels. Each of the new panels re-created several related subjects from the Old Testament, including the stories of Adam and Eve, Cain and Abel, Noah, Abraham, Joseph, and Moses. Because the individual panels were larger and the rectangular frame allowed him to craft figures of different sizes, Ghiberti was able to display his masterful use of linear perspective, a technique explained in detail by polymath Leon Battista Alberti in his book *On Painting*. As a result, Ghiberti created the illusion of spatial depth, perhaps the most striking feature of the doors, causing the planes of architectural elements in each panel to appear to converge at the center and making each scene look more like painting than sculpture.

While figures in the distance are smaller and flatter, those in the foreground are larger and in higher relief. Ghiberti's Eve is among the very first sensuous female nudes of the Renaissance. His facility with the illusion of depth did not detract from his ability to portray facial expression or wildly intertwined vegetation. Years later he wrote of his second pair of doors, "I sought to imitate nature as closely as possible, both in proportions and in perspective as well as in the beauty and picturesqueness of the composition."

Each panel is flanked by figurines of various Old Testament personages, such as Rachel, Judith, Aaron, Joshua, and Ezekiel, set in individual niches. Portrait busts, including one of Ghiberti himself—a bald, slightly rotund, self-assured figure—peer out from between the niche figurines.

So astonished were the Calimala members by this new set of doors that they moved his first pair from the more prominent east portal facing the cathedral to their current position on the north side, and hung the new doors in the east portal. According to custom, only New Testament scenes could embellish doors that opened on the *paradiso* (the walkway between a baptistery and a cathedral).

Replacing the doors depicting the life of Christ with those bearing the brilliant Old Testament reliefs is said to have marked the first time that aesthetics, rather than doctrine, had determined the placement of a religious work of art. It thus appears that, many years afterward, Michelangelo was indulging in a pun, as well as passing a famous judgment, when he pronounced Ghiberti's monumental doors "so beautiful they could stand at the entrance to Paradise."

Twenty-one

Cosimo and Lorenzo de' Medici, grand patrons of art and learning

> And what's the good of being wealthy
> If it doesn't make you happy?
> —Lorenzo de' Medici,
> "The Triumph of Bacchus and Ariadne" (c. 1490)

PLAGUE STRUCK FERRARA in early 1439, when the Council of Ferrara, convened in an attempt to bridge doctrinal differences between the Latin and Greek Orthodox Churches, had been in session for a year. Cosimo de' Medici (1389–1464), the unofficial ruler of the Florentine Republic, seized the opportunity to enhance his city's stature and his own prestige. Traveling north to Ferrara, he persuaded Pope Eugenius IV to move the council to the relative safety of Florence.

What a cast of characters Cosimo entertained back in Florence at his own expense: the pope, Byzantine Emperor John VIII Palaeologus, Patriarch Joseph II, and a retinue of nearly a thousand bearded clerics and scholars. The reunion of the two Churches, joyfully proclaimed in a final session held under Filippo Brunelleschi's astounding new dome in Florence's cathedral (see Essay 19), lasted only until the Byzantine group returned to Constantinople. Yet an acquaintance Cosimo made at the Council of Ferrara-Florence profoundly altered the intellectual history of his city and much of Europe besides.

Whereas Lorenzo de' Medici, *Il Magnifico*, is usually considered the artistic patron par excellence—a new Maecenas—his grandfather Cosimo was by far the greater subsidizer of genius in every form. Cosimo became the most generous and judicious patron of the arts in Italian history and presided sagely over a city that he helped make the intellectual and artistic capital of Europe. He was born on September 27, 1389, the elder son of Giovanni di Bicci de' Medici (1360–1429), a silk merchant of plebeian origin who founded the Medici Bank in 1397 and eventually secured the papal account.

It was Giovanni who established the Medici tradition of funding monuments and public buildings. In 1419, for the antipope John XXIII, he commissioned the first Renaissance-style tomb from the most eminent sculptor of the time, Donatello. The same year, Giovanni engaged Brunelleschi to rebuild the Medici parish church of San Lorenzo and add the so-called Old Sacristy, which Donatello decorated.

By the time Cosimo was a young man, he was established in his father's banking business, which had branches in ten major European cities (see Essay 15). His commercial interests were rivaled by his intellectual ones, and he befriended and supported leading scholars of his day, including Niccolò Niccoli, Ambrogio Traversari, and that tireless discoverer of ancient manuscripts Poggio Bracciolini. When Giovanni died in 1429, Cosimo assumed a more prominent public role and, like his father, proved popular with the common people.

In September of 1433 the noble family that headed the Florentine oligarchy, the Albizzi, decided to move against the rising Medici leader of the rival faction. Cosimo ended up imprisoned in the Palazzo Vecchio, but he may have paid off the authorities to banish rather than behead him. After a year in Padua and Venice, where he was received like a king in exile, his supporters at home won the elections and recalled him to Florence. He proceeded to expel or impoverish his enemies, actual and potential. When criticized for flouting God's will by ruining so many upright citizens, he replied that more could be created with two lengths of crimson cloth (the traditional citizens' garb)—and that states were not maintained by Paternosters.

The Florentine Republic, a mercantile oligarchy dominated by about seventy-five families, was on its way to becoming a de facto Medici princedom. Although Cosimo was technically a mere citizen of Florence (he held political posts for a total of only six months), he went on to become the city's éminence grise for three decades, a master of bribery, patronage, and subtle manipulation. His undisputed political primacy was manifested several years later when he scored the coup of attracting the Council of Ferrara to Florence. Among the outlandishly dressed Greeks, Syrians, and other easterners who thronged the city on the Arno was the most venerable of all Byzantine scholars, the octogenarian Neoplatonist philosopher George Gemistus Plethon.

This Greek patriot's fervid lectures to the Florentines on Plato opened up intellectual vistas largely unknown to Western Europe since the fall of Rome. Plethon's student, Cardinal John Bessarion, brought ancient Greek manuscripts to Italy, and some ended up in Cosimo's rapidly growing collection, which formed the core of the famed Laurentian Library, later named for Cosimo's grandson Lorenzo.

Many of the visiting Greek savants remained in Italy or returned after the fall of Constantinople to the Turks in 1453. In about 1456 Cosimo lured back to Florence the Byzantine scholar and translator of Aristotle, John Argyropoulos, who had been at the Council, making him professor of Greek at the university. At the same time, the Florentine ruler chose to have his physician's son, Marsilio Ficino (1433–99), instructed in Greek so that the young man could translate the texts that Cosimo's agents were acquiring for him overseas, or that were entering Italy with scholars fleeing Constantinople.

In 1462, acting on an old suggestion from Gemistus Plethon that he found a Platonic Academy, Cosimo gave Ficino a little farm near his own villa at Careggi, outside Florence, and supplied him with a rare complete Greek text of Plato's works. Ficino spent the rest of his life translating into Latin these and related works, such as the *Enneads* of the mystical Neoplatonist Plotinus (third century A.D.), and writing commentaries that attempted to reconcile Christian and Platonic thought. Finished by 1468 and published in 1484, Ficino's was the first complete translation of Plato's dialogues into any Western language, and it enabled vast numbers of European intellectuals and creative artists to immerse themselves in Platonic and Neoplatonic thought.

Ficino's brand of Neoplatonism and his doctrine of "Platonic love" (a term he coined) influenced the work of Botticelli, Michelangelo, and Castiglione (see Essay 27), among others. His notion of the Great Chain of Being colored European literature—including the work of Sidney, Spenser, Shakespeare, and Alexander Pope—for several centuries. Ficino also served as tutor to Cosimo's grandsons, Lorenzo and Giuliano, and as head of the remarkable group of thinkers and artists of the Platonic Academy in the days of *Il Magnifico*.

Cosimo once said to his friend and biographer Vespasiano da Bisticci, "Before fifty years have passed, we shall be expelled, but my buildings will remain." He and his son Piero (called *Il Gottoso*, the Gouty) expanded on the building programs started by Giovanni, and in the thirty years after Cosimo's return from exile, they rebuilt and redecorated the Dominican church and convent of San Marco and continued work on San Lorenzo and the Augustinian church and convent of the Badia at Fiesole. Their other projects included the Novitiate Chapel at the church of Santa Croce, a tabernacle fashioned by Michelozzo at San Miniato al Monte, a dormitory for students from Florence living in Paris, and an addition to the Franciscan House in Assisi, as well as numerous smaller churches and chapels scattered over Florence and its countryside.

The convent, church, and airy cloister of San Marco, Cosimo's first public commissions, employed a host of outstanding artists. The chief architect was Michelozzo, who had accompanied Cosimo into exile in Venice and who worked on the chapel at Santa Croce and several Medici villas. Michelozzo also built San Marco's library, with its core collection of eight hundred books supplied by Cosimo, the first public library in Europe. Andrea del Verrocchio cast San Marco's bronze bell, and Cosimo engaged Benozzo Gozzoli to create an *Adoration of the Magi* for the private chapel contiguous to his own cell (where he went to get away from it all).

For the most sublime works in San Marco—a lustrous altarpiece and approximately fifty religious frescoes in the monks' cells, chapter rooms, and corridors—Cosimo turned to Fra Angelico and his assistants. In an especially serene fresco on a dormitory wall, an angel Gabriel who has iridescent wings and casts no shadow announces the Incarnation of Christ to a modest Virgin in a setting of vaults, arcades, and classical columns beside a flowered lawn.

Inspired by the example of the Medici, wealthy Florentine families increasingly lavished funds on commissions, and an unprecedented period of artistic patronage blossomed in "The Flourishing City." Like Cosimo and Piero, other bankers and politicians believed they could expiate their sins, especially usury, by contributing to "God's account"—building churches, supporting religious orders, and helping the poor. But this is not to minimize the ingredients of familial propaganda, noblesse oblige, and genuine altruism that entered into the mix.

Cosimo was wary of arousing envy in his fellow citizens. When he built a palace for his family near San Lorenzo, he rejected a design by Brunelleschi as too ostentatious. Instead he accepted a more modest plan by Michelozzo for a structure now called Palazzo Medici-Riccardi. The building's fortresslike rusticated exterior concealed a palatial inner space of more than forty rooms, crowned by a superb collection of ancient and Renaissance art. The palace's courtyard, with ancient Roman masonry embedded in its walls, eventually acquired Donatello's nude androgynous *David* and his *Judith and Holofernes*.

The Medici family also fostered the work of some of the finest painters of the time, such as Paolo Uccello's three panels depicting *The Battle of San Romano*. Originally hung in the Medici Palace, they are now dispersed among the Uffizi, the Louvre, and London's National Gallery. Uccello told the story of Florence's 1432 victory over the Sienese with high drama and attention to fine details, with decorated golden bridles, distant trees, and a bristling forest of red and white lances. All three panels are distinguished by a central character wearing a *mazzocchio*, a huge, flashy Florentine turban.

In 1459, under the auspices of Piero, Benozzo Gozzoli started work on a sumptuous *Procession of the Magi*, which occupies three walls of the Medici Palace's Magi Chapel. The opulence of the long parade that snakes its way across a fantasy landscape to the Nativity scene is partly explained by the fact that some of the major figures are portraits of contemporary Florentines in heavy brocades and fine silks. Piero's son, Lorenzo, is pictured in front of a laurel tree (a play on his name) as the youngest of the Magi.

The Magi Chapel opens onto the sacristy, where the *Madonna Adoring Her Child*, the work of Fra Filippo Lippi, presides over the altar. This randy friar, the hero of a dramatic monologue by Browning, eloped with a nun who became the mother of the painter Filippino Lippi. Cosimo once even had to lock Filippo in his studio to prevent him from chasing women down the street. An indefatigable painter of sweet-faced Madonnas and a virtuoso with light and color, Lippi became a Medici favorite and did some of his finest work for them, including an *Annunciation* completed for their palace during the 1450s.

At age seventy-five, Cosimo died in his villa at Careggi on August 1, 1464, while listening to one of Plato's dialogues. Because Piero was frail and bedridden, Cosimo had despaired for the family's future. The old man had no way of knowing that Piero's fifteen-year-old son Lorenzo would be the greatest Medici scion, or that Lorenzo's son and nephew would ascend the papal throne as Leo X and Clement VII, world-class patrons of artists such as Raphael and Michelangelo. During his life, Cosimo gave away twice as much wealth as he left his heirs. At his death the government ordered that *Pater Patriae* (Father of His Country) be inscribed on the plain slab over his tomb at San Lorenzo.

Though *"Magnifico"* was a title of respect accorded to all men of lofty station at the time, Lorenzo de' Medici's versatile genius, charisma, and passion for life and the arts have kept him singularly "Magnificent" through the ages. Like his grandfather, Lorenzo (1449–92) was a munificent patron, although his interests tended more toward poetry, philosophy, and music than the visual arts, and his relatively restricted funds were spent on books, gems, objets d'art, and vases rather than on massive building projects, except for his palatial villa at Poggio a Caiano, built by Giuliano da Sangallo.

Lorenzo gave Leonardo da Vinci a stipend and recommended him to Ludovico Sforza in Milan (see Essay 23), housed the young Michelangelo at the palace, treating him like one of his own sons (see Essay 26), and greatly enlarged the family art collection. For Lorenzo, Verrocchio cast his gracefully slender bronze *David* with one hand on his hip, the other holding his sword, and with a self-satisfied aristocratic smile. Verrocchio's delightful *Putto with a Dolphin* was created for the villa at Careggi. Lorenzo also revived and lavishly funded the University of Pisa in 1472, and he continued to support the Platonic Academy, whose distinguished members constituted his circle of friends rather than any formal academic institution.

When Piero died in 1469, only five years after Cosimo, Medici supporters decided to entrust their fate and fortunes to twenty-year-old Lorenzo and his sixteen-year-old brother, Giuliano. In explaining why he accepted his friends' invitation to assume power, Lorenzo candidly voiced the plutocrat's credo: "In Florence, it's difficult to stay wealthy without controlling the State."

Not that his political career was serene. On April 26, 1478, in the climax of a dispute with the rival Pazzi family, who had the support of Pope Sixtus IV, the two young rulers of Florence were attacked during High Mass in the cathedral at the moment of the Consecration, when most heads were reverently bowed. Twenty-five-year-old Giuliano was killed, felled by a score of blows, but Lorenzo, wounded in the shoulder, was rushed to the sacristy by his friend, the poet Politian, and then helped back to his palace under escort.

The conspirators were ruthlessly punished, although Lorenzo saved some innocent Pazzi family members from the fury of Florentine mobs. He soon adopted a personal bodyguard, built up an army of spies, and swept aside most checks on his power. Although the republic was superficially preserved, Lorenzo would rule with a much more despotic grip than Cosimo had. The Florentine historian Francesco Guicciardini pronounced Lorenzo "a pleasant tyrant."

Lorenzo became a canny European statesman, however, developing the concept of the balance of power—and preserving it—among the peninsula's five major powers: Florence, Milan, Naples, Venice, and the Papal States. His peace policy depended on forging a precarious alliance between his own state and Milan and Naples to counterbalance the power of Venice, the strongest of the five. This maneuvering also discouraged France from invading Italy to press its dynastic claims to Milan and Naples.

Embroiled as he was in politics (and seducing women), Lorenzo tried to spend as much time as possible at one of his numerous country estates with his erudite friends. As he wrote to Ficino in about 1480, "When my mind is disturbed with the tumults of public business, and my ears are stunned with the clamors of turbulent citizens, how would it be possible for me to support such contentions unless I found a relaxation in learning?" Besides Ficino and artists such as Botticelli, Filippino Lippi, and the teenage Michelangelo, the luminaries of Lorenzo's circle included Politian and Pico della Mirandola.

Lorenzo first took notice of Politian (Angelo Poliziano, 1454–94) when the adolescent poet dedicated to him several books of his elegant translation of the *Iliad* into Latin hexameters. The young Florentine ruler made the precocious scholar his secretary and, eventually, tutor to his sons. An author of Greek epigrams and accomplished Latin verse, Politian wrote his greatest poetry in Italian. His masterpiece is an unfinished long poem in ottava rima, *Stanze per la giostra di Giuliano de' Medici* (*Stanzas for the Joust . . .* , 1475–78), which celebrates Giuliano's victory in a jousting tournament of 1475 and his love for his beautiful married mistress Simonetta Vespucci, who died in the following year. The poem helped inspire two exquisitely pagan and allegorical paintings by Botticelli: *Primavera* (*Spring*) and *The Birth of Venus*, the latter featuring the nude goddess of love, who has just sprung from the sea foam, riding a massive shell landward.

Among Politian's other works are a translation of the Greek Stoic philosopher Epictetus's *Manual*; the *Favola di Orfeo* (1480), the first secular drama in Italian, based on the story of Orpheus and Eurydice; and the Italian carnival and dance songs that rank him among the finest lyric poets of fifteenth-century Europe. In 1480 Lorenzo appointed Politian, the preeminent classical scholar of his age, to the chair of Greek and Latin eloquence at the University of Florence.

Another renowned protégé of Lorenzo's was the philosopher Pico della Mirandola (1463–94). At age twenty-three, Pico compiled nine hundred theological and philosophical theses, which he offered to defend against any scholar in Europe who dared face him in public debate in Rome. Since Pope Innocent VIII deemed some of the theses heretical, not only was there no debate, but Pico was briefly imprisoned in France, where he had fled. After his release, the young prodigy accepted Lorenzo's protection and hospitality, making his home in Florence from 1488 onward.

Pico's best-known work is the Latin *Oration on the Dignity of Man* (1486), planned as the introduction to his proposed debate. Reflecting the Neoplatonist thought of Ficino, Pico sees human nature occupying a fluid position in a great chain of being that stretches.from God, who created it, downward to angels, man, animals, plants, minerals, and primal matter. Because humans have free will and are uniquely composed of both matter and spirit, they are the only creatures that can move up or down on the chain—rising to angelic, even divine, essence by the acquisition of virtue and knowledge, or descending to bestial or vegetative depths by wallowing in vice and ignorance. Though a devout Christian, Pico also developed a philosophy of syncretism, which claimed that aspects of truth and wisdom resided in all philosophical traditions—Babylonian, Hebrew, Zoroastrian, Pythagorean, Platonic, Aristotelian, Islamic, Kabbalistic—and not uniquely in Christian revelation.

Politian and Lorenzo became the outstanding Italian poets of their day, doing much to revive the tradition of writing verse in the vernacular, as opposed to Latin. In championing the use of Tuscan as an apt literary medium, they cited the immortal works of Dante, Petrarch, and Boccaccio in that idiom. Lorenzo's hearty poetry celebrates his love of women, hawking, the Tuscan countryside, and its droll rustics. He is famed for his *canti carnascialeschi*—songs for Florence's spectacularly elaborate carnival celebrations with their festive floats, mythological backdrops, and singers in lavish garb.

Lorenzo also wrote realistic satiric verse about lovesick peasants and their wenches (whose teeth "are whiter than those of horses"), Petrarchan lyrics, religious poems, obscene dance songs, and works on classical themes, such as his *Apollo and Pan*. In *I Beoni* (The Tipplers), he recounts drunken escapades with his friends in various dives around the city. The proud and sagacious ruler of Florence also delighted in pranks and coarse humor, celebrated Plato's birthday with banquets and philosophical speeches, ruined the family banking business, and played with his children like a child. Machiavelli said of him, "If one examines the light and serious side of his life, one sees in him two different persons joined in an almost impossible conjunction."

Early in 1492, Lorenzo, who had long been tormented by the family affliction of gout, retired to his villa at Careggi, where he died on April 9, at age forty-three. Both Machiavelli and Guicciardini considered Lorenzo's death a national disaster, the latter writing, "It seemed that the concord and felicity of Italy had disappeared with him." The same year also saw the beginning of the catastrophic reign of the Borgia pope, Alexander VI. Then in 1494 Charles VIII of France invaded Italy, initiating a series of power struggles fought out on Italian soil by the armies of France, Spain, and the Holy Roman Empire. When the dust cleared, foreign rule was firmly entrenched in Italy, lasting until 1861 and beyond (see Essay 42).

In Florence itself, Lorenzo's incompetent young son, Piero the Unfortunate, was expelled in 1494, the same year the Medici Bank collapsed (signaling the end of Italian domination of European finance). Girolamo Savonarola, the fanatical Dominican preacher from Ferrara, soon set himself up as head of a theocratic republic in which he and his followers (called *piagnoni*—"snivelers"—by the aristocrats) burned books and paintings along with dice, cards, fancy clothes, luxurious furniture, and other worldly vanities.

A recurrent poetic theme of Lorenzo's had been the Horatian carpe diem, which laments the transience of beauty and youth. The first stanza of Lorenzo's most famous poem, the carnival song called "The Triumph of Bacchus and Ariadne," is the classic statement of the theme in Italian literature:

> *How lovely is our youthful time,*
> *Which flees and brings on endless sorrows!*
> *Let all who will, enjoy their prime—*
> *Not place their trust in vague tomorrows.*

These lines are often applied not only to their author but also to Florence and all of troubled Italy itself. Columbus may have discovered a new world only six months after Lorenzo's death, but the incomparably fresh and magical springtime of the Italian Renaissance was over.

Barely two years later, Politian and Pico followed Lorenzo to the grave, aged forty and thirty-one, whereas old Ficino fled to the country to get out of harm's way. In his small altarpiece of the *Adoration of the Magi*, now in the Uffizi, Botticelli included portraits of Cosimo (tenderly cradling the infant Christ's foot), Piero, Lorenzo, Giuliano, Politian, Pico, and the artist himself. It was quite a crew—a Florentine Camelot of sorts—and the world would not see its like in a secular court again until the times of Elizabeth I and Louis XIV.

Twenty-two

Sigismondo Malatesta: The condottiere with a vision

I am Sigismondo Malatesta, son of Pandolfo, king of traitors, a plague to both God and man, condemned to the flames by decree of the holy Senate.

—Inscription on a dummy burned in Rome by Pope Pius II
(April 27, 1462)

SIGISMONDO PANDOLFO MALATESTA, Lord of Rimini and its environs during Cosimo de' Medici's rule in Florence, lacked the means to subsidize the arts as lavishly as did his Tuscan neighbor, but on a much smaller scale he registered his aesthetic sensibility on his time (and ours) just as forcefully.[1] Art historian Giorgio Vasari referred to Sigismondo's so-called Tempio Malatestiano as "one of the foremost churches in Italy," and it's still one of the most richly sculptured. Whatever his strong points, this art-loving fifteenth-century mercenary general has not fared well at the hands of nineteenth-century cultural historians. Consider what John Addington Symonds had to say:

> Sigismondo Pandolfo Malatesta . . . might be selected as a true type of the princes who united a romantic zeal for culture with the vices of barbarians. . . . This Malatesta killed three wives in succession, and committed outrages on his children. . . . As condottiere, he displayed all the duplicities, cruelties, sacrileges, and tortuous policies to which the most accomplished villain of the age could have aspired.

[1]This essay is partly drawn from the introduction to Peter D'Epiro, *A Touch of Rhetoric: Ezra Pound's Malatesta Cantos* (Ann Arbor, Mich.: UMI Research Press, 1983), pp. xiii–xxiii.

In his classic study, *The Civilization of the Renaissance in Italy*, Jacob Burckhardt was even harder on Sigismondo:

> Unscrupulousness, impiety, military skill, and high culture have been seldom so combined in one individual as in Sigismondo Malatesta. . . . But the accumulated crimes of such a family must at last outweigh all talent, however great, and drag the tyrant into the abyss. . . . The verdict of history . . . convicts him of murder, rape, adultery, incest, sacrilege, perjury, and treason, committed not once, but often.

But in the first extended history of the Malatesta dynasty to be written since the nineteenth century, P. J. Jones begins his chapter on Sigismondo with the following observations:

> Sigismondo Malatesta is one of history's reprobates, a man burdened for centuries with the character of moral outcast. . . . Modern opinion is more circumspect. It is now understood that Sigismondo Malatesta . . . owes much of his evil reputation to hostile testimony. . . . The worst allegations against him were all transmitted to posterity by one authority: . . . Pius II, whose interests as ruler . . . envenomed him against the Malatesta, and whose published anathemas and, still more, his widely read historical *Commentaries*, represented Sigismondo with medieval gusto and indiscriminacy as a monster guilty of every possible public and private outrage. Many of these charges can be dismissed at once as the conventional invective of curia and church. Others, among the most grave, convicting him of the murder of his first two wives, Ginevra d'Este and Polissena Sforza, and of killing and dishonouring the corpse of a German noblewoman, were either inaccurate, improbable, or the offspring of malicious rumour.[2]

Whatever the truth about his private and political life, Sigismondo had the determination and the love of beauty that led him to construct what is informally called the *Tempio Malatestiano* (Malatesta Temple), although it is more precisely Rimini's cathedral church of San

[2]P. J. Jones, *The Malatesta of Rimini and the Papal State: A Political History* (London: Cambridge University Press, 1974), pp. 176–77.

Francesco. Designed by that human dynamo Leon Battista Alberti, the Tempio was the most classically inspired Renaissance edifice created up to that time.

In the days of Sigismondo (1417–68), the Malatesta family ruled a small principality in Romagna that included the cities of Rimini, Fano, Cesena, and Pesaro. Because Romagna was part of the Papal States, the Malatesta were technically vicars of the pope rather than independent despots. When his elder brother got religion in 1429, Sigismondo, aged twelve, succeeded to the rule of Rimini, the chief city of the Malatesta domains. In 1433 he married Ginevra d'Este; when she died seven years later, he was suspected of having poisoned her. In April 1442 he married Francesco Sforza's daughter, Polissena, two months after the birth, by another woman, of his son Roberto.

From 1433 onward, Sigismondo led numerous military campaigns, hiring himself out as condottiere to various Italian princes and communes. He also built a mighty fortress for himself and was the first man to make bombshells out of bronze rather than wood. In 1447, however, when he betrayed Alfonso of Aragon, the King of Naples (who had already paid him), and went over to the Florentine side, he saved Florence from destruction but made a dangerous enemy of a powerful Italian monarch.

In June of 1449, with Sigismondo fighting for the Venetians, Polissena Sforza died. A rumor arose that she had been strangled by her husband or at his orders. In reality, she seems to have succumbed to the plague, but Pope Pius II later pronounced on the case with all the impartiality of a sworn enemy. The fathers of both of Sigismondo's deceased wives continued to have dealings with the alleged murderer, nonetheless. In a similar vein, Malatesta was accused of the rape and murder of a German noblewoman who was on her way to Rome in the Jubilee year of 1450.

But this same man was also an avid scholar of Latin, Greek, the ancient world, and philosophy (even the vastly learned Pius II considered him erudite), as well as an assiduous patron of the arts. Indeed, it is the Tempio Malatestiano, one of the most original and unusual building projects of the Renaissance, for which Sigismondo is chiefly remembered. In 1447 he began remodeling the original thirteenth-century Gothic Franciscan church by building a Chapel of St. Sigismund, his patron saint, and commissioning carved figures of the Virtues on the walls. But within a few years he embarked on a massive refurbishment, inside and out, so that the church is today a "temple of fame" celebrating

Sigismondo himself, his classical learning, his ancestors, and the beautiful and witty Isotta degli Atti, the grand passion of his life, who had been his mistress since 1446 (when she was thirteen) and was to become his third wife a decade later.

In about 1450 Malatesta engaged Leon Battista Alberti (1404–72) to design the Renaissance shell of Istrian stone that was built around the Gothic brick cathedral (parts of which are still visible—Alberti couldn't knock down the original walls without destroying the extensive work already done inside). The austere façade was modeled after Roman triumphal arches, such as the one Augustus reared in Rimini in 27 B.C., which was only a few hundred yards away from the Tempio. Matteo de' Pasti of Verona was the on-site builder of the structure and the architect for the interior, which features a single nave, a wooden-beam roof, and, on both sides, chapels separated by ornamented marble balustrades.

Adorning the chapels are the elegant bas-reliefs of Agostino di Duccio (1418–81), who had fled to Venice from his native Florence in 1446 after being accused of stealing silver vessels from a church he was working on. This didn't faze Sigismondo, who stole (more accurately, "bought," from the Cardinal of Bologna) more than a hundred cartloads of marble, serpentine, and porphyry for the Tempio from Sant'Apollinare in Classe and other churches in Ravenna. The other chief sculptor of the Tempio was Matteo de' Pasti, who, along with the painter and novelist Pisanello, also created fine medals (based on ancient Roman coins) of Sigismondo and Isotta.

In a poem about Malatesta and the Tempio, Gabriele D'Annunzio (see Essay 43) insisted that "lovely Spring herself was the artist who sculpted the marbles." The church's carved splendors include classical deities such as Diana in her horse-drawn chariot of the sky, holding in her hand the moon's crescent; Saturn grasping a sickle (with which he castrated his father, Uranus) in one hand and one of his infant children (whom he is about to eat) in the other; and a splendid nude Venus holding large seashells and standing in shallow water behind her swan-drawn chariot.

The eye is dazzled by the profusion of reliefs, whose style owes more to Greek than Roman sculpture and also reveals the influence of Donatello: carved satyrs and bacchantes, sibyls and prophets, allegorical figures of the liberal arts, signs of the zodiac (including a massive crab for Cancer—Sigismondo's sign—hovering menacingly over Rimini), mirthful putti frolicking in water, and angels playing musical instruments.

Most appealing are the swirling motifs—the diaphanous draperies and transparent waves that invest many of these carved figures with an otherworldly aura.

One of the chapels houses the marble tombs of Sigismondo and his beloved mistress, the latter with a carved Latin inscription that may be translated, "For Isotta of Rimini, the ornament of Italy in beauty and virtue." In the Chapel of the Relics, Sigismondo is shown kneeling in prayer before his patron saint in a faded fresco by Piero della Francesca (who also painted a profile portrait of him, now in the Louvre). An artistic treasure from an earlier age is a crucifix painted by Giotto.

Everywhere in the church are the monograms of Sigismondo (looking just like our dollar sign, from the superimposed first two letters of his name) and his two dynastic emblems: the rose and the elephant. There are many Latin inscriptions (and even some Greek ones), and, on Alberti's façade, Malatesta's building of the structure is proclaimed in monumental capitals in the grand manner of ancient Roman patrons.

The Tempio was also to serve as the final resting place of the humanists of Rimini's court, such as Roberto Valturio (author of the military handbook *De re militari*, dedicated to Sigismondo) and the court poets Giusto de' Conti and Basinio Basini of Parma (author of the Latin epic *Hesperis*, which extolled Malatesta's exploits, culminating in his building of the Tempio). Basinio and other court poets also contributed to the *Isottaeus*, a collection of verse in praise of Isotta. These three humanists and other worthies were buried in seven Roman-style sarcophagi set deep within the arched niches of an exterior side wall of the church.

All in all, the building was a stunning cultural statement, coming as it did from a mercenary captain in the backwaters of Romagna, but it must be recalled that one of his neighbors was the condottiere duke Federigo d'Urbino, a hilltop princeling whose enlightened patronage and extraordinary level of classical culture rivaled Sigismondo's. (They detested one another, each threatening to rip out the other's internal organs.) An even more rabid enemy of Malatesta—Pius II—complained that the new church of San Francesco was so devoid of religious motifs and so embellished with mythological carvings that "it seemed less a temple of Christians than one of heathen devil-worshipers."

But Sigismondo ran out of money, and the Tempio remains a noble fragment, unfinished both inside and out. The second story of the façade was never built, and neither was the massive lead-roofed cupola projected by Alberti, which was probably to be modeled on the dome of

Rome's Pantheon (see Essay 5). Along with other condottieri, Malatesta found himself unemployed because of the Treaty of Lodi (1454), which pledged the major powers of Italy to peace.

When Pius II supported the Aragonese in the dispute over the throne of Naples, however, Malatesta threw in his lot with the French Angevin claimants. At the Congress of Mantua in 1459, Sigismondo was forced to accept Pius's arbitration of his feud with the House of Aragon (whose captains, including Federigo d'Urbino, were devastating Romagna). Furious at the harsh terms dictated by Pius, Malatesta blundered badly by making an agreement with the Angevins in the fall of 1460—which amounted to a vicar of the pope declaring war on his own overlord.

Sigismondo was excommunicated, and in January of 1461 Pius staged a mock trial, in which the main event was an unimaginably vitriolic diatribe by a papal spokesman, accusing Malatesta of almost every conceivable violent and sexual crime. Giovanni Soranzo, an early twentieth-century Italian authority on Pius's relations with Malatesta, claimed that not one of the grave charges against Sigismondo was conclusively proved. Some of the other accusations—such as the one about his filling a holy water font with ink so as to laugh at the worshipers unwittingly bespattering themselves as they emerged from a darkened church—could hardly have been fabricated.

On April 27, 1462, the pope had Sigismondo burned in effigy in Rome. The original sentence called for the man himself to be burned at the stake, but the accused had very wisely not shown up to answer the charges. In the bull *Discipula veritatis (The Disciple of Truth)*, Pius reexcommunicated Malatesta, placed his lands under interdict, consigned him to Hell while still alive (a unique event in the annals of the Church), and deprived him (at least on paper) of all his territories.

In the meantime, Sigismondo had soundly defeated the papal troops at Nidastore (July 2, 1461), but the triumph was short-lived. The pope's army, commanded by Federigo d'Urbino, trounced Malatesta's troops near Sinigaglia the following summer. Rimini was spared by its strong fortifications and an outbreak of the plague, both of which prevented Federigo from depriving Sigismondo of his last major holding.

Pius craved nothing less than the total destruction of Malatesta, but, fearing the Venetians (who wanted to keep papal power out of Rimini) and needing their support for his long-projected crusade against the Turks, he allowed Sigismondo to sue for peace in October 1463. The terms stipulated that Malatesta could retain only Rimini and only during his lifetime. The main beneficiaries of this despoilment were the pope's general, Federigo d'Urbino, who received more than fifty towns and castles, and Antonio Piccolomini, the pope's nephew. Most of the remaining lands reverted to the papacy.

In June 1464 Sigismondo departed for Greece, in command of Venetian troops against the Turks. The expedition was a failure, and when Malatesta returned to Rimini in April 1466, after Pius's death, his only spoils were the mortal remains of the Byzantine Neoplatonist philosopher Gemistus Plethon (see Essay 21), which he reverently buried in one of the Tempio's sarcophagi.

The new pope, Paul II, a Venetian businessman who had to be dissuaded from assuming the hardly papal name of *Formosus* (Handsome), was planning to exchange Foligno and Spoleto for Rimini. Malatesta was so enraged by the scheme that he rode to the Holy City in the fall of 1466, intending to murder the pope. But Paul suspected Sigismondo's motives for requesting an audience and surrounded himself with seven stalwart cardinals before receiving him. When Malatesta realized his plan had been foiled, he fell to his knees and begged forgiveness. On his part, Paul denied the projected exchange and took Malatesta into his service (on very paltry terms).

Sigismondo died in Rimini at age fifty-one on October 7, 1468, having named Isotta and his son Sallustio as his heirs. The young man was killed in the following year by Malatesta's bastard son Roberto, also a condottiere, who usurped the lordship of Rimini. By 1500 Cesare Borgia had ousted Roberto's son. After Julius II captured the city in 1512, it remained under papal control until the unification of Italy (see Essay 42).

A modern writer who celebrated Sigismondo's building of the Tempio and splendid patronage of the arts was Ezra Pound, who made the fifteenth-century despot the dominant figure in his early *Cantos* and the first historical figure in the eight-hundred-page poem to preside over a series of cantos (8–11). But in late 1943 and early 1944, Allied bombings completely destroyed the apse and roof of the Tempio and damaged its walls and arches, which required painstaking repairs after the war. Aside from the Tempio and a few antiquities and ruins, Rimini is now basically an Adriatic beach resort. Yet as Gabriele D'Annunzio (the last of the "Renaissance" princes) wrote about Sigismondo Malatesta (the archetypal one), "Through Art, the mighty tyrant conquers Time: He is more alive now than when he coursed through cities and provinces."

Twenty-three

Leonardo da Vinci: Renaissance man, eternal enigma

Di mi se mai fu fatta alcuna cosa. (Tell me if anything was ever done.)

—Leonardo da Vinci, *The Notebooks*

"Alas! This man will never do anything, for he begins by thinking about the end before the beginning of the work!" cried an exasperated Pope Leo X after watching Leonardo da Vinci prepare varnish for a painting he had not yet started and probably never finished. Art historian Kenneth Clark lamented Leonardo's "constitutional dilatoriness." Sigmund Freud suggested that the artistic works of this Tuscan lovechild were his children, and that "he created them and then troubled himself no more about them, just as his father did not trouble himself about him." Leonardo himself apparently pondered the seeds of his ruin, writing *Di mi se mai fu fatta alcuna cosa* endlessly in the margins of his numerous notebooks and beside his brilliant drawings.

None of Leonardo's sculptures survive, and we have only about fifteen of his paintings, although his hand may be seen in perhaps ten others. He wrote extensively on architecture, but no buildings are attributed to him. Scientists and engineers continue to debate the originality of his inventions and the prescience of his scientific observations—the emanations of "Faust's Italian brother," as French historian Jules Michelet called him. So how did Leonardo acquire his reputation as the "Universal Genius"? And why did the man who was arguably the greatest painter who ever lived dissipate his energies, often quite carelessly, among so many other fields?

Leonardo was born in the Tuscan town of Vinci on April 15, 1452, to a peasant named Caterina and her lover, Ser Piero, a notary. Within months, both parents had married other people and moved away, and the infant Leonardo was entrusted to Piero's parents. With his father at least a day's travel away in Florence and his mother living in a nearby village but preoccupied with new babies on a regular basis, Leonardo spent much of his childhood outdoors with an uncle who tended the family's olive and grape harvests. He received a rudimentary education in the basics, but not Latin, and he remained distrustful of classically educated men throughout his life. A left-hander, he began writing from right to left when still a child.

His illegitimate birth locked him out of his father's profession and most other fields. It is said, however, that ambidexterity may accompany unusual talent in the visual arts, and the boy could draw with both hands. When Leonardo was a teen, his father apprenticed him to Andrea del Verrocchio, a goldsmith, painter, and the finest Italian sculptor of the time, whose studio was one of the most renowned in Florence. Verrocchio's other students and apprentices, to whom he often consigned commissions for paintings and sculptures, included Sandro Botticelli, Pietro Perugino, and Domenico Ghirlandaio. Leonardo acquired a broad artistic education under his master's guidance, studying painting, sculpture, and related technical fields, and sometimes also working in the nearby studio of painter Antonio del Pollaiuolo. He was admitted to the painter's guild in Florence in 1472.

In a famous story, art historian Giorgio Vasari relates how Verrocchio, at work on *The Baptism of Christ* (c. 1475–78), asked Leonardo to add a second angel on the left side of the canvas. The master was supposedly so awed by the young man's expertise that he never painted again. Leonardo's lovely, gold-ringleted creature is portrayed in a three-quarter view from behind as he turns to look up at Christ, his eyes penetrating into some spiritual plane not visible to his angelic companion. Kenneth Clark notes that the other angel (which may actually be by Botticelli) kneels beside Leonardo's and gazes at his companion "as at a visitant from another world."[1]

The landscape in this painting, also credited to Leonardo, anticipates the misty, sfumato backdrops that would characterize his work. In his first signed piece, *Santa Maria della Neve*, a drawing completed in August 1473 that is a seminal landscape in Western art, he had already displayed a characteristic love of movement in nature, evidenced by the swirling strokes of his pencil that create realistic areas of light and shade, water that flows over rocks in a naturalistic way, and wind that the viewer can almost see. In his *Notebooks*, the man who was perhaps the

[1]Kenneth Clark, *Leonardo da Vinci*, rev. ed. by Martin Kemp (London: Penguin Books, 1993; 1939), p. 50. Subsequent quotations from Clark are from this edition.

greatest draftsman of all time would later instruct painters to "describe landscapes with the wind, and the water, and the setting and rising of the sun" (chapter 471).

Also at about this time he worked, perhaps in concert with others in Verrocchio's workshop, on an Annunciation now in Florence's Uffizi Gallery. The composition suffered because of an apparent preoccupation with achieving perfect linear perspective, but the Virgin's ethereal face is worth studying, if only to gauge Leonardo's increasing mastery of portraiture over the next few years.

A comparison of his work on *The Annunciation* with his portrait of Ginevra de' Benci (c. 1474) illustrates his growing skill with light and dark. In this portrait of an aristocratic lady, housed in the National Gallery in Washington, D.C., Leonardo subtly manipulates the shadows of her cheekbones and brows to create a powerfully modeled face. Behind her, sprigs of juniper (a play on her first name) echo the wispy curls at her temples. An exquisite deep landscape lies beyond the juniper: Tall trees are reflected in water, and bluish-gray sfumato hills extend into the distance. The painting shows Leonardo following his own advice when, in the *Notebooks*, he stressed to young painters the importance of knowing how to see, *saper vedere:* "As you go through the fields, turn your attention to various objects, and in turn look now at this thing and now at that, collecting a store of diverse facts. . . . Do not do like some painters who, . . . though they see various objects, do not apprehend them" (chapter 506).

In 1478, two years after surviving a court proceeding for sodomy in which the charges were dismissed, Leonardo received his first independent artistic commission for an altarpiece for the chapel of San Bernardo in Florence's Palazzo Vecchio. Establishing a pattern that would continue throughout his life, he began the altarpiece but soon abandoned it to Ghirlandaio and Filippino Lippi, the latter of whom finished it in 1486. The master did complete the beautifully composed, emotionally intimate *Benois Madonna,* and possibly one or two others, early in his career. For these and the uncompleted altarpiece, he left a sheaf of incomparable drawings and studies of babies, angels, gesturing hands, draperies, and faces.

His masterpiece of this period is the unfinished *Adoration of the Magi,* now in Florence's Uffizi. Drawings and studies associated with this revolutionary work are scattered in museums throughout Europe. Kenneth Clark observes (p. 80) that Leonardo labored on this canvas for just seven months, but that completing his creation of this complex world would have required seven years.

At the center of the composition, Mary holds the infant Jesus in her lap as he reaches out to a kneeling king. Around them, a tumultuous crowd of sculpturally rendered figures has gathered to gaze on the child or praise heaven, with no suggestion of the dignified procession of potentates that was de rigueur in formulaic depictions of this scene. Behind the gesticulating worshipers—who are overawed by the presence of the miraculous—is a strange backdrop of precisely rendered staircases and arches, fighting horsemen with their rearing horses, and a fantasy landscape vivified with chiaroscuro. In some ways, this *Adoration* is a preview of coming attractions: Many of the male figures reappear as Apostles in *The Last Supper*; the high-mettled horses recur in Leonardo's sketches for another famous (and lost) unfinished work, *The Battle of Anghiari*; and the sense of mystery carries over into the two versions of *The Madonna of the Rocks*. In 1482 Leonardo abruptly abandoned *The Adoration*, as well as an ascetically despairing *St. Jerome*, and left for Milan.

Leonardo had been taken aback when Pope Sixtus IV passed him over in favor of several colleagues, including Botticelli and Ghirlandaio, for commissions at the Vatican. Furthermore, Leonardo's scientific drawings and studies, which occupied an increasing amount of his time, were of little genuine interest to the Florentines. He believed that the intellectual climate in Milan favored men like himself with encyclopedic interests in science. When Lorenzo de' Medici, for whom the artist had restored ancient marble statues, asked him to go there in 1482, Leonardo seized the opportunity. Lorenzo wanted the artist to present a silver lyre, apparently crafted by Leonardo and shaped like a horse's head, as a gift to Ludovico Sforza, who had usurped power in Milan from his young nephew, the rightful duke. Among his many talents, Leonardo was also an excellent musician and had several music pupils, one of whom traveled north with him (and may have sat for Leonardo's portrait, *The Musician*, a few years later).

Ludovico, called *Il Moro* because of his dark complexion, aspired to make an ancient Athens of his duchy. But he also had pressing military and political problems, most notably an ongoing war with Venice. Canny Leonardo addressed the needs of this potential patron in a nervy, ten-point letter that he composed while traveling to Milan and that he may or may not have actually delivered. Reinventing himself, he proposed that Ludovico hire him as military engineer to construct great "machines of war," fire-resistant bridges, seagoing military vessels, mortars, and covered vehicles that eerily resemble modern armored cars and tanks in Leonardo's drawings.

He extolled his skills in draining enemy moats, digging secret underground tunnels in silence, and, in case peace broke out, constructing public and private buildings and transporting water. "By the way," he inquired in the last line of his letter, "how about a monumental bronze equestrian statue of your father?" Some historians suspect that the opportunity to create this massive memorial to Francesco Sforza, a project often discussed by Il Moro, was in fact the major attraction for Leonardo in Milan.

Immediate employment with Ludovico was not forthcoming. Instead Leonardo established his own painting studio, took on students, and began work on *The Madonna of the Rocks*, one of his most mystifying compositions. Because the first version (c. 1483–85, now in the Louvre) did not please his patrons, he and some assistants apparently did a second one (probably between 1491 and 1508, now in London's National Gallery).

The content of these paintings is somewhat unusual. In the foreground of a grotto, a seated Mary rests her right hand protectively on the shoulder of the infant John the Baptist, who extends his hands clasped in prayer toward the infant Jesus, who sits on the ground beside an angel on the other side of Mary. Jesus raises his hand in blessing. In the earlier version, the angel is pointing to John but gazing almost distractedly out of the canvas.

Questions abound. Why is the scene swathed in darkness and framed by ominous caves and jagged rock formations? Was some symbolic meaning intended—an identification of the scene of Christ's birth, sometimes portrayed as a cavern, with the cave of his sepulcher—or was Leonardo merely indulging his penchant for depicting nature in yet another mood? Why do the foot of the angel and Mary's left hand, which she holds suspended over Christ's head, look curiously bird- or serpentlike?

In 1489 Leonardo, by then a member of the ducal household, finally received a commission from Ludovico to paint a portrait of his mistress, Cecilia Gallerani. The work is as intriguing as the *Mona Lisa* and, according to historian Paul Johnson, "as close to perfection as a painting can well be." The elegant young woman turns her head as if to listen, her serene face lit by attentiveness and intelligence. Leonardo's mastery of anatomy is evident in her high cheekbones and her right hand, which strokes an ermine, an emblem of Ludovico. Kenneth Clark has written of this animal she cradles in her arms: "The modelling of its head is a miracle; we can feel the structure of the skull, the quality of skin, the lie of the fur. No one but Leonardo could have conveyed its stoatish character, sleek, predatory, alert, yet with a kind of heraldic dignity" (p. 98).

By the time he painted *The Lady with an Ermine* (and perhaps also the portrait of another mistress of Ludovico, Lucrezia Crivelli), Leonardo was already immersed in the most ambitious project he had yet undertaken—the recording of all his learning and musings into notebooks. More and more of his time was devoted to his scientific studies, and he adorned thousands of notebook pages with drawings and commentaries. Included in the *Notebooks* are treatises on painting, architecture, and human anatomy, as well as a book on mechanics. Other documents were compiled later in the *Codex Atlanticus*, now in Milan, a sister volume in Windsor Castle, England, and the Arundel Manuscript in the British Museum. Leonardo intended to publish the manuscripts, but this, too, he left undone.

These manuscripts are legendary for the so-called secret handwriting Leonardo employed. In fact, this was nothing more than the right-to-left handwriting in which he had been proficient since childhood and which is easily read with a mirror. These didactic texts, which he called "demonstrations," are noteworthy for relying heavily on illustrations rather than words to make their teaching points. Leonardo's detailed, remarkably accurate studies of human anatomy at rest and in action, for which he claimed to have dissected thirty cadavers, earned him a deserved reputation as the father of scientific illustration. His studies of plants and animals are no less exhaustive.

Other topics that attracted his attention, at least for a time, included astronomy, mathematics, geography, topography, the possibility of human flight, the functioning of gears, and naval warfare. In 1485, as Milan recovered from the plague, he focused on urban planning to promote a more functional, hygienic city, but none of these plans came to fruition. In each subject of inquiry, he fused scrupulous scientific observation with art. Historians of science are divided on the importance of his work in these various disciplines and on whether his lack of formal education was beneficial because it freed him to learn directly from nature, or detrimental because he worked in an intellectual vacuum. "Because I'm not learned in the classics," he complained, "I realize that some presumptuous men think they have reason to denigrate me by claiming that I'm an illiterate (*"omo sanza lettere"*). The fools! . . . They go about puffed up and pompous, adorned not with the fruits of their own labors, but those of others." Lovers of painting, however, find Leonardo's interest in so many fields frustrating because they believe it distracted him from his true genius.

In 1491 Leonardo helped design the entertainments in honor of Ludovico's marriage to Beatrice d'Este, daughter of the ruler of Ferrara. He loved the spectacle of theater because it was a means of indulging his taste for the fantastic. For this event, the first of several he directed, he concocted exotic wildlife costumes, set designs, and special sound and lighting effects that left the audience happily baffled.

Two years earlier, he had finally received the commission he was waiting for: the equestrian monument to Francesco Sforza. Perfectly in character, he prepared numerous studies of the horse and rider and finally completed a scale model in clay. But by that time it was all too late. In 1494 the French under Charles VIII bore down on northern Italy, and the sixty tons of bronze designated for the statue was rerouted to Ferrara for making cannons. When the French arrived in Milan, they reportedly used the clay model for target practice. Leonardo spent much of this time designing clockworks and fantastic machinery and, with some distaste, learning Latin so that he could read ancient manuscripts and unlock the intellectual treasures he surmised they might contain.

In 1495 Ludovico, now Duke of Milan in his own right, commissioned a mural of the Last Supper for the refectory of Santa Maria delle Grazie. Completed in 1498 with the relentless importuning of Ludovico, the work displays Leonardo's expertise in color, perspective, anatomy, and architecture. The dramatic focus of the classically symmetrical mural is Christ's head, framed by the central window of the three in the background (Christ is the second Person of the Trinity) and placed at the vanishing point.

Unlike earlier artists, Leonardo depicted not the institution of the Eucharist but the moment after a sadly serene Christ informs his followers that one of them will betray him. This is the reaction shot—querulousness, defensiveness, shock, denial, confusion. Their faces are so realistic and their gestures so vivid that the cacophony is almost audible. Leonardo's biographer Serge Bramly writes that the scene could have been cast by Fellini. Judas, the betrayer, is easily recognized—he's the detached one reaching for the bread.

It is tragic that the red chalk studies Leonardo did for *The Last Supper* probably provide a clearer approximation of what the original looked like than what remains of the mural today. He apparently wanted no part of fresco painting, in which pigments suspended in water are applied to wet plaster, and highly durable paintings are completed in days or weeks. He chose instead to work slowly in an experimental medium of tempera and oil on two layers of dry preparatory ground, with disastrous results.

By 1517 *The Last Supper* had already begun to deteriorate, and in 1556, less than sixty years after the mural's completion, Vasari reported that it was a "muddle of blots." Even with its recent restoration (1978–99), the existing work is largely the work of others who tried to mend it after botched touch-ups, flooding, and World War II bombing. Nonetheless, this spectral painting is cited by art historians as the initial High Renaissance work, whose monumentality, dignity, and expressiveness helped form the styles of Michelangelo and Raphael.

In 1499 Ludovico Sforza was deposed by the French, eventually dying in a dungeon in Touraine. Leonardo, who seems to have stopped painting for a while after completing *The Last Supper*, studied arithmetic and geometry with the eminent mathematician Luca Pacioli. (A letter of 1501 describes how Leonardo's "mathematical experiments have so distracted him from painting that he can't bear to pick up a brush.") With his patron gone, he and Pacioli left Milan, and Leonardo proved himself an able, if self-interested, diplomat.

First he mended fences with the French, who had deposed his patron and murdered a close friend. He then traveled to Venice and sold himself once again as a military engineer, helping the city prepare for a threatened Turkish invasion. A mercenary side of Leonardo emerged: Within months he was designing a bridge for the Sultan to link the Asian and European portions of Istanbul.

In 1502 he agreed to serve as military engineer for Cesare Borgia, the son of Pope Alexander VI and captain of the papal army. As a senior official for Borgia, Leonardo accompanied the feared despot on his brutal campaigns of conquest in the Marches and Romagna. Although Borgia was the main model for Niccolò Machiavelli's *The Prince* (see Essay 25), his ruthlessness apparently elicited no qualms of conscience in his new technical adviser. Freud noted that although Leonardo refused to eat meat because of his love of animals, he dispassionately sketched condemned men as they approached execution and seemed to have no clear sense of good and evil. Of the Borgia campaign, the good doctor wrote that not once in Leonardo's writings did he betray "any criticism or sympathy in the events of these days."

Of Leonardo's next painting, executed in Florence, Kenneth Clark has written, "Familiarity has blinded us to the beauty of the *Mona Lisa*'s pose" (p. 174). The subject of the most recognizable artwork in the world, begun in about 1503 and called *La Gioconda*—"the merry woman"—in Italian, was probably Lisa Gherardini del Giocondo, the wife of a wealthy Florentine. Credible evidence also suggests she might have been a mistress of Giuliano de' Medici, or Isabella d'Este (who hounded Leonardo for a portrait), or Leonardo's mother as a young woman, or a completely idealized woman, or even a gender-bending self-portrait.

Whoever she is, the power and mystery of her smile, hinting at an emotional richness and complexity unsurpassed in portraiture, captivate the viewer even today. Though Walter Pater saw in her an intimidating and vampirish archetypal woman, "older than the rocks among which she sits," we might respond with Shakespeare's assertion about Cleopatra: "Age cannot wither her, nor custom stale / Her infinite variety." After toiling over Mona Lisa for four years, Leonardo never parted with her.

In 1503 the versatile artist received a commission from Florence to paint an enormous mural (twenty-two feet high by fifty-five feet long) in the council chamber of Palazzo Vecchio. The subject was to be the Battle of Anghiari, in which Florence defeated Milan in 1440. Michelangelo was hired to work on the opposite wall on a depiction of the equally patriotic Battle of Cascina. Neither work was completed. What Leonardo did manage to finish in an unsuccessful experimental medium was later covered over by Vasari. In a spirited drawing of about 1615 by Peter Paul Rubens, however, based on copies of the central portion of Leonardo's lost mural, a potent harbinger of the Baroque may be seen in the lively and impenetrable tangle of horses and grimacing riders battling for a banner.

In the same year of 1503, Leonardo conceived a plan with Machiavelli to divert the Arno River away from Pisa. The goals were to cut off the enemy city's access to the sea and provide drinking water and irrigation for Florence. The scheme failed, but Leonardo's simultaneous efforts on two grandiose projects—a monumental mural and a river diversion (not to mention *Mona Lisa*)—provide an insight into why he came to be called the "Universal Genius."

Leonardo settled down in French-held Milan in 1508. For the next five years, with a studio and apprentices, he consulted on architectural projects and worked on paintings such as *Leda and the Swan* (now lost), *The Virgin and Child with St. Anne,* and the second version of *The Madonna of the Rocks*.

Among his last paintings were two of St. John the Baptist, whose principals, with pointing index fingers, are so disturbingly hermaphroditic that the later one has been considered to be a depiction of Bacchus. Unlike his archrival, Michelangelo, Leonardo was no more than nominally Christian.

In 1513, after the French were extricated from Milan, Leonardo traveled to Rome with some students, hoping to obtain commissions from Giuliano de' Medici, whose brother had just been elected pope as Leo X. Leonardo lodged at the Vatican, tinkered with mathematics, sketched ancient buildings, and drew plans for draining the Pontine marshes. In his letters, he seemed bitter and at loose ends. In a notebook he wrote: "As a kingdom divided against itself cannot stand, so every mind divided among different studies is confused and weakened." In 1516 he accepted the invitation of Francis I to work at the castle of Cloux, near the Loire, where his position was "first painter, architect, and engineer of the King," and there he died on May 2, 1519.

> O Time! Consumer of all things; O envious age! Thou dost destroy all things and devour all things with the relentless teeth of years, little by little in a slow death. Helen, when she looked in her mirror, seeing the withered wrinkles made in her face by old age, wept and wondered why she had twice been carried away (chapter 1163).

Leonardo's self-portrait in chalk, dating from 1512, shows an old man (the same one who wrote these words in his *Notebooks*) as a tangled whorl of beard and hair, with eyes that peer into a spiritual plane, but not the glorious one glimpsed by his angels. He seems to ask: "Tell me if anything was ever done."

Twenty-four

A new world beckons: Columbus, Cabot, Vespucci, Verrazano

Mannaggia Colombo! (Damn that Columbus!)

THIS INVECTIVE IS STILL heard among Italian immigrants in America who wish they had stayed home. More extreme variants were probably expressed by indigenous American peoples, whose ranks were decimated by the men who followed Columbus to the lands he discovered and claimed for Spain, places he called *Otro Mundo* (the Other World). Columbus himself, however, was apparently neither the blameless hero revered by earlier generations nor the greedy imperialist served up by revisionist historians.

Cristoforo Colombo, born in Genoa in 1451, made four voyages to the Western Hemisphere seeking a sea route to Cathay (China), where he hoped to find gold and claim territories for his sponsors, the Catholic Majesties of Spain, Ferdinand and Isabella. His life was a web of contradictions and false surmises. He endorsed Christian baptism for the native peoples he encountered, but members of his crews seduced or raped many female candidates for conversion. Based on the navigation problems he encountered, he concluded that the world was "the shape of a pear, round everywhere but the stalk where it juts out a long way, something like a woman's nipple." He had a marked mystical tendency and said the Divine Office more faithfully than most priests of his time. He died believing he had discovered an extension of the Malay peninsula, near the Garden of Eden, in Earth's single ocean. Preceded by the Vikings five centuries earlier, Columbus was hardly the first European to see the *Otro Mundo*.

But he was the first European whose visits had epic reverberations. The Vikings settled in Vinland (northeastern Newfoundland), but only briefly. Columbus, who discovered more new territories than even Ferdinand Magellan, initiated a four-hundred-year epoch of European exploration, conquest, and settlement.

Genoa, where Columbus lived until age twenty-two, was the maritime rival of powerhouse Venice and had a long tradition of exploration. In 1291 the Vivaldi brothers, Ugolino and Guido, sailed from the city and out through the Straits of Gibraltar in two ships, seeking a sea route to the Indies, but the expedition was lost. The legendary Venetian explorer and first European to traverse all of continental Asia, Marco Polo, dictated his marvelous *Travels* while imprisoned in Genoa in 1298–99. Columbus, the son of a Genoese wool worker, learned to sail as a child. By the early 1470s, he had traveled on several merchant vessels as far as Chios off the coast of Turkey. In 1476, while serving as first mate on a vessel attacked by pirates, he was shipwrecked off the coast of Portugal. He eventually settled in Lisbon.

On subsequent voyages across the Mediterranean and to Madeira, Ireland, and even the Arctic Circle, Columbus mastered the art of navigation. In 1477, near Galway, he and his shipmates encountered a small boat containing two corpses, which the Irish readily identified as Chinese (they were probably Finns). Columbus deduced that Cathay lay not too far to the west.

During his time ashore in Lisbon, Columbus overcame the most important barrier to his advancement in the merchant fleet—illiteracy. He learned to read and write Latin, Portuguese, Castilian, and Italian. Literacy changed the course of his life—and perhaps of history— because he could now peruse books that put ideas in his head, works such as Pope Pius II's treatise on the circumnavigation of Africa and Marco Polo's *Travels*.

The book that influenced him most was *Imago mundi* by Pierre d'Ailly (1350–1420), a French cardinal and Church reformer with a scientific avocation who suggested that the Indian subcontinent and China could be reached by sailing west. Columbus's personal copies of *Imago mundi*, Pope Pius's book, and his Latin edition of Polo's *Travels*, still preserved in Seville, are marked with copious marginalia and underlining. In the early 1480s he decided to sail west to China.

By mid-decade, after being turned down by John II of Portugal, Columbus began soliciting the support of other monarchs, including England's Henry VII and Ferdinand and Isabella of Spain. His plan was rejected twice by a panel of advisers to the Spanish monarchs, not because they thought the world was flat (educated Europeans had long before accepted the notion that the Earth is spherical), but because they believed, correctly, that Columbus had grossly miscalculated the distance to Cathay and Cipangu (Japan).

The error, which placed Japan where Cuba is and China in southern California, may have been a deliberate underestimate to make the success of the voyage seem more plausible. No one at the time knew that an enormous land mass—North and South America—stood in the way. Isabella gave her royal consent to the crossing in January of 1492.

The Queen's capitulation cannot be ascribed solely to Columbus's salesmanship. Although the Spanish had reclaimed Granada from the Moors on January 2, 1492, Islamic sea power was growing in the Mediterranean, and land routes to the East had been choked off—developments that Europeans viewed with alarm. The Spanish monarchs were also spurred by the news that their archrivals, the Portuguese, had attempted an alternate sea route to China by sailing south along the coast of Africa, rounding the Cape of Good Hope, and proceeding northeast. Eager to enhance their prestige in Europe and gain access to the gold and spices of Cathay and Cipangu, Ferdinand and Isabella saw in Columbus an opportunity to find their own ocean road to the fabled East.

Very early on August 2, 1492, Captain General Columbus, convinced that God willed him to discover a westward passage to the Indies, boarded his flagship, the 235-ton *Santa Maria* (crew of seventy), and, followed closely by the *Niña* and the *Pinta*, sailed down the Rio Tinto from Palos, Spain. Columbus's scrappy little caravels, crewed by local boys and only two other Italians, were accompanied out to sea by the last boatloads of Jews to leave Spain in that year of their expulsion. Ironically, the monarchs' chief finance official, a Jewish convert, Luís de Santángel, and several other Christianized Jews (*conversos*) staked their own money and exhorted the King and Queen to do the same. Columbus himself contributed about a third as much as their Majesties ventured.

Probably the finest navigator of his day, Columbus demonstrated his expertise on the first leg of the voyage. Rather than heading across the unpredictable North Atlantic—a route that had doomed many a vessel—he undertook a novel course, sailing south to the Canary Islands and then bearing due west. From the trading expeditions he had captained along the coast of Guinea and equatorial Africa a decade earlier, he knew the winds there would be favorable and the seas calm.

The seas may have been calm, but not the crews. On September 9, after a short stay in the Canaries (where the captain general had a romantic encounter with the beautiful and widowed lady governor), the ships lost sight of land, and Columbus wrote that his sailors wept. On that day, he decided to keep two navigation logs—a public one that underestimated the distances traversed and another with the true figures, which he kept hidden—a maneuver that would have failed to surprise their Majesties' advisory panel.

Three weeks passed. No European sailors had been out of sight of land for longer, and these men, with only hardtack and lentils left to eat, became increasingly restive. Columbus refused the request of Martín Alonso Pinzón, captain of the *Pinta*, to veer north, a course change that would have landed the fleet in Florida. Adding to the tension was the large cash reward promised by Ferdinand and Isabella to the first sailor to see land—and Columbus's threat of serious punishment for a premature alert. Only during the first week in October, when the men saw more and more birds and driftwood, did the general mood lift.

Then, at about 10 P.M. on the night of October 11, the crews spotted what looked like candlelights dancing on the horizon, probably bonfires on the island that lay dead ahead. The fleet sailed on with the *Pinta* in the lead and, at 2 A.M., her lookout finally shouted "*Tierra!*" Columbus and his two captains went ashore early the next day bearing Isabella's flag and claiming the island in her name. From the ship's log:

> **Saturday, 13 October 1492:** At daybreak many of the men came to the shore—all young and of a good height—a very fine people. . . . I watched carefully to discover whether they had gold. . . . The people are very gentle and eager to have the things we bring.

> **Tuesday, 16 October 1492:** The people have no religion, and I think they would be very quickly Christianized, for they have a very ready understanding.

It's unclear on which Caribbean island ("quite large, very flat, and delightfully green") Columbus made these entries, but it was probably San Salvador, or Watling Island, about four hundred miles southeast of Miami. After two days Columbus sailed on with captives, whom he hoped would help him find gold.

From Cuba, which he initially thought was Cipangu, and then Cathay, he ventured to a large island he named *La Isla Española*, or Hispaniola, where he found enough gold to prevent him from returning to his employers empty-handed. His men, the first Europeans to observe the "drinking of smoke from firebrands," soon afterward made tobacco fashionable in Europe. They also took home *Treponema pallidum*, the bacterial agent of syphilis, which was apparently unknown in Europe, but which soon spread across the continent.

When a boy taking his first unsupervised turn at the helm rammed the *Santa Maria* onto a reef off Hispaniola on Christmas Eve, Columbus took it as a divine omen to establish a garrison, which he built at the site with timbers from the beached ship and named *La Navidad* (Christmas). The Spanish received much help salvaging it from the local king and his family. As Columbus wrote to Ferdinand and Isabella, "Nowhere in Castile would one receive such great kindness.... They are so affectionate, have so little greed.... They love their neighbors as themselves." The king and his people lived to regret it.

Early in January 1493, leaving about two dozen men at La Navidad, Columbus headed home in his favorite vessel, the *Niña*, accompanied by the *Pinta* and bringing back some human captives, gold, exotic botanical specimens, and a few parrots. In one of his greatest accomplishments, Columbus discovered what later sailors recognized as the safest, fastest route back to Europe. Instead of simply retracing his course, he sailed north to the approximate latitude of Bermuda, where he found brisk westerlies to speed the homeward leg, although the two ships barely survived a fierce winter storm.

Columbus's prestige was at its zenith after his first voyage, as evidenced by the title bestowed on him—Admiral of the Ocean Sea—and the speed with which his second crossing was prepared, this time with seventeen ships, fifteen hundred men, some cavalry officials, six priests, the Admiral's two brothers, Bartholomew and Diego, and five returning, newly baptized Caribbean natives. After embarking in September 1493, the entire fleet arrived in the Lesser Antilles (dubbed by Columbus "the Eleven Thousand Virgins") in early November, not far from his original landing site on San Salvador. This was an astonishing feat for a sailor navigating primarily by dead reckoning, by which a ship's course is determined by assessing its direction (with a compass), elapsed time (in this case, with a half-hour glass), and speed (Columbus had to guess).

The Admiral and his men explored the islands of St. Croix, St. John, St. Thomas, and Puerto Rico, an area in which they discovered an indigenous people, the Caribs, engaging in cannibalism (which was named for them), usually at the expense of the hapless Taino tribe. Returning to Hispaniola, the Admiral found that La Navidad had been destroyed and its occupants slaughtered in retribution for the Spaniards' marauding for gold and women.

Columbus moved his settlement to another part of the island, a trading post he named La Isabella. He then left to explore Cuba and Jamaica but subsequently returned, convinced that most of the local gold must be on Hispaniola. The priests began to grumble about the maltreatment of the natives, which apparently occurred with the connivance of the Columbus brothers. Leaving Bartholomew and Diego in charge, Columbus sailed back to Spain after sending ahead five hundred slaves in hopes of obtaining backing for another voyage.

Less enthusiastic than before, but more distrustful of the Portuguese than ever (despite the agreement in 1494 to split the New World between Portugal and Spain), the Spanish monarchs bankrolled a third expedition, which set sail for Hispaniola in July 1498 with more than three hundred colonists, including thirty women. The only bright spots in this disastrous voyage were Columbus's discovery of compass variation, the discrepancy between magnetic north (in Greenland) and "true north" (at the Arctic), and his awe at reaching the Gulf of Paria in Venezuela near the outflow of the Orinoco. He later wrote to the King and Queen, "If this river does not flow out of the earthly Paradise, the marvel is still greater. For I do not believe that there is so great and deep a river anywhere in the world."

On returning to Hispaniola, however, the Admiral again found chaos. His brothers had lost control of the Spanish gentry and the native populations, much of the strife arising from a gold-producing operation. Many factors contributed to the disaster, but after a new Spanish administrator, Francisco de Bobadilla, sailed over to investigate, he sent all three Columbus brothers back to Spain—in shackles. This is how the Admiral saw the situation: "They judge me as if I had been sent to govern Sicily, . . . where the laws can be strictly applied without complete upheaval. I should instead be judged as a captain sent from Spain to the Indies to govern a large and warlike people with customs and beliefs very different from our own."

Nonetheless, after a humiliated Columbus wrote an obsequious letter to Ferdinand and Isabella en route, he was pardoned. Still fearing that the brilliant navigator—but awful administrator—might take his skills to Portugal, or even Genoa, their Majesties outfitted Columbus for his fourth voyage in 1502, but with only four ships. They also ordered him to stay away from Hispaniola.

Columbus made the fourth crossing in record time—twenty days to Martinique—but he noted signs of a looming hurricane, having sur-

vived two other such storms in those waters. He tried to make port in
Hispaniola and warned the governor, whose fleet was about to sail. The
governor laughed at the "soothsayer," denying him refuge. Columbus
rode out the storm a few miles down the coast, but the governor lost
nineteen ships and a large cargo of gold.

Columbus then sailed across the Caribbean to the shores of Hon-
duras. In search of the passage Marco Polo had traveled from China to
the Indian Ocean, he sailed against the wind and current along the
Honduran shore for twenty-eight days in a virtuosic feat of coastal navigation. The fleet continued along the shorelines of Nicaragua, Costa
Rica, and Panama but never explored deeply enough to realize they were
only miles from the Pacific Ocean—and that much nearer to Cipangu
and Cathay.

His vessels now ridden with shipworms, Columbus attempted yet
another landing at Hispaniola but was shipwrecked on Jamaica in mid-
1503. The captains of the other ships reached Hispaniola by canoe, but
the governor delayed Columbus's rescue for a year. It was August of 1504
before Columbus returned to Spain, just before Isabella's death. His last
years were marred by bickering with King Ferdinand over percentages
he believed were owed him on the gold discoveries in Hispaniola. He
died in Spain on May 20, 1506.

One of his many biographers, Samuel Eliot Morison, an expert sailor
himself and an official U.S. naval historian, wrote that Columbus's faults
were "defects of the qualities that made him great. . . . But there was no
flaw, no dark side, to the most outstanding and essential of all his qualities—seamanship. As a master mariner and navigator, no one in the
generation prior to Magellan could touch Columbus."

By 1496 Henry VII of England, who initially declined Columbus's offer
to sail west on his behalf, justifiably feared lagging behind in exploring
the new territories. The call went out to Giovanni Caboto (1450–99),
or John Cabot, a Genoese native and citizen of Venice, who was living
in Bristol, England.

Cabot shared Columbus's belief in the plausibility of sailing west to
China, and he set out with a single vessel and eighteen men on a
northerly route in May 1497. About a month later, he landed in or near
southern Labrador, claiming the land for England (but unfurling a
Venetian flag) and believing that he, too, was in Asia. A second voyage
in 1498 involved more ships and several hundred men. A vessel put in

for repairs in Ireland, but the others were not heard from again. Whether Cabot reached the New World a second time remains unknown, but England's subsequent stake in Canada derived from his explorations.

Like Columbus, the Florentine Amerigo Vespucci (1454–1512), who spent years in the service of the Medici family, also sailed for the Spanish. He was acquainted with Columbus and helped prepare vessels for his second and third crossings. During a voyage to Guyana in 1499 or 1500, Vespucci apparently discovered the mouth of the Amazon in northern Brazil and, like the others, believed he was near China.

On this expedition, Vespucci spent his spare time working on the new science of celestial navigation, by which he could estimate his latitude by measuring the positions of the sun and of a star such as Polaris and comparing his data with standard navigational tables. Vespucci also made the most accurate contemporary estimate of the Earth's circumference.

On a second voyage in 1501 for the Portuguese king, Manuel I, Vespucci sailed to Brazil and traveled as far south as Patagonia, where he wrote detailed descriptions of the flora and fauna. He and his men returned to Lisbon in 1502 with a startling and increasingly obvious conclusion: They had not been in Asia at all but in a "New World." In 1507 a German mapmaker first used the feminine form of the Latinized version of Vespucci's first name to designate "America," and the great Flemish cartographer Mercator first refined the appellation into its northern and southern components on a map dating from 1538.

Another Florentine, the nobleman Giovanni da Verrazano (1485–1528), was the last important Italian navigator to join the west-to-Asia exploration club. Seeking a more northerly route for King Francis I of France, he reached Cape Fear, North Carolina, in 1524. Sailing along the Outer Banks and unable to see the mainland, he assumed the water in the distance was the Pacific Ocean. Continuing north, he discovered New York Harbor, where a vast suspension bridge named for him now spans the Narrows between Brooklyn and Staten Island.

Anchored off modern-day Rhode Island, Verrazano displayed his celestial navigation skills by demonstrating that Newport lies on the same latitude as Rome. Several weeks later, he avoided disaster on the shoals of a hook-shaped peninsula he named Pallavicino after an Italian general. (We call it Cape Cod.) He continued on to Maine, which he referred to as "The Land of Bad People" because of some uncongenial bartering experiences with the locals.

Verrazano later made a profitable trading passage to Brazil, and his final voyage took him to Guadeloupe, in the Lesser Antilles. Apparently unaware that Columbus had reported cannibalism there, Verrazano blithely wandered ashore and, while his helpless brother watched from a small boat just beyond the breakers, was swiftly murdered and eaten by the inhabitants.

In a letter to Francis I at the conclusion of his first voyage in 1524, Verrazano had told the King that "the globe of the Earth is much larger than the ancients have held. All this New World which I have described is connected together, not adjoining Asia or Africa. . . . We hope to have better assurance of this, that we may see the perfect end of our cosmography and that the sacred word of the evangelist may be accomplished: 'Their voice carried over all the Earth and their words to the end of the world.'"

Some of the voices heard in the New World were those of the Gospel, while others were those of brutal exploitation. With time, European ideals of liberty and justice gradually prevailed over the two new continents that Italian explorers helped claim for the Western world.

Twenty-five

Machiavelli and the dawn of modern political science

I count religion but a childish toy,
And hold there is no sin but ignorance.
—Christopher Marlowe, *The Jew of Malta* (1589–90)
Prologue, spoken by "Machevill," lines 14–15

ALL THE DICTIONARIES AGREE on what Machiavellianism means. They speak of cunning, expediency, duplicity, deceit; of unscrupulousness in pursuing political objectives; of opportunism and power politics; of the irrelevance of morality in political life. Yet the man responsible for this dubious enhancement of the world's vocabulary was a high public official who served his city-state of Florence indefatigably and without any personal gain until he was ignominiously sacked. Niccolò Machiavelli (1469–1527), who was born and died in his beloved Florence, is regarded by many Italians as a fervent patriot who dreamed of national unification three and a half centuries before the fact. How did he also manage to acquire such an evil reputation?

Two years after the de facto despot of Florence, Lorenzo de' Medici ("The Magnificent") died in 1492, a republic was proclaimed. In 1498 the twenty-nine-year-old Machiavelli embarked on his political career as secretary of the council in charge of war and foreign affairs. He served on numerous diplomatic missions to wily rulers such as Louis XII of France, Ferdinand V of Spain, Pope Julius II, and Holy Roman Emperor Maximilian I, but the man who made the deepest impression on him was a ruthless general, Cesare Borgia. With the aid of his father, the profligate Borgia pope, Alexander VI, Cesare was carving out a state in central Italy by ejecting the petty tyrants of a dozen principalities.

Endlessly energetic and perfectly amoral, Cesare was the kind of man who showed off with stunts like decapitating bulls with a stroke of his broadsword in Rome's Piazza Navona. But the brutal young man was ruined when, after his father's death, an enemy became Pope Julius II. Harassed and broken, Cesare died while still in his early thirties.

In 1512 the Medici family was restored to Florence with the aid of Spanish military power. As a servant of the defunct Republic, Machiavelli was dismissed. Early the following year he was briefly imprisoned and tortured six times with the strappado when the returning Medici rulers falsely suspected him of being part of a conspiracy.

Retreating to his modest country house outside Florence, Machiavelli began composing historical and literary works. In a letter of December 10, 1513, he describes a typical day in his enforced retirement, spent mostly chatting and arguing over cards with the local yokels—except for several magical hours in the evening when, after changing into formal attire, he entered his study and communed with the ancient historians. He also mentions in the same letter having written a short work on principalities, "how they are acquired, how they are maintained, why they are lost." We know it as *The Prince*, the distilled essence of realpolitik.

Machiavelli thought it should be possible to devise general rules about politics because people are always motivated by the same desires and fears. That's how he put the "science" into political science, the discipline that inquires into the laws governing political life and change. But *The Prince* was chiefly a tract for the times. The many disparate states of Italy were helpless against foreign incursions. The Italian peninsula had become the field on which the great European powers contested for continental hegemony, beginning with the invasion of Charles VIII of France, who asserted his claim to the throne of Naples in 1494. The next French king, Louis XII, deposed the Duke of Milan, cut a deal with the Spanish for dividing up the Kingdom of Naples, and attacked Venice. The Spanish eventually defeated the French in southern Italy and took over that part of the peninsula. Foreign armies conquered or pillaged Venice's mainland possessions as well as Genoa and other northern Italian cities.

Machiavelli, who felt the shame of Italy like a wound, decided to compose a how-to manual for a Medici prince who might succeed to Cesare Borgia's mantle as a fierce ruler capable of driving out the invaders. Machiavelli's program in *The Prince* is articulated in Chapter 15: "I've thought it better to set forth the truth of things rather than what they're imagined to be. Many have imagined republics and principalities that have never been known to actually exist; and since the way life is lived is so far removed from how it should be lived, he who sets aside what is done for what should be done, learns how to ruin himself rather than how to survive. The fact is, the man who wants to be good all the time is ruined among so many who are not good. From this it follows that a prince who wants to stay in power has to learn how not to be good, and to use this skill, or not, as necessity may require."

This overriding goal determines the major themes of *The Prince*. After identifying the two main kinds of states, republics and principalities, and saying that he will address only the latter in this work, Machiavelli promises to explain how principalities can be governed and maintained. He drops his first bombshell in Chapter 3, claiming that "a new prince is always under the necessity of injuring those who helped him achieve power." This is an age-old problem faced by the leader of every successful revolution—what to do with his gunmen. Somehow, they must be subjected to controls they hadn't expected, yet, as Machiavelli blandly observes, the prince can't use "strong medicine" because he's indebted to them. True enough, but it's Machiavelli's matter-of-fact delight in phrases like "strong medicine" that immediately captures our attention.

He also notes that all a new prince has to do to hold on to a hereditary principality he has seized is "first, to extinguish the line of the former prince, and second, to avoid changing the laws and taxes." Thus a calculating respect for a conquered people's traditions is mentioned in the same breath as the extermination of the former ruling family, as if they were both just items on a to-do list. This notorious third chapter is also the source of one of Machiavelli's most quoted pieces of advice: "Men must either be coddled or crushed, since they avenge themselves for petty injuries, but they can't for fatal ones. Any injury done should be the kind from which the possibility of revenge is not to be feared." Chapter 5 teaches that "whoever takes possession of a city that is used to living free, and doesn't destroy it, can well expect to be destroyed by it himself."

Another famous generalization appears in Chapter 6: "All armed prophets have conquered; the unarmed ones have been destroyed." No doubt Machiavelli was thinking of Christ as the prime example of the unarmed prophet who comes to grief, but the one he mentions is Girolamo Savonarola, the fiery Dominican preacher who became the theocratic demagogue of the Florentine Republic. Savonarola proclaimed Jesus king of the city, presided over the famous Bonfire of the Vanities, and claimed he conversed with God. Soon afterward, pleasure-loving Florence—and Pope Alexander VI—grew tired of the ascetic preacher. They tortured and then hanged and burned Savonarola at the stake in

Piazza della Signoria on May 22, 1498, just days before Machiavelli started working for the Republic. For a leader to be naïve and credulous could be dangerous, even fatal.

Machiavelli obviously relishes the story of how law and order were brought to the feverishly violent Romagna that Cesare Borgia was trying to subdue. Cesare sent his henchman Ramiro de Lorqua to suppress brigands and factions with an iron fist. Once the dirty work was done, Cesare thought it was time to show the people that he himself had not condoned his underling's vicious methods. Accordingly, Ramiro's body was found sliced in two in a town square with a butcher's wooden wedge and a bloody knife beside it. This not only conveyed to the people how keenly Cesare felt their pain, but it also intimated that if he acted this way with his own men, they themselves had best behave.

In *The Prince* this crafty gangster is aggrandized into the embodiment of all the qualities that a new prince who is trying to consolidate his power should emulate. From the Cesare myth that Machiavelli weaves, a new prince can learn how to secure himself against his enemies, acquire friends, conquer territories through strength or fraud, destroy those who might injure him, gain the love and fear of the populace, and win the respect of his soldiers. As it was for Cesare, the chief preoccupation of a prince should be warfare, since a state that can't defend itself will soon be swallowed up.

The usefulness of fear looms large in *The Prince*. Machiavelli advises new princes to do any necessary killing or violence at once; stretching it out inspires hatred, which is bad, and not just fear, which is good. He urges the prince to play off the nobles against the people but also to make sure the people see the prince as their protector against the nobles. Establishing law and order often requires making an example of a few troublemakers. Allowing a state to lapse into chaos for fear of appearing cruel is wrongheaded because it harms the entire community. Misplaced compassion is self-defeating.

If a prince has to choose between being feared and loved, it's far better to be feared. Since men are generally ungrateful, vacillating, deceitful, cowardly, and greedy, they'll promise the prince their souls, but when their safety or self-interest is on the line, they'll desert or betray him, because love is fickle. Fear, on the other hand, is not.

Cruelty can reap both fear and respect, but taking men's property and their women brings only hatred: "Men sooner forget the death of their father than the seizure of their patrimony." While they can't bring back the dead, they can always try to regain their property.

The prince must be both a lion and a fox, making use of both strength and cunning as needed, since a lion has no defense against traps, and a fox has none against wolves. The fox par excellence, according to Machiavelli, was Pope Alexander VI, who, though he never thought of anything but deception, always found people to believe him because he was such an expert at dissimulation. The important thing for a prince is to appear to be compassionate, true to his word, upright, and religious—rather than to be so. People judge by what they see, and since few can see the prince from up close, the great majority can easily be strung along. If there is a cardinal sin in *The Prince*, it is to be gullible, pietistic, and naïve—in short, what Italians call being a *fesso* (it's an anatomic part).

Machiavelli advises against neutrality in foreign policy; the prince should be a true friend to other states, or a resolute enemy, rather than a fence-sitter. He must surround himself with competent advisers and shun flatterers, since people's first impression of a ruler's intelligence is based on the quality of his staff.

The Prince is a Dale Carnegie course with a vengeance. Since people understand only success, they admire a prince who attains an arduous goal, no matter how he goes about it, but they turn against one who adheres to his scruples and fails. But note that Machiavelli also urges the prince to honor and reward talented citizens and to encourage trade and agriculture. People shouldn't be reluctant to work hard for fear of losing their possessions or owing exorbitant taxes. The prince must never plunder his subjects or tyrannize for his own material gain.

Only in the hands of a shrewd ruler or governing body can the state bring enough power to bear to suppress revolts, repel invasions, and provide the peace and stability that are the indispensable basis of civilized life. The tacit assumption is that, in preserving his power, the prince is enhancing the well-being of his subjects by defending them from external threats and internecine strife. The relations of family and friendship, religion, economic life, the arts and sciences, ordinary human civilities—all are impossible amid political chaos, in which the state is militarily weak, its leaders feckless and dissipated, and the rule of law swept aside.

In his last chapter, Machiavelli adopts the tone and imagery of a biblical prophet to exhort one of the Medici princes to throw the "barbarians" out of Italy (meaning the French, Spanish, Germans, and Swiss). Italy is seen as "leaderless, lawless, beaten, despoiled, torn apart, overrun, and subjected to every manner of desolation." There once was a man—Cesare Borgia is meant—who was on the verge of rescuing her, but he was ultimately defeated by Fortune. The time is propitious for yet another attempt to unify a large part of Italy and make it strong.

Since the Medici family controlled both Florence and the papacy (in the person of Giovanni de' Medici, who had been elected Pope Leo X), it commanded considerable power, wealth, and prestige. Machiavelli hoped that one of the Medici would develop a powerful military and political machine to oust the invaders: "This barbarous domination stinks in everyone's nostrils." Italy needed nothing less than a "redeemer." Machiavelli ends his book with some lines from a patriotic poem by Petrarch, to the effect that *virtù* can triumph against barbarian fury, since ancient Roman valor still lives in Italian breasts.

The Prince, written in 1513, was published only in 1532, five years after Machiavelli's death, but it had circulated widely in manuscript form. Machiavelli dedicated the work to Lorenzo II de' Medici, grandson of the Magnificent and nephew of Leo X, who had made this kinsman Duke of Urbino. This younger Lorenzo, who had shown promise on the battlefield, was to die in 1519 at age twenty-seven. Machiavelli ended his dedication with a request for employment, but his attempt to curry favor with the restored Medici rulers of Florence flopped.

Because of his enforced retirement from the brutal politics of his day, the world has been enriched with the numerous historical and literary works he wrote over the course of a decade and a half. Then, in May of 1527, the new Medici pope, Clement VII, had to take refuge in Castel Sant' Angelo while Rome was sacked by twenty thousand starving and unpaid German, Spanish, and Italian mercenaries of Emperor Charles V. The capital of Christendom had to endure an orgy of bloodlust, rape, torture, looting, arson, and desecration that left more than ten thousand dead. This was the world Machiavelli had tried to reform.

The Florentine Republic was briefly restored in this dreadful year, but Machiavelli was passed over for office because of some minor jobs he had done for the deposed Medici rulers. He died the following month. The Republic did not long outlast him. The Medici were once again returned to power in Florence by the omnipotent Charles V in 1530, and they stayed put for two hundred years. We're told that the three books Charles kept by his bedside were the Bible, Castiglione's *The Book of the Courtier* (see Essay 27), and *The Prince.* As for Machiavelli's dream of Italian liberty, it remained just that during the centuries of Spanish domination ushered in by Charles V.

• • •

What was it about Machiavelli that made him the most important political philosopher of the Renaissance, a household word, and a detested symbol of Italian corruption? His novelty and power to shock depend largely on the fact that although many rulers had acted the way he describes, he was the first to formulate their behavior into a system. This introduced a profoundly discordant note into political writing.

For centuries before Machiavelli, Italian politics had been dominated by the factional strife of Guelfs and Ghibellines, the supporters of the Church versus those of the Holy Roman Empire (see Essay 12). The big question for political thinkers (who were usually theologians) was: Who was supreme in political affairs—the pope or the emperor? St. Thomas Aquinas stated a moderate position, according to which the Church can interfere in secular matters only when the ruler oversteps his mandate (see Essay 13). In 1302 Pope Boniface VIII argued for radical papal power over all the princes of Christendom (as had Pope Innocent III a century earlier). Marsilius of Padua, in *Defensor pacis* (*Defender of Peace*, 1324), claimed that the state rules supreme in temporal affairs.

But even Marsilius sought to prove his points by citing the Gospels and the Church Fathers, taking for granted that both church and state were ordained by divine Providence for the ultimate goal of mankind's eternal salvation. Medieval political controversies had raged over the respective spheres of church and state but left unquestioned the divine origin of these institutions.

Machiavelli, who had imbibed a century-old Florentine tradition of civic humanism, was the first important political thinker to adopt a totally secular perspective. Aquinas had insisted that "the common good of the state cannot flourish if the citizens are not virtuous—at least those whose job it is to govern." But Machiavelli knew that to regenerate a prostrated Italy, rulers would have to replace Aquinas's Christian virtue with a secular *virtù*, which may be defined as excellence, prowess, manliness, courageous resolution, and intelligent ability to get a job done. This quality, akin to the *arete* of the ancient Greeks and the *virtus* of republican Rome, had no religious, or even moral, connotations.

In communities like ancient Rome or the German and Swiss states of his own day, where the citizens were not hopelessly corrupt, Machiavelli believed that a republic functions well. This form of government is Machiavelli's chief focus in his other masterpiece, *Discourses on the First Ten Books of Livy* (1513–21), an extended commentary on the history of republican Rome based mainly on the Roman historian Livy. Although apologists claim "the true Machiavelli" speaks to us in the *Discourses*, the book rehearses all the major themes of *The Prince*. Whether discussing principalities or republics, Machiavelli always assumes that the survival of the free state is the prime directive.

The concept of Machiavellianism originated among the French out of antipathy to their wily Florentine queen, Catherine de' Medici (see Essay 31), but Elizabethan England got the most literary mileage out of it (and the allied stereotype of the treacherous, atheistic Italian). In *The Schoolmaster* (1570), righteous Roger Ascham quotes the Italian proverb, "*Inglese Italianato è un diavolo incarnato*" (An Italianate Englishman is the Devil incarnate). Shakespeare's Duke of Gloucester, aspiring to become King Richard III, boasts that he can "set the murderous Machiavel to school" (*3 Henry VI* 3.2.193). Francis Bacon, however, who pleaded guilty to accepting bribes, said we should be grateful to Machiavelli because he teaches "what men do, and not what they ought to do." In much the same spirit, German pessimist philosopher Arthur Schopenhauer pointed out two centuries later that "to reproach Machiavelli with the immorality of his work is just as much out of place as it would be to reproach a fencing master with not opening his instruction with a moral lecture against murder and manslaughter." T. S. Eliot claimed "no great man has been so completely misunderstood" and "no one was ever less 'Machiavellian' than Machiavelli."

On the basis of his *History of Florence* (1520–25), Machiavelli is considered one of the two creators of modern historiography, the other being his friend, Francesco Guicciardini. Among Machiavelli's works are poems, letters, diplomatic reports, translations from Latin, a treatise on the art of war, and a story about a devil named Belfagor who comes to Earth and marries a woman who ends up scaring him back to Hell. He also wrote one of Italy's greatest comedies, *La Mandragola* (*The Mandrake*, 1518), a fierce satire of Italian corruption, centering on a man's seduction of a virtuous young woman with help from her mother, her confessor, and her duped old husband, who wants to become a father at any cost. The play's moral is the triumph of intelligence over all other considerations.

When Machiavelli's tomb in the church of Santa Croce in Florence was erected in the mid-nineteenth century, Italian unification was finally becoming a reality. From that perspective, his role as a patriotic foe of foreign oppression overrode all hairsplitting moral discriminations. The inscription reads TANTO.NOMINI.NVLLVM.PAR.ELOGIVM: "To so great a name, no epitaph can do justice."

Twenty-six

Michelangelo: Epitome of human artistry

In the room the women come and go
Talking of Michelangelo.
　　—T. S. Eliot, "The Love Song of
　　　　J. Alfred Prufrock" (1915)

THOSE WHO HAVE BRAVED the hordes to admire Rome's Sistine Chapel might envy Goethe his comparatively unflustered access to it during his Italian journey in 1787, when he once even took a nap on the chapel's papal throne. Yet the artist whose Sistine frescoes prompted the German poet to assert that "the self-assurance, the virility, the grandeur of conception of this master defy expression" used to protest that he was no painter. Michelangelo Buonarroti (1475–1564), generally regarded as the greatest painter and sculptor of all time, was also a superb architect, a capable military engineer, and the most powerful lyric poet of the Italian Renaissance. In the course of his long life he earned the epithet "divine," but he was also tormented by religious scruples, guilt over his passionate desires, and the incessant demands of patrons and his own relentless genius.

He was born in the tiny town of Caprese, a craggy Apennine outpost in Florentine territory, on March 6, 1475, but within a month the family moved to Florence. His father, Lodovico, who spuriously claimed descent from the counts of Canossa, tried to beat the boy's interest in drawing out of him—it was unfit for a gentleman—before finally apprenticing him, at age thirteen, to the Florentine painter Domenico Ghirlandaio.

After a year, Michelangelo's talent came to the attention of Florence's ruler, Lorenzo the Magnificent (see Essay 21), who was delighted with a copy of an ancient faun's head made by the budding artist. The lucky adolescent was given a room at the Medici palace, where he supped with the Neoplatonist philosopher Marsilio Ficino; the greatest classical scholar and an outstanding poet of the age, Politian (Angelo Poliziano); and the polymath eclectic philosopher Pico della Mirandola. He might also have learned from a sculptor working for Lorenzo, Bertoldo di Giovanni, who had studied with Donatello (see Essay 19).

Michelangelo's earliest surviving sculpture, the marble *Madonna of the Stairs* (1489–92), carved in a Donatello-type low relief, shows a serene Virgin in profile nursing the infant Jesus. In his marble high relief *The Battle of the Lapiths and Centaurs* (c. 1492), whose mythological subject was suggested to Michelangelo by Politian, the contortion of the struggling nude forms already foreshadows the artist's lifelong project of portraying the human body as a vehicle of emotion.

During these years, Michelangelo heard the sermons of Lorenzo's great antagonist, the puritanical Dominican preacher, statesman, and, ultimately, martyr, Girolamo Savonarola. Even in old age, the artist recalled Savonarola's fire-and-brimstone voice. More important, he went to study the frescoes of Giotto at Santa Croce and of Masaccio in Santa Maria del Carmine. It was in the latter church's Brancacci Chapel that he got his nose broken by fellow sculptor Pietro Torrigiano, who was weary of Michelangelo's making fun of his drawings.

After Lorenzo de' Medici died in 1492, Michelangelo studied human anatomy from cadavers provided by the prior of Santo Spirito. In October of 1494 the first of his recurrent panic flights occurred, in which he made his way to Bologna just before the expulsion of Lorenzo's son, Piero the Unfortunate, and the establishment of Savonarola's short-lived theocratic republic. There Michelangelo studied the reliefs of Jacopo della Quercia in San Petronio, especially those on the creation of Adam and the expulsion of Adam and Eve from Paradise.

Moving to Rome in 1496 in quest of lucrative commissions, Michelangelo carved the larger-than-life-size marble *Bacchus* (1496–98), now in Florence's Bargello, depicting a slightly tipsy nude young god holding a wine cup and wreathed with grape leaves and clusters. Bacchus's sensual torso and the sly little faun at his side, nuzzling some grapes, create a convincingly pagan aura.

But the first of Michelangelo's masterpieces was the marble *Pietà* (1498/99–1500), expressing, according to Walter Pater, "the pity of all mothers over all dead sons." The Virgin Mary's small head and enormous lap, with the rhetorical flourish of her left hand, are minor distractions, while her youthful features, the exquisite folds of her garments, and the meticulously sculpted Christ evoke dignified sorrow. The technical virtuosity of this piece, in an artist who was not yet twenty-five, established Michelangelo as the foremost sculptor of his day.

On the strength of the *Bacchus* and the *Pietà*, Michelangelo was recalled to Florence to work on a huge marble block that two other sculptors had botched and abandoned in the previous generation. After the ouster of the Medici, the Florentine Republic wanted to display a massive emblem of its civic pride, a warning to all future tyrants in the person of David, the young slayer of Goliath.

Michelangelo accepted the challenge, and the result, now enshrined at Florence's Accademia, is a heavily muscled and gangling adolescent nude just a tad over fourteen feet tall. Dubbed *Il Gigante* (the Giant) by his earliest admirers, *David* (1501–4) frowns confidently in the direction of his opponent, the stone still in his huge right hand and the sling resting on his left shoulder. The colossus was set in front of the main entrance of Palazzo Vecchio, the seat of the Republican government, where it remained until it was replaced with a copy in 1873.

Michelangelo was summoned back to Rome in 1505 by the formidable warrior pope Julius II (Giuliano della Rovere, reigned 1503–13) to design and execute his tomb. Now began what the artist's biographer Ascanio Condivi called "the tragedy of the tomb"—Michelangelo's agreeing to sculpt more than forty figures for the pontiff's enormous monument, a project that would disrupt his life for the next forty years. It began inauspiciously: After Michelangelo had spent eight months in the Carrara quarries selecting and shipping the best marble blocks back to Rome, Julius refused to pay him or even receive him on his return, having in the interim decided to rebuild St. Peter's Basilica and wage war against his enemies.

In April 1506 the proud artist fled from his taskmaster to Florence. Seven months later, during an uneasy reconciliation between the two titans, the pope ordered Michelangelo to forge a fourteen-foot bronze seated statue of him, which Julius's enemies melted down three years later, refashioned into a cannon pointedly named La Giulia, and used in their wars against him.

After this diversion, instead of being allowed to continue work on the tomb, Michelangelo was ordered to paint the 45-by-128-foot ceiling of the Vatican Palace's Sistine Chapel, where popes are elected in secret conclaves. Although he tried to wriggle out of the assignment, which would take him four years (1508–12) to complete, he ended by creating the world's most sublime work of pictorial art.

The original plan called only for the twelve Apostles, but it was soon replaced by a cosmic thematic conception undoubtedly planned by a Vatican theologian. Seven Old Testament prophets were to be counterbalanced by five classical sibyls (among them the Libyan, with her lovely bare shoulders, reaching behind her for a massive book, and the Cumaean, with her old face and wrestler's biceps), all twelve of whom had supposedly foretold the coming of Christ.

The ceiling's nine central panels deal, in groups of three, with the creation of the universe, the story of Adam and Eve, and that of Noah. In the *Separation of Light from Darkness*, even God's face and form seem inchoate and primeval, whereas in the *Creation of the Sun and Moon*, his visage is sternly majestic as, with outstretched arms dazzlingly foreshortened, he hurls out the two spinning orbs, assigning them their places with imperious fingers. It is a curious feature of this panel that, next to this last depiction of God, he appears in rear view, with clearly outlined buttocks, soaring away to create the vegetation already seen in the distance. In the third panel, the *Separation of Earth from Land*, the patriarchally bearded Creator faces full front, arms extended.

The first panel on the story of Adam and Eve is the famous *Creation of Adam*, in which God's fingertip vivifies the languorously beautiful first man. The figure with girlish breasts who has God's left arm around her neck is the as-yet uncreated Eve, staring in wide-eyed wonder at Adam, who returns her gaze. In the *Creation of Eve* and the *Fall of Adam and Eve*, the mother of the human race is now a full-bodied mature woman (while Satan appears as a naked woman on top and a serpent below). In the *Expulsion*, in the same panel as the *Fall*, the angel's sword prods Adam's neck, while cowering Eve is already a crone. The three other main central panels show the *Sacrifice of Noah*, the *Deluge*, and the *Drunkenness of Noah*.

The semicircular lunettes and triangular areas portray some of the ancestors of Christ, and thus the general theme of the whole conception reveals itself as a dramatic representation of Christian time, from the very beginnings of Creation, through the Fall and Deluge, and onward to the promise of a Savior, both in the physical forebears of Christ and in the prophecies of his coming by the prophets and sibyls. Among the most remarkable features of the ceiling are nineteen surviving male *ignudi* ("nudes," also often called "athletes"), who support large painted medallions with dramatic gestures and in contorted postures while seated on pedestals of the illusionistic architecture.

"The nearer painting approaches sculpture, the better it is," Michelangelo later wrote. Indeed, the epic proportions and powerfully heroic molding of the 343 figures depicted on the ceiling in every possible posture owe much to two ancient marble sculptures in the papal collection: the trunk (probably of the Greek hero Ajax) known as the *Belvedere Torso*, with its rippling muscles, and the tormented *Laocoön*, a Roman copy of a Greek original that was dug up in Rome in 1506.

Perched sixty feet above the floor on a scaffolding of his own devising, Michelangelo worked not on his back but standing, as shown in a sketch he made of himself to accompany a sonnet in which he confided to a friend that he was not a painter. He claims that the strain of his posture, with his belly scrunched up beneath his chin, has made him sprout a goiter as he works all twisted out of shape while his brush spatters paint on his upturned face.

The restoration of the Sistine Chapel frescoes that ended in 1994 removed the accumulated candle and incense smoke of centuries, as well as the traces of earlier retouchings and botched restorations (once even using Greek retsina wine). Accustomed to the Chapel's dusky figures, the artistic world was so stunned by the originally bright palette of nine pigments that the newly revealed vibrant colors of the robes and vestments led one disparaging critic to speak of "a Benetton Michelangelo." Then again, the master is also said to have designed the bright dress uniforms of the pope's Swiss Guards.

After finishing the ceiling, Michelangelo resumed work on the tomb for Pope Julius, who soon needed it; the pontiff died only a few months after the unveiling of the Sistine Chapel. Sometimes said to be a portrait of the pope, the great marble *Moses* (1513–16), with his symbolic horns, stalwart body, and the most astounding beard in all of plastic art, evinces the rapt countenance of a man who has seen God. Also intended for the tomb were the so-called *Dying Slave* and the *Rebellious Slave* (now in the Louvre), nude male figures apparently meant to evoke the soul's attempt to escape the bonds of flesh and sin. Other unfinished pieces—four *Captives* and a *Victory*—are now in Florence. A much-contracted version of Julius's tomb in the Roman church of San Pietro in Vincoli was finally completed only in 1545.

The new pope, Leo X, who had been Michelangelo's boyhood companion as Giovanni de' Medici, sent the artist to Florence in 1516 to design the façade for the Medici church of San Lorenzo. When this project fell through, the artist was told to switch his attention to another part of the church—and to yet another mortuary monument, the Medici Chapel. This next project, the brainchild of Cardinal Giulio de' Medici, a cousin of Leo who became Pope Clement VII in 1523, was also never completed, though it occupied Michelangelo between 1519 and 1534.

As both architect and sculptor for the chapel, Michelangelo designed the rectangular, medium-sized room with elaborate classical niches and frames on the walls and a dome overhead. Its chief sculptural works are the seated statues, set in opposite niches on the side walls, of two recently deceased Medici princes in Roman armor, both of whom had died young. The statue of Lorenzo, Duke of Urbino, shows a melancholy and reflective commander, his chin resting in his left hand and his face receding into the shadow of his helmet. At his feet, resting on the curved lids of his sarcophagus, are two nude allegorical statues, reminders of inexorable Time. The figure of *Dawn* is a beautiful, frontally nude young woman with disturbed features, while *Dusk* is an older man in whose unfinished bearded face some have seen a hint of Michelangelo's.

Across the room is the tomb of Giuliano, Duke of Nemours, depicted as a figure holding a commander's baton while alertly surveying the field of action, ready to spring to his feet. The allegorical sculpture of *Day* is a very heavily muscled man, his face left unfinished, while *Night* sleeps fitfully with a star and crescent moon on her head and an owl nestled beneath the crook of her knee. The bearing of Giuliano suggests the active and that of Lorenzo the contemplative life, though neither of the statues is in any way a portrait. In a thousand years, Michelangelo said, no one would know that their faces bore no relation to the features of the deceased.

In the same San Lorenzo complex, Michelangelo next designed for Clement VII the Laurentian Library (1524–34), the first modern library, which was opened to the public in 1571. In 1557 Michelangelo sent Giorgio Vasari from Rome a description of his design for the library's small triple staircase, which looks like a wonderful musical instrument. The idea came to him "as if in a dream."

Meanwhile, the Florentines yet again threw off their allegiance to Medici rule and established a republic. Michelangelo was appointed superintendent of fortifications in 1529, not because he was a celebrity but for his engineering skills. After Florence capitulated to a siege in August of 1530, an order was issued for his assassination, but Pope Clement soon forgave him.

With yet a new ruler in the Vatican, Michelangelo was summoned back to the Eternal City in 1534, where he spent the last thirty years of his life. Although Clement VII had initiated the artist's next commission, work began in earnest only under the Farnese pope, Paul III, in 1536, when, at age sixty, Michelangelo agreed to paint *The Last Judgment* on the 2,100-square-foot wall over the altar in the Sistine Chapel. This epic feat, requiring five and a half years, would crown his labors in the world's most famous chapel, which now houses both his Creation and his Last Judgment, the alpha and omega points of Christian time.

Christ, so long awaited by the prophets and sibyls portrayed on the ceiling, is now come again, with his beardless face like Apollo's, his massive body like that of Hercules, and his right arm raised like thundering Jove's. He is not so much angry as disdainful and weary of sinful human recalcitrance. At his side, Mary, who can no longer intercede with him, averts her face, as if in sorrow.

Nowhere is Michelangelo's *terribilità,* or "sublime awesomeness," more evident than in this massive tableau of the wages of sin. Here he displays all he learned from the anguished writhings of the *Laocoön,* the Book of Revelation, Dante's *Inferno,* Luca Signorelli's *Last Judgment,* Savonarola's sermons, and the *Dies Irae,* the medieval hymn telling of how the angelic trumpets shall announce the dread day "when even the just man shall hardly be safe."

With its blue background sky of lapis lazuli, the fresco has the rhythm of a clockwise vortex as the dead (some of them just skeletons) rise from their graves at the lower left, the lucky ones ascending to Christ's level with the aid of wingless angels, while the unfortunate damned on the right are pulled downward by demons toward the depths of Hell. Shown holding the implements of their torment are martyrs such as St. Catherine of Alexandria (originally with pendulous breasts, now decently clothed) and St. Bartholomew, from whose left hand hangs his own flayed skin with Michelangelo's anguished self-portrait on its face.

Dante's influence may be seen in the figures of Charon (the old boatman of Hell, brandishing his oar at the sinners in his skiff) and of Minos, the infernal judge. This Minos is fitted with donkey's ears, however, and the features of Paul III's master of ceremonies, Biagio da Cesena, who had objected to all the nudity in the fresco. A serpent is shown biting his penis, thus decently covering him up.

Although Michelangelo provided Christ and half of his four hundred other figures with loincloths or covering, that still left a lot of bare flesh on the wall in the Catholic faith's holiest chapel. Even the pornographer Pietro Aretino felt obliged to weigh in after the fresco was unveiled, registering his shock at its indecency (see Essay 28). "Corrections" were ordered painted on more than forty figures over the next two hundred years. The latest restoration has spared the early corrections added by Michelangelo's pupil, Daniele da Volterra, and removed those of the later *Braghettoni* ("Breeches-makers"), as these artists were nicknamed. The sublime fresco—"the most overpowering accumulation in all art of bodies in violent movement," according to Kenneth Clark—barely escaped destruction at the hands of several popes in more prudish times after the artist's death.

We also have two hundred sonnets, madrigals, and other poems from the hand of this versatile genius, most of them composed between ages sixty and eighty, some penned on priceless drawings and sketches. Like his human figures, Michelangelo's poems are often contorted and muscularly energetic. Offering a window into his troubled private life, they abound in flashes of ecstasy and gloomy ruminations. His religious poems express his sense of abject sinfulness in the face of death and eternal damnation. In one, written when he was almost eighty, he renounces his art as an idle vanity that had reigned supreme—"his idol and monarch"—and he now seeks salvation in Christ, "who spread his arms upon the cross to clasp us." The poet Francesco Berni wrote in 1534 that whereas contemporary versifiers spoke words, Michelangelo spoke things.

Like W. B. Yeats, Michelangelo is a supreme singer of the pathos of love in old age. Death is approaching fast, he is old and decrepit, yet he's fiercely assailed by love for a middle-aged woman and a young man. He wrote some of his most memorable sonnets and madrigals for the widowed poet, religious enthusiast, and most venerated woman of her day, Vittoria Colonna, Marchesa of Pescara (1490–1547), whom he met in Rome when he was sixty-three and she was forty-eight. Several of these works feature imagery drawn from the art of sculpture, such as his most famous poem, which claims that even the greatest artist cannot conceptualize a form that does not already reside within the block of stone. The sculptor's task thus becomes one of liberating the statue that is already there by removing all the excess. When Vittoria died, Michelangelo almost went insane with grief, so ardently had he loved the pious woman, fiercely regretting that after her death he had kissed only her hand and not her face and forehead.

The handsome young Roman aristocrat Tommaso Cavalieri was only in his teens or early twenties when he met the fifty-seven-year-old artist. In some of his most fervid poems, Michelangelo addresses him as *Signore*—Lord—ending one with the wish: "and may I hold my sweet and longed-for lord / forever in my unworthy, ready arms." Tempestuous passion characterizes some of the poems to Cavalieri, often couched in Neoplatonizing terms as merely an affair of minds, souls, and earthly embodiments of heavenly bliss, though the poet concedes that ignorant slanderers think otherwise of their relationship.

The poems and letters to Cavalieri, who became a student of Michelangelo's, are rhapsodic compositions in which the lonely old artist sounds as smitten and rapturous as an adolescent. He loved other ephebes, too—Gherardo Perini, Febo del Poggio, Cecchino Bracci—but he may well have remained chaste all his long life, although, as he wrote, the beautiful features of anyone, of any age or either sex, went immediately to his heart.

From 1546 onward Michelangelo served as chief architect of the new St. Peter's, refusing any salary and working solely for the glory of God. Inspired by Brunelleschi's cupola for the Cathedral of Florence (see Essay 19), Michelangelo designed St. Peter's sixteen-ribbed dome, with its internal diameter of 140 feet, though he never lived to see it. His design called for a squatter shape, however, so his successor, Giacomo della Porta, deserves some of the credit for the magnificent final result. Michelangelo also designed the apse end of the basilica.

Another project of Michelangelo's old age was the refurbishing of Rome's Capitoline Square (Piazza del Campidoglio) with its monumental staircase leading up the Capitoline hill, past ancient statues of Castor and Pollux. The square is flanked by palaces on three sides: the Palazzo Senatorio in the center, for which Michelangelo rebuilt the façade and added its twin stairway; the Roman city hall, Palazzo dei Conservatori, which he designed; and, facing it, Palazzo Nuovo, which houses the Capitoline Museum, the oldest in the world, with its unparalleled collection of antiquities. Michelangelo had the ancient bronze equestrian statue of Marcus Aurelius placed in the center of the square, and he designed the rectangles-within-ovals motif on the surface of the piazza.

Toward the end of his life, Michelangelo worked on two unfinished marble versions of the *Pietà*, a theme he returned to after more than a half century. In the first (1550–55), originally intended for his own tomb and now in the Cathedral of Florence, the Virgin Mary, Mary Magdalen, and Joseph of Arimathea (according to some, Nicodemus) try to hold up

Christ's pathetically limp body, mangled by death. The face of Joseph is a self-portrait. In the *Rondanini Pietà* (1554–64), in Milan's Castello Sforzesco, the elongated figures of Christ and Mary seem as much a reversion to Gothic as an anticipation of twentieth-century sculpture. Mary is supporting her son's body from behind, clasping him closely, with her sorrowful face above his.

In one of his poems, Michelangelo had expressed these thoughts:

Ah me, ah me, how I have been betrayed
by these fleeting days of mine and by the mirror,
which tells the truth to all who gaze in it!
This happens to those who leave too much to the end—
as I have done, until my time has fled—
and find themselves, like me, grown old in a day.
Too late now to repent or to prepare,
too late for counsel, with my death so near.
My own worst enemy,
I spill my soul in tears and sighs—in vain,
for there's no greater evil than lost time.

The man whose artistic career spanned seventy-five years lost very little time. He worked at the *Rondanini Pietà* until six days before his death in Rome on February 18, 1564, a few weeks shy of his eighty-ninth birthday. At his bedside were Tommaso Cavalieri and the first "Breeches-maker," Daniele da Volterra.

The world's greatest artist lies buried in Florence's Santa Croce, in the company of Ghiberti, Machiavelli, Galileo, and Rossini. Vasari designed the monument, with three female figures representing the arts—sculpture, painting, and architecture—in which this devoted admirer and biographer claimed Michelangelo excelled all other artists: "The facility with which he achieved difficult effects was so great that they seem to have been created without effort."

The human body, especially the heroic male nude, was the beginning and end of Michelangelo's quest—the visible manifestation of an eternal beauty, goodness, and energy, God's image on earth. It was ironic that such a connoisseur of human beauty should himself be ugly, with his furrowed brow, small eyes, large ears, squashed nose, thin lips, and sparse forked beard. In periods of sustained creation, he subsisted for days only on bread and wine and hardly ever removed his clothes; in old age, he wore dogskin boots for months on end, which, when finally peeled off, took a layer of skin with them. He was a sarcastic and argumentative know-it-all, scornful of inferior talents, surly even with popes. "Michelangelo is terrible," Leo X once said, "one cannot deal with him." A haunted man who lived only for his art—sometimes working at night by the light of a candle stuck into a cardboard hat—he became very wealthy but lived like a poor man.

In one of his poems he describes himself as broken in body from his labors and cooped up in his tiny dark house with its thousand spiders and cobwebs and human excrement just outside the entrance. He wonders what good it has done him to have created so many "puppets" with his art, which has now left him "so poor and old, a slave to others' whims, / that if I die not soon I am undone."

Twenty-seven

Sprezzatura and Castiglione's concept of the gentleman

The courtier's, soldier's, scholar's, eye, tongue, sword . . .
The glass of fashion and the mold of form,
The observed of all observers.
— William Shakespeare, *Hamlet* (c. 1601)

IN THE ANCIENT WORLD, Confucius spoke eloquently of the literary and musical education, of the deference, courtesy, and service to one's prince, and of the ceremonious piety toward family and ancestors that marked the Chinese gentleman. Two thousand years later, Count Baldassare Castiglione (1478–1529) synthesized the chivalrous ideals of the medieval knight with the educational program of the humanists in his ground-breaking full-length portrait of the Renaissance gentleman, *Il libro del cortegiano* (*The Book of the Courtier*). Although there had been many medieval handbooks of manners throughout Europe, Castiglione's depiction of the model gentleman as a man of honor with refined taste would long serve as the Western world's counterpart of the Confucian ideal.

Castiglione was born into a noble family at Casatico, in the duchy of Mantua, on December 6, 1478. For his education, he was sent to Milan, where he learned Greek and Latin and also studied the Italian poets. At the splendid court of the Milanese duke Ludovico Sforza, he excelled in horsemanship and martial exercises, and he later saw action against the Spanish at the Battle of the Garigliano (1503), fighting under Francesco Gonzaga, Marchese of Mantua.

In 1504 Castiglione transferred his services to Guidobaldo da Monte-feltro, Duke of Urbino, whom he served as a diplomat for nine years. In the fifteenth century the court of this hill town in the Apennines, a tiny principality of forty square miles and 150,000 souls, twenty miles inland from the Adriatic, had been one of the most civilized places in the world. Not only had Urbino seen the birth of Bramante and his kins-man Raphael, but Guidobaldo's father, Federigo da Montefeltro (reigned

1444–82), had been an ideal Renaissance prince—scholar, outstanding condottiere, enlightened patron of the arts, meticulously just ruler, and refined gentleman. Piero della Francesca had painted his hook-nosed portrait in profile, and Luciano Laurana had built his famous palace. In a painting of 1476 Federigo d'Urbino is shown reading a book in his library (among the greatest in Europe) dressed in armor and with his young son holding a scepter beside him.

The little boy in the painting grew into Federigo's learned but hapless and gout-ridden successor, Guidobaldo. At his court, among other literary men, Castiglione found the poet Pietro Bembo and the comic dramatist Bernardo Dovizzi da Bibbiena (both of them later to become cardinals). For the carnival of 1506 Castiglione, an accomplished poet in both Latin and Italian, presented, in shepherd's dress, the eclogue *Tirsi*, which he had written with his cousin. The work paid homage to members of the court (many of whom reappear in *Il Cortegiano*) as rustic swains and bucolic lasses. In 1506–7 Castiglione visited England to accept the Order of the Garter for Guidobaldo from Henry VII.

In later life, Castiglione looked back on these years at Urbino as a kind of golden age. Not only did he form close friendships with the members of its court, but he also fell in love with the ailing Guidobaldo's wife, Duchess Elisabetta Gonzaga, whose austerely forbidding portrait in Florence's Uffizi features an eerily long forehead, complete with scarab, and a severely patrician face with narcotized eyes. She, too, was a semi-invalid, and seven years Castiglione's senior, but her gentle ways made him keep a portrait of her behind a mirror in his room, along with the sonnets and madrigals he composed about her.

The Book of the Courtier, written between 1513 and 1524, began as an act of nostalgia for the court the author described as "the very abode of joyfulness." The work fulfilled a desire to reevoke an Arcadia and leave behind a group portrait of the friends of his youth, many of them dead by the time of publication in 1528. In a phrase that William Butler Yeats especially recalled, which "often moved me till my eyes dimmed," Castiglione ends the roll call of his deceased friends with, "Never be it spoken without tears, the Duchess, too, is dead."

It is in the salon of the duchess that Castiglione sets his series of dialogues on four successive evenings in the spring of 1507. Since Guidobaldo always retired right after supper, the duchess's moderator for the discussions is Lady Emilia Pia, widow of Guidobaldo's brother. The book purports to be a transcription of a parlor game Elisabetta's courtiers play to while away the time amidst the music and dancing. They decide their topic of conversation will be "to form in words a perfect courtier," much as Machiavelli, at about the same time, articulated his notion of the ideal prince (see Essay 25). Castiglione's classical precedents, however, were Plato, who described an ideal state in the *Republic*; the Greek writer Xenophon, who portrayed an ideal king in his *Cyropaedia*; and Cicero, whose *De oratore* dealt with the training of an ideal orator-statesman.

Following in this distinguished tradition, Castiglione set himself a practical and far from trivial goal—to describe the formation of the members of a ruling class whose job was to advise their prince. As the book makes clear, one of the reasons the ideal courtier has to be such a pleasant, accomplished, and trustworthy companion to his prince is to ensure that the latter—who may be vicious and ignorant—will confide in him and allow his baser instincts to be guided by the courtier's virtue and wisdom. In addition to this public concern, Castiglione examines the art of self-cultivation, providing a Renaissance humanist perspective on the question of how best to live in this world. The book thus deals with crucial issues of political, social, cultural, and personal amelioration.

Sitting in a circle around the duchess, the group of about twenty men and women at the court of Urbino listen to a small number of main speakers, but interrupt and challenge them as they please. The dialogue format serves a dialectical purpose: Many of the viewpoints of the speakers are questioned or ridiculed by others, so that Castiglione's meaning is more complex and subtle than in any cookbook approach to becoming a model gentleman.

The author claims that although he missed these talks while away in England, a friend who was there reported what went on, and now he is trying to reconstruct what the four evenings were like. In the first two books of *Il Cortegiano*, the accomplishments of the ideal courtly gentleman, and the circumstances in which he should exhibit them, are discussed. Although noble birth may not be essential for a courtier, the first speaker, Count Lodovico da Canossa, believes it certainly helps, because living exemplars of refined manners and gentility should surround the budding young gentleman. Noble or not, he must at least be handsome and simpatico, so that he wins over at first sight all the high and mighty who set eyes on him.

Above all, the courtier must be an accomplished soldier and must demonstrate expertise in every kind of weapon and in the arcana of dueling. To help him prepare for this major role of his, he must master all sorts of physical exercises: horsemanship, hunting, jousting, fencing, hurling stones, running, leaping, wrestling, swimming, and even tennis. The courtier must demonstrate absolute bravery and unswerving loyalty in war and should try to perform his heroic deeds as nearly alone as possible and in sight of his prince and high-ranking officers. He must also be modest about his accomplishments—"talk little and do much"—since a braggadocio is universally despised.

Of course, the courtier must be a man of honor and integrity with nothing boorish, self-indulgent, or dissolute about him. His liberal education must include the study of Latin and Greek, the Italian poets, and other modern languages, especially French and Spanish. He must develop a fluent style in writing and speaking Italian, following the great Tuscan models of Petrarch and Boccaccio, but also more recent poets, such as Politian and Lorenzo de' Medici. The courtier must be able to write forceful prose and verse in Latin and, for the delight of the ladies, in the vernacular, too. Before he can write or speak well, however, he must acquire knowledge, since an ignoramus has nothing worthwhile to say.

The ability to provoke laughter is prized as a great asset, and the book incorporates a mini-essay on humor and a handbook of jokes and facetious sayings that was often mined by readers. The courtier should be able to converse wittily and tell amusing stories, though always with good taste, discretion, and decorum. Puns are fine, but scurrility, obscenity, buffoonery, or personal attacks on the unfortunate—or those who could make the mocker regret his words—are not advised. The company and the circumstances must be carefully weighed before the courtier can decide how best to speak or act at any time.

A gentleman should be able to draw and have an appreciation of painting. He should excel in music, and be able to read it, sing, play (but not wind instruments, which deform the face), and dance, since these skills are much admired by women, whose love spurs the courtier on to worthy pursuits. He must manage to be charming without exciting envy or ill will. His dress should be sober, not foppish, black being more pleasing for men than any other color.

Everything the courtier does must have a certain *grazia* (gracefulness), which should be acquired early from the best teachers. Yet it can also be achieved in another way. In a key passage in Book One, Castiglione explains that the "most universal rule" for acquiring grace is "to flee as much as possible . . . affectation; and, perhaps to coin a word, to make use in all things of a certain *sprezzatura,* which conceals art and presents everything said and done as something brought about without laboriousness and almost without giving it any thought" (26). What was this *sprezzatura?* Literally, it meant "undervaluing, setting a small price on," with the hint of a slightly superior disdain. Here it means an assumed air of doing difficult things with an effortless mastery and an air of nonchalance so as to make them look easy or like matters of small importance.

Castiglione's advice thus resembles that of the old Latin tag *ars est celare artem* (art consists in concealing art), or Ovid's *ars casum simulat* (art produces the illusion of spontaneity). How well the courtier does something is supposed to seem a matter of indifference to him, though of course he is acting, and his naturalness stems from long practice. In this studious avoidance of any appearance of affectation, his insouciance becomes a kind of affectation—but a well-concealed one. In the same mode, he should never volunteer to do what he excels at, but wait to be invited to do it, and then appear to have just "tossed it off"—although Castiglione advises him always to come prepared for such displays.

This notion of a social mask, or a disjunction between appearance and reality that is the very patina of civilization, reveals Castiglione's Renaissance aestheticism: The ideal gentleman, in creating an impression and feigning for effect, displays the characteristics of a work of art. Indeed, one "acts" the gentleman, and it is this artifice that allows social life to be a consciously shaped thing of beauty rather than a mere happenstance. This still-important Italian obsession—*far una bella figura* (to make a good impression, cut a fine figure)—is at the heart of Castiglione's vision of life as social artifact.

The formation of the ideal courtly lady is discussed in Book Three by Giuliano de' Medici, son of Lorenzo the Magnificent. Her accomplishments should be similar to those of the courtier, except that she must guard her virtue and reputation much more closely and avoid unsuitable activities, such as martial exercises and sports. In place of these, she must cultivate a sweetness and gentleness that "shall always make her appear the woman without any resemblance to a man" (3.4). But certainly "women can understand everything that men can" (3.12), and the great women of past and present are lauded in a long digression. Beauty is indispensable, however, for "that woman lacks much who lacks beauty" (3.4), but the ideal lady must also avoid vanity and frivolity in her dress and any brazenness of demeanor.

A courtly woman must know how to speak with every type of man but never in such a way as to allow her chastity to be impugned. She must never be confused with a courtesan: Although charming and delightful in conversation, dancing, and singing, and though vivacious,

witty, affable, and far from prudish, she must never be bawdy or lascivi-
ous. Since the courtly woman must also understand the niceties of love,
this third book contains advice on all the little feints and countermoves
of aristocratic courtship leading to marriage. Above all, if she marries,
the courtly lady must be a good wife, mother, and mistress of her household.

In Book Four, after Ottaviano Fregoso discusses the relation between
the courtier and his prince, the Venetian patrician, humanist, and historian Pietro Bembo takes center stage. This complex man, a Ciceronian
purist in Latin prose style and an ardent Petrarchan sonneteer in Italian,
a worshiper of Lucrezia Borgia and the father of three illegitimate children who later became an esteemed cardinal, gives a long and eloquent
description of what is often called Platonic love but owes much to the
Neoplatonism of Lorenzo the Magnificent's resident philosopher Marsilio Ficino (see Essay 21).

When the courtier becomes old, sexual love becomes ridiculous for
him, so Bembo outlines a more suitable course: the *scala d'amore* (ladder
of love) by which he can ascend from earthly beauty to the heavenly
beauty of God and his truth. Since all beauty is from God, physical
beauty in humans is only an outward manifestation of their inner goodness, and sexual possession is not the way to attain true enjoyment of it.

In this type of refined love, sexual union is an illusory pleasure, soon
giving rise to all the usual jealousies and petty concerns of the flesh. Sensual love, which brings more pain than pleasure, is excusable in youth
but not in an older man, who should feed exclusively on the lovely visage of his chosen lady and the melodiousness of her voice and singing.
He must strive to obey, please, and honor her in all things, loving the
beauty of her mind and virtue as well as the beauty of her form. Between
true Platonic lovers, kissing is allowed because, at least according to
Bembo, it is a commingling of souls, not of bodies.

But this is only the lowest rung of the *scala d'amore*. The love of
beauty in his lady should lead the lover to rise to the love of an abstract
beauty in all beautiful women, and, finally, since true beauty is incorpo-
real, to the intellectual love of the universal form of divine beauty itself.
Bembo, who ends with a prayer to God, "enemy of boorish savagery and
baseness" (4.70), is so rapt with his vision that Lady Emilia has to break
the spell by tugging at the hem of his gown and jokingly recalling him
back to earth lest his exalted soul depart from his body. The company is
surprised to find it is morning already, all the stars having disappeared
except Venus, the morning star of love.

As at the end, with Lady Emilia's humorous intervention, the book is marked by a genial tone, full of laughter and teasing repartee, and devoid of any pedantic insistence on arbitrary rules or pronunciamentos, making it a perpetual delight and one of the most civilized books ever written. Indeed, its Socratic open-mindedness and the obvious affection of all the characters for one another, different as they are, are among its most admirable qualities.

In April 1508 Duke Guidobaldo died at age thirty-six. Castiglione stayed on in the service of Guidobaldo's successor, Francesco Maria della Rovere, and of the widowed Elisabetta. Duke Francesco made Castiglione a count and in 1513 sent him as ambassador to Rome, where he met Raphael, Michelangelo, and Giulio Romano, and rejoined Bembo. In 1516, at age thirty-eight, Castiglione married a beautiful fifteen-year-old noblewoman, Ippolita Torelli, who bore him three children. Four years later, she died in childbirth, soon followed by his dear friends Raphael and Cardinal Bibbiena. Overwhelmed with grief, Castiglione became a churchman.

In his new life he journeyed to the court of Emperor Charles V in Spain as papal nuncio for Clement VII, who had to endure the terrible sack of Rome by Charles's troops in 1527. Although he hadn't seen this disaster coming, Castiglione was blamed by the pope for doing nothing to avert it, and he almost died of depression over it. Meanwhile, *Il libro del cortegiano,* Castiglione's *A la recherche du temps perdu,* was finally published in Venice in 1528 by the firm of Aldus Manutius in 1,030 copies.

Emperor Charles named Castiglione Bishop of Avila, but the disillusioned Italian died soon afterward in Toledo, on February 8, 1529, at age fifty. Charles, who knew whereof he spoke, praised Castiglione as *"uno de los mejores caballeros del mundo,"* and *Il Cortegiano* became one of the emperor's favorite books.

Castiglione's masterpiece went through more than sixty editions in Italy alone in the sixteenth and seventeenth centuries, and his vision of the ideal courtier was to be vastly diffused throughout the Western world. As Jacob Burckhardt observed, "In the sixteenth century the Italians had all Europe for their pupils, both theoretically and practically, in every noble bodily exercise and in the habits and manners of good society." Castiglione's courtier became a model for the civilized gentleman for almost four centuries, even beyond the French Revolution, until the First World War leveled all of society in its bloody trenches.

The book was translated into Spanish in 1534, French in 1537, Latin in 1561, and German in 1565. It was often reprinted outside Italy at a time when the European intelligentsia took for granted a knowledge of Italian, along with Latin and Greek. It also influenced hundreds of courtesy and etiquette books, including the Italian *Galateo* of Giovanni Della Casa (see Essay 29).

Sir Thomas Hoby's classic English translation of Castiglione, published in 1561, was immensely popular in the Elizabethan era. Sir Thomas Elyot's *Book of the Governor* (1531) and Roger Ascham's *Schoolmaster* (1570), both about the education of the English ruling class, were influenced by Castiglione. Toward the end of the sixteenth century, Sir Philip Sidney was seen as the perfect incarnation of Castiglione's cultured, sophisticated, and martial gentleman. John Milton's *On Education* (1644) and John Locke's *Thoughts on Education* (1693) continued in the footsteps of Castiglione. Samuel Johnson told Boswell that *Il Cortegiano* was "the best book that ever was written upon good breeding," and Lord Chesterfield's famous *Letters* to his son on how to be a gentleman (1774) were in the same tradition. As a young man, James Joyce read Castiglione and became more polite, though, according to his brother, also less sincere. W. B. Yeats, an ardent admirer of Castiglione, visited Urbino with Lady Gregory and had a friend read *The Courtier* aloud to him one summer. In "To a Wealthy Man. . . ," he calls Guidobaldo's court "that grammar school of courtesies / Where wit and beauty learned their trade."

Named Baldassare for one of the three Wise Men, Castiglione still gazes out at us from his portrait by Raphael in the Louvre: an unassuming man with hands modestly folded, self-sufficient in his integrity, half-hidden behind his huge hat, beard, and furs, but with his deeply intelligent blue eyes revealing the depths of a humane civilization. An even greater portrait of Castiglione remains that of the ideal gentleman he left behind in the pages of *Il Cortegiano*.

Twenty-eight

Aretino: Self-publicist, pornographer, "secretary of the world"

. . . that notorious ribald of Arezzo.
—John Milton, *Areopagitica* (1644)

THE ANCIENT GREEKS called them *anaischyntographoi*—"writers of shameless things." We call them pornographers, but the man who revivified the literary genre of the obscene in the Western world was called by his own contemporaries "divine." In a 1545 portrait by Titian, Pietro Aretino looks more like a bearded satyr or an old Silenus, stuffed with meat, than an Olympian or Judeo-Christian deity.

Yet a certain numinous quality must have inhered in this man of plebeian origin who, in the hierarchical sixteenth century, armed with nothing beyond his literary talents, coerced nobles, prelates, and kings to cough up rich gifts. With no formal education to speak of, Aretino set himself up as an enemy of the literary pedants of his day, developing a prose style that was popular in the best and worst senses—clear, colloquial, and forceful, but torrentially verbose and unrefined. Like the protojournalist he was, he threw his works together at breakneck speed, since he saw them as mere commodities. A pioneer in manipulating the power of the press, Aretino dictated the tastes of mass audiences as well as of society's elite, all to further his own selfish ends. Such swarms sought out his house in Venice to complain of this or that prince or priest that he referred to himself in a letter of 1537 as "the secretary of the world."

We don't even know his last name, but this Pietro of Arezzo—the Aretine, or Aretino—was born on April 20, 1492, only months before the European discovery of the New World. Although Aretino liked to claim he was a nobleman's bastard, the man who first figured out how to use the new world of print media to propel himself into fame and fortune was the son of a shoemaker named Andrea (or Luca) and Tita Bonci, who served as a model for the Madonna to painters.

After an early life of vagabondage, Aretino settled in Rome in 1517, where he amused Pope Leo X with his satirical poems and became a leading writer of pasquinades. These were lampoons, usually written in verse, that were appended to the ancient Roman statue popularly called *Pasquino* at the corner of the Piazza Navona, which served as a community bulletin board for anonymous wits who wished to lambaste the pope, the cardinals, or Roman politics in general. For the papal conclave of 1521–22, Aretino wrote a pasquinade sonnet in which he expresses no surprise that it was taking so long to choose a new pope—look at the candidates: One of the cardinals has a wife, another can't keep his hands off boys, while the others are gluttons, counterfeiters, flatterers, thieves, heretics, traitors, spies for Spain or France, or simoniacs who would sell God himself at any and all times. When a dour Dutchman was finally elected as Adrian VI, Aretino composed a pasquinade accusing the College of Cardinals of betraying Christ by choosing a "Teutonic barbarian" as pope. This said, he decided to skip town for a while.

When the candidate whom Aretino had backed, Cardinal Giulio de' Medici, mounted the papal throne as Clement VII in 1523, Aretino came hurrying back to Rome but soon found himself at the center of a pornographic storm. The artist Giulio Romano had created sixteen explicitly erotic drawings of couples having sex in more or less acrobatic positions. The drawings were copied as engravings by Marcantonio Raimondi, who was soon thrown into jail by the Church authorities. Aretino, a friend of both men, struck a blow for artistic license by writing a tailed sonnet (seventeen lines instead of fourteen) for each of the engravings. These *Sonnetti lussuriosi* (Lewd Sonnets), or *Sonnets for the Positions of Giulio Romano* (1524), have been called a Renaissance mini-*Kamasutra*, but they are only crude dialogues between the pictured men and women in which the latter mostly clamor to be sodomized. Nonetheless, the illustrated book became notorious throughout Europe. Even Ben Jonson had a character declare in his *Volpone*, "But, for a desperate wit, there's Aretine! / Only his pictures are a little obscene."

The sonneteer thought it best to flee from Rome a second time. After his return he was attacked in the street one night in 1525 for writing an insulting sonnet about (or for seducing) a kitchen maid of an ecclesiastical enemy of his. His assailant, the maid's beau, stabbed Aretino in the chest and right hand, two fingers of which had to be cut off. When his former protector, Clement VII, refused to arrest Aretino's attacker, the poet left Rome for good and soon started smearing the pope in his writings.

After some detours, Aretino headed for the only city in his day where his talents for pornography, satire, and self-promotion could blossom unmolested into a putrid *fleur du mal*. Settling in cosmopolitan Venice in 1527 at age thirty-five, he soon built up a menagerie of mistresses, literary secretaries, whores, servants, pathics, and parasites in the palazzo he rented on the Grand Canal opposite the Rialto. He continued to luxuriate in decadent Venetian splendor until his death almost thirty years later.

How did he pay for all of this? As Aretino well understood, "We rise from the world whenever we hear our name glorified, and are transported beyond mortality when it is sung." He would thus write to a nobleman or ruler offering to formally praise him in prose or verse and hinting at literary retaliation with one of his scurrilous satires if no payment was forthcoming. As incredible as it seems, the loot came pouring in from far and wide. It remains astounding how many huge fish he caught with this form of literary blackmail, especially since even his adulatory writings are so crammed with undigested hyperbole that they often sound like they're mocking the recipient instead of praising him.

All of Aretino's literary labors had the goal either of extorting cash, gifts, and pensions or of serving as a huge gossip mill that the cognoscenti, glitterati, and burgeoning middle class felt constrained to be aware of, like today's sitcom, shock radio, or blockbuster film du jour. His writings sold throughout Europe, since he himself proved to be an irresistible combination of international celebrity, scandal sheet columnist, bohemian, society reporter, muckraker, poetaster, stud, libeler, satirist, critic, literary gangster, bon vivant, name-dropper, buffoon, and pederast. Medallions were struck in his honor, and his bloated face appeared at his doorway in a laurel-crowned marble bust. He dressed like a lord and gave Lucullan banquets. All sorts of things, such as horses and types of Murano glassware, were given *Aretino* as their brand name, including several favorite groupies, who proudly called themselves "Aretines." Remaining a sensation and all the rage long after he should have become merely tiresome, he managed to fool everyone except himself.

This debauchee with the soul of a gifted pimp hobnobbed with all the rich and famous of his time. He became the artistic agent of his great friend Titian—each addressed the other as *compare caro* in their correspondence—selling his paintings to Francis I of France and arranging for Emperor Charles V, popes, and other notables to sit for his *compare*. Francis gave Aretino the thick gold chain that he wears in his portrait by Titian in Florence's Pitti Palace. (The Latin motto on the chain may be translated, "His tongue will always speak falsehood.")

But the self-styled *flagello de' principi* (scourge of princes) did his share of sucking up to them, too. He wrote a consolatory letter to Francis I on the king's defeat at Pavia and subsequent imprisonment by Charles V. He accepted a collar and pension from Charles, who enlisted him as a molder of public opinion in an era still without newspapers. Like Falstaff horning in on the serious affairs of Henry IV, Aretino wrote a letter urging Charles to make peace with Pope Clement VII in 1527—after the sack of Rome—and a letter of condolence to Clement in the same year. Henry VIII sent Aretino money for a literary dedication, and the future Philip II of Spain sent him yet another collar.

"Men of worth should consider the day I was born a truly memorable one," Aretino wrote in 1548. "I have forced all the great of the earth— dukes, princes, and monarchs—to become tributaries to my genius! All across the length and breadth of the world, fame has nothing but me as its topic." His parading as a champion of the common man against the mighty made him the idol of the small fry, but why princes should have feared and appeased him is harder to fathom.

Certainly, he must have possessed considerable charisma beyond that of the uninhibited charlatan, and his conversation must have been lively. Even his enemy, the satirist Francesco Berni, admitted "he talks well." Aretino corresponded with the Doge of Venice, the King of Algiers, popes, cardinals, dukes, counts, Michelangelo, Giorgio Vasari, Sebastiano del Piombo, the architects Jacopo Sansovino and Sebastiano Serlio, the poet and religious enthusiast Vittoria Colonna, and other scholars, artists, and literary figures. Tintoretto painted his ceiling, and among his other friends were the refined Cardinal Pietro Bembo (see Essay 27) and Lodovico Ariosto, who lauds Aretino in *Orlando Furioso*. The greatest Italian condottiere of his day, the short-lived Medici known as Giovanni delle Bande Nere, missing the orgies he and Aretino organized together, wrote that he couldn't live without him.

Beyond all the hype, Aretino was a writer of undeniable talent and verve. His most famous comedy, *La cortigiana* (1525), was probably meant as a satire of Castiglione's *The Book of the Courtier* (see Essay 27). In this play, when a man from Siena comes to Rome to get rich by learning how to become a courtier, his self-appointed tutor tells him it involves, among other arts, those of the blasphemer, gambler, whoremonger, heretic, flatterer, slanderer, ignoramus, and sodomite. Aretino's other four comic plays are predictably peopled by hypocrites, sluts, cuckolds, swindlers, and dupes, but he also managed to write a well-regarded tragedy, *Orazia* (1546), and an unfinished, nonlamented epic on the House of Gonzaga, *Marfisa*, a rip-off of his friend's *Orlando Furioso*.

His *Ragionamenti* (*Dialogues*, 1534–36), which take place among prostitutes, have also been seen as parodies of Castiglione's great conduct book, the implication being that courtiers, like whores, must learn to act and play a role. In Aretino's work the old courtesan Nanna expounds the obscene doings of women in their three Aretinian guises as nuns, wives, and prostitutes, in which the last come off best. The nunneries in these dialogues are replete with Murano glass dildos, obscene murals, monkish lovers, and proto-Sadean group sex scenes. The tales about wives are Boccaccian stories of deception, only far viler. In teaching her daughter Pippa how to be a whore, Nanna includes instruction in how to speak, laugh, dress, and sit at table in a debased version of the advice given in *The Book of the Courtier*. When dealing with noblemen, "so that they will think you adore the scholarly virtues," she says, "beg them to recite a sonnet, a song, a satire, or suchlike foolishness." *The Dialogues* and other pornographic works of Aretino's set the dubious standard for this species of literature throughout Europe.

More akin to his *Lewd Sonnets* are the *Dubbi amorosi* (Amorous Legal Cases), which purport to state and respond to cases in law that have arisen in a bordello. A stanza in ottava rima states the obscene legal question, and one in the same meter hands down the verdict, usually exonerating the perpetrators of any and all venereal acts. These sendups, which make use of Latin legalese tags, are also parodies of the *questioni d'amore* of Provençal, French, and Italian literature, which handed down decisions in matters of chivalric love.

Above all, Aretino was a best-selling letter writer and the first European author of letters in a vernacular tongue to publish them. There grew to be six volumes of them, and many of these three thousand missives were fulsome encomia designed to extort gifts. About a fifth of them deal with art and artists, and here Aretino, who had dabbled in painting when young, may be seen at his best, since he had a finely observant eye, an admiration for artists, and an appreciation of natural beauty.

His letters to Michelangelo are shameless, however. After servilely begging the great artist for some drawings—"there are many kings but only one Michelangelo"—but all in vain, Aretino had the effrontery to suggest what subjects *The Last Judgment*, then in progress, should contain. The painter replied that although Aretino had described the terrifying event as if it had already occurred (and he had been there to witness it), it was too late to change the plan for the fresco. Aretino subsequently wrote hypocritical letters in which he clucked his tongue at the indecent nudity of the finished masterpiece. Some have seen his features in Michelangelo's depiction of St. Bartholomew in the great doomsday fresco, along with the artist's self-portrait on the saint's flayed skin (see Essay 26).

Aretino's crowning impudence was his religious writing, which involved throwing together books about Christ (he had the temerity to call himself "the fifth Evangelist"), the Virgin Mary, St. Catherine of Alexandria, Thomas Aquinas, and other saintly figures. Charles V even entertained the notion of supporting this fat lecher for a cardinal's red hat, but when Aretino journeyed to Rome in 1554 for this express purpose, he had to settle for being made a Knight of St. Peter by Julius III. Prodigal he had always been, throwing away his vast unearned earnings as fast as they came in and always ready to help his friends, the poor, and those whose vices had landed them in misery.

After imbroglios past counting, clubbings and stabbings, and degrading literary and sexual quarrels, the most brazen of all self-publicists, who influenced Rabelais, Swift, Sade, and a host of other writers much greater than himself, died in his beloved Venice on October 21, 1556, at age sixty-four, a few months after making his confession—which must have been a lengthy one—and receiving Communion. He was buried in the little church of San Luca, and his complete works were placed on the Church's Index of Prohibited Books in 1559.

From a safe remove, Balzac called Aretino "the Voltaire of his century," but Francesco Berni, his contemporary, calls him "a rotten tongue, purulent and witless," and goes on in the same sonnet to accuse Aretino of having infected every nation, human, and animal, and of being hated by the heavens, God, and even the devil. He foresees Aretino's being beaten, stripped of his fineries, and quartered by the executioner, while his lickspittles spout prayers for his soul. None of this was to be— Aretino died suddenly of a stroke. But a more congenial legend claims he perished when he threw back his head and hit it on his chair, roaring with glee at a bawdy story his sisters had told him.

Twenty-nine

Giovanni Della Casa's *Galateo*: Etiquette book par excellence

After you're done blowing your nose, don't open your handkerchief and look in it, as if expecting pearls or rubies to have cascaded into it from your brain.

— Giovanni Della Casa, *Il Galateo* (1552–55)

WHEN ALLUDING TO someone's boorishness, Italians may still say, "He certainly never learned his *galateo*." Though there had been many earlier treatises on manners—William Caxton alone printed three in the late fifteenth century—there had never been one quite as useful or as witty as Giovanni Della Casa's, which soon became a classic in its field. Along with works like Machiavelli's *Prince*, Castiglione's *Courtier*, Guicciardini's *History of Italy*, Vasari's *Lives of the Artists*, Cellini's *Autobiography*, and Palladio's *Four Books of Architecture* (not to mention the epics of Ariosto and Tasso), Della Casa's much humbler contribution nonetheless became, according to philosopher Benedetto Croce, "one of those innovating books that sixteenth-century Italy gave to the modern world."

"We might accept it as a sequel to the *Courtier*," writes John Addington Symonds, "for while Castiglione drew the portrait of a gentleman, La Casa explained how this gentleman should conduct himself among his equals." The author of *Galateo ovvero de' costumi* (*Galateo, or On Manners*), usually referred to as Monsignor Della Casa, was powerfully influenced by Castiglione (see Essay 27), though without acknowledging his debt. Focusing on the details of behavior rather than on education, accomplishments, and an entire modus vivendi, the *Galateo*, though written only three decades after the *Courtier*, is the product of a more conservative age and urges the reader to avoid rocking the boat. Between the appearance of the two books, the Council of Trent had gotten under way, and the later work reflects some of the thought-policing and heightened conventionality of Counter-Reformation Italy.

Born to noble Florentine parents on June 28, 1503, in Mugello, Tuscany, about twenty miles outside of Florence, Giovanni Della Casa was sent to the University of Bologna to study law, but he also attended the lectures of the controversial materialist philosopher Pietro Pomponazzi. In those days some rebellious sons would defy their fathers by quitting law school and retiring to their villas to study Cicero and Virgil in depth, as Della Casa did in 1526, before journeying to Padua to study Greek. There he met the elegant Petrarchan poet, literary dictator, and future cardinal Pietro Bembo, whom Della Casa emulated in both his literary and his ecclesiastical endeavors.

Moving on to Rome, Della Casa, without the least trace of a religious vocation, took minor orders by way of embarking on a lucrative career in the Church. He also tried his hand at some fashionably obscene verses, notably the *"Capitolo sopra il forno"* ("Satire on the Oven"), which were published in Venice in 1538. Among his Latin compositions was a jocularly misogynist work, *Lepidissima quaestio, an uxor sit ducenda* (A Most Elegant Treatise on Whether to Take a Wife—the answer being a resounding no for men who wished to pursue high-powered political or scholarly careers). In 1540 Pope Paul III appointed Della Casa collector of tithes in the Florentine territories, and the exacting tax man took his work seriously indeed.

On returning to Rome, he was made papal treasurer, then the (totally absentee) Archbishop of Benevento, then the prestigious papal nuncio to Venice. Things were progressing smoothly for a man who was only forty-one. In Venice, Della Casa established the Inquisition in 1547 and prosecuted heretics with gusto, most prominently Pier Paolo Vergerio the Younger, the Bishop of Capodistria, who reminded everyone of his accuser's youthful dirty poems before seeking sanctuary in Protestant Germany. The monsignor replied with a few harrumphing Latin blasts of his own, but his early literary indiscretions would continue to haunt him throughout his life.

Once again in Rome, Della Casa compiled the Church's first Index of Prohibited Books (1548) in accordance with the Council of Trent. But he had an indomitable ambition to be named a cardinal, and once his hopes for appointment faded, he abandoned both his ecclesiastical career and Rome itself, retiring to private life in Venice and then the Abbey of Nervesa, near Treviso, in 1552.

Besides those infamous poems of his, the fact that he had an illegitimate son, Quirino, also may have militated against that cardinalate—although the irrepressible Cardinal Bembo's three illegitimate children had proved no obstacle. Della Casa now began composing a life of the late Bembo, as well as some intriguing lyrics in which the word *ostro*, or "cardinal's purple"—his one true love—resounds obsessively and plaintively. He also started writing the *Galateo*.

This masterpiece of Tuscan prose was hurled out a window by Vittorio Alfieri after the eighteenth-century poet and dramatist had read only its first word, a pretentious literary term for "since"—*Conciossiacosaché*—although a far greater poet, Giacomo Leopardi, pronounced the book "one of the most elegant and Attic prose works of the sixteenth century" (see Essay 41). Its title was formed from the first name of Della Casa's friend Galeazzo Florimonte, Bishop of Aquino and Sessa Aurunca, who urged him to write a manual of etiquette.

Adopting the persona of a *vecchio idiota*—ignorant old man—who has learned by experience and is now instructing a youngster of his, the author assumes a colloquial, cracker-barrel diction, replete with rustic images, for lightheartedly teaching his favorite nephew, Annibale Rucellai, "the modes of conduct that are to be observed or shunned in our dealings with others." Although many consider the subject frivolous, the speaker asserts that "good manners, pleasantness, and refinement, . . . if not virtues, are nonetheless very similar to them."

Besides, the great virtues—justice, fortitude, magnanimity—can be employed only rarely, whereas common etiquette is needed every day. Many individuals with little going for them beyond their social skills have risen higher in the world than more genuinely gifted people who don't know how to behave. Most people despise rude and unpleasant persons as much as they do those who are actually wicked—or even more so. Even a poor person with good manners has a rich and powerful patrimony.

Far from Castiglione's lofty courtly ideal, Della Casa is attempting to shape decent, everyday behavior by encouraging consideration for others' wishes and sensibilities, deference toward the group, and the taming of selfish desires by reason and decorum. His advice to the young who are just setting out in life is often very basic but still worth remembering: Don't talk too much or too little, don't regale the company with a blow-by-blow of your senseless dreams, don't interrupt, lie, bad-mouth, flatter, brag, engage in false modesties, or make fun of the deformed. Don't comb your hair or get drunk in public.

Acts to be avoided are those displeasing to the senses, the appetites, the imagination, or the intellect, and Della Casa goes through these various faculties, pointing out how each may be offended. Not only should you avoid *doing* ugly, dirty, or disgusting things in front of people, but even *mentioning* them. A few simple guidelines on hygiene and toileting are offered first: no touching certain body parts in public, no beginning to disrobe on your way to the bathroom, nor finishing to do so on your way back. A bit more advanced is this one: Don't wash your hands in public after coming back from the bathroom.

Regarding the sense of smell, it's always bad form to stick something under someone's nose and say, "Take a whiff of this! Doesn't it stink?" Be easy on others' ears, too: Don't grind your teeth, whistle, scream, drum with your fingers, make screeching noises with metal, or sing if you can't carry a tune. Don't deafen your company when you cough or sneeze, and try not to wet their faces. Don't bray like an ass when you yawn—or continue talking while yawning, like a mute trying to speak. Apropos of yawning, try not to overdo it in the first place, since it tells your company you're bored and betokens a dormant mind.

Table manners are the centerpiece of any treatise on etiquette, and the *Galateo* does not disappoint:

- Don't stick your nose in a glass of wine or over a dish that someone else has to drink or eat from in order to savor it (or even in your own glass or dish, since something could fall out of your nose—and the mere thought is revolting).
- Don't stuff both cheeks with food, or blow the ashes off a piece of toasted bread, because "never was there wind without rain."
- Don't wipe sweat off your face with a napkin (much less blow your nose in it) or get your fingers so greasy that the napkin gets loathsomely dirty from them.
- Don't leave the table, toothpick in mouth (like a bird making a nest) or behind your ear—and certainly not around your neck on a string.

Dressing is not a matter of self-expression; it should be done with the aim of avoiding offense to others by wearing clothes that are appropriate for one's age and class, following local usage. Lack of conformity in sartorial or tonsorial matters is equivalent to reproving or contradicting one's fellows. Men shouldn't deck themselves out like women, using curling irons on their hair (or beards). Here's a stricture with a cogent modern application: Clothes shouldn't have writing on them.

Conversation should avoid vulgar, trivial, or gross subjects. It shouldn't be too subtle or esoteric for the company to follow, nor should it cause anyone embarrassment or shame. It shouldn't be blasphemous or irreligious, and here Della Casa singles out the loose talk of Boccaccio's young narrators in the *Decameron* as a bad example (see Essay 17). At a party or at table, one shouldn't tell lugubrious stories or talk about "wounds, diseases, deaths, plagues." Men shouldn't always be droning on about their wife and kids: "My little guy really cracked me up last night. . . ." Offering unsought advice implies that the recipient has urgent need of one's superior wisdom: "That wine you drink isn't good for you—stick to the red!" If you're going to tell a story, make sure you've got it straight in your head beforehand, and don't torture your hearers with irrelevant details: "The guy who was that guy's son who lived on Watermelon Street—didn't you know him?—who married that Gianfigliazzi woman—the little skinny one who used to go to Mass in San Lorenzo. Whaddaya *mean*, 'No'? *Sure*, you knew him!"

Harmless practical jokes and gentle ribbing are fine in their place, but some people should *never* be trifled with. Witty rejoinders "should bite like sheep rather than dogs." Those who aren't good at it shouldn't tell jokes—it's as painful as watching a fat man dancing in his underwear. Only buffoons make faces to get people to laugh, and nothing is more plebeian than infantile puns and wordplays.

If Castiglione's keyword is *sprezzatura*, Della Casa stresses *leggiadria*, an elegant grace that emanates like an aura from one's actions, words, sentiments, and gestures, deriving from the Renaissance virtues of harmony, concordance, reasonableness, and proportion. Walking in the street, for example, shouldn't be too hurried or too shambling, limbs shouldn't be thrown every which way, and stomping along should be avoided. Don't stare at people (still critical advice for those riding the New York City subways), and don't shake your butt like a peacock wiggling its tail.

Della Casa's patriotic and anti-Spanish policy is evident where he decries the recent proliferation of fulsome ceremonious observances. All that bowing and scraping, all that fondness for empty titles, came into Italy as "foreign and barbarous" importations from Spain. Although you can't ignore prevailing customs—even bad ones—you can tone them down as much as possible.

Needless to say, chugging down toasts is bad form and another foreign custom, as the Italian word for *toast*, *brindisi* (from the German *Ich bringe dir*, "I offer to you"), makes abundantly clear. "I thank God," the sober monsignor declares, "that with all the other plagues that have descended on us from beyond the Alps, we haven't yet seen among us the very worst of them all: the notion that drunkenness is not only amusing but even admirable."

The book ends with a torrent of prohibitions, as if the monsignor's mind, at the end of his task, had been swamped with all the images of gross behavior he had encountered in his half century of life. Don't expose your tongue, pick at your beard, rub your hands together, or stretch while blissfully shouting out "*oimè, oimè*" like a peasant awakening beneath a haystack. Don't cluck or tsk with your tongue; don't laugh like an imbecile or at your own jokes. When telling a story, don't become so animated that you toss your head, roll your eyes around, stretch one eyebrow halfway up your forehead and the other way down by your chin, twist your mouth, spit in the faces of those you're talking to, and flail your arms about as if swatting flies.

"And what should I say of those who come out of their home office into company with a pen behind their ear? or carry their handkerchief in their mouth? or drape a leg over the table? or spit in their hands? or other innumerable gaucheries? They could never all be listed, and I'm not even going to try. In fact, some would perhaps venture to say that I've already mentioned too many."

Thus ends the golden little book of Giovanni Della Casa. From his melancholic literary retreat, a new pope, Paul IV, summoned him to be his secretary of state in April of 1555, though the gouty monsignor, disenchanted with the stormy court of Rome, would have preferred to decline. Yet again his hopes of a coveted red hat were frustrated, and he died little more than a year later, at age fifty-three, on November 14, 1556.

The *Galateo* was first published in Venice in 1558, almost two years after Della Casa's death. Read throughout Europe and first translated into English by Robert Peterson in 1576, it was the ancestor of works as different as Emily Post's *Etiquette*, Paul Fussell's hilarious *Class: A Guide through the American Status System*, the flustered columns of Miss Manners, and the various "gentlemen's guides" to this or that.

Far from being all fluff and fuss, Della Casa also left behind many somberly beautiful poems. A master Petrarchan sonneteer, he often employed enjambed (rather than end-stopped) lines and an intricate syntax and word order, profoundly influencing the prosody of John Milton's sonnets and even of *Paradise Lost*. "O bed / heaped high with bitterness! O harsh, hard nights!" he laments in one of his gloomy poems, and in another the feisty monsignor, who had descended into the political and religious maelstroms of his day, reminds us that "A fierce spirit once was mine—and warlike."

Thirty

Andrea Palladio and his "bible" of building

*Beauty will result from the form and correspondence of the whole,
with respect to the several parts, of the parts with regard to each
other, and of these again to the whole; that the structure may appear
an entire and complete body.*

—Andrea Palladio, *The Four Books of Architecture* (1570)

IN NOVEMBER 1817 Thomas Jefferson wrote to fellow Virginian James
Madison: "We are sadly at a loss here for a Palladio. I had three different
editions, but they are at Washington, and nobody in this part of the country has one unless you have. If you have, you will greatly aid us by letting
us have the use of it for a year to come." The book Jefferson sought was
I quattro libri dell'architettura (The Four Books of Architecture) by Andrea
Palladio,[1] still at that time the standard authority in its field. The ex-
president urged another friend, who was building a house, to obtain a
copy of "The Bible," as he referred to the book, "and stick close to it."

Andrea Palladio (1508–80), or Andrea di Pietro della Gondola, as he
was christened after his humble birth in Padua, was apprenticed to a
sculptor at a young age. In 1524 he moved to Vicenza, where he was
admitted to a stonemasons' guild. Within a short time he gained the
notice of poet, scholar, and diplomat Gian Giorgio Trissino, when he
was hired to help rebuild the poet's newly acquired villa in what was
thought to be ancient Roman style.

Impressed by the stoneworker's intelligence, Trissino schooled the
young man in music, science, mathematics, and Latin. More important,
he introduced his protégé to *The Ten Books on Architecture* by the architect and engineer Vitruvius, the only such treatise to survive from
ancient Rome. As a measure of his regard, Trissino bestowed on Andrea

---

[1]Andrea Palladio, *The Four Books of Architecture*, trans. by Isaac Ware (New York: Dover
Publications, Inc., 1965). Quotations from Palladio are from this edition.

the name *Palladio*, a reference to a character who helps expel the Goths from Italy in an epic poem of his.

Under Trissino's tutelage, Palladio became acquainted with the buildings of notable northern Italian architects, including the classicist Michele Sanmicheli; Jacopo Sansovino, who designed the Library of St. Mark's in Venice; Sebastiano Serlio, author of several influential tomes on architecture; and Alvise Cornaro, whose work was deeply influenced by Renaissance buildings in Rome. By this time, Palladio would also have read the outstanding treatise on the subject, *The Ten Books of Architecture*, published in 1452 by the ultimate Renaissance man, Leon Battista Alberti.

This remarkable character—architect, engineer, mathematician, poet, classical scholar, musician, athlete, and art theorist—espoused the concept of *concinnitas* (harmony). Like the ancient Greeks, Alberti believed that the mathematical relationships responsible for harmony in music can be embodied in the material world, such as piazzas laid out in a specified width-to-length ratio, to produce pleasing aesthetic effects. Throughout his career, Palladio, too, although less rigid about mathematical relationships than Alberti, would always strive for a classical proportion and symmetry in his structures.

The nascent architect traveled to Rome with Trissino in 1541 on the first of his five visits to the Eternal City. There Palladio studied the works of earlier Renaissance masters, including Bramante and Raphael, and scrutinized, measured, and sketched ancient buildings. Based on his diligent studies, he wrote *Le antichità di Roma* (*The Antiquities of Rome*), a guidebook first published in 1554 that remained a travelers' favorite for several centuries.

In 1546 Palladio received his first major public commission to construct a buttressing shell around the huge old town hall of Vicenza, the Palazzo della Ragione. He provided the rectangular structure, not fully completed until forty years after his death, with a two-story façade influenced by Sansovino's St. Mark's Library in Venice, which Palladio praised as the "richest" edifice since ancient times. The hallmark of the Palazzo della Ragione is the series of arched openings supported by small columns, an architectural composition henceforth known as the "Palladian motif."

Palladio's design for the Basilica in Vicenza demonstrated his mastery of the classical architectural vocabulary, while his work on numerous villas and palaces showed how creatively he could apply these same forms and aesthetic ideals in novel contexts. In 1550 he started work on the Palazzo Chiericati in Vicenza, one of the first of many edifices he would build for his wealthy clientele. The Palazzo Chiericati was a radical departure because, except for a solid wall in the center portion of the second story, the entire façade was open, punctuated only by Tuscan and Ionic columns.

The most renowned of the private dwellings that Palladio built for Venetian patricians and magnificoes, the Villa Capra, better known as the Villa Rotonda, dates from the mid-1550s and was completed after his death by his pupil, Vincenzo Scamozzi. Atop a small hill on the outskirts of Vicenza, the cube-shaped villa is crowned by a prominent central dome, a form previously used almost exclusively in churches, temples such as the Pantheon, and the Imperial Roman baths. On each of the four sides are stately porticoes that recall the façades of ancient Greek temples, complete with triangular pediments supported by Ionic columns and approached by steep banks of stairs.

The porticoes afforded the inhabitants different views of the countryside, as well as protection from the midday sun, a feature that may have accounted for the popularity of the design centuries later in Virginia and other southern states. Indeed, Palladio's villas were the first dwellings meant to achieve a harmonious unity with the landscape, since, as he wrote, "Architecture, . . . being an imitatrix of nature, can suffer nothing that either alienates or deviates from that which is agreeable to nature" (p. 25).

In the interior of the Villa Rotonda, the central space beneath the dome was intended as the main reception area. Lit only by the dome's oculus, it was surrounded by four symmetrical groups of rooms—parlors and bedrooms—each designed in accordance with mathematical ratios vis-à-vis the other rooms and the entire structure. The harmony and classical proportions of Villa Rotonda, one of the most gracious and elegant human dwellings ever devised, were ideally intended to mirror (and foster) the rationally ordered souls of its inhabitants.

Palladio experimented with several villa and palace designs. The Villa Barbaro at Maser, commissioned in 1555, is dominated by a two-story rectangular central-hall structure with a pitched roof. The building is flanked by single-story colonnades connecting to ancillary wings that might have housed servants, horses, or farm equipment. The villa's first floor opens out into a nymphaeum, a spring-fed, semicircular pool ringed by statuary.

Palladio might well have had the Villa Barbaro in mind while writing that as much as a gentleman may appreciate his house in the city, "perhaps he will not reap much less utility and consolation from the country house, where the remaining part of the time will be passed in seeing and adorning his own possessions. . . . The body will the more easily preserve its strength and health, . . . and the mind, fatigued by the agitations of the city, will be greatly restored and comforted" (p. 46). Stupendous edifices like the Villa Barbaro and Villa Rotonda dot the entire Veneto countryside, in the former mainland empire of the aristocratic Venetian Republic (see Essay 40).

In 1556 Palladio illustrated an Italian-language edition of Vitruvius, but he completed the book for which he is most revered only in 1570, after twenty years of building villas. True to his origins as a manual laborer, Palladio begins the first of *The Four Books of Architecture* with practical chapters on building materials, site selection, foundations, and wall construction. He continues with a lengthy discussion of the proper use of the five architectural orders—Doric, Ionic, Corinthian, Composite, and Tuscan. In a pivotal section of the first book, the master underscores his sensitivity to harmonic proportions and the congruity of structures and landscapes. The second is a pattern book that includes many of his designs for town and country homes. The third book presents bridge designs and plans for ancient buildings, and the fourth deals with reconstructions of ancient edifices. This four-part work was translated into nearly every European language.

Among Palladio's masterpieces are two Venetian churches, San Giorgio Maggiore (1566) and Il Redentore (1576), which dominate the city from across the Giudecca Canal. In these churches Palladio solved a problem that had long vexed Renaissance architects: how to attach a façade to a cross-shaped Christian basilica without the two components appearing to be simply tacked together. His solution integrated two temple fronts, one with single-story Corinthian pillars connecting the side aisles, and, superimposed on that, a narrower, taller central portion faced with Colossal Corinthian pillars fronting the lofty main aisle. That his classicizing church façades resembled those of his villas served both to domesticate the divine and to proclaim the right of humans to live in dwellings fit for the gods.

Andrea Palladio died in 1580, leaving Scamozzi to finish several works, including San Giorgio Maggiore and an architectural jewel, the Teatro Olimpico at Vicenza, with its classical, semicircular stage and three-dimensional backdrop depicting the streets of ancient Thebes in perfect perspective.

In the early seventeenth century, after the theater designer Inigo Jones was appointed surveyor to the British Crown, he traveled to Italy to study its buildings. Palladio and the *Four Books* became his ideal, and Jones returned to England convinced that buildings should be designed as rational and clearly organized wholes. With his Queen's House in Greenwich (1616) and the Banqueting House at Whitehall Palace in London (1619), Jones ignited the Anglo-Palladian movement, which eventually filled the English countryside with Palladian homes. The movement was reinvigorated during the Georgian period, starting about 1716, when James (Giacomo) Leoni published the first English translation of the *Four Books*, including high-quality engravings.

Palladio became the most influential Renaissance architect in England and the United States. Prominent British Palladians included Richard Boyle, Earl of Burlington, whose house at Chiswick is a copy of (and possibly an improvement on) the Villa Rotonda; Colen Campbell, Burlington's student and builder of Mereworth Castle in Kent; and the creator of London's sublime St. Paul's Cathedral, Christopher Wren. In America, Thomas Jefferson followed Palladio in designing Monticello as well as various buildings for the University of Virginia and the Capitol in Richmond, as did Peter Harrison, architect of King's Chapel in Boston. The Palladian style also spread to Ireland, Denmark, Sweden, Poland, and Russia.

Of Palladio, Goethe wrote, "There is something divine about his talent, something comparable to the power of a great poet."[2] The dozens of magnificent villas Palladio and his followers built in Venice and the Veneto still bear eloquent witness to his genius for visual poetry.

---

[2] J. W. Goethe, *Italian Journey (1786–1788)*, trans. by W. H. Auden and Elizabeth Mayer (London, Penguin Books, 1962), p. 64.

Thirty-one

Catherine de' Medici: Godmother of French cuisine

The Italians . . . made the French acquainted with the art of dining well, the excesses of which so many of our kings tried to suppress. But finally it triumphed in the reign of Henry II, when the cooks from beyond the mountains came and settled in France, and that is one of the least debts we owe to that crowd of corrupt Italians who served at the court of Catherine de' Medici.

—The French *Encyclopédie*, vol. 4 (1754)

CATHERINE DE' MEDICI (1519–89) was a fourteen-year-old orphan when she arrived in France in 1533 to marry Henry, son of King Francis I. Parentless, but indulged by her relatives, including Pope Clement VII, Catherine traveled to Marseilles with forks (the French still ate with their fingers), an acting troupe, dancers, high-heeled shoes, several copies of Machiavelli's *The Prince*, and a retinue of perfumers, embroiderers, firework makers, confectioners, and pastry cooks. But it was the Italian chefs accompanying Catherine to France who helped create the legend of how she transformed French cooking, which still languished in the Middle Ages, into what eventually became the *grande cuisine* of France.

Catherine, the great-granddaughter of Lorenzo the Magnificent (see Essay 21), lost both her parents, Lorenzo II de' Medici, Duke of Urbino, and his wife Madeleine de La Tour d'Auvergne, a princess of the House of Bourbon, within three weeks of her birth in Florence. It was to Catherine's father that Machiavelli had dedicated *The Prince* (see Essay 25), and Michelangelo immortalized him as one of the two Medici princes he sculpted for Florence's church of San Lorenzo. When Catherine was six months old, her grandfather's cousin, Cardinal Giulio de' Medici, brought her from Florence to Rome, where her great-uncle, Pope Leo X, could more carefully supervise her upbringing.

She lived in Rome until age six, when the cardinal, now Pope Clement VII, had her removed to Florence before Rome was viciously sacked by the armies of Emperor Charles V in 1527. In Florence, although she was shuttled between convents, she received a meticulous education from the nuns. By the time she was fourteen, Catherine was regarded as one of the most cultured young women of her day. This was quite an achievement considering her unsettled circumstances, which included late-night transfers through the streets of Florence to escape politicians who thought the interests of their short-lived Republic might best be served by the demise of this young heiress of the former ruling family.

When she was safely able to return to Rome after Florence surrendered to the Medici pope in 1531, the subject of her marriage became a preoccupation in Vatican circles. Clement VII prevailed, and Catherine was betrothed to Henry of Orléans, second son of King Francis I of France. The Pope presided over the marriage at Marseilles on October 28, 1533, and if contemporary reports can be trusted, he himself peeked through the curtains of the royal bed the next morning to make sure that all nuptial responsibilities had been fulfilled.

Francis I grew fond of his new daughter-in-law. She was a particularly good equestrienne and is credited with inventing the sidesaddle. The king, a well-read, sophisticated man, also discovered that Catherine was far better educated than the other ladies of the court and, delighting in her company, admitted her to his circle of intimates.

But Catherine could not captivate her husband. A major impediment was Diane de Poitiers, a beautiful and wealthy widow twenty years older than Henry who had become his mistress several years before his marriage. More important, Catherine at first failed to conceive, and popular opinion turned even more decisively against the princess the French had long derided as "The Italian Woman."

It was probably during the unhappy time before her children were born that Catherine made the changes in court cooking that lived on as France's *grande cuisine*. Italian cooking had achieved European prominence more than half a century earlier with the publication in 1474 by Bartolomeo Platina of the first cookbook ever printed, *De honesta voluptate et valetudine*, sometimes called *Platina's Book*, an influential work reprinted in six editions over the next thirty years. In 1498 further interest in the culinary arts was kindled by the publication of fragments of gastronomic learning from the ancient Roman gourmet Apicius, who provided recipes for such exotic dishes as peacock meatballs, crane, ostrich, parrot, and flamingo, "whose tongue is of unsurpassed taste."

On a more practical plane, Italian cooks had begun using spices to enhance the flavor and piquancy of ordinary meats and vegetables rather than merely to cover up the odor and taste of spoiled food. When Catherine arrived at the French court, its cuisine still largely consisted of thick, heavily spiced meat stews. Catherine's dowry included, in addition to her Florentine chefs, beans and vegetables that had never been seen in France, most notably broccoli, savoy cabbage, and the exotic artichoke.

Over the next several decades, she and her cooks helped cultivate a taste in the French court for delicacies such as liver crépinettes, quenelles, aspics, veal, sweetbreads, and the most sublime sauces. Truffles, which Italians had learned about from the Arabs, became a particular favorite. Catherine, a true *buona forchetta* (a good fork, or hearty eater), was partial to tournedos of beef and eventually became quite obese. Someone—Catherine or her cooks—displayed considerable imagination in naming some of her signature dishes, including Sea Bat in a Sulphurous Cauldron with Satan's Shrimp (skate and shrimp with marjoram, basil, red pepper, and garlic) and Witch's Snake Burnt at the Stake (eel).

Catherine also made ice cream popular at court, as well as iced aperitifs. (A century later, a Sicilian named Francesco Procopio opened a wildly successful ice cream shop on the Left Bank in Paris that remains in business today—Café Procope.) Catherine's confectioners introduced such tempting Italian treats as zabaglione, macaroons, custard cakes, and frangipane tarts (created in Italy for Catherine by her friend Cesare Frangipani). Melons, which, like truffles, came to Italy from Arab countries, also graced French tables by the mid-sixteenth century. Catherine's culinary innovations later influenced the legendary chef La Varenne, author of *Le Cuisinier français*, who worked in the kitchens of Maria de' Medici at the French court.

Forks, which Catherine reportedly introduced into France, evoked even greater fascination than the artichoke. Known in the Byzantine Empire many centuries earlier, forks had come to Venice and Italy by way of Constantinople. Other Europeans considered the Italians extremely fastidious for using them. Catherine also brought to the king's table elegant Venetian crystal goblets and may have inspired Francis I to commission the exquisite gold salt-cellar from Benvenuto Cellini that is now in the Vienna Kunsthistorisches Museum.

Catherine restored women, long absent from formal dining in France, to the banquet table. Before her time, court women ate in private because chewing was thought to "deform" their faces. Perhaps they had good reason to be self-conscious, since the level of table etiquette was appallingly low. In his *Galateo*, an urbane book on table manners and general decorum published in 1558 and widely read throughout Europe (see Essay 29), another Tuscan, Giovanni Della Casa, speaks of certain people at table "who resemble pigs with their snouts totally buried in their slop, never lifting their faces or raising their eyes (much less their hands) from their food, with both cheeks so stuffed that they look like they're playing the trumpet or blowing on a fire." Backed by the *Galateo*, Catherine discouraged such abominations in the court dining rooms.

During her time in France, printed menus and the organization of dinner courses were also introduced. She choreographed elaborate garden festivals that included feasts served by bare-breasted women, ballet, dramatic performances, and floating orchestras disguised as whales. Her ancestor, Lorenzo the Magnificent, had similarly delighted in arranging the spectacular carnivals of Florence.

These accomplishments alone would have secured Catherine's place in history, but she also had a full and turbulent personal and political life. After a decade of marriage, she finally gave birth to the first of her ten children. Her French subjects whispered that Catherine had laced her incomparably delicate white sauces with aphrodisiacs to lure her straying husband to bed.

It was Diane de Poitiers, though, not Catherine, who ran the royal nursery, procured wet nurses, and directed the staff. Contemporaries said that Catherine loved her husband deeply and tolerated his relationship with Diane in good humor. More likely, this apparent steadiness was the product both of her practical Medici temperament and the formidable self-control instilled in her during her convent days. To add to Catherine's humiliation, during Henry II's coronation in 1547 Diane became de facto queen, even sitting in the place that should have been Catherine's. Catherine later wrote to a friend that if she had been polite to Diane, "it was for the King's sake, yet I always told him that it was against my will, for no wife who loves her husband has ever loved his whore."

For the next dozen years, except when serving as regent of France while Henry was away at war, Catherine lived in the shadow of Diane. Yet the queen began to emerge as a distinguished patron of the arts, a fact acknowledged by Diane when she relinquished the royal heirs to Catherine for their education. The queen, a product of the finest Italian learning, devoted herself to the details of her children's studies. So renowned was the royal nursery that Mary Stuart, the future Mary Queen of Scots, was sent there at age five. It was Catherine who schooled the future tragic queen in Latin, molded her into a Renaissance woman, and eventually married her off to her eldest son.

In July of 1559 Henry II was killed during a tournament. Over the next decade and a half, Catherine managed, amid a series of fierce civil wars between Catholic factions and the Protestant Huguenots, to see three of her sons, the last kings of the Valois dynasty, ascend the French throne. Her conduct in the three tumultuous decades between her husband's death and her own in 1589 has been characterized by many historians as dictatorial and unscrupulous. Others have ascribed her policies to an obsession with the fate of her children at a time when widowed queens and their offspring were often violently swept off the scene.

The most notorious blot on her reputation was the St. Bartholomew's Day Massacre, which she ordered, or convinced her young son, Charles IX, to order. The planned "antiseptic strike" against the chief Huguenot leaders got out of hand, and several thousand Protestants were slaughtered in a bloodbath that started in Paris on August 23 and 24, 1572, and spread to the provinces.

As a result, many in France and Protestant England saw Catherine as the female counterpart of her fellow Florentine, Niccolò Machiavelli (see Essay 25). In Christopher Marlowe's tragedy *The Massacre at Paris* (c. 1592), Catherine plays the scheming, power-mad villainess to the hilt: "Tush, all shall die unless I have my will; / For, while she lives, Catherine will be queen" (3.2.66–67).

Even during these stormy times, her influence on the cultural life of France continued. In addition to chefs, she also brought Italian dance masters to France, most notably Baltazarini di Belgioioso, who renamed himself Balthazar de Beaujoyeulx and produced the *Ballet comique de la reine* for Catherine in 1581. The ballet recounted the ancient myth of the enchantress Circe and ended with her relinquishing her sovereignty to the king of France. This was the first performance of the highly allegorical *ballet de cour,* an idealized genre that glorified the absolute monarchy of France that was to become so redoubtable in the days of Louis XIV. Catherine also had a hand in several notable architectural achievements, helping to design the gardens of the Tuileries, a wing of the Louvre, and the château at Monceau.

Caterina de' Medici left an indelible and unmistakably Italian mark on French culture, especially its cooking and table, although the transformation of French cuisine took many decades and continued for years after her death. This development was an evolution, not a revolution, and it probably reached its peak in the early decades of the seventeenth century, during the troubled reign of her distant cousin, Maria de' Medici, the second member of the illustrious Florentine house to become queen of France.

Thirty-two

Peri's *Euridice*: The birth of opera from the spirit of tragedy

*I believed that the ancient Greeks and Romans used a kind of music
more advanced than ordinary speech [in their tragedies], but less than
the melody of singing, thus taking a middle position between the
two. . . . Taking note of this usage and those accents that serve us in
grief, joy, and similar states, I made the bass move in time, now
faster, now slower, according to the affections.*

—Jacopo Peri, Preface to *Euridice* (1600)

WITH THESE WORDS, a man better known to his contemporaries as a
singer than a composer described his remarkable musical innovation,
stile rappresentativo (representational style), the half-spoken, half-sung
vocal technique that distinguishes his *Euridice*, the oldest surviving
opera, from all earlier extant musical works. October 6, 1600, the day
Peri's *Euridice* received its first public performance at Florence's Pitti
Palace, marks the birth of opera. It is one of the few dates in the genesis
of art forms that can be established with such precision.

How surprised the first spectators must have been, since they were
attending the glittering nuptials of Maria de' Medici and King Henry IV
of France and expected an elaborate dramatic and musical celebration
like those of other Medici weddings. By contrast *Euridice* must have
seemed quite subdued. The singers, Peri among them, had only the sparest
instrumental accompaniment, and some members of the audience later
complained that the *stile rappresentativo* was "boring." Present-day listeners might even have trouble identifying *Euridice* as an opera. Lacking
the rapid repartee or more pointed musical phrasing of recitative in
operas by Mozart or Verdi, for example, the *stile rappresentativo* sounds
flat and flaccid to us. Nonetheless, the creative artists associated with
Euridice were convinced they had revived the musical spirit of ancient
Greek tragedy.

Florence was accustomed to propagandistic spectacles in honor of the Medici family (see Essay 21). Births, weddings, and political victories were celebrated with ballets, pageants, elaborately staged dramas, miniature naval battles reenacted in garden ponds, and banquets unlike any others in Europe. The pinnacle of these extravagant festivities was the 1589 wedding of Grand Duke Ferdinando de' Medici to Christine de Lorraine in a monthlong celebration fabled as the most spectacular of the Renaissance.

Among its highlights was the drama *La Pellegrina* (The Pilgrim Woman), remembered today because of its excellent *intermedi* or intermezzi, which were allegorical musical numbers performed as prologues or interludes between the acts of a play. In *La Pellegrina*, classical and Medici mythology were intertwined in an iconography that lauded Ferdinando (represented by Apollo) for restoring the earth to its ancient golden age of peace.

The *intermedi* were an important step toward opera, fusing drama and music in the minds of composers and audiences. Comprising any combination of vocal solos, choral music, madrigals, instrumental pieces, and dances, they often became more compelling than the plays they accompanied.

A highly regarded performer in the *intermedi* of *La Pellegrina* was Jacopo Peri (1561–1633), a young tenor who moved audiences to tears and whose elegant blond-red mane gave rise to his nickname, *Zazzerino*. The most eminent artistic figure associated with the 1589 celebration, however, was the musician and scholar Count Giovanni de' Bardi, who is credited with the overall conception of *La Pellegrina* and some of the words and music of its *intermedi*.

For nearly twenty years, Bardi had been the leader of a group of amateur musicians, poets, and philosophers known as the Florentine Camerata (salon), which met at his palace several times each month to discuss the history and aesthetics of music. Among the most prominent musicians of the Camerata were Vincenzo Galilei, father of the astronomer Galileo (see Essay 33), and Giulio Caccini, who contributed music to the 1589 Medici wedding and similar events. Jacopo Peri and the poet who would become his librettist, Ottavio Rinuccini, were probably students of Camerata members at this time.

The self-imposed mission of the Camerata was to determine what sort of music the ancient Greeks wrote. Many cultured Florentines of the time believed in the nearly magical power of ancient Greek music to move the soul and influence human behavior for good or ill. Members of the Camerata found this characteristic to be lacking in contemporary music and wished to recapture it.

Music played an essential role in the verse tragedies of ancient Greece, such as those of Aeschylus, Sophocles, and Euripides. In a passage from the *Poetics* with which Bardi and his colleagues were familiar, Aristotle discusses the components of Greek tragedy and emphasizes the importance of "pleasurable language, by which I mean language that has the embellishments of rhythm, melody, and meter. In some parts meter alone is employed, in others, melody."

Therefore it was reasonable to assume that at least some portions of ancient Greek drama were sung. Certainly this was true of the formal odes assigned to the chorus, whose members performed elaborate dances, interacted with the characters, and periodically commented on the action by singing in unison, with one note allotted to each syllable. Instrumental accompaniment was limited to one or two lyrelike and double-reed wind instruments.

Based on his research and his correspondence with Girolamo Mei, a humanist and scholar of Greek drama, Galilei concluded that ancient Greek music consisted largely of "singing with attention to the words." He attributed the legendary emotional effects of Greek music to the use of a single melodic line that imitated natural speech patterns. Spareness was the key to the power of this music, Galilei said, because it allowed the emotional message to emerge unencumbered from the text.

The Camerata believed that "singing with attention to the words" could get to the heart of what was wrong with contemporary music. Although all members of the salon had composed *madrigali*, their notions about ancient Greek music now led them to fault this popular musical form because the words were nearly impossible to discern among the intricacies of three or four melodies sung in counterpoint. As a result, the Camerata decreed that words set to music should be sung by one vocalist with minimal accompaniment and with the inflections and rhythms of speech.

While Galilei was formulating his theories about Greek tragedy, Giulio Caccini was developing a type of musical shorthand known as *basso continuo*, or figured bass, which would be widely used in Europe until about 1750. This compositional technique employed single notes in the bass clef accompanied by scant markings suggesting harmonies that a lutenist, harpsichordist, or cellist could add. The method also allowed the singer to improvise to a certain extent, affecting a nonchalant singing style, or *sprezzatura di canto*.

The 1589 Medici wedding was the last pageant Bardi devised for the family, since he left for a post as protocol chief with Pope Clement VIII in 1592. Jacopo Corsi, a wealthy amateur composer who had participated in the work of the Camerata, assumed Bardi's role and eventually became a generous patron of musical events in Florence. Under his wing, Peri and Rinuccini developed the distinctive recitative style that became an essential component of opera.

The earliest complete opera, or *dramma per musica*, attempted by the two collaborators was *Dafne*, first performed in Corsi's palace during Carnival in 1597 and subsequently at the Florentine court in 1599 and 1600. Only a few phrases have survived, but contemporary accounts confirm that Rinuccini based the libretto on the story of Apollo and Daphne in Ovid's *Metamorphoses* (see Essay 7). Although *Dafne* may have been regarded as experimental, the second opera by Peri and Rinuccini, *Euridice*, the direct inspiration for Monteverdi's *Orfeo* (see Essay 35), was destined for a far grander opening.

The wedding of Grand Duke Ferdinando's niece, Maria de' Medici, to France's King Henry IV in 1600 was the culmination of protracted diplomatic and dowry negotiations in which Corsi played a key role. As a token of his appreciation, Ferdinando allowed Corsi to produce *Euridice* at the nuptials in lieu of a gift.

Euridice was the first of about thirty operas, including those by Monteverdi and Gluck, that tell the story of Orpheus, son of Apollo and the Muse Calliope, and his short-lived wife Eurydice, who succumbs to a snakebite. Renowned for his ability to move men, animals, and even trees and rocks with his music, Orpheus journeys to the Underworld and convinces Pluto, its ruler, to release Eurydice. The god agrees, but on condition that Orpheus not look back at his spouse as they depart from Hades. Unable to resist the temptation, Orpheus turns, and Eurydice falls back into the pit of Hell. Disconsolate, Orpheus forswears women and turns to the love of boys, enraging a band of Maenads, fierce female worshipers of Dionysus, who rip him to pieces and send his head, still singing, floating down the River Hebrus to the island of Lesbos.

The story, told by both Virgil and Ovid, and dramatized by the Florentine poet Politian in 1480, was a shrewd choice for the wedding. Although the Medici could not compete with the political and military power wielded by Henry, the groom still ate with his fingers, while the

Medici were unrivaled patrons of all the arts. With his power to move all of nature—and even the god of Hell—Orpheus, son of the god of music, was the symbol par excellence of the creative artist as hero.

The short opening prologue of Peri's *Euridice*, the first surviving opera, is followed by the marriage of the mythological lovers. The death of Euridice, which takes place offstage in standard Greek fashion, is announced by the nymph Dafne. This scene is followed by the lamentation of Orfeo and his friends. After the goddess Venus urges Orfeo to demand Euridice's return, he descends into Hell and persuades Pluto to free his wife. (In this version, no conditions are imposed.) In the last scene, a messenger announces that both the newlyweds have returned safely. Everyone lives triumphantly ever after, since, in consideration of the happy occasion on which the work was performed, Rinuccini had rewritten the familiar tragic ending of the tale. Orfeo and Euridice, of course, represented Henry and Maria in an elaborate compliment that was typical of the times.

Peri's *Euridice* has two elements in common with the *intermedi*: the chorus, which apparently remained onstage throughout the performance, and the songs at the beginning and end of scenes. The body of the text, however, was performed in the chantlike *stile rappresentativo*, the novel achievement of Peri and Rinuccini that propelled the operatic drama forward via dialogue set to music. The accents and inflections are consistent with those of normal speech, and the melodic vocal line is accompanied only by the basso continuo. The harmonies and melodies are crisp and unobtrusive, allowing the words to be clearly understood.

Peri, who apparently sang the role of Orfeo, wrote that four instruments accompanied the singers at the first performance: a harpsichord (played by Corsi), a lute, a chitarrone (a large bass lute), and a large lyre, all of which were hidden behind a curtain to avoid distracting the audience. Because the score provides little more than the bass line and the melody for the vocalists, the instrumentalists improvised with simple harmonies, in keeping with the philosophy of the Camerata.

Modern listeners note the pleasant but nearly static nature of the music of *Euridice*, which sounds pallid to our jaded ears. Renaissance restraint and decorum in dramatic action, speech, and musical expression pervade the work, even in the first words we hear from a stunned Orfeo after he learns that Euridice has died:

I neither weep nor sigh,
O my dear Euridice,

For I cannot sigh, I cannot weep.
Hapless lifeless body,
O my heart, my hope, O peace, O life!

The words are emphatically clear, and the music, as Peri and Rinuccini intended, is subordinated to the expression of feelings, however stereotyped and, in this example, severely muted. Despite Peri's goal of highlighting the emotions inherent in the text, Orfeo's grief is more plangent on the silent page than in performance. The musical texture of this earliest opera is sober and chaste, lacking the range, complexity, subtlety, and pacing that modern listeners expect. No bone-chilling shrieks or elaborate laments mirror the characters' psychic swings.

Until the day of its first performance, backstage drama compensated for the drama lacking in *Euridice*. In honor of the bridal couple, Caccini, by then a fierce rival of Peri's, had been commissioned to write a spectacular production that contained no recitative and thus resembled a series of *intermedi*. Caccini refused to let his musicians perform in *Euridice*, and he even rushed his own operatic version of the ancient story (with the same title) to the printer weeks before Peri did, although it was not publicly performed until 1602. Nonetheless, Caccini was unable to prevent his daughter Francesca from performing the title role in Peri's *Euridice*.

Reaction to Peri's opera was mixed. At court, some favored the more familiar fare provided by Caccini, even though his production lacked sets and costumes, which did not arrive in time for the curtain. The impresario Corsi's reputation was greatly enhanced by the performance of *Euridice*, however, which suggests that Duke Ferdinando was pleased.

Corsi rewarded Peri by making him a partner in his textile business, though the latter also continued composing and performing. In 1625 Peri was asked by the two reigning Medici widows to write a protofeminist piece advocating the political rights of women, *La precedenza delle dame*, to celebrate the visit of a Polish prince. The same festivities featured the first opera written by a woman, *La liberazione di Ruggiero dall'isola d'Alcina* (The Liberation of Ruggiero from the Island of Alcina), by Peri's old and dear friend Francesca Caccini.

The first opera faded from artistic consciousness in much the same way that its music tends to fade into the background today. The centerpiece of the next Medici wedding, in 1608, was a comedy with *intermedi* more in line with the 1589 model of entertainment. But Peri and Rinuccini, along with envious Caccini, had paved the way for the genius who would be widely regarded as the father of modern operatic and orchestral music, Claudio Monteverdi—not to mention a glorious succession of operatic composers, from Pergolesi to Gluck, Mozart, and Weber, from Rossini to Donizetti, Wagner, Verdi, and Puccini.

Thirty-three

Galileo frames the foundations of modern science

When Galileo caused balls, the weights of which he had himself previously determined, to roll down an inclined plane . . . a light broke upon all students of nature. They learned that reason has insight only into that which it produces after a plan of its own. Reason . . . must approach nature in order to be taught by it. It must not, however, do so in the character of a pupil who listens to everything that the teacher chooses to say, but of an appointed judge who compels the witnesses to answer questions which he himself has formulated.
—Immanuel Kant, *Critique of Pure Reason*, 2d ed. Preface (1787)

"PUT FORWARD THE ARGUMENTS and demonstrations, Simplicio—either yours or Aristotle's—but not just texts and bare authorities, because our discourse must relate to the sensible world and not to one on paper." This challenge, thrown down by Salviati, one of three characters in Galileo's *Dialogue Concerning the Two Chief World Systems* (1632), epitomizes the author's chronic dissatisfaction with the scholars of his time: Instead of presenting arguments based on observation, experiment, and reflection, they quoted books believed to contain absolute, unquestionable truths.

Note that Salviati, who tends to speak for Galileo, demands arguments and demonstrations, whether new or from Aristotle. Contrary to common opinion, Galileo was not anti-Aristotle. He was merely opposed to those who substituted someone else's teachings for the evidence of their own senses. Aristotle himself, he says, would have had to be "a man of intractable mind, of obstinate spirit, and barbarous soul" to prefer his own decrees to "the senses, experience, and nature itself."

The problem lay not with Aristotle but with his followers, who, in Galileo's time, constituted virtually the entire learned world—the universities and the Church. Across the myriad courts and emerging nation states of Renaissance Europe, these institutions taught succeeding generations to see the world not through their own eyes, but through the texts of Aristotle, Galen, Ptolemy, and other ancient authorities.

Here and there, some had the courage to think for themselves. Copernicus certainly had done so, but he kept the book describing his revolutionary heliocentric theory a secret until he lay dying in 1543. Galileo's correspondent Johannes Kepler embraced the Copernican theory, which inspired his famous three laws of planetary motion, although his thought continued to be saturated with mysticism. In his *Novum Organum*, England's Sir Francis Bacon (1561–1626) called for methods of inquiry that required careful data collection and experimentation, along with a healthy absence of servility toward authorities like Aristotle, whose veneration, in Bacon's view, hindered mankind's ability to discover useful truths about the world. But these and a handful of others were the exceptions. For the most part, Galileo Galilei (1564–1642) was born into a world that had no interest in confronting nature directly and, as Kant says, compelling her through observation and controlled experiment to answer questions.

To go from the lecture halls of Pisa or Padua, where he taught mathematics, to Galileo's workshop, must have seemed to many of his contemporaries like stepping out of an abstract world of monkish texts and into the wards of Bedlam. In one area, workers assembled sectors—multipurpose calculators invented by Galileo; in another, students peered through telescopes at the phases of Venus. Some, turning in circles, intently watched balls float in bowls of water they held in outstretched arms; others rolled balls down planes of various inclinations, noting elapsed times. Visitors might find hand-drawn images of the moon's surface next to painstaking sketches of sunspots and of the motions of Jupiter's four largest moons, discovered by Galileo in 1610. There were identical weights swinging from pendulums of varying lengths, and varying weights swinging from pendulums of identical lengths. In tanks of water, some objects floated, others sank; straining under assorted weights, some columns crumbled, others held firm. Amid the silent interactions of magnets rose the incessant racket of pulleys, levers, winches, screws, and scales—in short, a hubbub of attention directed to how things on Earth and in the heavens move, fall, and break—a test facility that would have seemed unremarkable to Edison, Feynman, or Fermi.

How did a man born in Pisa to a Florentine musician and cloth merchant come to interrogate nature via the scientific method we take for granted today? Clues are strewn throughout Galileo's works. In one passage he tells how he began to question Aristotle's notion that the speed of a falling body was proportional to its size. Having noticed large and small hailstones striking the ground at the same time, he writes that he could not believe that all the big ones originated farther up, or started falling later, than the little ones.

Many such epiphanies led Galileo to a fundamental starting point for inquiry: that the human mind, simply using its faculties, could arrive at a profound apprehension of the workings of nature. It was for this reason that he chose to write all his major works in Italian, rather than in Latin, the language of institutional learning in his day.

> I wrote in the colloquial tongue because I must have everyone able to read it. . . . I am induced to do this by seeing how young men are sent through the universities at random to be made physicians, philosophers, and so on. . . . Now I want them to see that just as nature has given to them, as well as to philosophers, eyes with which to see her works, so she has also given them brains capable of penetrating and understanding them. *(Letters on Sunspots)*

If there is a unifying thread in Galileo, it is this contention that the mind can gain direct access to understanding the world—it requires no ceremonial ribbon, no Latin or Greek, no logic-chopping *Organon* or four Aristotelian causes—just "horse sense," as he put it. This is so because mind and world share a "vernacular" as well—the vocabulary of form and motion:

> Philosophy is written in this grand book, the universe, which stands continually open to our gaze. But the book cannot be understood unless one first learns to comprehend the language and read the letters in which it is composed. It is written in the language of mathematics, and its characters are triangles, circles, and other geometric figures without which it is humanly impossible to understand a single word of it. *(The Assayer)*

This declaration emancipated students of nature from what Galileo called "enslavement" to masters who were seen as holding the keys to all knowledge, and left them free to formulate, postulate, challenge, and refute, using the universal language of mathematics. The full impact of this blow to the hieratic medieval worldview would register only when, by unifying Galileo's laws of local motion with Kepler's laws of planetary motion, Isaac Newton expressed the law of universal gravitation, the defining scientific achievement of the Enlightenment.

But the idea that the mind has the mobility to reach out and grasp the truth about nature goes deeper, with even more subversive implications. In Galileo's day, the prevailing world order, formulated by Aristotle almost two thousand years earlier and backed by the Church's imprimatur, required that nature assume two distinct modes.

Below the moon, flux and impermanence characterized our earth—a stationary, base, and volatile milieu, subject to time and decay (a notion rich in moral overtones stemming from the Fall of Man). Above the moon, however, nature was perfect, immutable, constantly in circular motion, and composed of unknowable elements. Only the revealed truths of Scripture, as interpreted by the Church with the aid of assimilated ancient sages like Aristotle, could disclose its mysterious quintessence.

The project of Galileo's *Dialogue Concerning the Two Chief World Systems*—indeed, of his lifelong inquiry into motion—was to put this dichotomy to rest. By claiming that all nature shared a common language of mathematics, he had already implied that earth and the heavens belonged to a single nature. When in 1609 he perfected the telescope (after hearing about a rudimentary one devised by a Dutchman) and aimed it at the heavens, he became the first human to see the craggy face of the moon and, somewhat later, four of the moons of Jupiter and the phases of Venus. To anyone else, these would have been discrete, unrelated observations. To Galileo they were jigsaw pieces of evidence helping build a case that Copernicus had it right—that the earth rotated on its axis and revolved around the sun, no differently from the other planets.

But just as important, this meant that Aristotle had it wrong: There were not two natures, only a sole vast one that could be read by means of the same vernacular we use on earth. Not only does the earth move, but the human mind itself can travel to unimaginably remote worlds without going astray in its assumption that all of them move in the way mundane material objects move—what modern physicists call *symmetry*.

Galileo's accomplishment was to reveal a world that operated according to predictable and measurable behaviors, much like a pulley. "In my judgment," he wrote to Grand Duchess Christina of Tuscany, "one should first be assured of the necessary and immutable truth of the fact, over which no man has power." But it would be wrong to take Galileo for some freethinker, a proto-Diderot or incipient Voltaire. The tenor of his life and work bespeaks a profound religious faith and solicitude for the Church. The complexity of the man can be better appreciated if we see him situated on the fissure riving the medieval and modern worlds.

In the *Dialogue*, immediately after challenging Simplicio the Aristotelian to offer arguments for the immobility of the earth, Salviati looks back on their conversation of the day before: "In yesterday's argument the earth was lifted up out of darkness and exposed to the open sky, and the attempt to number it among the bodies we call heavenly was shown to be not so hopeless and prostrate a proposition that it remained without a spark of life." The goal of this book that drew down the wrath of the Vatican on Galileo was not merely to unify nature, but to accomplish a transvaluation. Did viewing the stars and planets as changeable physical bodies have to mean that all heavenly nature was as corrupt and foul as earth? Why couldn't the argument be made that earth possessed the beauty and serene grace of the stars? In part, the revolution that moves from Copernicus through Galileo to Newton involves a reconfiguration of systems of value concerning heaven and earth, high and low, celestial and terrestrial, permanence and mutability, divine and human, which had been in place for roughly two millennia.

One of many ironies of Galileo's story is how he ultimately met his fate at the hands of a man who had been his lifelong admirer. Maffeo Barberini, elected pope as Urban VIII in 1623, fancied himself a man of learning and valued his fellow Florentine as a friend, a cultivated man (Galileo's skills as a lute player and a writer of artful plays were well known), and a leading Catholic intellectual.

This last asset took on greater significance as the religious hatreds fueling the Thirty Years' War (1618–48) led Catholic princes to look to the pope for moral and doctrinal leadership. Galileo was precisely the man to represent the Catholic worldview with the requisite force and intelligence to stand up to withering criticism from Germany and other Protestant lands.

A major source of contention was the Copernican theory, which, thanks to Kepler and Galileo, was considered by many north of the Alps to be a striking advance over the Ptolemaic model. That the Church still adhered to the earth-centered system was grist for the Protestants—evidence that it was lapsing into dotage. Aware that Galileo was composing his *Dialogue*, Pope Urban expected him to restore the Church to its former intellectual preeminence.

It was a no-win situation for Galileo. One of his major concerns, both in writing the *Dialogue* and in defending himself from charges of heresy, was that if the Church took the step of making the Ptolemaic universe an article of faith (and declaring the Copernican view to be heretical), it was staking a huge portion of its credibility on a conjecture about the physical world that had a very good chance of eventually being refuted.

For its part, the Church was pleased to have Galileo as its champion and valued his contributions to the understanding of nature, including his work on Copernicus. But—and it was a big but—he was expected to adhere to a view that in essence asserted that Copernicus's hypothesis, while brilliantly useful in helping calculate the motions of the stars and planets, was false.

Galileo faced a dangerous quandary. He could only maintain Catholicism's intellectual leadership by preventing the Church from fatally confusing matters of faith with the findings of science. By insisting he affirm the "truth" of geocentrism, the pope gave Galileo a fateful choice: either betray his honor, his life's work, and ultimately the credibility of the Church, or risk the agonies reserved for heretics. His enemies and the Inquisition were watching.

What was so threatening about claiming the earth moved? (After all, Copernicus was not the first to advance the idea—Aristarchus of Alexandria had put forward a heliocentric model some 270 years before Christ.) One oft-cited reason was that such a notion conflicted with the Old Testament passage in which Joshua made the sun stand still at the Battle of Jericho, the implication being that the sun moves and the earth doesn't. But this wasn't the real reason. Even the Jesuit who took Galileo to task on the matter—Cardinal Roberto Bellarmino, the subsequently canonized "Hammer of the Heretics" who had consigned the philosopher Giordano Bruno to the flames in 1600—had written that if Copernicus was ultimately proved correct, the biblical passage could be interpreted another way.

The real threat lay in the Promethean thrust of Galileo's assumptions—in the possibility that a human could obtain such certain knowledge of the world as to essentially possess divine understanding. As Karl Popper observes in an essay on Galileo, "They saw in its [science's] success the power of the human intellect, unaided by divine revelation, to uncover the secrets of our world—the reality hidden behind the appearances." Positing such human power would be hubristic, to be sure. But it would also imply a limit to God's power—and this was an article of faith about which the Church had no doubts whatsoever.

The underlying conflict stemmed from the demonstrable advances of scientific inquiry in the early seventeenth century. If man could obtain absolute knowledge of the world, it was because the world necessarily follows discoverable and predictable causes. But if the world is so determined, then what becomes of the miraculous? If God is not free to ordain things any way he pleases, God is not God. The stakes were enormous. Galileo was expected to reinvigorate the intellectual prestige of the Church while clearly demarcating the limits of human knowledge and asserting the omnipotence of the Creator.

Anyone who reads the *Dialogue* will probably concede that Galileo's strategy of stacking two brilliant Copernican sympathizers against one pathetic Aristotelian called Simplicio was ill-advised. Near the end, the infinite power of God receives an obligatory nod. Galileo quite simply could not call everything he had learned about the world through a lifetime of indefatigable inquiry a "false hypothesis." And the Church felt it couldn't afford to let him do anything else.

Pope Urban VIII faced other threats and pressures at the time. By 1631 he was being excoriated by the King of Spain for failing to support the Faith vigorously enough. Isolated, paranoid, and insomniac, the pope ordered all the singing birds in his garden to be killed. At this unsettled juncture, enemies of Galileo—including Aristotelians who felt threatened by his science (some still smarting from his caustic ridicule) and ambitious Jesuits who saw in the fall of Galileo a chance to replace him as the scientific voice of the Church—hinted to the pontiff that the Church and the pope cut foolish figures in the *Dialogue* and were represented in it by a simpleton called Simplicio.

Although Galileo produced a letter from the late Cardinal Bellarmino stating that he was free to discuss the Copernican theory, his fall from grace in 1633 was swift. Nearly seventy and in bad health, he was not declared a heretic but was judged "vehemently suspected of heresy." Under threat of torture, he was compelled to kneel before his inquisitors, abjure his errors, and promise never to repeat them. His *Dialogue* was ordered burned. It is unlikely that he chose this tense moment to mutter his stubborn belief in the earth's motion, *"Eppur si muove,"* as has often been claimed.

For the final decade of his life Galileo remained under house arrest, receiving visitors including the young John Milton and Thomas Hobbes at his home in Arcetri, outside of Florence. During this time he set to work on his final book, *Dialogue Concerning Two New Sciences*, using the same three characters who appeared in his *Dialogue Concerning the Two Chief World Systems*.

This last work, a summa of his insights into matter and local motion, contains the seeds of Newton's synthesis. It also continues his lifelong inquiry into the fundamental structure of nature. At the opening of the "Third Day," Galileo drops the fictional characterization and speaks in his own voice: "There is in nature perhaps nothing older than motion, concerning which the books written by philosophers are neither few nor small; nevertheless I have discovered by experiment some properties of it which are worth knowing and which have not hitherto been observed or demonstrated."

Without saying it in so many words, this is Galileo's "*si muove*." It was here that he described how his assistants rolled balls hundreds of times down planes at various angles, finding that the "spaces traversed were to each other as the squares of the times," regardless of the inclination. This manuscript, which physicist Stephen Hawking considers "the genesis of modern physics," had to be smuggled out of Italy. By the time it was published in Leiden, Holland, in 1638, Galileo was blind. He died at age seventy-seven in 1642, the year of Newton's birth.

How did the devout faith into which Galileo was born coexist in him with the scientific temper he helped engender? A clue might reside in how he saw the limits of human understanding. He believed that the mind was made to inquire and to discover truths about nature, but that nature is so rich, so full of infinite motions and causes, that we will never be in danger of getting to the bottom of it. Does our power to predict and control nature diminish the God we are supposed to believe in? Judging from Galileo's example, the mind need never shrink from its quest: Watch the hailstones, and trust divinity to take care of itself.

—Thomas Matrullo

Fortepiano: This excellent instrument is—bless us!—again an invention of the Germans.
— C. F. D. Schubart, *Ideas on the Aesthetics of Music* (1777)

Cremona, n. A high-priced violin made in Connecticut.
— Ambrose Bierce, *The Devil's Dictionary* (1911)

WHAT A PAIR OF JOKERS, Schubart and Bierce. Italy gave us not only the violin, the vibrant heart of orchestral music, whose timbre and expressiveness most evoke the human voice, but also the piano, the instrument fittest for accompanying the voice in song. Schubart, a high-living musician, poet, and fantasist, almost certainly knew he was wrong—the piano was invented by Bartolomeo Cristofori in the early eighteenth century. Granted, Cristofori was the only first-rate Italian piano maker of the period, and it was the Germans who subsequently refined the instrument until it attained its present form.

As for Ambrose Bierce, his facetious definition of *Cremona* (actually one of the exquisite violins made in that city on the Po between the sixteenth and eighteenth centuries) alludes to the rampant violin forgery that occurred in the nineteenth century. Although Antonio Stradivari was still making violins past his ninetieth birthday, he would have had to live for several hundred years to craft all the violins attributed to him.

The violin is an end product of Renaissance science, mathematics, and craftsmanship—musical passion concretized by the laws of acoustics. It evolved from the rebec, the *lira da braccio* (arm-lyre), and the Renaissance fiddle (the vielle or fiedel). From the rebec, the violin inherited strings tuned in fifths (though the rebec had three strings, one fewer than the violin's g, d, a, and e strings), a playing position at the neck, an overhand bow, and strings anchored by lateral tuning pegs. The *lira da braccio* contributed the sound post (which transmits vibrations from the front soundboard to the back), an arched top, a shaped waist, and f- or c-shaped sound holes. The Renaissance fiddle bequeathed to the violin its soprano register; a top and back with connecting ribs; a separate neck, pegbox, and fingerboard; and its oval shape.

Despite their similar names, the viol was a more distant and slightly older relative of the violin that had guitarlike frets on the fingerboard. Viols and violins coexisted for about two hundred years until the viol, with its curiously reticent music, was left behind by the brilliant complexities of the Baroque. One of the earliest Baroque composers and the father of the modern orchestra, Claudio Monteverdi, himself a native of Cremona, was among the first to write orchestral music that included integral parts for the violin. His intricate and demanding compositions exploited the violin's dazzling speed and range (see Essay 35).

The violin first emerged from northern Italian workshops in the mid-sixteenth century with two other members of the modern string family, the viola and the cello. By the end of the century, the violin had assumed the basic form and proportions we recognize today. Some of the earliest masters of violin making lived in Brescia and included Gasparo Bertolotti da Salò (1540–1609) and his apprentice, Giovanni Paolo Maggini (1579–1630), who later influenced both Giuseppe del Gesù and Antonio Stradivari. But the man generally credited with the creation of the modern violin was the former fashioner of rebecs and viols, Andrea Amati (1520–1611), founder of the Cremona school of violin making, whose earliest known violin dates from 1564.

It was his grandson, however, Nicolò Amati (1596–1684), who went on to produce some of the world's finest violins. Nicolò's elegant instruments are noted for their deep, vibrant tone, beautifully grained wood, richly hued amber varnishes, and meticulously fashioned sound holes and scrolls. They also evinced a shallower, flatter form than earlier violins.

So eagerly have violin connoisseurs sought the "secret" of Cremonese violins that a luthier (a maker of stringed instruments) and a radiologist recently performed CT scans of a Nicolò Amati violin. Modern imaging technology revealed fine gradations in thickness and delicate archings of the violin's front and back plates—clues, perhaps, to the secret of its near perfection.

Nicolò Amati's students included Andrea Guarneri (1626–98) and Antonio Stradivari. Guarneri produced about 250 violins and several violas and cellos. His grandson, known as Giuseppe del Gesù (because of the monogram *IHS*, the first three letters of the Greek word for *Jesus*, on his violin labels), made the most famous and esteemed of the Guarneri family violins.

More interested in the tone than in the beauty of his instruments (some have stains or streaks in the varnish), del Gesù (1698–1745) followed the path of Giovanni Maggini rather than that of the Amati family, and his violins tend to be more massive than others of the Cremonese school. Their lush tones rank second to none, however, not even those of Stradivari. When fifteen-year-old Niccolò Paganini (1782–1840), composer and incomparable violin virtuoso, lost his Amati in a card game, he reluctantly pressed into service a del Gesù, which he played for the rest of his life. In our own time, Isaac Stern performs on a del Gesù.

Another of Nicolò Amati's pupils, Antonio Stradivari (1644–1737), became the most celebrated violin maker in history. At age twenty-two, while still apprenticed to Amati, Stradivari started putting his own labels in the violins he made. Like del Gesù, Stradivari later experimented with larger violins and deeply colored varnishes. He patiently designed and redesigned pegs, fingerboards, and tailpieces.

In about 1690, Stradivari completed his first so-called long violin. By 1700, the beginning of a twenty-five-year "golden period," he had settled on a proportion for the instrument and redesigned the bridge, which transmits the vibrations of the strings to the soundboard. (The wooden body of a violin is essentially an amplifier, its front soundboard and back being analogous to a tweeter and a woofer.) Stradivari increased the air space inside his violins by about 10 percent, and his long, shallow instruments produced a penetrating, robust tone that made them legendary. Contemporary violinists who perform and record with Stradivarii include Joshua Bell, who plays the 1732 *Tom Taylor* (most of these instruments acquired proper names over the years), Gil Shahan with his 1699 *Countess Polignac,* and Itzhak Perlman with the 1714 *Soil* and the 1721 *Sinsheimer.*

For years, the inimitable tone of Stradivari's violins was attributed to some unknown property of the varnish, whose formula has never been discovered. Modern acoustical research, however, has confirmed that the tone of any violin is the result of complex interactions among the thickness and curvature of the pine soundboard and sound post, the maple back, and the pine-lined maple sides of the instrument, as well as the varnish recipe. Antonio Stradivari, a tireless experimenter, had apparently achieved an optimal admixture of components. The master made his last violin in 1737, when he was ninety-two. He may have crafted more than 1,100 violins, guitars, violas, and cellos, of which about 650 survive.

Even if Stradivari had not made a single violin, he would be remembered for his refinements of the cello. Like Maggini before him, he decreased the dimensions of this instrument, which was outsized and difficult to play. His new cello (and similar ones emerging from other Cremonese workshops) helped foster a new generation of cello virtuosi. Since they are fewer in number, Stradivari's cellos command even more astronomical prices than his violins.

Yo-Yo Ma inherited his—the 1712 *Davidoff* left to him by the British cellist Jacqueline Du Pré at her death in 1987. For an album of Bach and Boccherini pieces to be played on period instruments, Ma's *Davidoff* was restored to nearly the condition in which it left Stradivari's hands. This included removal of the end-pin, which supports a modern cello and also carries some sound down through the stage. Ma likened playing without an end-pin to riding a horse, since he had to grip the instrument with his legs. The sound was fuller and richer, however.

Two of Antonio Stradivari's sons, Francesco and Omobono, worked with him, along with another collaborator, Carlo Bergonzi. The violins made by this trio originally carried a label reading "*sotto la disciplina d'Antonio Stradivari,*" acknowledging that the instruments were made "under the supervision" of the master. Much of the Stradivari mischief down to this day stems from the underhanded substitution of these labels with others that attributed the instruments to the great man himself.

When the violin first appeared, it was used, like the rebec and viol, to double voices or provide dance music. Soon it achieved a loftier and more independent artistic status as composers began to exploit its capability in the hands of a skilled musician to express the gamut of emotions at a dizzying tempo or with the heart-stopping plangency of a human plea. In addition to Monteverdi, Italian composers including Antonio Vivaldi (himself a violin virtuoso), Arcangelo Corelli, Giuseppe Torelli, Giuseppe Tartini, and Pietro Locatelli began to write increasingly complex music for the violin and small orchestras. Vivaldi's *The Four Seasons* (actually a set of twelve violin concertos) became popular immediately after its first public performance in 1725.

Today violins constitute nearly one third the instruments in a symphony orchestra, and they figure prominently in the solo and chamber music repertoire. With the possible exception of the piano, the violin is the instrument most written for in the classical tradition. Nearly every major composer, from the eighteenth century on, has composed solo violin music, including Bach, Mozart, Beethoven, Mendelssohn, Schumann, Brahms, Grieg, Bartók, and Schönberg.

If, by the early eighteenth century, violinists wielded the most sublime, evocative, and subtly emotive of musical instruments, their keyboard counterparts were not so fortunate. In 1711 French composer François Couperin, the preeminent harpsichordist of his time, wrote that he would be indebted to anyone "who by the exercise of infinite art supported by fine taste contrives to render this instrument capable of expression," a sentiment with which anyone who has attended a protracted harpsichord recital—unless it was an all-Bach program—can fully sympathize.

The root of the harpsichord's deficiencies was a string-plucking mechanism, the plectrum, that made it extraordinarily difficult to vary loudness or tone color. The result, even for a virtuoso like Couperin, was the tedium of a narrow expressive range. The clavichord, a brass-hammered instrument that is the piano's closest relation, was touch sensitive, but its tone was far too soft to be heard in a large room.

Enter Prince Ferdinando de' Medici of Tuscany, who, since he owned dozens of harpsichords, apparently needed an in-house technician to keep them in good repair. In about 1690 he hired a renowned harpsichord maker from Padua, Bartolomeo di Francesco Cristofori (1655–1731), to whom he also entrusted the care of his vast collection of other musical instruments.

The first clue we have that Cristofori had exceeded his curatorial duties is a 1711 magazine article by littérateur and publisher Marquis Scipione Maffei describing a *"nuova invenzione d'un gravicembalo col piano e forte,"* or "new invention of a harpsichord that has soft and loud [tones]." By replacing the plucking mechanism with a hammer, Cristofori revolutionized keyboard music.

Cristofori had designed the piano's action—an intricate mechanism that includes keys, hammers, levers, and many other components—in such a way that when a key is depressed, it sets a hammer in motion toward the strings. The most ingenious aspect of Cristofori's design is the escapement, which causes the hammer to fall away from the strings immediately after striking them so that they can continue to vibrate freely. Another innovation is the back-catch, which prevents the hammer from rebounding against the strings and creating an echo. And to stop the strings' vibrations, Cristofori added dampers, which come to rest on the strings when the player releases the key.

For each note, Cristofori used dual strings tuned in unison, which increased the instrument's flexibility. With the soft, or shift, pedal (the left pedal on a modern piano), also his invention, the hammers could strike only one of a pair of strings, thus softening the tone. With his damper pedal (our right pedal), the dampers were prevented from descending on the strings once the key was released, thereby prolonging the tone.

By 1726 Cristofori had perfected the action in his pianoforte, which had only four octaves (modern pianos have seven and one third). He died five years later. The total number of pianos he made is unknown, but only two survive: one in New York's Metropolitan Museum of Art and the other in a museum in Leipzig.

Cristofori's invention was little known in his lifetime, but German keyboard builders ultimately learned of it through Maffei's writings, and by 1730 Gottfried Silbermann had used Cristofori's mechanism to construct the first German piano. By the mid-1750s, it was widely assumed that Silbermann had invented the piano, or *Hammerclavier*, as it was called in Germany. There it was soon understood that the piano was a novel instrument, not simply a harpsichord with hammers instead of plectra.

Subsequent changes made by German, British, and American piano builders through the nineteenth century included increasing the number of keys to the current eighty-eight, replacing wooden soundboards with metal ones, and fortifying the instrument so that string tensions could be increased to broaden the dynamic range and tonal gamut.

In 1732 Lodovico Giustini became the first composer to write a piece of music exclusively for the piano: a set of twelve sonatas, *12 sonate da cembalo di piano e forte detto volgarmente di martellati*. Mozart and Muzio Clementi were the first to write music for the piano that fully exploited its lyricism and delicate expressiveness. The likes of Haydn, Beethoven, Schubert, Schumann, Chopin, Liszt (the "Paganini of the Piano"), Brahms, Tchaikovsky, Debussy, Ravel, and Rachmaninoff have written dazzling solo works and concertos that showcase the piano, perhaps the most versatile—and certainly the hardest-working—of musical instruments.

Thirty-five

Claudio Monteverdi, father of modern music

The end of all good music is to affect the soul.
—Claudio Monteverdi, Preface,
Eighth Book of Madrigals (1638)

CONSIDERED A REVOLUTIONARY in his time, Claudio Monteverdi (1567–1643) was the creator of both the modern opera and the orchestra. His compositional skills, paired with his psychological insight, gave him a vast range of emotional expression in his use of voices and instrumentation. Furthermore, he was heir to a fertile musical inheritance, which he both exploited and refined, leaving a rich legacy for the composers who came after him. On the cutting edge of music from a very early age, he wrote four operas in three years while in his early seventies. Of his extant operatic works, *Orfeo*, the first truly modern opera, and his last, *The Coronation of Poppea*, are still recorded and widely performed.

Monteverdi was baptized on May 15, 1567, in Cremona, only three years after Andrea Amati produced his first violin there (see Essay 34). Little is known of the composer's early life except that he received private musical training with Marc'Antonio Ingegneri, maestro di cappella of Cremona's cathedral, who instructed him in choral technique and string instruments. Monteverdi's precocity, however, revealed itself in his musical compositions. Between the ages of fifteen and twenty-three, he published four books of music, including his first two books of madrigals, love songs for several voices that were all the rage in the sixteenth and seventeenth centuries, especially in Italy, Flanders, and England.

In 1590 he took a position as a string player with a small ensemble at the court of Duke Vincenzo I Gonzaga of Mantua, where he came under the tutelage of the local cathedral's maestro di cappella, Giaches de Wert, one of the *Oltremontani*, as the Italians called northern European composers. The vocal works of the Franco-Flemish school, including

Dufay, Ockeghem, and Josquin des Prez, were revered throughout Europe as the *ars perfecta*. These polyphonic compositions, in which several groups of vocalists or entire choruses sang different melodic lines simultaneously, were, as *perfecta* implies, considered the epitome of vocal musical expression.

Within two years of his move to Mantua, Monteverdi produced a third book of madrigals. Showing the influence of Wert and the *Oltremontani*, this book includes musical settings of texts by the late-Renaissance poets Torquato Tasso and Battista Guarini. While adopting the principles of the *ars perfecta*, in these compositions Monteverdi experimented with dissonance, soon recognized as a hallmark of his compositions, to enhance the emotional impact of his texts.

By 1600 Monteverdi was Europe's premier avant-garde composer. His books of madrigals were in great demand, and the works were widely performed. His reputation was unintentionally enhanced by Bolognese musical theorist Giovanni Maria Artusi, who published pamphlet tirades against Monteverdi, attacking his increasingly novel uses of harmony, melody, and rhythm, and taking particular aim at his use of dissonance.

While Artusi ranted, Monteverdi, now maestro di cappella in Mantua, published his fourth and fifth books of madrigals in 1603 and 1604, to critical and popular acclaim. Monteverdi's first opera, *Orfeo* (1607), sounds like the work of a polished operatic composer because he had laid much of its groundwork in the fifth madrigal book, which he himself considered a demarcation between his old and new styles. Clearly showcasing Monteverdi's dramatic talent, sixteen of the nineteen madrigals in this book were based on highly sensuous poems by Guarini.

Stretching the boundaries of the madrigal, the composer included declamatory passages sung by small choruses, portions for a solo voice opposed by a small chorus singing in counterpoint or in imitation, as well as solos, duets, trios, and passages with rich musical accompaniment. The focus is on the melody, and the emotional pitch of the music mirrors that of the verse. The poems he selected featured short dramatic scenes for which he composed such crisply paced yet fully developed musical settings that it was a relatively small step from a collection of these miniatures to a full opera.

The madrigals of the fifth book sound remarkably modern, primarily because of how harmonies are used to punctuate the most heart-rending lines of Guarini's texts. Dissonance is expertly manipulated to convey nuances of emotion. This music astounded Monteverdi's contemporaries, who heard harmonies with which they were completely unfamiliar, unusual rhythmic sequences, and novel pairings of instruments and of instruments with voices. In the preface to a Milanese edition, the publisher called the music of the fifth book "the most pleasant tyrant of the mind."

Amid the flurry surrounding these publications, Claudio's brother, Giulio Cesare, crafted a lengthy rebuttal to Artusi, in which he wrote that Monteverdi saw himself as the product of at least fifty years of musical evolution and that Claudio now defined modern music as consisting of two styles. The *prima prattica* (first "practice" or style) was essentially the *ars perfecta,* the old, mostly religious polyphonic music that exemplified Netherlandish ideals and manifested strict rules for counterpoint and harmony. Of paramount importance in this style was the perfection of the musical phrase, which often had little emotional relationship to the text. Somber verse, for example, might be set to light, pleasant music. Unusual harmonies and uneven rhythms had no place in the *prima prattica.*

Monteverdi derived the *seconda prattica* (second style) from Plato's discussion of the three musical elements essential for moving the listener's soul: text, harmony, and rhythm. Primacy was given to the expression of the text, as summarized by Giulio Cesare Monteverdi: "The word, the text, with all its values and qualities, should be the master, not the servant, of the musical harmony." The composer did not mean that each syllable had to be discernible, and he saw no reason to dispense with the polyphony of the *prima prattica,* in which individual words and phrases were often obscured. Instead, he believed that the music should embellish the mood and passion of the poetic text.

Orfeo, subtitled *Favola in Musica* (Play Set to Music), was commissioned by the Accademia degl'Invaghiti, an aristocratic arts salon, and first performed on February 24, 1607, at the Gonzaga Palace in Mantua. It was an immediate success, dwarfing *Dafne* (1597) and *Euridice* (1600), the pioneering operatic efforts of Jacopo Peri, which now seemed rudimentary, insipid, and overly academic (see Essay 32).

In contrast, Monteverdi produced a deeply emotional and highly dramatic work that told the familiar story of Orpheus and Eurydice in a libretto by Alessandro Striggio the Younger. Emboldened by his power to sway all of nature with his music, Orfeo follows his recently dead wife Euridice down to Hades, where local autocrat Plutone agrees to release her, but with one condition—that Orfeo not look back at his wife during the ascent. Alarmed by a sudden noise, Orfeo turns to check on her, and she disappears before his eyes. In Monteverdi's revised ending, after

Orfeo returns to the upper world, he laments for Euridice so movingly that his father, Apollo, takes him up into heaven. There Orfeo will admire his beloved's likeness in the sun and stars.

Besides being a fully mature operatic work, *Orfeo* is Monteverdi's musical curriculum vitae, showcasing his facility with all the musical genres of the time. An opening toccata serves as an overture, choruses comment on the action, pop songs (not an invention of the twentieth century) are incorporated in jocular scenes, somber music marks the sober passages, and ballet music is occasionally heard. Most important, Monteverdi fuses the *intermedi* (the elaborately staged musical allegories slotted between scenes of court plays of the time) with the simplicity of the recitative, the new hybrid of singing and speaking first used by Jacopo Peri to further the dramatic action in operas.

Monteverdi's first opera also marked the debut of the first truly modern orchestra, containing up to three dozen instruments: two harpsichord-type instruments, two double basses, ten arm-viols, a double-strung harp, two small (or French) violins, three violas da gamba, two bass lutes, two wooden pipe organs, a portable organ, four trombones, two cornets, a flute, and four trumpets. At a time when composers typically specified that vocal pieces be accompanied by a harpsichord and a lute or two, this was an outlandish collection of instruments. It became the model for all orchestras that followed.

The instrumental score also had some novel features and made great technical demands on the instrumentalists. No composer had written more difficult music, and Monteverdi owed some of his success with the premiere of *Orfeo* to the unusually well-trained musicians in Mantua. He also made some startlingly novel instrumental couplings, specifying, for example, that trombones and double basses play simultaneously.

In *Orfeo*, Monteverdi uses musical climaxes to reflect the dramatic climaxes in Striggio's text by composing lines with emotionally powerful instrumental sonorities that demand virtuosity from the singers. Agitation builds steadily through the passage in which the nymph Silvia brings news of Euridice's death to Orfeo and his shepherd friends, who first wonder at her unexpected appearance, and then, sensing disaster, beg the gods to "turn not your benign gaze away from us." For any listener who has had to impart tragic news, Silvia's agony is palpable when she sings, "Ah me! Must I then, even as Orfeo delights heaven with his songs, pierce his heart with my words?"

After the first performance of *Orfeo*, Monteverdi returned to his father's home in Cremona and, following his young wife's death there, was incapacitated by depression. Although he initially resisted the demands of his Gonzaga patrons that he return to Mantua to compose a new opera for the marriage celebrations of Francesco Gonzaga and Margaret of Savoy, Monteverdi was eventually lured back to the city, and he immediately started writing the music for *L'Arianna* (Ariadne), for which Jacopo Peri's librettist, Ottavio Rinuccini, had written the text. He was also pressed to write *intermedi* and ballets for the Gonzaga nuptials.

Then, weeks before the wedding day, the composer suffered another blow when the young vocalist who had been cast as Arianna, and who had lived in Monteverdi's home as his wife's pupil, died of smallpox. The part was reassigned, and the opera was subsequently performed to overwhelming acclaim, as were the ballet and *intermedi*. Only one aria, the enormously popular "Lament" that the composer reworked at least twice, survives from the score of *L'Arianna*. It has been said that while *Orfeo* launched modern opera, *L'Arianna* kept the art form afloat until it was more firmly established. Monteverdi was now recognized as the preeminent composer of Europe.

In 1610, after another bout of depression and ongoing bickering with the Gonzagas, Monteverdi wrote a Vespers for the Feasts of the Blessed Virgin Mary and, obviously seeking a position at the Vatican, dedicated it to Pope Paul V. Like *Orfeo*, the Vespers displayed Monteverdi's skills with a variety of forms, including old-style counterpoint, modern psalm settings, plainsong chants, virtuoso solos, and two nearly operatic settings of the Magnificat. The Vespers also marked the introduction of secular elements, including instrumental interludes, into liturgical music, which may be the reason the Vatican didn't hire him.

In 1613 Monteverdi was asked to audition for what turned out to be his happiest professional post and one that he would retain for thirty years, maestro di cappella at St. Mark's Cathedral in Venice, whose musical programs had declined since the recent death of Giovanni Gabrieli. Liturgical composition was serious business in Venice: A priest saying Mass could receive a stiff fine for interrupting the music. Within several years, Monteverdi had restored musical glory to St. Mark's.

By this time, most of Monteverdi's enemies in Mantua had died, and he was again accepting commissions from its court. He wrote numerous works for Mantuan patrons, including the ballet *Tirsi e Clori* (1616), as well as several cycles of *intermedi* and his seventh (1619) and eighth (1638) books of madrigals. In the 1624 cantata *Combattimento di Tancredi e Clorinda* (The Battle of Tancredi and Clorinda), he put the orchestra to novel use by having the violinists pluck their instruments to mimic the clashing of swords and directing them to play brief passages softly then loudly in rapid succession to suggest the irregular breathing of the dying Clorinda.

Monteverdi continued to write and publish secular and liturgical works, including a 1631 Mass of Thanksgiving to mark the end of the plague. Shortly afterward, he was ordained a priest. Then, in 1637, Venice opened the first public opera house in Italy and, a year later, his *L'Arianna* was revived.

With a venue for operas in his beloved Venice, the seventy-year-old master embarked on a second phase of operatic production, from which only two works survive, *Il ritorno d'Ulisse in patria* (The Return of Ulysses to His Country) and *L'incoronazione di Poppea* (The Coronation of Poppea). More than ever, Monteverdi emphasized the importance of depicting realistic human emotions in dramatic situations. *Poppea*, one of the first operas based on historic events rather than on mythological, biblical, or pastoral themes, tells the story of conniving Poppea and the Emperor Nero, an adulterous pair of antiheros who achieve happiness after destroying statesman-philosopher Seneca and banishing Nero's wife, Octavia, and Poppea's former lover, Otho.

After a farewell trip to Cremona and Mantua, Monteverdi returned to die in Venice on November 29, 1643, "as a swan, feeling the final hour near, approaches the water and, in it, passes on to another life singing," according to a contemporary. The composer's tomb lies in Venice's church of the Frari.

Opera, the first culturally unifying force in a politically fragmented Italy, quickly became a ubiquitous entertainment. Nearly four hundred different operatic works had been produced in Venice's seventeen opera houses by 1700. From its epicenter in Venice, the craze for opera quickly spread to Naples, Vienna, Paris, Hamburg, Salzburg, London, and elsewhere. European composers, including Handel, Gluck, and Mozart, invariably traveled to and trained in the cradle of opera, and Italian became the language of music, with its wealth of terms like sonata, soprano, allegro, andante, piano, forte, crescendo, prima donna, and castrati. Italian composers were commissioned to write operas in Germany, Austria, France, and England. Eventually, national schools of opera developed in these and other countries, but the inspiration provided by Italian composers permeated every salon and stage, as it does to this day, when most of us, Wagner's horn-helmeted sopranos notwithstanding, still think of opera as "Made in Italy."

Thirty-six

The Baroque splendors of Bernini

The opinion is widespread that Bernini was the first to attempt to unite architecture with painting and sculpture in such a manner that they make a beautiful whole.
—Filippo Baldinucci, *The Life of Bernini* (1682)

AGAINST A BACKGROUND of alabaster, surrounded by blue-green marble, and illuminated by golden light descending from an unseen source, a swooning woman is buoyed by a bank of clouds while an angel, as much rascal as heavenly messenger, is poised to strike her breast with a fine-tipped arrow. This is Gian Lorenzo Bernini's best-known sculptural group, depicting the ecstasy of St. Teresa of Ávila, her mystical union with Christ effected by an angel who pierced her heart with divine love, "the sweetest caressing of the soul by God," as she called it. The mesmerizing, erotically charged sculpture is the embodiment of the Baroque.

St. Teresa resides above the altar of the Cornaro Chapel in the church of Santa Maria della Vittoria in Rome. Conceived and executed by Bernini in the late 1640s and early 1650s, the chapel exemplifies his intensely dramatic artistic vision, with its elaborate, multicolored marbles, light emanating seemingly from the heavens, and architectural settings for sculptures that are meant to be viewed from only one angle, including two groups of cardinals (members of the illustrious Venetian Cornaro family) whimsically perched in what appear to be opera boxes on either side of the altar. Some of the cardinals converse animatedly about the mystical event before them, while others meditate on its significance.

Bernini was born in Naples on December 7, 1598, to a Florentine sculptor, Pietro, and his Neapolitan wife, Angelica, who, according to art historian Rudolph Wittkower, endowed him with Tuscan precision and a Neapolitan temperament, both of which are discernible in his works. On being hired by Cardinal Scipione Borghese and his uncle,

Pope Paul V, Pietro moved his family to Rome in 1605, where seven-year-old Gian Lorenzo trained with his father and spent hours in the Vatican Museum, studying and sketching ancient Greek and Roman statuary, as well as works by Raphael and Michelangelo. The younger Bernini's earliest surviving sculpture, *The Goat Amalthea Nursing the Infant Zeus and a Young Satyr,* dates from 1615, when Gian Lorenzo was sixteen. This depiction of an indulgent Almathea with two playful youngsters was sometimes mistaken for a Hellenistic work.

Between 1615 and 1624, Bernini's talent matured rapidly. He produced several busts before 1620, but the *Anima Dannata (Damned Soul),* howling in terror as he encounters the torments of hell, is notable because its artistic antecedents were not sculptures but paintings, especially several works by emotional powerhouse Michelangelo da Caravaggio. Bernini worked primarily on commissions for Cardinal Scipione Borghese and his family until 1624, including works such as the highly realistic busts of beefy Scipione himself and of Paul V.

Not limiting himself to "talking statues" of prelates, Bernini also sculpted a bust of his married mistress, Costanza Bonarelli, which Howard Hibbard has called "a petrified fragment of passion." With her full, parted lips, startled expression, rumpled hair, and décolleté chemise, *Costanza* anticipates by more than a century similar depictions of women, captured as if by surprise in the throes of emotion. When Bernini caught Costanza cheating on him with his own brother, the hot-blooded artist severely beat his sibling and paid a servant to slash his lover's face, whose beauty he both immortalized and destroyed. After the ugly scandal blew over, Bernini settled down with a young Roman woman in a marriage that produced eleven children, assuming a pious, orderly life that included daily attendance at Mass. His son Domenico later described him as "stern by nature, steady in his work, passionate in his wrath."

The major sculptural achievements of this early phase of Bernini's long career are three life-size works: *Pluto and Proserpina, Apollo and Daphne,* and *David.* In each, the crux of a narrative is etched on the figures' faces and forms. Pluto abducts the thrashing Proserpina with lust and even a glint of amusement visible in his eyes, while the girl's marble tears and contorted limbs project blind despair. Beyond the eerie expressiveness of the figures, we note for the first time Bernini's genius to shape marble like soft clay. Where Pluto grasps her, Proserpina's flesh is indented by his fingers in a brutally realistic fashion.

Apollo and Daphne is based on Ovid's story of Daphne's transformation by her river-god father into a laurel tree to spare her from being raped by Apollo (see Essay 7). Still in pursuit, a startled Apollo sees the metamorphosis of her splayed fingers into leafy twigs before she is even aware of her transformation, and Bernini captures him in the instant that he starts recoiling from her. Daphne's O-shaped, shrieking mouth (again invoking Caravaggio) seems like the portal to an unfathomable pit of grief as she arches away from her pursuer. Although the work was created early in his career, Bernini considered *Apollo and Daphne* his most virtuosic sculpture. The intimate, disturbing impact of both groups is enhanced by their illusion of motion, as suggested even by Daphne's billowing hair.

The *David* of 1623–24 was a marked departure from earlier depictions by Donatello and Michelangelo (see Essays 19 and 26). Bernini's young hero is all motion and emotion as he twists back to fire his slingshot at an unseen Goliath. David's face, said to be a self-portrait, reveals a steely will with its set jaw, pursed lips, and ridged brow.

Although these three works can be seen in the round today at Rome's Galleria Borghese, Bernini intended them to be installed so that they could be viewed only from a single angle (the *Apollo and Daphne* being particularly incoherent from certain viewpoints). Bernini, who created more than two hundred paintings himself, was thinking like a painter as well as a sculptor. Like the Renaissance sculptors before him, he also understood that since these works represented an instant of dramatic action, it was entirely suitable that the viewer first see them from the single angle he intended. This made it crucial that his sculpted figures and groups be fully integrated into the surrounding architectural space, and in this strategy he was followed by most seventeenth-century sculptors.

In 1623 one of Bernini's patrons, Cardinal Maffeo Barberini, became Pope Urban VIII. Baldinucci reported that "the Pope had conceived the lofty ambition that in his pontificate Rome would produce another Michelangelo." Perhaps the gracious prelate was sincere—not merely practicing a seventeenth-century form of motivational psychology—when he told the young artist, "It is your great luck, Cavaliere, to see Maffeo Barberini Pope, but We are even luckier that the Cavaliere Bernini lives at the time of our pontificate."

Bernini's first commission from Urban was to create a new façade for the church of Santa Bibiana, his maiden architectural venture. He was also to redecorate the interior and design new vestments for the priests. His statue of the teenaged ancient Roman martyr, his first fully clothed subject, which stands behind the altar, exhibits the fiery physical energy of his earlier pieces but transmuted by Bibiana's radiant acceptance of her cruel fate. Sunlight accentuates her upraised hand (and originally shone also on her face, before a hidden source was sealed during the next century) in this first instance of Bernini's use of light to illuminate sculpture.

In 1624 he was appointed architect of St. Peter's Basilica, which had been under construction since Julius II laid the first stone in 1506. By Bernini's time, nearly all the greatest Italian architects had worked in this largest church in Christendom, which was now set to undergo a transformation from a Renaissance to a Baroque edifice.

For nearly sixty years, Bernini would labor on the architectural, sculptural, and theatrical vision that is St. Peter's. The first task assigned him by the Barberini pope was to follow through on an idea originally proposed by Carlo Maderno, who designed the church's façade, to create a towering canopy, or *baldacchino*, over the main altar, which lies under Michelangelo's dome and over the tomb of St. Peter. Bernini completed this massive, magnificent fusion of sculpture and architecture in 1633 after nine years of work. Some of the required bronze was pilfered from girders on the Pantheon's portico, a bit of papal vandalism that gave rise to the epigram "What the barbarians didn't do, the Barberini did."

Four bronze spiral columns, a motif borrowed from the old St. Peter's, sinuously twist their way up to a superstructure populated by putti (holding the papal tiara, St. Peter's keys, and the emblems of St. Paul) and by four gigantic bronze angels at the corners, and capped by a gilt-bronze orb supporting a large cross. Fluting, with gilded ridges and dark grooves, marks the bottom third of each column, infusing the structure with even more swirling energy. Along with scampering, mischievous putti, lush laurel branches and bees (emblems of the busy Barberini family) grace the upper two-thirds of each column.

While the ninety-foot *baldacchino* was being erected, Bernini began transforming the four great crossing piers beneath the dome into shrines for relics. Commissions for statues for three of the niches were given to other artists, but in 1638 Bernini completed the fourteen-and-a-half-foot Carrara-marble *St. Longinus*, a masterpiece of his mature style. In that work he captured the moment when the Roman centurion, still clutching the lance with which he had pierced Christ's side, gazes at him on the cross and exclaims, "Truly this man was the son of God."

According to Baldinucci, after the pontificates of Urban VIII and Innocent X, Pope Alexander VII asked to see the famous artist on the very day of his election in 1655, and the following year he commissioned him to design a new piazza in front of St. Peter's, an area that had been neglected since medieval times. Bernini's creation, St. Peter's Square, is now one of the world's most visited, photographed, and televised open architectural spaces.

The square had to be large enough to contain thousands of pilgrims, with shelter also provided from the rain and the hot Roman sun. In addition, the two sites at which the pope appeared, the Benediction Loggia and his window in the Vatican Palace, had to be visible from as many vantage points as possible.

The solution Bernini devised, probably with assistance from the pope and one of his associates, Virgilio Spada, was to enclose an elliptical area equivalent to that enclosed by the Colosseum with two semicircular colonnades. These structures were to be connected to St. Peter's by colonnaded corridors, which delimited a trapezoidal space, modeled on Michelangelo's Campidoglio and located immediately in front of the church. Nearly three hundred Tuscan columns were arranged in rows of four, which delineated two narrow pedestrian paths flanking a wider carriage path. The devout Bernini, preeminent artist of the Counter-Reformation, wrote that the colonnades would envelop Catholics in a kind of maternal embrace, encouraging them "to reinforce their belief, heretics to reunite them with the Church, and infidels to enlighten them with the true faith."

In the same year that Pope Alexander commissioned St. Peter's Square, he directed Bernini to create a setting for the *Cathedra Petri* (Throne of Peter), a wooden throne that was believed to be that of the first pope, but that probably belonged to Carolingian emperor Charles the Bald, who was crowned in the old St. Peter's in the ninth century. After encasing the ancient chair in bronze gilt, Bernini set it afloat on stucco clouds in the apse of St. Peter's, above the choir, flanked by four Church Fathers, each highly individualized and with agitated robes like St. Teresa's in the Cornaro Chapel. In an archetypally Baroque synthesis of painting, sculpture, and architecture, light descends on the throne through a dove representing the Holy Spirit, painted on an oval sunburst window adorned with gilded rays.

Another project for Pope Alexander, completed during the 1660s, attests to Bernini's imaginative engineering. The artist considered the Scala Regia (Royal Staircase), linking St. Peter's with the Vatican

Palace, his most difficult technical challenge, requiring columns to be repositioned and windows to be added for dramatic and functional lighting. At the main landing, he placed one of the great sculptures of his later career, an equestrian statue of the Emperor Constantine on a rearing horse, both rider and mount astonished by the blazing Cross that has appeared in the heavens. By manipulating light and illusionistic perspectives, Bernini made the ascent of the long staircase appear more difficult than it actually proves to be.

In the late 1660s a new pope, Clement IX, a close friend of Bernini's, commissioned statues of angels to decorate the Sant'Angelo Bridge, which spans the Tiber, linking its far bank with an approach to the Vatican. The ten grieving, larger-than-life angels, who carry the instruments of Christ's passion, are among the most hauntingly expressive of Bernini's sculptures, and, unlike many of his statues, they can be viewed from all angles. All of them stand in marked contrapposto (one knee bent, one hip higher than the other), swathed in billowing drapery. The originals were apparently never intended to be placed outdoors, but at least one of the copies standing on the bridge today was crafted by Bernini.

With the angels in place, Bernini's creations now beckoned travelers from across the Tiber into the piazza of St. Peter's and the magnificent church itself, drew them to the main altar surmounted by the *baldacchino*, encouraged contemplation of the relics in the niches of the crossing, and finally brought them to the *Throne of Peter*, the most potent symbol of the Church Triumphant.

Bernini's son recalled his father saying that when he wanted "a relief from my duties [and] to console myself with my work," he went to Sant'Andrea al Quirinale, a small church sometimes called "the Pearl of the Baroque," which the Jesuits had commissioned from him in 1658. Bernini had addressed the long but narrow site with an unusual oval plan.

Complex Baroque curves upon an oval shape make a striking exterior. Passing through a projecting porch on the short axis of the oval, worshipers immediately face the altar, which is set behind fluted columns of rich, red-flecked marble. Guglielmo Cortese's painting of the martyrdom of the church's patron, St. Andrew, hangs on the rear wall, illuminated from an unseen source. Above the altar a statue by one of Bernini's students portrays the saint in the act of ascending to heaven, which is represented by a gilt-coffered oval dome ringed by large windows adorned with putti. The dramatic qualities of Sant'Andrea remind us that Bernini was also a renowned theatrical set designer known for his frightening special effects, including an onstage fire and a simulated flood that sent panicked audiences scurrying for the exits.

If Rome is a city of fountains, Bernini deserves the credit. Only a handful of his creations remain, but his emulators were legion, as visitors to the Eternal City can attest. Water flowing over stone intrigued this artist who, from his earliest works, sought to embody animated movement in his sculptures. His most celebrated creation in this genre is the *Fountain of the Four Rivers* in Piazza Navona, built between 1648 and 1651 in honor of Pope Innocent X.

Dominating the huge square, the work features an ancient obelisk topped by the dove of the Holy Spirit and resting apparently weightlessly atop a naturalistic rock formation. Four rivers—the Danube, Nile, Plate, and Ganges—gush out from it accompanied by geographically appropriate flora and fauna and crowned by papal insignias. Although the fountain was designed by Bernini, the head and torso of a horse were probably among the only portions actually carved (or touched up) by his own hand.

Bernini suffered a few setbacks during his life, too. A bell tower he designed for the façade of St. Peter's proved structurally unsound and had to be demolished in 1646. When Louis XIV invited the artist to Paris in 1665 to rebuild the royal residence, the Louvre, Bernini apparently made so many disparaging remarks about the state of the arts in France—including the suggestion that all the Court's painters and sculptors be sent to Italy for training—that he was sent packing after five months, and his plan for the Louvre was ignored. Nonetheless, his bust of the Sun King, completed during this ill-fated trip, became the most imitated portrait bust over the next hundred years.

Bernini died on November 28, 1680, just days shy of his eighty-second birthday, having toiled for eight popes. His death came after a series of strokes that left his right arm paralyzed. The dying artist consoled his nine surviving children with the notion that it was only fair to rest an arm that had worked so very hard during its long life—a life, he might have added, that transformed the visual arts in all of Europe—the life of the greatest sculptor since Michelangelo and of a titan of Baroque architecture.

Thirty-seven

Pioneers of modern anatomy: Eustachio, Fallopio, Malpighi, Morgagni, et al.

For the unloosing of these knots I have destroyed almost the whole race of frogs.
—Marcello Malpighi, *De pulmonibus, Observationes anatomicae* (1661)

MEDICINE OWES MUCH TO Malpighi's frogs, not to mention many unfortunate humans who met their deaths on the scaffold and ended up on the dissection table. Marcello Malpighi was a pioneer in using the microscope to investigate the structures of animal and plant tissues, and we all carry around several anatomic structures named in his honor. But Malpighi was only one of numerous Italian anatomists who, beginning in the thirteenth century with that most fundamental part of a physician's education—dissection and study of the human body—helped transform medicine from a folk craft into a science.

The chief ancient anatomic texts to survive the Dark Ages were Arabic translations of the Greek writings of Galen (d. c. A.D. 200), the Greco-Roman physician who compiled the writings of other medical scientists and his own observations on anatomy and physiology. Although by 1200 many of Galen's medical works had been translated into Latin, his two major anatomic treatises would not be available in the European language of science and learning until the fourteenth and sixteenth centuries. Nonetheless, Galen long remained Europe's most prestigious authority on human anatomy. Observations that contradicted his writings were often attributed to a gradual degeneration in the human species since ancient times, rather than being considered evidence that his work might contain some inaccuracies.

Except for the Alexandrian scientists Herophilus and his rival Erasistratus, most ancient physicians, including Hippocrates and Galen, apparently confined themselves to animal dissections. The Muslims, who dominated medieval medicine, forbade human dissections outright. Physicians gained anatomic information only by treating open wounds or through the fortuitous discovery of skeletons. Galen had correctly determined that blood flows from the right side of the heart to the lungs and back to the left side of the heart only by attending gladiators dying of massive chest wounds.

The first dissections of animals of any kind since antiquity were performed at the University of Salerno in the twelfth century (see Essay 10). Pigs were used for these early studies, as in courses today, because of their anatomic similarity to humans. Much of the credit for shifting the focus of medical studies to human anatomy belongs to Emperor Frederick II (see Essay 12), who in the mid-thirteenth century decreed that the bodies of two executed criminals be delivered every two years to the medical school at Salerno for a public dissection that all medical practitioners were required to attend. Human dissection was gradually adopted at the universities of Paris, Montpellier, and Bologna.

In 1316 Mondino de' Liuzzi (1270–1326), a professor of practical medicine at the University of Bologna who conducted public human dissections, wrote the first modern European anatomy text. Since Mondino relied more heavily on Galen than on his own observations, his *Anathomia* is riddled with errors, but it was superior enough to anything else available to serve as the standard handbook for human dissections for two hundred years.

The most important anatomic studies during the fifteenth and early sixteenth centuries were those of Jacopo Berengario da Carpi (1460–1530), a professor at Bologna and the author of the first known descriptions of the appendix and heart valves. Berengario, who also described in detail the thymus and pineal glands and the opening of the common bile duct into the intestine, was among the first scientists to posit that Galen's anatomic lore was often inaccurate. His *Commentaries* on the work of Mondino de' Liuzzi was the first printed book to provide anatomic illustrations. Berengario also produced the first known printed work on the surgical management of head injuries after he successfully treated Lorenzo de' Medici, Duke of Urbino, for a serious skull wound.

The pace of discovery accelerated in 1537, when the Flemish physician Andreas Vesalius was appointed lecturer at the University of Padua, from which he had just received his medical degree. As was the custom, Vesalius lectured while assistants did the actual cutting. Because his blade men were inept, Vesalius soon took over both tasks—and was surprised by what he found.

Literally up to his elbows in human corpses, Vesalius, like Berengario, found that much of Galen's teaching was erroneous, and he concluded that the Greek master must have dissected only animals and extrapolated his findings to humans. Not yet thirty, Vesalius challenged much of Galen's dogma in his landmark *De humani corporis fabrica* (*On the Structure of the Human Body*), published in 1543 with drawings made in Titian's studio. Vesalius left Padua the next year, but his legacy endured. The *Fabrica* and the earlier, exquisitely detailed anatomic drawings of Leonardo da Vinci (see Essay 23), who dissected numerous cadavers, launched the modern era of anatomic illustration. Physicians now realized that only by examining many human bodies could they determine whether a particular anatomic structure was normal or pathological.

Vesalius was succeeded at Padua by his student Matteo Realdo Colombo (1516–59), a native of Cremona, who in 1545 was recruited by Duke Cosimo de' Medici to be the first professor of anatomy at the University of Pisa. Three years later, Colombo became chairman of the anatomy department at the Papal University in Rome, where prelates often joined medical students at his dissections. He also served as personal physician to the elderly Michelangelo, who, writes Vasari, "for many years was syringed by the hand of his dear friend" for bladder stones.

Colombo wrote one of the first accurate descriptions of the movement of blood within the pulmonary circulation, which, along with that of the contemporary Spanish anatomist Michael Servetus, confirmed Galen's observations on this point. He described systole, the pumping or contraction phase of the heart, and diastole, its relaxation or filling phase. He discovered the valves that permit only one-way movement of blood in the vessels leaving the right and left ventricles of the heart and noted that the beating heart was "most beautiful to behold." Colombo may have been the first modern scientist to deliberately expose living organs for observation (the heart and lungs of small animals). English physician William Harvey, who wrote the most complete early description of the circulation of the blood in 1628, gave Colombo due credit as a predecessor.

Bartolomeo Eustachio (1520–74), born near Ancona, was a student of Vesalius and succeeded Colombo at the Papal University. He described the stirrup bone in the ear, as well as the canal or tube joining the ear and throat that bears his name, although credit for discovering these structures apparently belongs to a lesser-known Sicilian physician, Giovanni Ingrassia (1510–80), who wrote about them in 1546. Eustachio also studied the insertion and attachment of several muscles in the head, face, neck, and upper back and wrote a treatise on dentistry.

His meticulous descriptions of the human fetal circulation included a crucial feature: the valve (still called eustachian) that directs blood from the inferior vena cava to the foramen ovale, the opening between the right and left atria of the heart that closes within minutes of birth. He made an accurate study of renal anatomy and discovered the adrenal gland. His most distinguished work may have been his copper plate engravings of the sympathetic nervous system and his description of the thoracic duct of the lymphatic system.

Gabriello Fallopio (1523–62) made discoveries that advanced the study of several organ systems and also contributed to diagnostic and therapeutic practice. After a brief stint as a cleric in his native Modena, Fallopio, who came from an impoverished family, scrimped to obtain a medical education at the University of Ferrara, where he became a professor of anatomy in 1548. He also taught at the universities of Pisa and Padua before his death at age thirty-nine.

Fallopio, most famous for his description of the fallopian tubes, the conduits from the ovaries to the uterus, made a detailed study of the reproductive systems of both sexes. In *Observationes anatomicae* (1561) he named the vagina from the Latin word for "scabbard" and gave the name *placenta* (Latin for "flat cake") to that life-sustaining interface between mother and child. The uterine artery, which he first described, is also known as the fallopian artery.

Fallopio made detailed studies of the head, especially the inner ear, the circular and oval windows, and the tympanic membrane. He named the cochlea, the labyrinth-like structure of the inner ear, from the Latin word for "snail." He studied and named the hard and soft palate from the Latin for "vault" and elucidated the workings of the tear ducts. His study of anatomy led him to write several texts on surgery, in addition to others on drug therapy and syphilis.

Hieronymus Fabricius ab Aquapendente (1537–1619), also known as Girolamo Fabrizio, was a student of Fallopio at the University of Padua and, at twenty-five, succeeded him as chairman of anatomy. Fabricius's patients included Galileo, and he trained William Harvey, who traveled to Padua to study with him. In Venice the Senate built Fabricius an anatomic theater for his visiting lectures. In his 1603 work *De venarum ostiolis* (*On the Valves of the Veins*), Fabricius gave the first systematic description of how the valves in the leg veins assist the return of blood to the heart and prevent it from pooling. This work was another seminal influence on Harvey, who expanded on it to describe the circulation throughout the body.

Continuing the work of Fallopio, Fabricius made a more complete study of the human placenta and, with the publication of *De formato foetu* (*On the Formation of the Fetus*) in 1600, he founded modern embryology. He also identified the larynx as the organ of speech and described how the pupil of the eye changes size in response to varying light intensities.

Marcello Malpighi (1628–94), born near Bologna in the same year that Harvey's book on circulation was published, supplied the answers to questions that had puzzled the great English scientist: How does blood recirculate? Where do veins and arteries meet? This is how Malpighi recounted his discovery of capillaries: "Although in the lungs of animals a vessel sometimes appears to end and gape . . . , it is probable that, as occurs in frogs and turtles, it has minute vessels that are propagated farther in the form of a network, though these elude even the keenest sight because of their small size."

Malpighi, who received his medical degree at the University of Bologna in 1653, began wide-ranging research that entitles him to be called the father of microscopic anatomy, or histology (the study of minute tissue structures). His grand contribution was his exploitation of modern optics, in the form of the microscope, for studying anatomy and embryology. His histologic studies were an essential step toward a better understanding of human physiology.

In 1660 Malpighi wrote two letters to a colleague in Pisa that were published in 1661 as *De pulmonibus*, a groundbreaking work in the history of science. Harvey had inferred the existence of capillaries, but without the benefit of optical advances he had been unable to observe them. Malpighi described viewing the capillary bed in frog lungs with the aid of his microscope. He produced detailed engravings of the capillary network and observed a similar capillary mesh on the surface of a distended frog bladder, demonstrating that the arteries and veins eventually meet in a web of fine vessels that allow blood to recirculate.

Based on the amount of envy Malpighi's discovery engendered, its magnitude must been evident to his colleagues. Unwilling to endure their harassment, he took a job at the University of Messina. While practicing and teaching medicine in Sicily, he continued his microscopic studies, discovering the taste buds and correctly associating them with nerve endings. He described the cortex of the brain and studied the minutiae of cerebral tissue, identified the optic nerve, and was one of the first researchers to see red blood cells, which he likened to a "rosary of red coral." Returning to Bologna in 1667, he continued his work on organ tissues, detailing the structure of the liver, spleen, kidney, bone, and skin. In 1669 Malpighi became the first Italian to be made an honorary member of London's Royal Society.

In that same year he wrote a detailed anatomic study of the silkworm; four years later, he published his studies on the development of the chick embryo. Not content with the animal world, he detailed the structure of plants and wood, eventually proving that a tree's age could be determined by the number of rings in a cross section of its trunk. His major work in botany, *Anatome plantarum* (1675), contained drawings that were completely understood by other botanists only in the nineteenth century.

Giovanni Battista Morgagni (1682–1771), a native of Forlì, graduate of the University of Bologna, and for sixty years professor at the University of Padua, was the founder of pathologic anatomy. His magnum opus, *De sedibus et causis morborum per anatomen indagatis* (*The Sites and Causes of Diseases as Investigated by Anatomy,* 1761), which he published when almost eighty, contains five hundred case studies that illustrate his signal achievement: the correlation of risk factors, symptoms, organ dysfunction, and diseases.

In one case, Morgagni details the final illness of a gouty, fleshy, vertiginous cardinal "troubled with cares and anxieties of the mind," who lost feeling and motion on his left side and subsequently died. In describing the autopsy of this victim of stroke, he says the internal organs were in their "natural state," but the brain was "flaccid" with areas of pooled blood and ulcerated tissue. Morgagni ascribed the stroke to the cardinal's anxious state and gout and correctly associated the brain damage with the paralysis. Such conclusions represented a huge leap in Morgagni's time, when illness still was often blamed on imbalances among the four humors of ancient medicine—blood, phlegm, black bile, and yellow bile.

Morgagni's studies, which were translated into French, English, and German, produced the first crack in the humoral model of disease, and the link he established between anatomic lesions and disease symptoms made pathology one of the leading medical disciplines of the nineteenth century. He was the first physician to describe cirrhosis, kidney failure, and Adams-Stokes disease, in which irregularities of cardiac electrical conduction cause loss of consciousness. Morgagni insisted that surgery provided the best chance of curing malignancy and made a systematic study of aortic aneurysms. Unlike other physicians of his time, who focused on symptoms and how to eliminate them, Morgagni delved deeper, seeking structural explanations.

Morgagni's versatile student Antonio Scarpa (1752–1832) described the pathology of clubfoot and the innervation of the heart and wrote the first Italian ophthalmology text. His contemporary, Domenico Cotugno, made exquisite studies of the inner ear and described sciatica and cerebrospinal fluid.

The Italian contribution to anatomic and medical studies in more recent times is evidenced by several Nobel laureates in physiology or medicine, starting with Camillo Golgi, who shared the award in 1906 for his detailed studies of the nervous system. Golgi was followed by Salvador Luria, who shared the 1969 prize for his work on viral replication, and Renato Dulbecco, who, with two others, won the award in 1975 for their work on tumor viruses. Rita Levi-Montalcini, a Jewish Italian neuropsychiatrist who had to work out of a secret home laboratory in Turin during World War II and became professor of neurobiology at Washington University in St. Louis, Missouri, in 1947, won a Nobel Prize in 1986 for her work on nerve growth factor. This world-class standard of medical research continues into the twenty-first century with major Italian clinical trials on heart disease, cancer, diabetes, and all the other scourges of humankind, which will someday yield their secrets to painstaking investigation of the type that went into the Italian anatomic breakthroughs.

Thirty-eight

Founder of modern penology: Cesare Beccaria

> In order for punishment not to be, in every instance, an act of vio-
> lence . . . , it must be essentially public, prompt, necessary, the least
> possible in the given circumstances, proportionate to the crimes, dic-
> tated by the laws.[1]
>
> —Cesare Beccaria, On Crimes and Punishments (1764)

AT THE BEGINNING OF his detailed commentary on a short book published in Italian two years previously, French philosophe-in-chief
Voltaire wrote in 1766 that On Crimes and Punishments (Dei delitti e delle
pene) was "in the realm of morality what only a very few remedies for our
ills are in the field of medicine. I was expecting this work to mitigate
whatever remains barbarous in the jurisprudence of so many nations . . .
when I learned that, in one of our provinces, an 18-year-old girl had just
been hanged." Her crime had been to abandon her newborn outdoors in
an attempt to hide her pregnancy from her parents. "Because the infant
died," Voltaire asked, "is it absolutely necessary to make the mother die,
too? . . . Isn't this law unjust, inhuman, and pernicious?" That both his
commentary and the book that sparked an international movement to
rethink criminal justice and capital punishment were at first published
anonymously bears eloquent testimony to the dangers still facing
reformers in the heyday of the European Enlightenment.

The Italian author Cesare Bonesana, Marchese di Beccaria
(1738–94; pronounced beck-ah-REE-ah), was born into an aristocratic
Milanese family and earned a law degree from the University of Pavia,
where he had been an undistinguished student. Shortly afterward he
married a young woman against his father's wishes and, when poverty
loomed, had to beg for forgiveness. The reconciliation was the first of

---

[1]Cesare Beccaria, On Crimes and Punishments, trans. by Henry Paolucci (Englewood Cliffs,
N.J.: Prentice Hall, 1963), p. 99. This and subsequent quotations are from this edition.

several events in which the introverted Beccaria was encouraged by two friends, the brothers Pietro and Alessandro Verri, who had founded the *Accademia dei Pugni* (the Academy of Fists). This fiercely named society of Milanese intellectuals was imbued with the ideals of the Enlightenment and dedicated to political, economic, and literary reform in a reawakening Lombardy that was still under Austrian rule. As a member, Beccaria studied the writings of Enlightenment thinkers such as Montesquieu, Helvétius, d'Alembert, Hume, and Diderot. Preferring to listen at the group's meetings, which often addressed humanitarian issues, he would set down his ideas on paper only when the Verri brothers coaxed him.

In 1763 Pietro Verri asked Beccaria to conduct a systematic study of criminal law, which would incorporate some of Pietro's original research on the history of torture as well as the experiences of Alessandro, who was then a prison administrator. The result, *On Crimes and Punishments*, first published in 1764 when the author was only twenty-six, was spectacularly successful, with numerous Italian editions and French, German, English, Spanish, Polish, and Dutch translations appearing within months. The first coherent statement of the argument against capital punishment and a seminal work in penology, the book sent shock waves throughout Europe and America.

Underlying the work is the conviction that legal systems should try to ensure the greatest possible good for the greatest number. Beccaria thus advocated punishments that would protect the integrity of the social contract and motivate citizens to abide by just laws: "A wrong already committed, and for which there is no remedy, ought to be punished by political society only because it might otherwise excite false hopes of impunity in others. . . . The true measure of crimes is, namely, the harm done to society" (pp. 31, 64). In this view, the worst crime was treason, which harms everyone, followed by violence against individuals and property.

Beccaria argued against retaliatory or vengeful punishments in favor of those that were commensurate with the associated crimes and that reestablished security and order in the community: "Whoever sees the same death penalty, for instance, decreed for the killing of a pheasant and for the assassination of a man or for forgery of an important writing will make no distinction between such crimes, thereby destroying the moral sentiments, which are the work of many centuries" (p. 63). He believed that the certainty of punishment was a greater deterrent than its severity. When punishments were deemed necessary, he urged that they be administered promptly, so that crime and punishment would become linked in the public mind.

Detailing his arguments against the use of torture to extract confessions, Beccaria reasoned that "the guilty man . . . finds himself in a favorable situation; that is, if, as a consequence of having firmly resisted the torture, he is absolved as innocent, he will have escaped a greater punishment by enduring a lesser one" (p. 33). Of innocent men who are tortured, he noted that they may confess to a crime they did not commit and thus be forced to endure an undeserved sentence.

Beccaria spoke out against the corrupt magistrates of his day, asking that laws be made clearer so the need for judicial interpretation would be minimized. He opposed asking courtroom witnesses leading questions and forcing them to take oaths, because "no oath ever made any criminal tell the truth" (p. 29). He also insisted that women could serve as reliable witnesses in legal proceedings.

In his reasoned arguments advocating the abolition of the death penalty, Beccaria linked the social contract to an unquestionable right to life, pointing out that capital punishment could not possibly be useful to society because it sets a barbarous example and reduces sensitivity to human suffering. Long-term imprisonment is a better deterrent to capital crime, he wrote, since "it inspires terror in the spectator more than in the sufferer" (p. 48).

He concludes, however, that "it is better to prevent crimes than to punish them" (p. 93). As a means of reducing the number of duels, for example, Beccaria advocated stronger measures to protect people against insults. But above all, he believed that preventing crime involved enacting clear laws, ensuring that "enlightenment accompanies liberty" (p. 95), rewarding virtue, and improving education.

Several of Beccaria's idols, including Hume and Helvétius, praised his book unstintingly. Soon the author was lionized by the European intelligentsia, and Alessandro Verri dragged him off to Paris. But shy and retiring as he was, Beccaria cut a very poor figure there and soon returned to Milan, never to leave. Until his death in 1794, however, he continued his work as an eminent economist, anticipating some of the ideas of Adam Smith and Thomas Malthus. He also lived to see the birth of a grandson, Alessandro Manzoni, who went on to write *I promessi sposi* (*The Betrothed*), often considered the greatest Italian novel.

Beccaria's book helped undermine the assumptions of political and religious absolutism by outlining a purely practical and secular approach to the role of punishment in civil society. As a direct consequence of his ideas, legislative reforms were enacted in the Austrian Empire, Sweden, the Russia of Catherine the Great, and the Grand Duchy of Tuscany, and within a third of a century of his book's publication the use of judicial torture had been banned from most European legal systems. His focus on the general welfare of society, rather than on the prerogatives of rulers, paved the way for documents such as the Declaration of the Rights of Man in France. In England, Beccaria's ideas came to fruition in the utilitarian philosophy of Jeremy Bentham, who lavished praise on the Milanese reformer.

When John Adams opened his controversial defense of the British soldiers accused in the Boston Massacre, he quoted a passage from Beccaria's book. Later the American Constitution and Bill of Rights would bear the strong imprint of Beccaria's work in their emphasis on due process of law and the prohibition of "cruel and unusual punishments." By any measure, Beccaria's intellectual and moral achievements must be seen to outweigh the man's personal inability to sparkle in the Parisian limelight.

Thirty-nine

Trailblazers in electricity: Galvani and Volta

Then there is electricity—the demon, the angel, the mighty physical power, the all-pervading intelligence! . . . [B]y means of electricity, the world of matter has become a great nerve, vibrating thousands of miles in a breathless point of time.
—Nathaniel Hawthorne, The House of the Seven Gables (1851)

IN ABOUT 600 B.C. Greek philosopher Thales of Miletus discovered an unusual property of amber (*elektron* in Greek): When rubbed with a piece of fur, it attracts feathers and other light materials. Centuries later, in A.D. 70, Roman encyclopedist Pliny the Elder conducted simple experiments that corroborated Thales' findings. With the passage of many more centuries, Pliny's northern Italian birthplace, Comum, had become Como, birthplace of Alessandro Volta.

Volta (1745–1827) and his Bolognese contemporary Luigi Galvani (1737–98) played a crucial role in harnessing the practical applications of electrical phenomena. These two Enlightenment scientists, although often in fundamental disagreement, made seminal contributions to the modern study of electricity and thus to the switched-on world we all inhabit.

After Galvani received his medical degree from the University of Bologna, he lectured on comparative anatomy and obstetrics, becoming professor of anatomy at his alma mater in 1775. At about this time he began investigating how nerves cause muscles to contract. In 1786, during an electrical storm, Galvani observed that the muscles of a dissected frog leg contracted when he touched the nerves with scissors.

Later that year Galvani was entertaining some friends with an electrostatic machine (a simple device used to generate static electrical charges). His wife noticed that when one of them touched a skinned frog's nerve ending with a knife, a spark emanated from the machine and the animal's leg kicked. In similar experiments Galvani was able to replicate the results.

He was also able to cause muscular contractions without his machine by suspending frog legs by a copper wire from the iron balcony of his house. Ruling out the electrostatic machine as the source of the electrical impulse, he concluded that he had discovered a new kind of electricity that was a sort of fluid originating in the animal itself.

Although Galvani earned support for his findings, which he expounded in 1791 in a Latin essay whose title may be translated *Commentary on the Effect of Electricity on Muscular Motion*, he also drew criticism. In response he conducted further experiments and, in 1794, anonymously published *On the Use and Activity of the Conductive Arch in the Contraction of Muscles*. In this work he described experiments in which, by touching a frog's nerve with another frog's muscle, he achieved muscular contractions without any intervening metal.

Alessandro Volta, who had made an extensive study of the properties of electricity on his own, was not convinced by Galvani's conclusions. A professor of physics at the University of Pavia since 1779, Volta had invented the electrophorus, a static electricity generator, and had also discovered and identified methane gas. While experimenting on how electricity affects the senses, he found that placing coins of different metals above and beneath his tongue and connecting them with a wire produced a tingling sensation accompanied by a salty taste. In 1796, however, he observed the generation of a current when he placed a brine-soaked piece of pasteboard between the coins instead of his tongue. He concluded that the current did not depend on animal tissue but on metals and moisture.

Galvani had sent Volta a copy of his 1791 paper on the effect of electricity on muscular contraction, and the latter now had support for his belief that Galvani had misinterpreted his own experiments. The observed charge did not result from an innate "animal electricity," but the frogs' legs had simply functioned as a conductor and detector of the charge emanating from two unlike metals in what Volta called "metallic electricity." Although the controversy went on for years, the two gentlemen at its center did not allow their disagreement to degenerate into an egoistic squabble. It turned out that both had been correct, but each had been studying different phenomena.

Galvani was right to assert that the muscular contractions in his experiments resulted from the fundamental property (now called *excitability*) of nerves and muscles to generate electrical forces (as detected by modern electrocardiograms, electroencephalograms, nerve conduction studies, and so forth). Volta was right to claim that some metals can generate electrical forces when brought into contact with each other. Galvani's experiment with the frog legs, the copper wire, and the iron balcony had blurred the issue by accidentally bringing together two types of electrical forces.

After Galvani's death, Volta invented the "voltaic pile," the world's first battery, in Pavia in November of 1799. The voltaic pile was made of numerous alternating disks of silver, zinc, and pasteboard that had been immersed in salt water. When the two dissimilar metals at the ends of the stacked column were connected with a wire, current flowed continuously from one to the other, just as it does between the oppositely charged terminals of a modern battery. Volta described his invention as having "an inexhaustible charge, a perpetual action or impulse on the electric field."

The creation of the voltaic pile secured the apparent victory of the "Voltians" over the "Galvanians." A year later, Volta conveyed his findings on the first source of a continuous electric current in a report to the Royal Society of London, which published his work in *Philosophical Transactions* and granted him the society's Copley Medal.

In 1801 Volta traveled to Paris at the invitation of Napoleon to demonstrate his voltaic pile at the Institut de France. The French dictator and the Institut were so pleased with the results that they awarded Volta 6,000 francs and minted a gold coin in his honor. Bonaparte also made Volta a count and a senator of the short-lived Napoleonic confection, the Kingdom of Lombardy. (In contrast, toward the end of his life Galvani lost his post at the University of Bologna for refusing to swear allegiance to Napoleon's Cisalpine Republic of northern Italy and died in poverty.) Volta later received the Cross of the French Legion of Honor, and the Austrians made him head of the philosophical faculty at the University of Padua in 1815. Since 1881 the volt (the unit of the electromotive force that drives the current) has commemorated his achievements.

Immediately after Volta's article appeared in *Philosophical Transactions*, the science of electrochemistry was born. English scientists William Nicholson and Anthony Carlisle used the voltaic pile to initiate chemical reactions, isolating hydrogen and oxygen from water. Stronger batteries were soon developed, and by 1809 English chemist Sir Humphry Davy had used such devices to first isolate various metals, including sodium and potassium, from their liquid compounds.

In 1827 German physicist Georg Ohm was able to determine the precise relationship among current, voltage, and resistance. Seven years later, English scientist Michael Faraday enunciated his law governing the relationship between the amount of electrode material produced in batteries and the quantity of electrical power generated. In 1873 the brilliant Scottish physicist James Clerk Maxwell provided a thorough formulation of the laws linking electricity, magnetism, and light.

While Volta's work gave rise to the sciences of electrochemistry and electromagnetism, Galvani's research paved the way for electrophysiology. In 1848–49 German electrophysiologist Emil Du Bois-Reymond used the galvanometer that was named for the Italian scientist to prove that nerves do indeed carry electrical impulses from one area of the body to another. Galvani's asserted link between electricity and life set the stage not only for neuroscience but also for Mary Shelley's 1818 Gothic thriller, *Frankenstein*, which centered on the artificial creation of life by means of electricity. Galvani's observation in 1791 that an electric current applied to the heart of a dead frog resulted in myocardial contraction eventually led to the emergency technique of cardioversion, the restoration of the heart's normal rhythm via electrical shocks.

Through their ongoing scholarly disagreement as much as through their research, Luigi Galvani and Alessandro Volta initiated an interest in electrical studies that grew into a veritable mania as the nineteenth century progressed. Today the applications of the work of these two men remain practically boundless—cars, computers, space shuttles, medicine, myriad forms of entertainment, communication, and illumination. We have come quite a way since Thales and his amber.

—Dante D'Epiro

Forty

Venice: Rhapsody in stone, water, melody, and color

I sat on the Dogana's steps
For the gondolas cost too much, that year.
—Ezra Pound, "Canto 3"
(1917, referring to 1908)

WHEN GUSTAV VON ASCHENBACH, the famous elderly author in Thomas Mann's *Death in Venice*, feels an overwhelming compulsion to travel from Munich to the City of Lagoons, "the most improbable of cities," we witness the spectacle of a self-repressed man succumbing to love and death, both of them supreme expressions of a total loss of control. Yet despite the cholera epidemic he finds there and the riot of his own chaotic emotions, Aschenbach first experiences true eros and ecstasy, although it is no accident that the discovery of his id in decadent Venice coincides with the demise of this bourgeois artist from the solid, industrious north.

Venezia, Queen of the Adriatic, *La Serenissima*—former seafaring mercantile republic and seat of empire, with its stone palazzi rising from the water, its pastel colors and narrow lanes, its dank odors and paludal aura—is less than three square miles in area, only twice as big as New York's Central Park. Built on 118 mudflat islets, whose 177 canals are spanned by 450 bridges, the city has often assumed mythic proportions in the world's imagination: as a triumph of human will over Nature, an impregnable bulwark, Wordsworth's "eldest Child of Liberty" that held "the gorgeous east in fee," a beehive of espionage, a vast museum, the mecca of all Grand Tours, Europe's pleasure capital and mumming carnival. Proust made it his ultimate image of a lifelong dream that fades into the light of common day when actually attained: "The town that I saw before me had ceased to be Venice. . . . I saw the palaces reduced to their constituent parts, lifeless heaps of marble with nothing to choose between them, and the water as a combination of hydrogen and oxygen, eternal, blind, anterior and exterior to Venice, unconscious of Doges or of Turner."[1]

The reversed S shape of the two-and-a-half-mile Grand Canal, Venice's main artery, with its Rialto Bridge, is one of the most recognizable thoroughfares in the world. Set in a lagoon in the Gulf of Venice, an arm of the Adriatic, the romantic city of the Grand Canal was built with much unglamorous sweat: Pine and oak piles—many millions of them—were pounded twenty-five feet into the marshy ground onto a solid layer of clay as a foundation for Venice's twenty thousand buildings.

It's unclear exactly which invaders the first settlers were fleeing from. The traditional year of the city's founding is A.D. 421, and we know that Alaric and his Goths had gorged on the nearby Roman city of Aquileia in 402 before sacking Rome in 410. Desperate souls no doubt fled from the Veneto mainland to some islands in the lagoon in 452, when Attila's Huns destroyed Aquileia again. By 523 the monk and scholar Cassiodorus was comparing Venetians' houses to seabirds' nests afloat on the waves. In 539 neighboring Ravenna fell to Emperor Justinian's general Belisarius, and the old provinces of Venetia and Istria became part of the Byzantine Empire. In 568 more refugees fled to islands in the lagoon to avoid the invading Lombards under King Alboin.

Orso Ipato, the first well-attested Venetian doge (like *duke* and *duce*, from the Latin *dux*, "leader"), took office in 726. Founded in freedom, Venice was to remain an independent republic for more than a millennium, setting the European record for the longest unbroken form of government. The Byzantine emperor formally recognized Venice's independence in 803, and in 1000 the pugnacious city-state sent out a fleet to conquer or receive the submission of the Dalmatian coast of the Adriatic to protect her lifeline to the trading ports of the east.

The Feast of the Ascension, the day the fleet set sail, was commemorated by a yearly ceremony of thanksgiving that later developed into the "Marriage of Venice to the Sea." Amidst hordes of dignitaries and to the singing of motets, the doge recited the formula *"Desponsamus te, mare, in signum veri perpetuique dominii"* (We wed thee, O sea, in sign of true and perpetual dominion) and dropped a gold ring into the Adriatic from the *Bucintoro*, the gilded state barge.

---

[1]Marcel Proust, *Remembrance of Things Past*, vol. 6, *The Sweet Cheat Gone*, trans. by C. K. Scott Moncrieff (New York: Vintage Books, 1930), p. 165.

The spectacular success of Venice's trading ventures allowed it to erect a monument to its own magnificence—the five-domed Byzantine-style St. Mark's Basilica, consecrated in 1094. With its double tier of arches crowned with religious mosaics, it was, in the opinion of Petrarch several hundred years later, the most beautiful sight on earth. Above the main doors are copies of the four gilded bronze horses (the originals are now inside) that the Venetians plundered from Constantinople's Hippodrome. The treasures of the church include the jewel-encrusted enamels of the tenth-century Pala d'Oro altarpiece and scores of rich mosaics and multicolored marble columns.

"Venetians prospered," wrote historian Brooks Adams, "because they were bolder and more unscrupulous than their neighbors." What other city, under the personal leadership of a fierce, crafty, and blind octogenarian, could have diverted the Fourth Crusade of 1204 to the very Christian city of Constantinople, the richest in the world, and sacked it mercilessly? Enrico Dandolo, the "incomparable Doge" in John Milton's phrase, leaped down, in full panoply, from his vermilion-painted galley and led the first wave of the assault on the battlements of Constantinople, drawing heavy fire. From its act of cynical piracy, Venice emerged with stupendous riches, incomparable artistic spoils, and strategic possessions.

The city now ruled three-eighths of Constantinople and its broad realms—"one quarter and half a quarter of the Roman [Byzantine] Empire"—emerging as mistress of the eastern Mediterranean and the Black Sea. Venice waged four wars against its great trading rival Genoa (during one of which Marco Polo was captured and imprisoned in Genoa, where he dictated the story of his marvelous adventures). In 1381, using cannon for the first time in Italy's history, Venice decisively defeated the Ligurian metropolis and became the leading maritime power in Europe. These were times of rapid expansion when Venice was building, next to St. Mark's, the Gothic Doges' Palace (1309–1438), with its graceful colonnades and loggias (and linked to the prisons by the Bridge of Sighs in 1614).

In Venice the wealthy patrician merchants—the magnificoes—ran the show. These men made up the oligarchic *Maggior Consiglio* (Great Council), whose members were legally given the hereditary right to rule the state in the so-called "Closing of the Council" in 1297. The *Libro d'Oro*, or Golden Book, was later established to keep track of the marriages and births within this closed ruling caste of about two hundred families. From their ranks the Senate and all other state officials were chosen, including the feared Council of Ten, which became a permanent body in 1334, ferreting out plots and conspiracies with the help of its secret police. The doge—resplendent in his robes and pointed cap, the *corno*—was reduced to a mere figurehead, although he reigned for life. In the sixteenth century, when Venice's population was 170,000, and that of its subject territories more than two million, a mere 2,500 patricians controlled the state.

Although they lacked a voice in the government, the middle classes manned the civil service, and the craftsmen had plenty of work, as well as judicial recourse against injustice, including the right to counsel. These legal benefits existed in Venice much earlier than they did in England and France. Members of the ruling classes were often called on to make large forced loans to the state, and they could not retire from or evade political office without official permission. Political stability was achieved (there were no popular revolutions in the city's history) while tyranny was avoided for ten centuries. All Venice's rulers were elected, though by a small part of the citizenry, as was generally true even of modern democracies until the twentieth century. In the view of Jacques Barzun, "Taken all in all, Venice was the nearest approach ever made to Plato's system of rulers by duty and dedication who govern soberly."[2]

The source of Venetian wealth was trade, and this circumstance led, as in most mercantile powers, to colonial expansion. In 1082 the Venetians won the right from the Byzantine emperor to trade without paying taxes or customs duties anywhere in his realms. Soon afterward, in 1124, they captured Tyre, the first possession in an overseas empire that lasted almost seven centuries, longer than any other in European history. Other pawns subsequently fell: Crete, the Peloponnesus, the western coast of Greece, the Ionian Islands, Cyprus.

The nine decades between 1339 and 1428 saw Venice, at the height of its power, accumulating possessions on the Italian mainland, including the cities of Bergamo, Brescia, Verona, Vicenza, Padua, Treviso, and Udine. The rationale for the takeovers was the need to protect Venice's routes to Alpine passes for the reexport trade of eastern luxury items against fierce enemies such as expansionary Milan, 160 miles away. The mainland area called the Veneto became the site of splendid villas, which noble Venetians enjoyed during their summertime *villeggiatura*.

---

[2]Jacques Barzun, *From Dawn to Decadence: 500 Years of Western Cultural Life, 1500 to the Present* (New York: HarperCollins Publishers, 2000), p. 171.

By the end of the fourteenth century, 36,000 seamen earned their livelihood aboard Venice's merchant vessels and warships. Its vast Arsenal, which gave the word to English and other languages, is cited in Dante's *Inferno* as an example of busy activity. Founded in 1104 and rebuilt in the fifteenth and sixteenth centuries, it was the shipbuilding wonder of the world. At its height, it employed 16,000 men in Europe's largest industrial complex and could produce a fully armed galley in one day.

In huge convoys, the fabled argosies of Venice plied the Mediterranean, the Black Sea (at the terminals of caravan routes to Persia, India, and China), and the waters off Alexandria. Laden with timber, wine, and other bulky raw materials, as well as woolens from Europe's growing textile industry, the ships exchanged these items for silks, drugs, spices, precious stones, and perfumes. To keep a finger on the political pulse of their trading partners, which included all the peoples of the Levant, Christian or Muslim, Venice developed the first modern diplomatic service, requiring its ambassadors to send back daily reports.

After Constantinople fell to the Ottoman Turks in 1453, the religious and military hackles of Christian Europe were raised. When Pope Pius II tried to interest Venice in a last hurrah for the Crusades, he sarcastically remarked on the city-state's crass attitude toward the proposed endeavor: "To a Venetian, everything is just that is good for the State, everything pious that increases the Empire." But Venice's dominance began to falter as progress occurred elsewhere: Columbus was voyaging to America; Vasco da Gama discovered a sea route around Africa to India in 1499; Pope Julius II arrayed much of Europe against Venice in the League of Cambrai (1508); the Turks achieved naval hegemony over the eastern Mediterranean; and ruthlessly efficient Dutch traders expanded their empire in the East.

Venice began to decline into a mercantile backwater. Yet in 1571, shortly after the Ottomans relieved Venice of Cyprus, when a combined Christian fleet sank or captured 230 Turkish ships in a spectacular sea battle off Lepanto, more than half the allied ships were Venetian. The victory gave Venice only a temporary respite from its troubles. In 1576 the plague killed almost a quarter of Venice's people (including Titian), and the Turks had by no means been swept from the seas. Crete fell to them in 1669 after a long, excruciating war. In 1687 Venetian admiral Francesco Morosini captured Athens (badly damaging the Parthenon in a bombardment), but in the next generation Venice lost almost all of its overseas possessions. About all that remained of the city-state's "one quarter and half a quarter" of the long-defunct Byzantine Empire were the Ionian Islands.

Venice ultimately found a fitting last nemesis in Napoleon, who threatened to become "an Attila to the Venetian state." The once-haughty city decided to capitulate without a fight. On May 12, 1797, after presiding at a meeting of the Maggior Consiglio that voted to depose the government, Lodovico Manin, Venice's 118th doge, removed his *corno* and handed it to his secretary, saying he wouldn't be needing it anymore. It had been 1,071 years since the first attested doge took office. For the first time, the city was occupied by foreign troops, and later in the year Napoleon presented it to Austria. Vincenzo Cuoco, a young Italian historian writing in 1801, claimed "the destruction of that old, imbecile Venetian oligarchy will always be a great advantage to Italy," but Wordsworth had a different take on the demise of the Most Serene Republic: "Men are we, and must grieve when even the Shade / Of that which once was great, is passed away." Venice became part of a united Italy in 1866 (see Essay 42).

Trade and empire were far from the sole Venetian preoccupations. Aldus Manutius (1450–1515), the humanist scholar and founder of the Aldine Press, with its anchor and dolphin logo, settled in Venice and produced the inexpensive editions of the Greek, Latin, and Italian classics that made the city the printing capital of Europe. For several centuries, Venice was also in the forefront of musical and operatic composition. Its architects, apart from the splendors lining St. Mark's Square, have created some of Italy's loveliest churches, such as the jewel box–like Santa Maria dei Miracoli and Palladio's San Giorgio Maggiore and Il Redentore (see Essay 30). And Venetian painting, one of the glories of world art, reflects the rich, sensuous, pleasure-loving qualities of the people, as evidenced in the costumes, draperies, landscapes, feasting, sumptuous palaces, seductive nudes, and bacchic events portrayed in hundreds of color-drenched canvases and frescoes.

Giovanni Bellini (c. 1430–1516), founder of the Venetian school, adopted the use of oil paint instead of egg tempera in his soulful, dreamy-eyed Madonnas and his dignified portraits, such as that of Doge Leonardo Loredan in full regalia. His pictures of saints—*St. Francis in Ecstasy* or *St. Jerome Reading*—are noteworthy for the evocative landscapes in which the figures are placed.

The most stunning work of the short-lived and enigmatic Giorgione (1476/77–1510), Bellini's pupil, is the mysteriously romantic *Tempest*, with its nursing young woman and a soldier holding a long staff and looking on. In a poetic landscape of classical ruins with a city in the far background, a thunderbolt cleaves the blue-green storm clouds. Giorgione's *Sleeping Venus* (completed by Titian) was the first of the great reclining nudes of the Renaissance.

Titian (Tiziano Vecellio, 1488/90–1576) became an outstanding Venetian master in religious subjects (such as *The Presentation of the Virgin in the Temple* and *The Assumption of the Virgin*) and the unrivaled creator of lovely nudes and classically inspired erotic works. He was also one of the very greatest of portraitists. Among his approximately one hundred surviving paintings in this genre are the *Portrait of a Bearded Man* (the so-called *Ariosto*, perhaps an assertive self-portrait); the suave *Man with the Glove* and *Man in a Red Cap*; the massively powerful old man, *Doge Andrea Gritti*; and the portraits of Emperor Charles V.

The Venetian Mannerist painter Jacopo Tintoretto (1518–94) brought his deeply religious temperament to his dramatic religious works and depictions of biblical scenes. The play of light and shadow and the deep perspective in his *Last Supper* in San Giorgio Maggiore—the scene lit only by a smoky hanging lamp and Christ's halo—create a mysterious effect like that of El Greco or Van Gogh.

The superb colorist Paolo Veronese (1528–88) decorated the Doges' Palace, painted portraits, and created sprawling banquet scenes such as *The Feast in the House of Levi* and *The Marriage at Cana*. He also produced frescoes for villas and palaces, most extraordinarily Palladio's Villa Barbaro at Maser in the Veneto.

The tradition of Veronese's grand epic frescoes was revived in the eighteenth century by the Venetian painters Giambattista Tiepolo (1696–1770) and his son Giandomenico (1727–1804), who adorned many ceilings and walls with rococo mythological scenes. This century also gave birth to the Venetian panoramas of Giovanni Antonio Canaletto (1697–1768) and Francesco Guardi (1712–93), the satiric genre paintings of Pietro Longhi (1702–85), and the phantasmagoric architectural etchings of *Le Carceri* (*The Prisons*) by Giovanni Battista Piranesi (1720–78). Straddling the nineteenth century were the neoclassical sculptures of Antonio Canova (1757–1822), considered greatest sculptor of his day.

Venice became the European capital of music publishing when Ottaviano dei Petrucci first printed musical scores there in 1501. Later, after Giovanni Gabrieli (c. 1554/57–1612) was named organist of St. Mark's, musicians from all over Europe flocked to Venice to study the art of composition for multiple choruses with him. After its birth in Tuscany, the new musical form of opera received a major impetus from the genius of Claudio Monteverdi (1567–1643; see Essays 32 and 35). The year 1637 saw the opening of the world's first public opera house, the Teatro San Cassiano, and three others opened within the next four years. From 1640 to 1700, about eight hundred operas were composed in Venice, which was the European opera capital of the time.

Antonio Vivaldi (1678–1741), the Baroque master with his bright, lyrical, upbeat, slightly frenetic melodies, strong instrumental color, and marked tendency to plagiarize from himself, was the greatest Venetian composer of the eighteenth century. A violin virtuoso, he became violin master and then musical director at a female orphanage, L'Ospedale della Pietà, whose residents performed in an illustrious choir and orchestra. Vivaldi wrote more than forty operas, but he is far more esteemed for his groundbreaking concertos, which Bach so admired that he transcribed twenty-one of them for keyboard instruments.

In the eighteenth century, Venice was famed for its seven full-time opera houses, as well as its theaters, which featured the comic plays (more than two hundred of them) of Carlo Goldoni (1707–93), whom Voltaire dubbed "the Molière of Italy," and of Carlo Gozzi (1720–1806), both of whom drew on the Italian commedia dell'arte stock characters and plots. Gozzi also made use of folklore in plays that became the basis of the operas *The Love of Three Oranges* and *Turandot*.

Like other huge entrepôts in history, Venice was known for its easy mores and tolerance. To say *"Siamo a Venezia"* (we're in Venice) implied that one had the freedom to do pretty much as one pleased as long as it didn't threaten the public interest or the state. This most cosmopolitan city of Europe adopted a don't-ask, don't-tell attitude toward religious belief and practice and never burned a heretic. Repeatedly placed under papal excommunication and interdicts, which they usually ignored, the Venetians never let religion interfere with their business or statecraft. Jews worshiped in their synagogues in the original Ghetto (named for the iron foundry in the district); Protestants, Greek Orthodox, and Armenians had their churches, and Muslims their mosque.

Venice's greatest historian, Paolo Sarpi (1552–1623), though Provincial of the Servite Order, wielded such a wicked pen as spokesman for Venetian independence against the impostures of the papacy and its interdict of the city that he was almost assassinated. His masterpiece, *History of the Council of Trent* (1619), portrays the papacy in a less than flattering light.

Luigi Barzini reminds us that Venice was also "the brothel and gambling casino capital of Europe." It could boast of the most beautiful, skillful, and learned courtesans, like the poet Veronica Franco (1546–91), who once entertained Henry III of France; and the singer, semicourtesan, and much greater poet Gaspara Stampa (1523–54). The Ridotto, the famed gambling house, was in operation between 1638 and 1774. Players had to come disguised in masks, as in a Pietro Longhi painting named for the casino.

The annual Carnival was magnificently celebrated with masks, pomp, music, dance, and dissipation. Venice was also home of a custom by which well-to-do women were usually escorted to balls and other public functions by a *cicisbeo*, a cross between a gallant, a gigolo, and a *cavaliere servente*—instead of by their older, busier, and more boring husbands.

The world's most gifted have always found their way to Venice. Dante got the cold shoulder on a diplomatic mission there; longtime resident Petrarch was insulted there and left in a huff; Dürer, who said of it, "Here I am a gentleman, at home a sponger," came to paint (as did Rubens, Turner, Whistler, and Monet); Michelangelo thought the entire city a "beautiful painting"; Aretino delighted in it, boasting that from his window overlooking the Grand Canal he enjoyed "the loveliest view in all the world"; Ruskin, D'Annunzio, and Mann wrote about it; Byron cavorted there while working on *Don Juan;* Henry James did not cavort while working on *The Aspern Papers* there; Wagner, Browning, Stravinsky, and Pound died there; Hemingway threw them back at Harry's Bar there, home of carpaccio and the Bellini cocktail.

Of the twelve million somewhat less gifted who currently visit Venice each year, most are glad that the city has ignored the demand of Futurist poet and showman Filippo Tommaso Marinetti: "Let us burn the gondolas, rocking chairs for cretins." The Regatta, held on the first Sunday in September, still features a gondola race, and the Carnival, abolished when Venice fell to Napoleon, was revived in 1979. Visitors buy lace, jewelry, and Murano blown glass and gaze at the old palaces with the magical names: Ca' Giustinian, Ca' Rezzonico, Ca' d'Oro. Then there's the Venice Biennale, the international art exhibition held in odd-numbered years; the International Film Festival at the Lido; and several dozen art galleries and museums. La Fenice, which has featured operatic premieres ranging from Verdi's *La Traviata* to Stravinsky's *The Rake's Progress*, is being restored, after barely escaping total destruction in a 1996 arson fire.

But Venice is slowly sinking. In November of 1966, the water level rose six feet in three days, causing $100 million in damage, and in January 2001, the city suffered the worst spate of sustained flooding in its history. Various engineering proposals are being considered, including a $3 billion plan (Project Moses) for the construction of seventy-nine movable floodgates at the three inlets of the outer bank of the lagoon. The gigantic gates would block off the lagoon only during periods of exceptionally high tides, but critics say the contraptions would have to be used so often that they would only exacerbate Venice's pollution problems, which are already critical. The sea level, which rose by 9.8 inches from 1897 to 2000, is projected to rise 39 inches between 2000 and 2100. When Thomas Mann imagined his dying protagonist Aschenbach sitting on a beach chair at Venice's Lido and admiring the beautiful young Polish boy, Tadzio, Mann may well have suspected that the Adriatic tide slowly washing over the shore would someday threaten death to proud old Venice itself.

Forty-one

Europe's premier poet of pessimism:
Giacomo Leopardi

*Every human life is tossed backwards and forwards between pain
and boredom.*

—Arthur Schopenhauer, *The World as Will and Representation* (1819)

WHAT A HIT THOSE TWO—Schopenhauer and Leopardi—would have
made at a party. The German prophet of pessimism and ascetic renunci-
ation of the world was familiar with the uncompromisingly gloomy work
of the greatest Italian poet of modern times, as witnessed by Schopenhauer's claim that the misery of existence has never been treated "so
thoroughly and exhaustively as by Leopardi in our own day. . . . He presents it on every page of his works, yet . . . with such a wealth of imagery
that he never wearies us."

In Leopardi's verse, the old certainties of the metaphysical realm are
dissolved, while the emotionalism and intense subjectivity of Romanti-
cism are combined with the elaborately formal elegance of ancient verse
and of classic Italian poets such as Petrarch and Tasso. His later poetry
embodies an anti-Rousseauist view of Nature and a theory of the void
and the absurd that foreshadows authors such as Nietzsche, Sartre, and
Beckett, and the stark verse of Giuseppe Ungaretti and Eugenio Mon-
tale. How Leopardi would have enjoyed Ibsen's ironic plays, in which
the characters who see clearly and try to dispel others' illusions only end
up ruining everything. How he would have wept at the plays of
Chekhov, in which the tedious futility of existence and the pathetic
quality of unrealizable dreams assume an almost palpable presence on
the stage.

Count Giacomo Leopardi was born on June 29, 1798, in his family's
redbrick palace in the torpid little hillside town of Recanati in
the Marches, not far from the Adriatic coast and the city of Ancona.
"Horrible, detestable, execrated" was how he described the town, which

was part of the reactionary Papal States. The poet was the eldest child of Count Monaldo and Countess Adelaide, the latter of whom pinched pennies to restore the family's fortunes, which her husband's disastrous financial speculations had destroyed. Monaldo was a studious man who wrote treatises on politics and theology but allowed his ice-cold, emotionally warped, and religiously fanatical wife to bully him and his children.

At age twelve, Giacomo, who was already more learned than his private ecclesiastical tutor, embarked on an orgy of study in his father's library of 25,000 volumes. For seven years, he devoured literature, history, and philosophy in Latin, Greek, Hebrew, Italian, French, German, and English; translated extensively from Greek and Latin; and wrote poetry, tragedies, philological works, and a history of astronomy. He emerged as the most erudite poet of the modern world, perhaps outstripping even John Milton.

And then he looked in the mirror one day and saw a pale, frail, and ugly little hunchback who had weakened his eyes and exacerbated his scoliosis by his "insane and totally desperate studies." Realizing that no woman would ever love him, he began to give voice to the jaundiced philosophy that permeates his writings. Sickly and asthmatic, plagued by constipation, insomnia, ophthalmia, and depression, he felt he had thrown away his youth—indeed, his entire life: "I have miserably and irremediably ruined myself."

Leopardi made several vain attempts to escape the family and town that had blasted his youth: "Here I spend the years, abandoned, hidden, / Without love, without life." Aside from a brother and sister, he had no friends, and street urchins threw stones and snowballs at him while shouting "fucking hunchback!" When he managed to leave home for the first time at age twenty-four for a visit to Rome, he hated it. His only pleasure during his five-month stay was in weeping at Tasso's tomb. He subsequently wandered to Bologna, Milan, Florence, Pisa, and ultimately Naples in search of friendship and poetic recognition.

For fifteen years he made entries in his *Zibaldone* (Literary Miscellany, 1817–32), which is more than four thousand pages long in manuscript. This work, described by literary scholar Luciano Rebay as "perhaps the most fascinating diary ever kept," is crammed not only with autobiographical information but with extracts from and commentaries on Leopardi's vast reading. His *Operette morali* (*Little Moral Works*, 1824) consists of twenty-four essays and dialogues brimful of political and social satire. The work ended up on the Church's Index of Prohibited

Books for aperçus such as this: "Who could be deriving any pleasure or gain from the miserable life of this universe, perpetuated only by the pain and death of all things that constitute it?" In the 1830s Leopardi put together a volume of 111 *Pensieri* (Reflections), the first of which sets the bitter tone: "I say that the world consists of scoundrels in league against honest men, and of cowards in league against the brave. . . . If a decent man lapses into poverty, nobody comes to his aid. If a crook becomes poor, the entire city flocks to his rescue." But Leopardi's masterpiece is the *Canti* (Songs), published in two editions during his lifetime (1831 and 1835). The posthumous edition of 1845 contained forty-one poems—thirty-six lyrics, many of them elaborate odes, and five fragments—which established Leopardi's reputation as Italy's greatest lyric poet.

An advocate of a united Italy (see Essay 42), Leopardi wrote a number of patriotic odes that were confiscated by the Austrian censorship as too inflammatory. In each of them the heroic *virtus* of ancient Rome and the genius of earlier Italians such as Dante and Tasso (part of "that infinite company of immortals") are contrasted with the debasement of the fragmented and colonized Italy of Leopardi's time. In 1818, at about the time he refused to continue dressing in the priestly garb forced on him at home, he published *"All'Italia"* ("To Italy"), which begins like this:

> My native land, I see the walls and arches,
> The columns, and the statues, and the empty
> Towers of our forebears,
> But I do not see their glory,
> The laurel and the armor that once decked
> Our ancient fathers.

In the same poem, here is his personification of the Italy of his own day:

> Both of her arms are weighted down with chains,
> So that, with locks disheveled and unveiled,
> She sits upon the ground, distraught, unkempt,
> Buries her face
> Between her knees, and weeps.

In early poems like this one, Leopardi adopts the austere voice of a Pindar or Simonides to excoriate his age. (French critic Sainte-Beuve called him "an ancient born too late.") He also enunciates the theme of how expanding knowledge and science have stripped the world of beauty, mystery, and poetry.

In *"L'infinito"* ("The Infinite," 1819), Leopardi's Romantic preoccupations come to the fore. In a brief fifteen lines, he conveys the Pascalian terror that overwhelms him at the thought of the infinite expanses and empty silences of the universe, which drown him in their immensity. The final verse pays homage to the sublimity of boundless Nature, the mere contemplation of which is enough to destroy him: "And shipwreck in a sea like this is sweet."

"La sera del dì di festa" ("The Evening of the Holiday," c. 1820) introduces Leopardi's metaphor of life as a feast that, although eagerly awaited, turns out to be joyless. In his *Pensieri*, he had evoked the boundlessness of infinite space, only to claim that human desire dwarfs it all. Here he expresses how dreams always fall far short of expectations by recalling how, as a child, sleepless and disappointed in his bed on the night of a holiday, the sound of a wayfarer's song "dying bit by bit" in the distance "wrenched his heart." The poem is also notable for its depiction of a cruel Nature that informs the speaker, "Your eyes are doomed to sparkle only with tears."

The feast metaphor becomes central in *"Il sabato del villaggio"* ("Saturday in the Village," 1829), Leopardi's best-known poem. On Saturday evening, after the week's work is done, a small town—Recanati—prepares for its day off:

> The sweet young girl heads homeward from the fields
> At the setting of the sun,
> Bearing her sheaf; and in her hand she brings
> A trim bouquet of roses and of violets
> With which, as is her custom,
> For tomorrow's holiday,
> She makes ready to adorn her breast and hair.

We then see an old woman sitting on her steps and gabbing with her neighbors about how, when she was young, she would dress up on Sunday and dance with her friends. Within a few lines, the young girl, so full of expectations, has been merged with an old crone whose best days are far behind her. After describing hordes of children shouting and leaping in a little square (in front of Leopardi's house), the poet cuts to a man with a hoe whistling in anticipation of his day of rest as he returns from his day's work in the fields, and then to a carpenter who works all night in his shop to finish his week's work before the holiday. But as Leopardi wrote in the *Zibaldone*, "Pleasure is always past or future, never present." Indeed, Saturday turns out to be the best day, not Sunday, the nominal holiday, which proves to be cheerless. Soon everybody can't wait to get back to work on Monday, just to escape from tedium and disillusionment:

> *Of seven days, this is the best of all,*
> *Filled with hope and filled with joy;*
> *Tomorrow's hours will bring*
> *Sadness and boredom to all, who in their thoughts*
> *Will all return to their accustomed labors.*

Childhood itself is like Saturday night; adult life, so eagerly awaited, is as depressing as Sunday. The poem ends with an admonition to a young child:

> *O playful little boy,*
> *This flowering age of yours*
> *Is like a day that's filled with happiness—*
> *A bright and cloudless day*
> *That comes before the holiday of your life.*
> *Enjoy yourself, my child; these are good times,*
> *This is a joyful season.*
> *I'll say no more; but if your holiday*
> *Is long in coming, let it not disturb you.*

The inexpressibly delicate "*A Silvia*" ("To Silvia," 1828) recalls the times when the young Leopardi would take a break from his books in his father's library and go over to the balcony overlooking the little cobbled square. From there he could see, through her window, the family coachman's young daughter, Teresa Fattorini, seated at her loom and singing in the little house across the way: "No mortal tongue can express / What I then felt in my heart."

The young woman died of consumption at age twenty-one, a decade before Leopardi addressed her as Silvia in this poem. He asks her whether she still remembers her earthly life, when beauty radiated from her smiling eyes and bright dreams filled both of their minds. Of Nature, he bitterly asks, "Why don't you afterward give / That which you promised before?" Silvia died before she ever knew love, and the speaker's expectations for his own future did not long survive her. He, too, was denied youth, and his shattered hope could offer only the prospect of "cold death and a naked tomb."

As the years went by, Leopardi's verse grew increasingly more somber. In *"La quiete dopo la tempesta"* ("Calm after the Storm," 1829), he presents humans, birds, and chickens reemerging from shelter after a tempest. Everyone seems so cheerful and chirpy, but Leopardi sees in it an image of human life. What we conceive of as happiness is nothing more than a momentary lull in life's dreadful storm: "For us, pleasure / Is mere respite from pain."

The Romantic preoccupation with death is taken to new heights in Leopardi's works. In *"Canto notturno di un pastore errante dell'Asia"* ("Night Song of a Nomadic Shepherd from Asia," 1829–30), the senselessness of existence is conveyed via an extended simile of a frail and ill-clad old man who, after dragging a heavy burden over the harshest landscapes in every weather, arrives at his destination: a horrid, immense abyss that grants him oblivion when he throws himself into it. The poet points out that the first thing parents do is to console their bawling infant for having been born. He also expounds on *tedio*, the *noia* of "Saturday in the Village," both of which anticipate Baudelaire's *ennui*. Although it is humanity's worst affliction, boredom is also "the most sublime of human sentiments" (*Pensieri*, 68) because it chiefly afflicts the intelligent.

The poet who wrote of himself, "With its cold hand, / Misfortune seized my heart, and wrapped it in ice / In the flower of my years," was not destined for a fulfilling love life. Leopardi's single infatuation during his youth was formed during the three-day visit of a married cousin to Palazzo Leopardi when the poet was nineteen. In his notes to a poem of 1823, he had spoken of his true love as *"la donna che non si trova"* (the woman who cannot be found)—except perhaps in the stars above or among Plato's Forms. But eight years later, at age thirty-three, he offered his otherwise "indomitable heart" to a woman he called Aspasia, after the learned courtesan who was the mistress of Pericles.

Fanny Targioni was the wife of Antonio Tozzetti, a noted Florentine physician and botanist. Her nickname for Leopardi—*"il mio gobbetto"* (my little hunchback)—says it all. His two surviving letters to her feature phrases like "I haven't written until now so as not to annoy you" and "it's a joy and a glorious thing to serve you." He ended up practically serving as a go-between for her and his handsome friend Antonio Ranieri. "Excess of love had made him a slave and child," he wrote in the autobiographical poem *"Consalvo,"* and in *"Aspasia"* he bitterly remembers himself timid and trembling like an officious fool before his beloved's "haughty contempt." When the inevitable disillusionment set in, he composed the brief but shattering "*A se stesso*" ("To Himself") in 1833:

Rest now for evermore,
My weary heart. The last deceit has perished,
Which I had thought eternal. Perished. And now,
Not only the hope but
Even the desire for dear deceits has fled.
Rest forever. Too much
Have you pounded. Nothing whatever is worth
Your flutterings, nor is the earth itself
Worth your sighs. Bitter and dull
Is life, as always, and the world is mud.
Be quiet now. Despair
No more. To us, one gift was given—to die.
And now, despise yourself, and that brute force
Of Nature madly ruling,
Which only works for universal harm—
And the infinite emptiness of all things.

When asked in her old age why she hadn't reciprocated the great poet's love, Fanny Targioni promptly replied, "*Puzzava*" ("He stank").

Leopardi's most ambitious poem, "*La ginestra o Il fiore del deserto*" ("The Broom Plant, or The Desert Flower," 1836), placed in the final position among the *Canti* at his instructions, was first published posthumously in 1845. Written at the end of his life, when Leopardi was living in Naples, the long poem celebrates the sturdy humility of the scented golden broom—the sole plant blooming on the lunarlike slope of Mt. Vesuvius. The plant functions as a symbol of precarious life but also of the poet and his attempt to beautify a grim world:

Here, on the barren back of
The formidable mountain,
Exterminator Vesuvius,
Which no other tree or flower gladdens,
You scatter your lone clumps of bushes round—
You, fragrant, fragrant broom plant,
Content to live in deserts.

For Leopardi, the desolate lava slope of the volcano that destroyed Pompeii and Herculaneum in A.D. 79, and had last erupted violently only twenty years earlier, is a reminder of human helplessness in a hostile universe. Leopardi proceeds to mock the self-deluded optimism of his "proud and foolish century," with its simplistic belief in progress, which is belied by the facts of experience. In thundering periods and exalted diction, he defines humankind's true state on "this obscure grain of sand that has *Earth* for name."

Unlike his Romantic contemporaries, who saw Nature as a kindly mother, Leopardi considers it a charnel house. Since life is a "common war" against Nature's ravages, there is no room for hatred in the world. Despair should lead to brotherhood and solidarity, by which humans can at least attain some dignity.

But the speaker doesn't know whether to laugh at or feel sorry for this creature, man, who gives himself airs and thinks the gods have often descended to earth to converse with him. Vesuvius's stupendous eruption, when it extinguished countless lives, is a more accurate indicator of the human condition. Meaningless chance governs all, and there is no afterlife to make amends for the terrors of this one. Far from being the Lord of Nature, man is merely a tiny, insignificant part of it.

At the end of the poem, the broom plant emerges as an ideal model for humankind: It is born, lives with no pretensions, and dies without either abasing itself before its destroyer or considering itself immortal. A creature of pathetic transience, but wiser than man, it sheds its fragrance in the air before submitting to its ineluctable fate. All in all, *"La ginestra"* presents a view of life even bleaker and more tragic than that of later poets such as Thomas Hardy and A. E. Housman.

In his "Dialogue between Plotinus and Porphyry" (1827), Leopardi wrote the following as an argument against suicide:

> Let us live, my Porphyry, and comfort one another; let us not refuse to bear our share of the ills of our species that destiny has allotted us. And let us diligently keep one another company and keep encouraging one another and lending a helping hand to each other, so as to get through this weary life, which, at least, will surely be brief. And when death arrives, let us not lament. Even in those final days, our friends and companions will comfort us, and we will be cheered by the thought that, after we are dead, they will often remember us, and they will love us still.

It is a message of love as the sole flickering light illuminating an otherwise empty and pitch-black universe.

Leopardi himself finally experienced the loving friendship of Antonio Ranieri, a young Neapolitan who, with his sister Paolina, took care of the invalid poet during his last years. Despite extreme poverty, Antonio and Paolina bore patiently with the nocturnal habits of their friend (who, because of his eye problems, needed them to read to him and take dictation), as well as with his knuckle-cracking, his changing his shirt only once a month, and his dribbling food all over his clothes.

The poet died of chronic heart failure (probably a result of his deformity) on June 14, 1837, two weeks short of his thirty-ninth birthday. "The world can offer," he had written, "only two beautiful things: love and death." A friend of his wrote that "a naturally purer, nobler, and more generous soul never lived on this earth." In 1939 the poet's remains were buried near what is called Virgil's tomb, a site of Leopardi's frequent pilgrimages, across the bay from the slopes of "exterminator Vesuvius."

In one of the *Operette morali*, we read this:

> There will come a time when this universe, and Nature itself, will be extinguished. And just as today there remains no trace or knowledge of some of the mightiest human kingdoms and empires, so there will not remain a single vestige of the entire world and the infinite vicissitudes and calamities of created things—only a naked silence and a profound stillness will fill up immense space. And so, all this marvelous and terrifying mystery of universal existence, before being either explained or understood, will evaporate and disperse.

Yet Leopardi also wrote, "The knowledge of truth, even if harsh, has its pleasures." It is in this vein that the literary critic Francesco De Sanctis, who as a schoolboy once saw Leopardi, summarized Count Giacomo's work: "Life remains intact when it still has the ability to imagine, feel, and love—which is life itself. The intellect says: 'Love is an illusion; the only truth is death.' And yet I love and live and want to go on living. The heart re-creates the life that the intellect destroys."

Forty-two

Giuseppe Garibaldi: A united Italy emerges

What a lucky generation! We are entrusted with the sublime mission of regenerating Italy after fifteen hundred decadent years during which she dithered and groveled before the stupid soldiery of the oppressor!

—Giuseppe Garibaldi, proclamation to his volunteers (1866)

THREE MEN WHO heartily disliked one another made Italy. The movement for Italian liberation and unification—the Risorgimento (Resurgence)—succeeded because of Giuseppe Mazzini's patriotic idealism, Count Cavour's realpolitik, and Garibaldi's boundless bravery. Giuseppe Garibaldi (1807–82), a brilliant guerrilla warrior who became the greatest Italian general of modern times, owed as much to his experiences on the Argentine Pampas as he did to Caesar's *Commentaries* on the Gallic and civil wars of ancient Rome. A born commander, fearless and monumentally self-assured, this "Hero of Two Worlds" made freedom fighting fashionable in the West.

With his captivating voice, bearded and long-haired messianic look, rough-hewn swagger, and South American getup, he always remained a bit of a pirate and charmed almost everyone. Nationalistic "catechisms" identified him with God and Christ, and he himself thought nothing of baptizing infants, though he would shoot followers of his who had turned criminal without even bothering to take the cigar out of his mouth. He was Italy's George Washington, John Paul Jones, Andy Jackson, Honest Abe, Buffalo Bill, and Teddy Roosevelt all rolled into one. Women stole kisses from him and collected locks of his hair and nail clippings. Even Roberto Rossellini, who made a film about him, inherited a relic of his beard and his bloody boot. Garibaldi always acted like a sovereign state rather than an individual, but since he lived and breathed for human liberty alone, his larger-than-life persona seemed entirely appropriate.

This champion of the rights of labor and of women's emancipation was a lifelong believer in racial equality and freedom from oppression and repression in any form—even ordering the fig leaves to be removed from public statues in Naples in 1860 and the erotic art of ancient Pompeii to be made available for viewing. Yet after Italian liberation was finally achieved, at so much human cost to himself, he gave vent to this bitter reflection: "It was a different Italy that I had dreamed of all my life, not this miserable, poverty-stricken, humiliated Italy that we now see, governed by the dregs of the nation."

Garibaldi was born on July 4, 1807, in the seaport of Nice, which had long been part of the Kingdom of Piedmont and Sardinia but was annexed by France in 1793. Only when he was seven did Nice revert to Piedmont, whose Savoy monarchs were the oldest ruling house in Europe. In addition to his native Ligurian dialect, the boy grew up speaking French. He later learned standard Italian but always spoke it with an accent.

Like his father and grandfather before him, he became a sailor. His mother, a washerwoman, so overwhelmed him with love that her roughneck son always kept her picture above his bed. When he was eighteen he sailed to Rome with a cargo of wine, and the sights of the Eternal City haunted his imagination for the rest of his life. As a young merchant captain he plied the waters of the eastern Mediterranean and the Black Sea before being drafted into Piedmont-Sardinia's navy in 1833.

That same year, he joined Mazzini's *Giovine Italia* (Young Italy), whose goal was to unify the peninsula as a republic. In those days, Italy was divided into a number of fairly reactionary and autocratic states:

- Independent Piedmont-Sardinia, which also ruled Liguria;
- The Austrian provinces of Lombardy, Venetia (Venice and the mainland Veneto), and the Trentino (South Tyrol);
- The Spanish Bourbon Kingdom of the Two Sicilies (or of Naples), comprising Sicily and all southern Italy;
- Tuscany, ruled by an Austrian archduke;
- The smaller duchies of Parma (another Spanish Bourbon principality) and Modena, both controlled by Austria;
- The Papal States, including Latium, Umbria, the Marches, and Romagna.

In late 1833 Garibaldi took part in an insurrection of Genoa against Piedmont concocted by the exiled revolutionary and saturnine intellectual Mazzini (1805–72). When it flopped, both men were condemned to death in absentia for treason.

Garibaldi hightailed it home to Nice, then France, and eventually to South America, where he began fighting for Rio Grande do Sul (a small breakaway republic from the Brazilian Empire) as a freebooter with a vessel he named the *Mazzini*. One day, from aboard ship, he scoped out a woman (literally), strode ashore, and announced, "You must be mine." Though the beautiful Anita Ribeiro da Silva was already married, she escaped with her dashing Italian suitor in October of 1839, fought beside him in the futile rebellion, and later became his wife.

In 1841 Garibaldi, out of a job, drove a herd of cattle to Montevideo. After trying to settle down as a commercial traveler and a teacher, he found employment more congenial to his skills and interests: commander of Uruguay's naval forces in its attempt to fend off Argentina's dictator. In 1843 Garibaldi formed an Italian Legion of his exiled or idealistic countrymen and began learning how to wage guerrilla warfare. His flamboyant red shirt uniform dates from this time, when he got his hands on a shipment of clothes intended for slaughterhouse workers. His heroism in the protracted struggle for the besieged Uruguayan capital won him the sobriquet "The Hero of Montevideo."

In 1848—that tumultuous year of revolutions all over Europe—Garibaldi, dreaming of Italian liberation from its foreign rulers, returned to Italy with sixty of his men and headed for Milan, where pale, black-garbed Mazzini was directing a rebellion against the Austrians. Garibaldi was made a general, but after Piedmont, which had taken advantage of the insurrection to declare war against the Austrian Empire, was defeated in battle that summer and signed an armistice, he carried on the hopeless fight for a few more weeks on his own before wending his way back to Nice and rejoining Anita and their three children.

Where next? The restless freedom fighter set out for rebellious Sicily, Tuscany, and Venice; but soon after political turmoil forced Pope Pius IX to flee to the King of Naples for protection on November 24, a bearded man in a poncho and ostrich-plumed hat was seen riding his white horse into Rome at the head of a multinational group of volunteers, including his gigantic black orderly from South America. Garibaldi was made a colonel, Rome was declared a republic on February 9, 1849, and Mazzini, who arrived in March, was elected one of the ruling triumvirs.

But the desperate pope called on a foreign supporter, Louis Napoleon, the new president of France who would crown himself emperor as

Napoleon III in 1851. When Louis sent troops to Rome to restore the pontiff, Garibaldi, now a general commanding more than a thousand men, trounced them as they attacked the Janiculan hill on April 30, where he himself was wounded. Garibaldi also defeated a Neapolitan army that had been ordered in, and he gallantly directed the defense of Rome against the French siege in June, thrilling all of Europe. But he was endlessly quarreling with Mazzini.

Garibaldi left Rome on July 3, when defense of the city became impossible, and about 5,000 soldiers went with him. On the day before, he had warned his men in St. Peter's Square: "You can hope for no wages but hard work and danger, without roof, without rest, without food, and there will be long night watches, forced marches, and fighting at every step. Let him who loves his country follow me."

With 65,000 enemy troops dogging him—Austrian, French, Spanish, Neapolitan—Garibaldi led a brilliant retreat that enabled his followers to escape (by deserting his cause). He laid down his arms and accepted asylum in the neutral republic of San Marino, and then tried to flee across the Adriatic. But in Romagna, on August 4, his pregnant wife, Anita, who had joined him in the last days at Rome, died of disease and exhaustion while her husband cradled her in one of his red shirts. After another month of subterfuge, he was captured by the Piedmontese and told to make himself scarce.

After six months at Tangier, where he hunted and fished with some fellow Italians, made cigars, and wrote his South American memoirs, Garibaldi sailed for New York in June of 1850 to obtain U.S. citizenship so that he could work as an American ship's captain. There he lived in the Staten Island home of Antonio Meucci, a Florentine immigrant who went on to build the first (albeit unpatented) working telephone, years before Alexander Graham Bell. Meucci employed the newcomer in his factory, where the Hero of Two Worlds made candlewicks. After nine months, Garibaldi took off for Peru, where he spent three years as a ship's captain hauling guano. No one could blame him for heading back to Europe in 1854.

By this time the prime minister of Piedmont-Sardinia was Count Camillo Benso di Cavour (1810–61), a brilliant, Frenchified Turinese aristocrat once described as "an iron bar painted like a reed." Cavour allowed Garibaldi to return home to his family in Nice, hoping to extricate him from Mazzini, whom Cavour hated, and the other radical republicans. In turn, Garibaldi promised to fight in the future only for Piedmont and its ambitious king, Victor Emmanuel II (1820–78).

Cavour, the greatest Italian statesman of modern times, was so Machiavellian that he sent Piedmontese troops to fight against Russia in the Crimean War for the sole purposes of gratifying his powerful allies, France and Britain, and securing his tiny country a forum for the vexed "Italian Question" at the peace conference afterward. He now convinced Garibaldi to accept the notion that all the revolutionary factions should rally to Piedmont—a constitutional monarchy, the strongest and most liberal native Italian power, and the only truly independent one—as a nucleus of five million souls around which the rest of Italy could grow.

In 1855 Garibaldi bought half the desolate island of Caprera, off the northern coast of Sardinia, where his friends and his son Menotti helped him build a four-room *Casa Bianca,* or White House. A private dream of this patriot who always rose at dawn and went to bed with the sun was to become self-sufficient by farming, hunting, and fishing. When Cavour had him summoned to Turin in August of 1858, Garibaldi was found milking his cows.

Cavour was planning to incite a war against Austria the following spring. With the aid of French troops and Garibaldi, Piedmont-Sardinia hoped to snatch Lombardy and Venetia. Impressed by his meeting with the king, Garibaldi accepted an appointment as a major general, although he was put in charge only of a volunteer brigade, not the entire volunteer force. His men were issued blue pants and gray coats—none of that red shirt nonsense for Cavour.

In April of 1859 Piedmont went to war against Austrian Emperor Franz Joseph. Garibaldi's 3,500 *Cacciatori delle Alpi* (Alpine Huntsmen) defeated the Austrians and captured Como, but after the Battle of Solferino on June 24, Napoleon III called for an armistice because of the casualties suffered on both sides. Cavour, who had not been consulted, fumed and resigned (although he was back in the saddle in six months). Piedmont had acquired the wealthy region of Lombardy, but Venice was still in Austrian hands. "The Italians have too much individual egoism," Garibaldi observed about the lack of popular involvement in the war, "and too little love of their country."

Meanwhile, the Austrian Archduke of Tuscany, Leopold II, had fled; Modena and Parma had revolted; and Emilia-Romagna had declared its independence from the pope. These states banded into a Central League, and Garibaldi was made second in command of its forces. But the idolized guerrilla leader was being manipulated by the king, by the new Tuscan leader Baron Ricasoli, and even by his fiancée, the young

Marchesina Giuseppina Raimondi, whom he abandoned a few hours after their marriage in January 1860, when he found out she was pregnant by one of his own officers.

In April Cavour announced the transfer to France of the provinces of Savoy and Nice, which he had exchanged for Napoleon III's pledge of military aid to prevent the Austrians from interfering with Piedmont's plans to annex Tuscany and the rest of the Central League. Garibaldi was enraged with Cavour for bargaining away his birthplace, but at least a kingdom of northern Italy had been cobbled together—Piedmont, Lombardy, Parma, Modena, Emilia-Romagna, and Tuscany—right up to the border of the Papal States. The Italophile British prime minister, Lord Palmerston, eager to see a strong Italy for keeping France in check, warned Austria to let bygones be bygones.

After Mazzini had incited popular insurrections in Sicily, Garibaldi embarked on the most extraordinary achievement of his career, gathering volunteers from all over Italy for a mighty enterprise. These were the immortal "Thousand" (*I Mille*), many of them university students, nearly half younger than twenty, including one intrepid lad of eleven.

On the night of May 6, 1860, they set out from Quarto, a suburb of Genoa, on two hijacked paddle steamers, *Piemonte* and *Lombardia*, with Garibaldi now resplendent in his red shirt, big black hat, and silk neckerchief. Evading the navy of the Bourbon Kingdom of Naples and Sicily, the force of 1,088 men and one woman (the mistress of future Italian prime minister Francesco Crispi), armed with only 993 rusty rifles, landed at Marsala, in western Sicily, on May 11. Three Bourbon ships were in the harbor with their cannons aimed, but they were discouraged from firing on the steamers because of the presence of two British warships whose captains had had a gentlemanly talk with their Italian counterparts.

Garibaldi's liberators landed and took over, their general springing for a dozen bottles of the local Marsala wine that night to celebrate. Cavour had opposed the expedition but was reluctant to alienate the masses, who worshiped the Redshirt leader. Garibaldi also had the support of the king, who had privately egged him on. He now declared himself dictator of Sicily in the name of Victor Emmanuel II.

It must be emphasized that, until only a year earlier, the Sicilians had been the unwilling subjects of Ferdinand II, who earned his nickname of "*Bomba*" by ordering his navy to bombard restive Sicilian cities like Palermo and Messina in the aftermath of the 1848–49 revolutions. The new Bourbon king of Naples, Francis II, had 20,000 troops defending the Sicilian capital of Palermo, 3,000 of whom were now sent out against the Thousand.

The forces met at Calatafimi, halfway to Palermo, on May 15, near the ancient Greek temple of Segesta. Shouting "Here we make Italy or die," Garibaldi staked everything on this skirmish, and his troops fought fiercely. The Bourbon soldiers, poorly led, retreated from the Redshirts' bayonet charges, and the angry locals cut the Bourbon force's lines of communication and murdered stragglers. The way to Palermo lay open.

The dictator of Sicily entered the capital on June 1 and, five days later, when the Bourbon garrison surrendered, declared Sicily independent of Naples. To avoid being murdered by their vengeful peasants, many landowners came out for Garibaldi. Cavour, who now pretended that he had been solidly behind the expedition, sent money, supplies, and 3,000 more volunteers. Alexandre Dumas *père*, in part to get material for his swashbuckling novels, was covering the amazing international story for a Paris newspaper from aboard his yacht, where his entourage made red shirts for the *garibaldini*.

On July 20, despite serious losses, Garibaldi won a battle at Milazzo. With 10,000 to 15,000 men under his command, he had captured all of Sicily except Messina in the northeast. On August 18 and 19, an advance force of 3,500 crossed the Strait of Messina, bombarded Reggio's garrison, and soon received the surrender of most of the 16,000 troops who were holding Calabria.

The Bourbon soldiers defending southern Italy were demoralized, and their own political and military leaders were accepting bribes from Cavour. In advance of his troops, Garibaldi rode a train into Naples from Salerno with a handful of men on September 7, the day after King Francis fled north to his fortress of Gaeta. Bourbon soldiers presented arms as Garibaldi rode through the streets in an open carriage, and crowds cheered when he later addressed them from his hotel balcony. "The royal nest, still warm," Garibaldi wrote, "was occupied by the emancipators of the people, and the rich carpets of the royal palace were trodden by the heavy boots of the plebeian."

For six weeks Garibaldi ruled Naples, Italy's largest city, as dictator. He now wanted to cap it all by wrenching the Papal States from Pius IX, but crafty Cavour seized the initiative. In late September, after secretly fomenting uprisings there, Cavour sent an invading force to Umbria and the Marches, in the northern Papal States, under command of the king himself.

Under the pretext of restoring order, Cavour set about his real agenda, which called for annexing these regions and preventing Garibaldi from seizing Rome, a move that would have inflamed Napoleon III (and the French Catholics he had to appease). The king then marched south to demand from Garibaldi the lower half of the peninsula conquered in his name—which Mazzini was clamoring to proclaim an independent republic.

But the fighting wasn't over yet. On October 1 and 2, pitting his 30,000 men against 40,000, Garibaldi won a pitched battle—the greatest victory of his career—on the River Volturno, near Caserta, where the Bourbons had made a major last stand. He dutifully surrendered his astounding conquests—the whole of southern Italy in four months—to Victor Emmanuel at Teano, near Naples, on October 26, and was the first to salute him as king of Italy, a title officially promulgated by the first Italian parliament in Turin on March 17, 1861. Italy would remain a monarchy under the House of Savoy until June of 1946.

Garibaldi left Naples after his request to be made interim governor was refused and his edicts were nullified. When the king tried to appease him by offering him land and an appointment to full general, Garibaldi crumpled up the missive and flung it out a window. Once more a private citizen, he returned to Caprera. Proudly listing "farmer" on his census returns, he relished following in the footsteps of the Roman dictator Cincinnatus who, after crushing the enemy, returned to his humble agricultural pursuits. Garibaldi made sure to name his donkeys Louis Napoleon, Franz Joseph, and Pius IX.

Encouraged by Garibaldi's conquests of 1860, aggrieved peasants committed barbarities all over southern Italy. To cite just one, in the hill town of Esperia, in the province of Frosinone, halfway between Rome and Naples, the local baron, Don Francesco Roselli, was murdered and decapitated. His head, with his pipe stuck in his mouth, was propped on a low wall at the entrance to the town, where his former underlings came to dip their bread in his blood. The Piedmontese government claimed such acts were perpetrated by brigands, but they were often spontaneous outbreaks of social revolution on the part of a desperate underclass.

More than a hundred thousand soldiers were needed to quash these spontaneous rebellions, and the north had to impose martial law on the south, which teemed with atrocities, insurrections, bandits, the Sicilian Mafia, and the Neapolitan Camorra. For decades southern Italy was an occupied territory, and the experiences of this catastrophic honeymoon fueled animosities that are far from forgotten. As a Sicilian army officer says in Lampedusa's *The Leopard*, "We've never been so divided as since we were united" (see Essay 48).

In 1861, in the elections for the first Italian Parliament, Naples chose Giuseppe Garibaldi. The general caused quite a stir in the assemblage at Turin, Italy's first capital, in his red shirt, poncho, and sombrero among a sea of frock coats and top hats. That was nothing compared with the uproar triggered by his speech—a vehement attack on Cavour (who was present), blaming him for "a fratricidal war provoked by the government," for shabby treatment of his volunteers, and for having made Garibaldi "a foreigner in Italy" by ceding Nice to France. But only two months later, on June 6, Cavour died suddenly—a disaster for Italy, since there was no one of his stature to guide the infant nation's destinies. Venetia and Rome still remained outside the fold.

In July 1861 President Lincoln offered to make Garibaldi a major general in command of an army corps in the Civil War, but the intransigent guerrilla leader demanded to be made commander-in-chief and wanted Lincoln to come out strongly against slavery. Besides, Garibaldi told the Americans, he had unfinished business at home.

During a visit to Marsala in 1862, when Garibaldi heard the crowd chanting *"Roma o morte"* (Rome or death!), he immediately went to the cathedral to take an oath to liberate the ancient city from papal rule, later raising a force in Sicily for this purpose. At Aspromonte, near the Strait of Messina, his troops were fired on by the Italian army, and he himself was wounded and captured but soon released. His king, who owed him so much, was talking to him out of both sides of his mouth.

In 1866 Austria was attacked by both Prussia and Italy, the latter with the aim of winning Venetia. Garibaldi was put in command of volunteers and won the only notable Italian victories while fighting in the Trentino, but the territory he conquered was given back in the peace treaty. Although the Austrians were ruinously defeated by the Prussians at Sadowa during this Seven Weeks' War, they scorned to hand over Venetia directly to Italy, which they had defeated on land and sea. Instead, they gave the former Queen of the Adriatic and the rest of Venetia to France, and France, in turn, passed them on to Italy like hand-me-downs.

Once again Garibaldi set out to capture Rome, but the French were protecting the pope, and Italy was still frightened of openly defying Napoleon III. On September 24, 1867, Garibaldi was arrested on his way to Rome and sent back to Caprera, but he managed to get through the island blockade of nine warships in a small boat (probably with government connivance). At Mentana on November 3, Garibaldi's volunteers were defeated by French and papal troops. When he escaped into Italian territory, he was arrested and kept in custody for three weeks. Weary of the tawdry politics, of the under-the-table encouragement combined with public hostility to his actions, all of which were designed only to keep Napoleon III fooled, Garibaldi lashed out against the pope, Mazzini, the Italian Parliament and ministers, and even the king.

Finally, in 1870, when its participation in the Franco-Prussian War caused France to withdraw its garrison from Rome, Italian troops (with all the usual pretexts) were dispatched to seize the city. On September 20, which became Italy's national holiday, General Raffaele Cadorna shelled and breached the city walls at Porta Pia, and Rome fell at a cost of fewer than seventy lives all around. ("When the Savoy marched into Rome, it was like Saddam marching into Kuwait," said Roman prince Sforza Ruspoli for the benefit of *W* magazine in February 2001.) The city became Italy's capital, and the pope was left with only the Vatican.

But this crowning event of the Risorgimento took place without Garibaldi, who had chivalrously gone off to fight for the French Republic after Napoleon III was deposed. As usual, the red-shirted leader fought bravely, winning battles at Châtillon, Autun, and Dijon. Victor Hugo claimed that Garibaldi was the only general on the French side who remained undefeated.

Except for the Trentino and Trieste, acquired after World War I, Italy had been liberated and unified. Clad in his omnipresent red shirt, Garibaldi retired to Caprera, crippled by arthritis and his numerous wounds. He occasionally sang arias from Verdi and Donizetti, and liked to read Greek and Roman history, Voltaire, mathematics, agriculture, and poetry, especially the patriotic verse of Ugo Foscolo. Besides his memoirs, he wrote three novels and some poems in French and Italian.

Refusing any last rites, he died on Caprera on June 2, 1882, not quite seventy-five. The man who had fought sixty-seven battles and countless skirmishes on land and sea wanted to be burned on a wooden pyre like Hector or Achilles, but the Italian government forbade it. Carved on his statue on the Janiculan hill, overlooking the Rome he was not allowed to liberate, is one of his favorite slogans: *"Roma o morte."*

Forty-three

The last "Renaissance" prince—D'Annunzio at Fiume

Memento audere semper. (Remember to always dare.)
—Gabriele D'Annunzio, one of his numerous mottoes

ON SEPTEMBER 12, 1919, a world-renowned poet, novelist, and dramatist took over the city of Fiume on the eastern coast of the Adriatic and proceeded to rule it for the next sixteen months as his own private fiefdom. One literary critic has pointed out that this was "a unique case in the history of world literature: a major poet and narrator conquers, and holds, a city-state."[1]

But Gabriele D'Annunzio (1863–1938), a native of the Adriatic city of Pescara in the Abruzzi, was no garden-variety littérateur. During World War I, Lieutenant Colonel D'Annunzio had volunteered for action at the advanced age of fifty-two and had fought heroically in all three services of the Italian armed forces. He won the maximum permissible number of medals for deeds such as charging Austrian trenches at night with dagger and pistol, leading a torpedo-boat squadron into a heavily defended port and blowing up an enemy ship, and bombing Austrian-held Trieste twice in one day (once with his own propaganda leaflets and once with bombs). In an accident during a forced landing, he lost his right eye and was temporarily blinded but managed in the interim to write a book on ten thousand strips of paper that were specially prepared for him.

This bald, pale, goateed, highly perfumed, and monocled (later eye-patched) little man, an ardent Nietzschean who undoubtedly saw himself as an *Übermensch*, also enjoyed a string of beautiful mistresses,

---

[1]Paolo Valesio, *Gabriele D'Annunzio: The Dark Flame*, trans. by Marilyn Migiel (New Haven, Conn.: Yale University Press, 1992), p. xvii. This scholar claims that D'Annunzio "is not only the most creative writer of the Italian twentieth century but also the most intelligent writer of his times, and the most modern and cultured" (p. 175).

principally noblewomen and artists, including the greatest Italian actress of all time, Eleonora Duse (1858–1924). He fought duels, played the dandy, rode to hounds, served in Parliament as a member of the extreme Right who dramatically crossed over to the extreme Left, threw away other people's fortunes, created well-received dramatic works in French (scored by Debussy and Mascagni), got his entire oeuvre placed on the Vatican's Index of Prohibited Books, wrote the intertitles for a silent movie, had a price put on his head by the Hapsburgs, and influenced writers such as Thomas Mann and James Joyce.

His writings—vitalistic, pagan, allusive, nature- and Italy-worshiping, patriotic, militaristic, sensuous, symbolist, decadent, hedonistic, bombastic, polemical, exotic, Homerically violent, precious, sensationalistic, highly musical, vatic, megalomaniacal, classically inspired, overwrought, and vastly learned—eventually filled forty-nine volumes of a government-subsidized set of his complete works, including a dozen major collections of poems, well over a dozen plays, at least seven novels, and numerous short stories, journalistic pieces, and memoirs. All in all, Luigi Barzini had to conclude that Gabriele D'Annunzio was "perhaps more Italian than any other Italian."

Why did this force of nature and most flamboyant of authors take over Fiume (or Rijeka, as the Croats call it—it means "river" in both languages), a seaport that had belonged to the recently dissolved Austro-Hungarian Empire? Like all the eastern Adriatic littoral, including cities with large Italian populations such as Pola (Pula) in Istria and Zara (Zadar) and Spalato (Split) on the coast of Dalmatia, Fiume had been part of the old Venetian Empire and had acquired Italian settlers in medieval times. But its former Hungarian rulers had also much more recently wooed Italian businessmen to Fiume to counterbalance the restive native working class of Croats. After World War I, Fiuman Italians numbered about twenty-five thousand—just half the population— but the city council rebaptized itself the Italian National Council of Fiume and declared the city to be part of Italy rather than of the new ramshackle state of Yugoslavia. Allied troops assumed control on November 17, 1918, until the dispute could be resolved by the Paris Peace Conference the following year.

The city soon became a sticking point between the Italian and the other Allied negotiators at the conference. A few years earlier, Britain and France had persuaded Italy to enter the war on the Allied side by promising extensive Austrian territories in the Adriatic such as the Istrian peninsula and Dalmatia (basically the Croatian coast). Even though Italy had treaty commitments with Germany and Austro-Hungary at the time, it signed the secret Treaty of London in April 1915. D'Annunzio, with mesmerizing speeches to vast crowds (some 100,000 swarmed to hear him in Rome's Capitol alone), had built public support for joining the Allies.

But after 600,000 Italian soldiers had lost their lives in the war, the Allies were reneging on their promises, and Italian nationalists like D'Annunzio were furious. The Italians blamed President Woodrow Wilson, whose nation had not been a signatory to the Treaty of London, since the United States had entered the war only in 1917. Wilson was determined to settle postwar disputes according to his own Fourteen Points, through which he tried to map out humane and commonsensical solutions to the highly complicated political questions caused by the collapse of the German, Austro-Hungarian, Russian, and Turkish empires. A crucial principle underlying his Fourteen Points was self-determination, according to which formerly subject peoples would be given a voice in deciding which larger national entities, if any, they wished to join.

Italy's delegation at the peace talks, led by Prime Minister Vittorio Emanuele Orlando, allowed itself to get seriously sidetracked over Fiume, demanding that the city be ceded to Italy according to the doctrine of self-determination (although the Treaty of London had stipulated that Fiume must go to Croatia). But Italy also wanted the Treaty of London territories it had been promised—even though, according to self-determination, many of these regions, such as Slavic-speaking Dalmatia, should become part of the new state of Yugoslavia.

The other Big Four Allied representatives at Paris, Lloyd George of Great Britain and Clemenceau of France (to whose demands stiff-necked Wilson had proved much more amenable than to Italy's), shared the American president's growing exasperation with Orlando's seemingly contradictory rationales for his various claims. When Wilson decided to make an appeal directly to the Italian people—in effect, trying to pull the rug out from under the feet of their own representatives at Paris—he succeeded only in unleashing a wave of outraged anti-Americanism throughout the country.

Orlando himself was sacked in June, and Francesco Saverio Nitti succeeded him as Italian prime minister. A few months later, after some violent clashes in Fiume, the Allies decided to pull out their troops (including the Italians), remove the Italian influence from the city's governing council, and send in a British police force to assume control of the city on September 12, 1919.

Enter D'Annunzio again. The aviator-poet was contemplating a flight to Tokyo at the time but quickly turned his attention to remedying what he called the "mutilated peace." Although Italy had received Trieste from Austria, as well as the Italian-speaking Trentino and the German-speaking Alto Adige (south Tyrol) right up to the Brenner Pass, it had been cheated of Dalmatia—and Fiume.

Writing to Mussolini that "the die is cast," the fifty-six-year-old poet, although weak with fever, set out from Ronchi, about fifty miles north of Fiume, down the coast road toward the city. Dressed in a huge fur overcoat and riding in a general's staff car with the horn blaring, he was accompanied by about two hundred Sardinian grenadiers who had been ordered out of Fiume by the evacuating Allies. On the way he picked up some disgruntled veterans, especially the ultranationalist elite shock troops, the *Arditi* (the "ardent" or "burning" ones), as well as other Italian soldiers and officers who deserted to join his cause. *"O Fiume o morte!"* was their inevitable slogan—"Fiume or death." By the time D'Annunzio got to the gates of the city, he led about 2,500 men in a long column of tanks, armored cars, trucks, and other vehicles.

The commanding Allied general (Pittaluga, an Italian), dispatched from Fiume with orders from his government to shoot the poet if necessary, warned D'Annunzio that he was committing an act of sedition. When this approach failed to have the desired effect, Pittaluga ordered a colonel of the Arditi to shoot the traitor, but the officer merely saluted. After some pleading by Pittaluga, the histrionic poet opened his coat, displayed his array of war medals, and said, "Just have me shot, General." Since he was getting nowhere, Pittaluga made a virtue of necessity and accompanied D'Annunzio into the city, which had erupted into celebration—people were singing and cheering, church bells pealing, sirens wailing, banners and streamers flying everywhere. When the other leaders of the march appointed D'Annunzio the new *comandante*, he did not demur. The remnant of the Allied forces soon moved out as scheduled to avoid confrontations.

On his first evening in the city, in a harangue from the balcony of the Governor's Palace (now his), D'Annunzio thrilled the crowd in Piazza Dante by announcing the annexation of Fiume to Italy (although the latter hadn't been consulted). Adopting the black flame emblem of the Arditi as the city's symbol, he dubbed his new principality "the City of the Holocaust," claiming a fire would be started there that would consume the old regime in Italy and regenerate the rest of the world.

A brilliant demagogue endowed with a beautiful voice, D'Annunzio delivered balcony speeches at Fiume almost daily, keeping tens of thousands hanging on his every word, without the aid of loudspeakers, or whipping them up into mystically patriotic frenzies, especially when he accompanied his words with the waving of huge flags stained with the blood of Italian war heroes. Sometimes he led them in song, including anthems of his own devising; sometimes they would antiphonally chant *eja, eja, eja, alalà!*—which he told them was the war cry of Trojan Aeneas, ancestor of the Romans. He called his stalwart followers *teste di ferro* (Ironheads), while the nickname he coined for Italian prime minister Nitti—*Cagoia*—may be roughly translated as "Shitter." When the warrior-bard occupied the city of Zara in November, as a prelude (he vainly hoped) to the conquest of all of Dalmatia, the crowds there were so moved by his oratory that they all knelt in the cold rain and mud as he unfurled a patriotic banner.

While Wilson blustered about the need for "absolute firmness" in dealing with the embarrassing Fiume situation, Cagoia clapped an embargo on the city but let food, medicine, and other essential supplies through. The Italian government didn't want to risk civil war—the loyalty of Italian troops was highly suspect, given how many had defected to D'Annunzio—and it was also exploiting the crisis to ratchet up the pressure on the Allied diplomats.

Fiume was noted for its thriving nightlife, its cafés and dance halls swarming with people in a party mode. An air of festivity reigned in the city after the Italian takeover, and D'Annunzio's legionnaires found the Fiuman women very congenial. Drug use was common, and the *comandante* himself, like other war pilots, probably used cocaine. While Capuchin priests clamored for the right to marry, the city soon became something of a divorce mart, too.

Not long after the coup, the Futurist poet, propagandist, and proto-Fascist Filippo Tommaso Marinetti blew into town, but his fire-eating addresses to the troops, and loose-cannon approach to life in general, proved too much even for D'Annunzio, and Marinetti was asked to leave within two weeks. Mussolini, who had founded the Fascist Party five months earlier, flew in to confer with the *comandante*. When the latter evinced a desire to march on Rome and seize the government, Mussolini said the times weren't ripe yet, although he obviously let the idea percolate. Visits by members of the Italian royal family conferred a patina of respectability on D'Annunzio's regime. Arturo Toscanini and his orchestra visited, too, but there was a problem when live grenades exploded during an entertainment in the maestro's honor, and several legionnaires were wounded.

Much like Garibaldi's 1860 expedition to Sicily (see Essay 42), D'Annunzio's venture became a magnet for thugs, bored students, idealists, the underemployed, and some lazies and crazies. Some of his followers, whom he called *uscocchi* after the dreaded pirates of the ancient Adriatic, preyed on cargo ships. Others stole horses from a nearby Italian army stable. Soldiers started shaving their heads and growing goatees in homage to their *comandante*. Decked out in black shirts, capes, and fezzes with black tassels, they swaggered through the city armed with daggers. So many Arditi, veterans, and officers—even generals—flocked to him, 9,000 in all, that D'Annunzio had to beg them to stop because he couldn't feed and house them all.

One of D'Annunzio's most irritating schemes against the Allies was an Anti–League of Nations consisting of Irish, Arabs, Palestinian Jews, Indians, and others he considered to be oppressed by the Big Four powers, whose activities at Paris he saw as "a conspiracy of privileged thieves and robbers." The major coup of this League of Oppressed Peoples was its sale of 250,000 rifles to anti-British Egyptians, but lack of funds kept the league from getting off the ground.

When the Allies finally resolved to make Fiume an independent state, D'Annunzio decided to beat them to the punch. On September 8, 1920, he promulgated *La Carta del Carnaro*, a constitution that declared Fiume to be the autonomous *Reggenza Italiana del Carnaro* (Italian Regency of the Gulf of Carnaro). As might be expected, the document, drafted by the anarcho-syndicalist head of D'Annunzio's cabinet, Alceste De Ambris, and reworked and expanded by the *comandante* himself, was unique in the annals of government. It set up a corporative and syndicalist state (later imitated by Mussolini) in which the two parliamentary bodies (whose deliberations were to be "laconic") were elected by universal suffrage and composed of representatives of various professions and trades (each citizen having to belong to one of these "corporations," too). Local governing bodies—the communes—exercised self-rule in day-to-day affairs.

Although he ruled as if above the law, D'Annunzio proved to be a benevolent despot, often pardoning criminals, even traitors. His constitution was an egalitarian document that guaranteed the freedoms of religion, speech, the press, and privacy, provided for the complete equality of women, and stressed the dignity of work: "Labor, even the most humble, . . . if it is well done, tends toward beauty and ornaments the world." It established a minimum wage, medical insurance, and social security for illness, injury, unemployment, and old age. As in ancient Rome, it also provided for rule by a dictator for short periods during emergencies (such as at the time of its promulgation).

D'Annunzio's constitution, which placed "the culture of the people at the summit of its laws," also established a College of Aediles to "keep the city beautiful, organize the civic festivals, and instill a sense of beauty and elegance in the citizenry." No wonder it has been called "a kind of Napoleonic Code rewritten by an Ezra Pound." Like any self-respecting state, Fiume had its own currency, stamps, and flag (yellow, wine-red, and blue). As a historian of D'Annunzio's statecraft has written, "he wished to re-create . . . the ferment of activity that had produced the Renaissance."[2]

In June of 1920 Italy elected a new prime minister, Giovanni Giolitti, who took a tougher stance than Nitti had toward D'Annunzio's shenanigans. During the debates on whether Italy should enter World War I, Giolitti had come to hate D'Annunzio for his viciously obscene public attacks, which had incited the crowds to violence against Giolitti and his fellow neutralists. Giolitti tightened the embargo on Fiume so that food had to be rationed, electricity and heating oil were scarce, unemployment grew, and labor troubles led to the arrest of hundreds of workers. The good times had clearly come to an end in the city.

The Allies finally threw up their hands over the situation, letting Italy and Yugoslavia settle their remaining differences. After the Treaty of Rapallo in November of 1920 arranged for Fiume to be declared an independent city and for Italy to keep Zara but to cede the rest of Dalmatia to Yugoslavia, D'Annunzio quixotically declared war on his native land. When skirmishes left a few dozen dead, Giolitti ordered the Italian navy to bombard D'Annunzio's palace on "Bloody Christmas." Barely missed by a shell from the battleship *Andrea Doria*, the poet, who had vowed a fight to the death, decided that the better part of valor was discretion.

Although he was received in Italy like a conquering hero, D'Annunzio had lost some of his verve and ebullience. He retired to a villa in the hills above Lake Garda in 1921, explaining that "I have come to enclose

[2]Michael A. Ledeen, *The First Duce: D'Annunzio at Fiume* (Baltimore: The Johns Hopkins University Press, 1977), p. 169. All quotations from D'Annunzio's constitution are from this work.

my sadness and my silence in this ancient rustic house, not so much to humiliate myself as to put to a more difficult test my powers of creation and transfiguration."

His last great creative act was to enlarge and transform his villa into what he named *Vittoriale degli Italiani* (Victory Place of the Italians), a walled compound with parks and gardens that he bequeathed to Italy in 1923 and that is now a national monument. When he heard that an Italian cruiser was to be decommissioned, he had its prow brought there, still armed with cannons, and set up on the grounds. Thundering gun salutes welcomed visitors, the number of blasts determined by their rank. He proceeded to cram the villa with as many books, art objects, exotic pieces of huge furniture, Oriental rugs, casts of ancient Greek sculptures, war mementos, and mistresses as would fit. Thousands still visit the Vittoriale daily.

Taking a page from D'Annunzio's voluminous book, Mussolini finally orchestrated his march on Rome in late October 1922. ("Rome, Rome, will you give yourself to a butcher?" D'Annunzio had rhetorically asked, but he hardly furthered the cause of liberal institutions by referring to the Italian parliament as "a great mephitic sewer.") D'Annunzio himself didn't take part in the march on Rome. Just before he was to meet with Mussolini, he had mysteriously fallen out a window after an assignation with a woman and found himself indisposed.

But Europe's first fascist leader borrowed much from D'Annunzio. In addition to the Arditi and other followers of the *comandante* who drifted back to Italy after the fall of Fiume, Mussolini appropriated D'Annunzio's Roman salute and Roman eagles, his balcony addresses (which had also been a specialty of Garibaldi), his passionate exchanges with the crowds, the black shirts and other distinctive garb, the Arditi anthem *"Giovinezza"* (Youth), and various slogans, including Aeneas's war cry. D'Annunzio himself never joined the Fascist party.

Italy did get Fiume by treaty in 1924, after Mussolini took over, but lost it again in the chaos after World War II. Called Rijeka today, it is a Croatian city of about 170,000 residents. As for the man who ruled it like a Renaissance prince, he was finally made a real prince (of Monte Nevoso) at age sixty-one by King Victor Emmanuel III.

On March 1, 1938, not quite seventy-five, Gabriele D'Annunzio died of a cerebral hemorrhage while at his desk at the Vittoriale. The great lyric poet Petrarch, too, had died in old age while writing (see Essay 16), and the two men share some other points of similarity. Both were steeped in Roman history and literature, patriotically harked back to the glories of the ancient Roman Empire, crafted the Italian language to supreme heights of musicality in their verse, freely associated with tyrants, and ardently admired Cola di Rienzo, the medieval revolutionary who seized Rome in an attempt to revive the Roman Republic.

An unlikely devotee of St. Francis of Assisi, D'Annunzio, who would sometimes don the Franciscan habit at home in the Vittoriale, had expressed the wish to die in his bare *Schifamondo* Room (Contempt of the World Room or, better, *De Contemptu Mundi* Room). His body was dutifully transported there by his staff. Of course, he had ordered that a death mask be made and that he be buried on the premises.

The Fiume takeover is often cited as the first ominous outbreak of international violence in Europe after the end of World War I, although it was not very violent at all, especially in light of the 9 million soldiers and millions of civilians who had perished in the Great War. In 1934, when the Prince of Monte Nevoso was an old man, Ezra Pound, another political poet, saw fit to praise him: "The only living author who has ever taken a city or held up the diplomatic crapule at the point of machine-guns, he is in a position to speak with more authority than a batch of neurasthenic incompetents."

A man of thought who was also a man of action, D'Annunzio was a progenitor of the *poètes engagés* of the 1930s and the partisan intellectuals and Resistance fighters of World War II, who devolved into the legions of ivory-tower revolutionaries of the 1950s, 1960s, and beyond. Whatever D'Annunzio's ultimate poetic worth or ambiguous human legacy, few would quarrel with literary scholar Sergio Pacifici's bottom-line assessment: "He was, this much is sure, a man of genius."

Forty-four

La Dottoressa: Maria Montessori and a new era in early childhood education

Multiply the sensations, and develop the capacity of appreciating fine differences in stimuli, and we refine the sensibility and multiply human pleasures.

—Maria Montessori, *The Montessori Method* (1909)

OUR TOY STORES and preschool classrooms are stocked with bead mazes, sorting boxes, peg puzzles, play kitchens, child-sized furniture, stacking blocks, and other toys that are said to enhance dexterity, eye-hand coordination, fine motor skills, creative thinking, and personal independence. The notion of "educational toys" is so ingrained in our culture that it's difficult to imagine that a century ago the concept would have been considered an oxymoron.

The woman largely responsible for the shift in thought about how young children learn would be displeased to hear her educational theory described as a "fun and games" approach. Maria Montessori (1870–1952), often called *La Dottoressa* (The Woman Doctor) in her day, was admired by the likes of Sigmund Freud, Jean Piaget, Thomas Edison, Alexander Graham Bell, and even Benito Mussolini, but not for the undisciplined classroom environment sometimes erroneously associated with her.

She was born in the small town of Chiaravalle in the Marches, on August 31, 1870, less than a month before the final unification of Italy. Maria's father, Alessandro, was an inspector for the Ministry of Finance. Her mother, Renilde, was a widely read and remarkably well-educated daughter of a prosperous local farmer. A strong supporter of a liberated, unified Italy, Renilde was the niece of Antonio Stoppani, a priest and eminent professor of geology at the University of Milan. One of the relatively few Italian clergymen to champion the goals of the Risorgimento, Stoppani founded a journal dedicated to the reconciliation of natural science and religious thought. Seen in this context, Montessori's accomplishments—breaking ground for Italian women educationally and professionally and revolutionizing the schooling of "defective" and poor children—seem to be a natural outgrowth of her progressive family environment.

Maria was an ordinary grade-school student whose early academic career was notable only for prizes in needlework. At the time that most Italian girls left school, however, she became interested in mathematics and engineering. At age thirteen, with her mother's backing, she entered a technical school in Rome and then continued at a technical institute, where she majored in mathematics and also studied the biological sciences. Contrary to her aghast father's wishes, but with Renilde's support, Maria declared her intention to become a physician.

After completing her premed studies in 1892, Montessori applied to the University of Rome's medical school. No woman had ever attended the school, and Montessori apparently owed her admission to the intervention of no less a personage than Pope Leo XIII, who later declared medicine to be an ideal profession for women. In 1896 she became the first woman in Italy to receive a medical degree, graduating near the top of her class.

Montessori now began working in the psychiatric clinic at the University of Rome, where she developed an interest in the education of disabled and retarded children. Through careful observation, she became convinced that at least some of the children suffered more from a lack of training and sensory stimulation than from any serious organic problem. She found confirmation of her intuitions in the writings of Jean-Marc-Gaspard Itard (1775–1838), a French military physician who had helped train deaf-mutes and gained fame for his efforts to tame and educate the so-called "Savage of Aveyron," a young boy who had grown up wild in a forest. Itard argued that the feral child did not suffer from "idiocy" but from sensory and social deprivation.

Montessori also studied the writings of Itard's pupil, the psychiatrist Edouard Séguin (1812–80), a pioneer in providing the mentally retarded with sensory training as a means of increasing their level of functioning. Viewing childhood as a series of developmental stages during which distinct physical and intellectual skills emerged in succession, Séguin adapted conventional educational methods for use with disabled children. Other strong influences on Montessori included Friedrich Froebel (1782–1852), the German educator and social reformer who founded the first *kindergarten* (garden of children), and Johann Heinrich Pestalozzi (1746–1827), a Swiss pioneer in educating the poor and an advocate of helping children to think independently.

Working closely with Giuseppe Montesano, a colleague at the psychiatric institute, Montessori began to formulate practical methods of educating children who were labeled feebleminded. She lectured frequently on her findings, emphasizing that most of these children could be trained to some degree and that society owed them that much. Among the leading nations of the West, she told her audiences, only Italy lacked educational institutions for teaching basic skills to the mentally handicapped.

By the late 1890s the charismatic Montessori had lectured to growing audiences in most European capitals on what we now call special education, in which she had become the preeminent authority. In 1900 she and Montesano were asked to be codirectors of the new Scuola Magistrale Ortofrenica (the Orthophrenic School) in Rome for training teachers of retarded children.

In keeping with Montessori's belief that young children should be schooled in practical, everyday activities, the pupils assigned to the student teachers were taught simple skills such as using a spoon and walking in a straight line. They spent hours in gardens, looking at, smelling, and feeling the flowers. Gymnastic training was included as a child's physical condition permitted. Once these activities had aroused the child's senses and interests, "real instruction" began.

Montessori and Montesano based much of the curriculum on teaching materials originally developed by Itard and Séguin. Initially, the children were presented with objects to sort according to shape, size, and texture, frames for lacing and buttoning, cylinders of graduated diameters and heights, and bead-stringing sets. "The aim," Montessori later wrote in *The Montessori Method*, "is to educate the eye to the differential perception of dimensions."

Children achieved greater success, she found, when they were well-prepared to undertake a task. A child who could not learn to use a needle and thread might first be helped to weave wide strips of colored paper together. Relying on detailed observation of which approaches worked, Montessori refined what she called her "didactic materials" and what we call educational toys. For example, she ordered the construction of wooden letters with consonants and vowels painted in different colors. After spending time observing and touching the letters, the children eventually learned to write the alphabet on a chalkboard.

Within the first three months of the Orthophrenic School's operation, government and educational officials marveled at the progress being made there. Some of the less disabled children eventually learned to read and write and were able to pass examinations given to children in conventional schools.

Then Montessori's career took an abrupt turn. She bore Montesano's child, but the affair ended badly when he married another woman shortly afterward. As a result Montessori left the Orthophrenic School in 1901, severed her professional alliance with her son's father, and returned to the University of Rome to study philosophy, pedagogy, and the new discipline of educational psychology. Shifting her focus to normal children, she began to apply what she had learned from working with the mentally disabled. During this time she continued to lecture on education, anthropology, the emancipation of women, and the protection of children.

In 1907 she embarked on the project for which she remains known throughout the world. A group of bankers sought her advice on a problem they were having at some apartment houses in the San Lorenzo district of Rome. The buildings, formerly inhabited by squatters, had been rehabilitated by the bankers, who recruited working-class families, including about fifty children, to live in them.

In most of the families both parents worked, and even the smallest children were left to their own devices during the day, often doing damage to the property. The bankers realized the children needed daytime supervision, and Montessori agreed to establish a child-care center, which was known as *Casa dei Bambini* (Children's House). Not only did she see the venture as an altruistic one, but she also considered it an opportunity to test her educational theories on economically deprived children of normal intelligence.

By this time Montessori was convinced that normal children should be helped to teach themselves and that the teacher's proper role was chiefly that of observant guide. She had designed classroom materials to be self-correcting, so that a child who tried to place a cylinder in a hole that was too small could see his own error and search for the right opening. "When the child educates himself," she wrote, "and when the control and correction of errors is yielded to the didactic material, there *remains for the teacher nothing but to observe.*"

As with disabled children, Montessori began by educating the senses of her new charges before engaging their intellect. Soon her success at the Orthophrenic School was repeated at Casa dei Bambini. The initially rowdy children were captivated by the didactic materials, which had been designed to prepare them for reading (by training their eyes to move from left to right) and for developing math skills. Within months some of the four- and five-year-olds were reading and writing, a feat that astonished educators and the public because of the students' ages (children typically learned to read one to two years later) and their deprived backgrounds.

The students also made strides in the practical activities of daily living, in keeping with Montessori's belief that children should be made independent in these matters as early as possible. When the bankers and educational inspectors came to visit, they saw very clean children (Montessori insisted that the parents maintain a high standard of hygiene) serving themselves hot soup and tidying up after meals. The head of a religious order exclaimed that Montessori's discoveries were even more important than Marconi's (see Essay 45).

Visitors remarked on the children's diligence and concentration as they went about their individual tasks, often preferring to work with the didactic materials rather than to draw or color. At the Casa, children had considerable freedom of movement in contrast to conventional classrooms of the day, whose students Montessori compared to butterflies mounted on pins. Children at the Casa were also free to choose from among the didactic materials that were available to them. All work was voluntary, but most students found the materials irresistible.

Poise, orderly behavior, and conversational skills were also emphasized. Weather permitting, the children spent time outdoors learning about nature, and they eventually maintained their own gardens and cared for small animals. Those who misbehaved were isolated and kept from their activities for a time.

Other Montessori schools soon opened in Rome and throughout Europe, and La Dottoressa was hard-pressed to train teachers to staff them. The schools attained widespread popularity in England, Austria, and the Netherlands, and the first American Montessori School was opened in Tarrytown, New York, in 1912.

Although the Montessori system had its roots in a Roman slum, it found adherents in all social strata. Alexander Graham Bell, who started his career as a teacher of the deaf, and his wife, who was deaf, were early American admirers, and they established Montessori schools for their grandchildren in Washington, D.C., and Nova Scotia. Bell, who later served as president of the Montessori Educational Association, and Thomas Edison were among Montessori's hosts when she made her first widely publicized trip to America in 1913. Leo Tolstoy's daughter

Tatiana took a strong interest in the Casa, and *The Montessori Method* was published in Russia in five separate editions. A Montessori classroom was even established for Czar Nicholas's children.

The Montessori Movement, as it was soon known, became increasingly organized, ensuring that teachers were trained only by the founder herself and that the classroom materials were endorsed by the newly formed Association Montessori Internationale (AMI). Sigmund Freud became an official sponsor of the AMI, and his daughter Anna, who would later pioneer the psychoanalysis of children, was a Montessori disciple. Other notable AMI sponsors included developmental psychologist Jean Piaget, who led the Montessori Society of Switzerland, and physicist Guglielmo Marconi.

During the 1920s Montessori served as government inspector of schools under Mussolini, who hoped to capitalize on the international prestige of her Method by associating it with his regime. By 1934, however, La Dottoressa had clashed with Il Duce. After resigning her post, she left her native land for Barcelona. Soon all Montessori schools in Italy were closed, as well as those in Germany. Americans, who were initially enamored of the movement, also became disenchanted because of fears about erosion in classroom discipline.

Many other early supporters and protégés, especially in England and the United States, left the movement because of Montessori's increasingly strident insistence that all teachers be trained by her and that only her materials be used in all classrooms identifying themselves as Montessori establishments. These requirements were, in part, business decisions. The income thus generated supported not only Montessori but also her son, his family, and several other individuals.

Driven from Spain by the Civil War, Montessori moved first to Holland and then, in 1939, to India, where she trained teachers and established schools until after the end of World War II. Ultimately she settled in the Netherlands. For her efforts to further world peace through the enlightened education of children, she was nominated for the Nobel Peace Prize three times. Well into her later years, Montessori continued to travel and lecture widely. On May 6, 1952, aged eighty-one, she died in the Netherlands. Although in 1913 she had been one of the most celebrated women ever to visit New York, by the time of her death most Americans had lost all memory of her.

The Method experienced a major resurgence in the United States in the late 1950s, however, and remains a vital force in early childhood education throughout the world. Although its practitioners have modified the Method in accordance with recent advances in educational psychology, it retains the essence of Maria Montessori's original philosophy.

For Montessori, each child comes into the world with a unique potential: "Humanity reveals itself in all its intellectual splendor during this tender age as the sun shows itself at dawn, and the flower in the first unfolding of its petals; and we must respect religiously, reverently, these first indications of individuality." As she wrote toward the end of her life, "The teacher must have faith that the child will reveal himself through work."

Forty-five

Marconi invents the radio

Che orecchi grandi ha! (What big ears he has!)
—The Marconi family gardener on first seeing
the newborn Guglielmo (1874)

He will be able to hear the still, small voice of the air.
—Annie Marconi, mother.

ON A BLUFF OVERLOOKING the Atlantic Ocean in South Wellfleet, Massachusetts, stand the remains of a transmitting station that once included four towers, each rising 210 feet high and linked with steel cables to hold them aloft against the harsh winds of Cape Cod. From this site, on January 18, 1903, President Theodore Roosevelt tapped out a message in Morse code, which was received by King Edward VII at a similar station in Cornwall, England. The message read: "In taking advantage of the wonderful triumph of scientific research and ingenuity which has been achieved in perfecting a system of wireless telegraphy, I extend on behalf of the American people most cordial greetings and good wishes to you and to all the people of the British Empire." The king responded with thanks "for the kind message which I have just received from you, through Marconi's transatlantic wireless telegraphy." This interchange was the first two-way telegram across the Atlantic, the fulfillment of a dream by the young Italian electrical engineer and inventor Guglielmo Marconi.

Only a little more than a year earlier, on December 12, 1901, sitting in a shack in Newfoundland, twenty-seven-year-old Marconi had received the first transatlantic signal—a faint dot, dot, dot—Morse code for the letter S—sent by a colleague from England. With that feeble signal, the twentieth century opened as an era of high-speed mass communications, although even Marconi himself could hardly have foreseen the potentialities of his invisible waves, which would be put to use in inventions from television to cell phones. Nor could he know that his radio devices and their progeny would ultimately provide the greatest number of jobs in the history of civilization.

Born in Bologna on April 25, 1874, to a wealthy retired businessman, Giuseppe, and a young, strong-willed Irishwoman, Annie (of the Jameson whiskey-distilling family), Guglielmo inherited his father's business acumen and his mother's independence, chafing at formal schooling and learning mainly from his mother and a series of tutors. Fortunately, his father had amassed an impressive library in which the boy studied the achievements of Washington, Benjamin Franklin, and Garibaldi, while admiring the scientific wizardry of men such as Michael Faraday and Thomas Edison.

By the time he was in his teens, Guglielmo had ensconced himself in a laboratory on the third floor of the family home, Villa Grifone, in Sasso-Pontecchio, about fifteen miles from Bologna. There he performed primitive sound transmission experiments with wires and simple oscillators and reflectors, ringing bells and buzzers throughout the house. His informal education included tutoring by Vincenzo Rosa, a physics professor from a nearby technical college.

Marconi became acquainted with the work of the German mathematician and physicist Heinrich Hertz, who in 1888 had demonstrated that electromagnetic waves produced by sparks from a transmitting circuit could be detected by a second circuit on the other side of a room, proving the accuracy of the mathematical calculations of Scottish physicist James Clerk Maxwell more than two decades earlier. Maxwell had determined that there must exist in space electromagnetic waves that, although invisible, behave in the same way as light. Hertz's experiments were the first to confirm the reality of electromagnetism under controlled laboratory conditions.

With the help of his older brother, Alfonso, Marconi tinkered with oscillators, batteries, and currents, finally developing an apparatus that included a voltage induction coil of the type invented by Michael Faraday. The device was similar to that used by Hertz in his experiments, but Marconi added a pair of grounding wires as well as a pair of vertical aerial wires attached to upright metal plates supported on posts. By manipulating this aerial-and-grounding arrangement Marconi could greatly increase the range of transmission and send Morse code messages to his brother over a mile away.

In late 1895, convinced that his apparatus had scientific and commercial significance, and accompanied by his enthusiastic mother, Marconi journeyed to Rome, where he attempted, unsuccessfully, to interest the Ministry of Posts and Telegraphs in his invention. After their rejection in Rome, the pair set off for England. Marconi believed that the primary application of his invention lay in its ability to link ships with shore, and, given England's dominance of the seas, he expected to find greater interest there for an invention with the potential to improve maritime communications.

He was ultimately proved correct, but he first met with a hostile reception by English customs officials, who feared the foreigner with his boxes of wires and induction coils was a bomb-carrying Italian anarchist. Only after they dismantled his transmitter (and were unable to reassemble it) were the Marconis allowed to enter the country. But having cleared this bureaucratic hurdle, Guglielmo made rapid progress toward gaining recognition for his achievement.

By June 1896 Marconi had received a British patent for his electromagnetic wave transmission device, and he had arranged for an introduction to William Preece, chief of the Engineering Department of the General Post Office. Preece, who had himself performed experiments with telegraphy, was most impressed with Marconi's demonstrations, in which the young man successfully transmitted signals from the GPO rooftop to other nearby government buildings. Preece then arranged for larger demonstrations on Salisbury Plain to be observed by representatives of the army and navy.

Using essentially the same apparatus he had developed in Italy (copper plates suspended 10 and 25 feet above the ground that were connected to 90-foot aerial wires) Marconi succeeded in transmitting signals up to four miles—as well as in creating a scientific sensation. Further interest was generated when he was able to send wireless reports on the progress of the August 1898 Kingstown Regatta to England from distances up to ten miles offshore. He also sent bulletins to Queen Victoria on the medical condition of her son, the Prince of Wales, as the future King Edward VII watched the regatta from the royal yacht while recovering from an injury.

In 1897 Marconi registered his own company, the Wireless Telegraph and Signal Company, Ltd., in Chelmsford, England, and began selling transmitters and stock in his venture. During a trip to the United States to demonstrate the device he caught the attention of U.S. Navy officials, who became interested in equipping their ships with the new radio transmitters for navigational messaging. But a final refinement would be needed before radio could come into widespread use. In 1900 Marconi received the auspicious-sounding British patent No. 7777 for "Improvements in Apparatus for Wireless Telegraphy," which allowed tuning and transmission on different wavelengths, so that separate signals did not interfere with one another.[1]

Many scientists and mathematicians were skeptical about Marconi's continuing attempts to increase the distance of his demonstrations, claiming that long-distance electromagnetic transmissions were scientifically impossible because of Earth's curvature. Unaware of the existence of the ionosphere, a layer of the upper atmosphere where ionizing radiation reflects radio waves back toward Earth, many of Marconi's contemporaries believed that, over long distances, his radio waves would simply disperse into distant space. Although the existence of the ionosphere was not confirmed until 1924, the naysayers were proved wrong on that day in December 1901 when Marconi, at his station in Newfoundland, heard that Morse code signal from England.

During the early years of the twentieth century, as Marconi continued to extend the distance of his transmissions, from Ireland to Buenos Aires and from England to Australia, the radio was often used at sea to send frivolous dispatches, predominantly private messages and reports to passengers. All that changed on a cold night in April 1912 in the North Atlantic, when the "unsinkable" luxury liner *Titanic* rammed into an iceberg and sent this Morse code radio message: "CQD [Emergency!]. We've struck a berg. Sinking fast. Come to our assistance. Position, Latitude 41.46 North, Longitude 50.14 West. SOS. Titanic."

Tragically, the telegrapher of the *Californian*, a passenger ship only ten miles away, had already turned off his equipment and retired for the night when the *Titanic*'s SOS shot through the frigid air. A *Californian* watchman assumed that the white flares he saw emanating from the *Titanic* were celebratory fireworks. Some sixty miles away, the radio signal was picked up by another luxury liner, the *Carpathia*, which had been heading in the opposite direction but abruptly changed course

---

[1]In 1943 the U.S. Supreme Court overturned this patent, claiming that several other inventors had priority. The hugely controversial attribution of the invention of the radio depends on what facets of this device's long and complex development one chooses to emphasize as most crucial—but it also tends to follow certain ethnic lines. Thus, many Americans attribute the radio to Lee De Forest, John Stone, or the Serbian-American genius, Nikola Tesla; the English to Sir Oliver Lodge; the Germans to Heinrich Hertz; the Russians to Alexander Popov; and the French to Édouard Branly. Being of Irish descent, the present writer opts for Marconi.

after receiving the distress signal. The *Carpathia* raced northwest through the night, receiving on its wireless the message, "Come quick, our engine room is flooded to the boilers," while the *Titanic*'s band played "Nearer My God to Thee." By the time the *Carpathia* arrived, all that remained above water were sixteen lifeboats with 717 passengers.

The outside world knew of the drama playing out on the Atlantic because signals were received at the Marconi shore station in Cape Race, Newfoundland, and Marconi himself was present on the New York dock when the *Carpathia* arrived with its cargo of rescued passengers. The survivors later presented Marconi with a gold medal, likening him to the Greek god Apollo releasing sparks from his fingertips into the air.

Three months after the *Titanic* sank with the loss of 1,500 passengers and crew members, disaster inquiries in the United States and Great Britain prompted the meeting of an International Radio-Telegraphic Convention in London to establish procedures and guidelines for emergency wireless transmissions at sea. Then, in November of 1913, representatives of sixty-five nations convened in London for the Safety of Life at Sea Conference and adopted sweeping regulations, including the requirement that ships' communications nerve centers be on alert twenty-four hours a day.

Marconi continued to investigate the potential applications of different frequencies of radio waves, and he contributed to the development of shortwave and microwave wireless communication, as well as of radar. He received numerous awards, including a 1909 Nobel Prize in physics. He also served as a delegate to the 1919 peace conference in Paris, where he signed treaties with Austria and Bulgaria. In 1929 he was appointed to the Italian Senate and made a marchese. In the following year, he was chosen president of the Royal Academy of Italy. When he died in Rome on July 20, 1937, all radio stations around the world observed a two-minute silence.

Among the dilapidated transmission towers in South Wellfleet, where much of the bluff that was the site of those early transatlantic transmissions has been lost to erosion, a bronze bust of Marconi was set up with the following inscription:

GUGLIELMO MARCONI
PIONEER OF WIRELESS COMMUNICATION
SON OF ITALY
CITIZEN OF THE WORLD

—Nancy Walsh

Forty-six

Enrico Fermi: Father of the atomic age

Some recent work by E. Fermi and L. Szilard . . . leads me to expect that the element uranium may be turned into a new and important source of energy in the immediate future. . . . [I]t may become possible to set up a nuclear chain reaction in a large mass of uranium, by which vast amounts of power . . . would be generated. . . . This new phenomenon would also lead to the construction of bombs, and it is conceivable . . . that extremely powerful bombs of a new type may thus be constructed.

—Albert Einstein, letter to President Franklin D. Roosevelt
(August 2, 1939)

JUST MOMENTS AFTER humankind first torched the heavens with a brilliance many times that of the sun, while Manhattan Project director J. Robert Oppenheimer was reciting passages from the Sanskrit philosophical classic, the *Bhagavad Gita,* the Italian physicist Enrico Fermi, nine miles from the blast, was scattering small scraps of paper on the ground to measure their displacement when the shock wave hit. With the aid of these crude observations, knowledge of his distance from ground zero, and a table of calculations he had prepared, Fermi was able to accurately gauge the awesome power of the explosion on that summer day in New Mexico in 1945.

There was always a rule-of-thumb, build-it-yourself, figure-it-out-in-your-head, Italian-artisan-and-craftsman quality about Enrico Fermi, who was born in Rome on September 29, 1901, to Alberto Fermi, an administrator for the Italian national railroad, and Ida de Gattis, an elementary school teacher who instilled a serious work ethic in her three children. Enrico, the youngest, excelled in school, especially in mathematics, and enjoyed building mechanical and electrical toys with his brother, Giulio, but this beloved playmate died from complications of anesthesia during minor throat surgery when barely a teen.

The surviving son turned to his studies for consolation. Discovering a two-volume mid-nineteenth-century textbook on physics in a Rome bookstall, he brought it home and soon devoured it, barely noticing it was written in Latin. A colleague of his father's who had studied engineering then lent the fourteen-year-old a text on projective geometry, followed by others on trigonometry, algebra, analytical geometry, calculus, and theoretical mechanics.

After reading these books, Enrico claimed he could easily derive any of the formulas himself, in the unlikely event that he forgot one. "I studied mathematics with passion," he said at the time, "because I considered it necessary for the study of physics, to which I want to dedicate myself exclusively." His prodigious memory was not limited to mathematics, since he could also recite long passages from the *Divine Comedy* and *Orlando Furioso*.

Young Fermi graduated at the top of his class from the *liceo* (roughly equivalent to high school) in two years, rather than the usual three. Having received a solid grounding in Latin, Greek, and French, as well as in mathematics, physics, history, geography, and philosophy, he also began to study German (and later English) on his own, so that he could keep abreast of the latest scientific research. When Fermi applied for a fellowship at the elite Scuola Normale Superiore, associated with the University of Pisa, he flabbergasted the professor who read his competition essay on the characteristics of sound. At Pisa, his physics professor would often ask Fermi to teach him about Einstein's theory of relativity.

Although Enrico's true interest was in relativity, a dissertation in theoretical physics would have gone against the grain of the predominantly experimentalist mind-set at the university. Deciding that X rays were a promising field for original research, Fermi spent two years working in this area while building and modifying lab equipment, which he found to be outdated and in disrepair. These experiences at the University of Pisa, where the young Galileo had studied and briefly taught, prompted Fermi in later life to devise his own equipment whenever feasible, tailoring it to his specific requirements.

Fermi's first paper, on the dynamics of electrical charges, was published in 1921, the year before he received his doctorate in physics, magna cum laude, for a dissertation on images derived from X-ray diffraction with bent crystals. Concurrently, Fermi was making his first significant contributions in general relativity and becoming increasingly intrigued with the possibility of nuclear energy release.

Through the Italian Ministry of Education, Fermi won a fellowship to study quantum mechanics in Germany with Max Born at the University of Göttingen, and at Leiden in the Netherlands, before returning to Italy to teach mathematics at the University of Florence. In 1926 he developed the so-called Fermi-Dirac statistics for determining the quantum characteristics of a major class of subatomic particles.

Fermi's paper on a perfect hypothetical gas so impressed the physics department at the University of Rome that he was offered a full professorship in theoretical physics with lifetime tenure. Once in Rome, he decided to take three important steps: to write articles on modern physics that a wide audience could understand, to write a textbook on atomic physics, and to assemble a group of young physicists at the university (who soon nicknamed him "the pope" because of his apparent infallibility). In 1929 Fermi was named a member (the youngest) of the distinguished Royal Academy of Italy, and he subsequently lectured at the University of Michigan at Ann Arbor and in Argentina and Brazil.

In 1933, the year after James Chadwick posited the existence of an electrically neutral particle, the neutron, Fermi presented his theory of beta decay, which led to the discovery of one of the four fundamental forces of nature, the so-called weak nuclear force, the basis of radioactivity. In this phase of his research, he also coined a word for a newly postulated subatomic particle, *neutrino*, Italian for "little neutron."

Along with experiments in France, Fermi's theory of beta decay opened the door to research involving the bombardment of chemical elements with neutrons in an attempt to create new radioactive elements. Noting that the experiments worked better when performed on a wooden table, which scattered the neutrons and thus slowed them down, in 1934 Fermi developed a method of decelerating the neutron stream by passing it through paraffin. These slow neutrons, he found, were particularly effective in producing radioactive particles (and they are still used in nuclear reactors). After experimenting on most of the elements in the periodic table, he finally came to uranium, which produced unusual results. Fermi's colleagues believed he had formed a new "transuranic" element with atomic number 93, but he himself was unconvinced. In 1938 he was awarded a Nobel Prize in physics for discovering new elements (which he hadn't) and for pioneering nuclear reactions via slow neutron bombardment.

When his work was replicated in Germany, the scientific community realized Fermi had unknowingly discovered fission; that is, he had split the nucleus of the uranium atom into several smaller particles, including the elements barium and krypton. This process, which converted into energy just tiny amounts (0.1%) of the mass of the uranium atom, could nonetheless liberate tremendous amounts of energy, in accord with Einstein's famous equation, $E = mc^2$.

After traveling to Sweden for his Nobel Prize, Fermi, with his wife, Laura, and two small children, boarded a ship for the United States. Laura was Jewish, and Enrico was becoming wary of the increasing anti-Semitism of Mussolini's regime. Shortly after arriving in New York, Fermi learned of the fission discovery and immediately sought out Niels Bohr at Columbia University, where Fermi was soon appointed professor of physics. They discussed the possibilities of fission for chain reactions and determined that the uranium-235 isotope would be best for the purpose.

Fermi and his colleagues, including Leo Szilard, a Hungarian Jew who had fled Hitler's Germany in 1933, asked Albert Einstein to communicate this news to President Roosevelt. By the time the letter, dated August 2, 1939, was delivered to Roosevelt on October 11, World War II had erupted, and the president immediately appointed a Committee on Uranium. Arthur H. Compton, a physics professor at the University of Chicago, was placed in charge of producing the chain reaction, and he brought the chief workers on the project, including the Columbia group, to his campus. By October 1942 enough uranium had been collected, and Fermi proposed building the hundred-ton nuclear pile in the basement squash court beneath the stands of the university's Stagg Field.

On December 2, with subzero temperatures in Chicago, everything was ready for the big test. The events of the frigid morning proving inconclusive, Fermi called for lunch (with which nothing in his career, no matter how momentous, had ever yet interfered). After the break, at 2:20 P.M., the pile attained criticality and remained operative for twenty-eight minutes at a power not exceeding half a watt (to minimize the production of radioactivity), with Fermi overseeing the insertion and withdrawal of the neutron-absorbing cadmium rods that controlled the rate of the chain reaction.

This was the first production of a controlled flow of energy derived from a source other than the sun. Fermi had demonstrated that bombarding uranium nuclei with a neutron stream could split them and liberate enough other neutrons to, in turn, split other uranium nuclei in a geometrical progression, liberating greater amounts of radiation and thermal energy as the fission reaction continued. One of his colleagues uncorked a bottle of Chianti, but there was no toasting or speechifying.

Meanwhile Compton reported the news cryptically over an open phone line to Harvard scientist James B. Conant: "The Italian navigator has just landed in the New World."

When Fermi's former student, colleague, and biographer, the 1959 Nobel laureate in physics Emilio Segrè, asked him why he had named the equipment for the first self-sustaining nuclear chain reaction an atomic *pile* (thinking he was obviously alluding to the voltaic pile of Alessandro Volta [see Essay 39]), Fermi indicated, in his imperfect English, that he had merely intended to refer to a *heap* of things—uranium scattered between layers of graphite. Soon afterward, a second pile built at the nearby Argonne Laboratory operated at one hundred kilowatts—200,000 times more power than the first one.

In November 1942, Los Alamos, New Mexico, had been chosen as the site for developing and testing the first nuclear weapon, with a team of six thousand assembled, all intent on one goal—the construction of a bomb so terrible it would put an immediate end to the war that was devastating the world. J. Robert Oppenheimer, a professor of theoretical physics at Berkeley and the California Institute of Technology, was appointed director of the Los Alamos Laboratory. Enrico Fermi, with his fairly transparent code name of "Henry Farmer," was among the leading scientists chosen for the top-secret project. At 5:30 A.M. on July 16, 1945, thirty-one months after Fermi had split the atom, the first atomic bomb was exploded near Alamogordo, in the New Mexico desert, with a power equivalent to fifteen thousand tons of TNT. The blast vaporized the metal tower on which the bomb had been perched and melted the sand at the detonation point into glass.

Losing no time, Harry Truman, who had assumed the presidency after Roosevelt's death on April 12, unleashed the new weapon against Japan only three weeks after its first test. When an atomic blast over Hiroshima on August 6 failed to end the war, a second bomb was dropped on Nagasaki three days later. Japan finally surrendered on August 14. Truman said he never lost any sleep over his decision, claiming that at least several hundred thousand U.S. lives and two million Japanese lives would have been lost if an invasion of Japan had proved necessary to defeat the last remaining Axis power.

Before Roosevelt's 1942 Columbus Day declaration that Italian nationals living in the United States were no longer considered enemy aliens, Fermi's mail had been censored by the American authorities. He and Laura became U.S. citizens in 1944, and two years later Fermi received the Congressional Medal of Merit and became Distinguished-Service

Professor for Nuclear Studies at the University of Chicago, where he was chief adviser on the construction of the synchrocyclotron, a particle accelerator.

Fermi opposed U.S. development of the hydrogen bomb in 1949, writing that "the fact that no limits exist to the destructiveness of this weapon makes its very existence . . . a danger to humanity as a whole." The following year, he was made a member of the Royal Society of London. He also served as an adviser to the U.S. Atomic Energy Commission, receiving its first annual award. The Fermi National Accelerator Laboratory (Fermilab), in Batavia, Illinois, outside of Chicago, was dedicated posthumously in 1969.

Among the numerous scientific terms named after the Italian physicist are *fermium*, the artificially produced radioactive element with atomic number 100; *fermions*, matter particles such as protons, neutrons, electrons, and their antimatter counterparts; and the *fermi*, a unit of length equivalent to a femtometer (10^{-15} meter). In Chicago, on November 28, 1954, a man who made gigantic contributions to both theoretical and experimental physics succumbed to metastatic stomach cancer at age fifty-three. Even in the hospital, he calculated the flow of his IV nutrients, stopwatch in hand. The chaplain at the University of Chicago chose as his text for the memorial service St. Francis of Assisi's "Canticle of the Creatures" in recognition of Fermi's fascination with nature (see Essay 11). A lifelong agnostic, Fermi had once told his wife, "With science one can explain everything except oneself."

Enrico Fermi was an outstanding teacher, whose unfulfilled wish was to instruct an entire cohort of physics students from their elementary college courses through advanced work. In his biography, Emilio Segrè says of Fermi's "extremely lucid lectures" that "the very simplicity of his reasoning conveyed the impression of effortlessness. But this impression is false: The simplicity was the result of careful preparation and of deliberate weighing of different alternatives of presentation." The 1965 Nobel laureate in physics, Richard Feynman, recalled how Fermi once immediately laid out the contours of a complicated experiment Feynman was working on, "ten times better" than he himself could have, even before the young American scientist had finished describing it to him.

Fermi's chief legacy to the world is beset with ethical quandaries, but he himself always believed his work had been for a good cause. Besides, he explained, "the sequence of discoveries leading to the atomic chain reaction was part of the search of science for a fuller explanation of nature and the world around us. No one had any idea or intent at the beginning of contributing to a major industrial or military development."

Forty years after Fermi's death, a KGB spymaster claimed in a book that Fermi and other prominent Los Alamos scientists had helped pass along atomic secrets to the Soviet Union. Edward Teller, who led the production of the hydrogen bomb for the United States and was Fermi's close friend for more than twenty years, repudiated the charge, saying, "Fermi was apolitical. But he simply and clearly opposed the Stalinist nightmare even more than he opposed Mussolini." He hadn't even told his wife what he was working on at Los Alamos.

The words *Hiroshima, Nagasaki, Chernobyl,* and many others will remain inextricably associated with Fermi's gift of Promethean fire to the human race. Whether we rise to the challenge of taming this immense force for peaceful purposes—finding ways to power our cities and further the sophistication of diagnosis and therapy in the field of nuclear medicine—or whether, despite attempts at stockpile reduction, nonproliferation, and sensible nuclear waste disposal, it proves to be, like John Milton's characterization of gold, a "precious bane," still remains to be seen.

—Dante D'Epiro

Forty-seven

Roberto Rossellini: Neorealist cinema and beyond

Art can make you understand through emotion what you are absolutely incapable of understanding through intellect.
— Roberto Rossellini (1962)

Among all the many liars I've known in life, Rossellini occupies a place on the highest level in that he had the great merit of living his lies.
— Franco Riganti (1989)

AT THE END OF World War II, Italy lay broken in strength and spirit. The excesses of two decades of Fascism under Mussolini had been crushed: In place of the public spectacle and military adventures that had incited dreams of a reborn Roman Empire, there remained only a shattered nation, occupied by foreign troops and so stripped of amenities that it lacked the electric power to run a movie projector, let alone a studio.

Yet even before the Allies had driven Nazi forces from Florence and northern Italy in 1945, Roberto Rossellini (1906–77) had sold his bed to help finance a film that would take New York and Paris by storm, transform the image of the Italian people in the eyes of the world, and inspire a new critical term to describe the work's cinematic power: Neorealism. Rife with scenes of brutal Nazi decadence and partisan resistance in locations that still reeked of the Fascist occupation, *Roma città aperta* (*Open City*) launched Rossellini's career as a world-class director and established Italian film as a revitalizing artistic force. In quick succession and under conditions of astonishing scarcity, he produced *Paisà* (1946) and *Germany Year Zero* (1947), completing his war trilogy.

As Giotto and Masaccio had revolutionized pictorial representation, as Monteverdi had revolutionized the relation of word to music, so Rossellini's work was immediately recognized as a radical break with stylized convention and hackneyed studio technique, offering a cinema at once strange, humble, solid, and powerful. At roughly the same time, Vittorio De Sica, Giuseppe De Santis, Luchino Visconti, and others were also making films that came to be called *Neorealist*. In the years ahead, Federico Fellini, Michelangelo Antonioni, Pier Paolo Pasolini, Bernardo Bertolucci, Lina Wertmüller, the Taviani brothers, and others would extend the reach, variety, and styles of Italian film, seducing generations of filmgoers and filmmakers.

Some of these artists, like Fellini, got their start working with Rossellini; others worked against his influence to achieve their own styles and voices. But it was Rossellini—in his choice of subjects, in his refusal to conform to traditional studio technique, in taking filmmaking to the streets, in challenging every aspect of cinematic craft as it was then practiced—who changed what it meant to make a film, and how films were made. Like the unquiet volcano in *Stromboli*, his first feature with Ingrid Bergman, his influence is still rumbling today.

Roberto Gastone Zeffiro Rossellini was born into an eccentric Roman family in 1906—his great-uncle, Zeffiro, was a wealthy contractor and developer who as a young man had briefly run off to join Garibaldi's Redshirts (see Essay 42). The family led a bohemian life of extravagance, their home open to artists and intellectuals, princes and beggars.

After a youth of la dolce vita that exhausted his inheritance, Roberto found work as a dubbing assistant at a film studio. He also earned extra cash ghostwriting scripts for black-market films, which quickly took the mystery out of filmmaking. "It was so mechanical," he later said, "that the experience really disenchanted me completely." In the late 1930s and early 1940s, he worked as a director on several projects produced by Vittorio Mussolini, son of Il Duce. Benito Mussolini had given his blessing to Cinecittà, the vast Roman film studio, and had taken many other steps to help revivify the Italian film industry. Neither Rossellini's family nor his wastrel acquaintances were prepared for the independence and originality that came with Roberto's maturity.

In 1942 Rossellini directed *A Pilot Returns*. He was still working with Vittorio Mussolini, but Jean Renoir's *La Grande Illusion* was a greater influence. Critics marveled at the film's seemingly unbiased depiction of the brutality of war. "A film without rhetoric," was one critic's assessment. What is more remarkable is that Rossellini continued to work in the industry, given that the Fascists wanted something more compatible with their aim to glorify the war effort. Fortunately, Fascist political support evaporated like morning dew as the Allies entered Rome. The studio system was in disarray—a fact that Rossellini later claimed was decisive in his being able to make *Open City*, his first Neorealist film.

Open City was shot at night, without sound, to cut costs. Lamp bulbs, hard enough to find, produced a sickly, yellowish tinge. When the technicians complained, Rossellini replied that everything was perfect for what he wanted—a look of everything "thrown away."

The most famous scene in *Open City*—the shocking moment when the Germans take away Anna Magnani's lover, a Resistance hero, in a truck, and she runs behind it, only to be gunned down in cold blood—had its origin in sheer chance. When Magnani's real-life lover visited her on the set, they quarreled; he jumped on a production truck to escape; she, hurling scatological abuse, chased the truck down the street. Rossellini quickly "stole" that volcanic emotion and transmuted it into a sequence of raw power. "With Rossellini," Magnani later recalled, "we didn't rehearse, we filmed."

The initial reaction of Italian distributors to *Open City* is telling: They charged that Rossellini had broken his contract by delivering a newsreel instead of a film. By contrast, one Communist critic exclaimed that after twenty years of Fascist rhetoric, "At last we've seen an Italian film!" Another critic noted that for the first time in an Italian movie, common people were the makers of history, not merely its victims. The critics were more on the money than the distributors: The film broke attendance records, with crowds fighting to get in.

It was *Open City*'s fidelity to recent historical events, coupled with its naturalistic dialogue, costumes, and settings, that gave currency to the Neorealist label. But while these elements were undoubtedly present, there is more to Rossellini, as evidenced by the range and richness of his subsequent films—from his take on St. Francis of Assisi, *Francesco giullare di Dio* (1950), to *Voyage in Italy* (1953), to *The Rise of Louis XIV* (1966).

Indeed, throughout his long odyssey as a filmmaker, Rossellini was attacked for failing to adhere to the criteria assigned to Neorealism by the critics. (He was also pilloried for failing to toe the Marxist ideological line that some believed was implicit in Neorealism.) Other directors ended up conforming to the label more closely than Rossellini, who had no use for programmatic approaches to anything.

Several of Vittorio De Sica's films, for example, including *Shoeshine* (1946), *Bicycle Thieves* (1948), and *Gold of Naples* (1955), can be seen as fulfilling many of the literary, formal features of Neorealism: The anecdotal action is shaped by conventions of the realist novel; the characters tend to be types that crystallize concepts of entire classes; and the plots follow fateful, predictable patterns of pathos and loss. The protagonists are powerless to alter their destinies, underscoring the useless pity inherent in a generic and, at times, patronizing view of society. De Sica's quintessential moment is the crazed delusion of Antonio, the protagonist of *Bicycle Thieves*, as he wanders amid the maze of Rome, believing he sees his stolen bicycle—on which his livelihood depends—everywhere he turns.

At the other pole of the Neorealist spectrum is the conceptual approach of a director like Luchino Visconti. In a nation where even "hard news" malleably morphs to reflect a host of political and social viewpoints, it should come as no surprise that many films would be marked by one ideology or another, from extreme leftist Marxism to extreme right-wing Catholicism. A film like Visconti's *La terra trema* (*The Earth Will Shake*, 1948) divides all of society neatly into rich exploiters—the fishing-boat owners—and poor exploited—the crewmen laborers who never earn enough to do more than subsist. In this world, protagonists discover economic injustice and try to introduce change.

The quintessential moment in Viscontian Neorealism occurs when the hard facts of the unfair social system bring someone to his knees. In *La terra trema*, Antonio—the only laborer who envisions an alternative life in which honest men and families work for themselves—must swallow every last bit of pride and return to slave for the bosses he once spurned.

In contrast with Visconti's apparent endorsement of a particular view of the world, Rossellini characteristically sought to mediate between opposing factions of Italian society. At the end of his life, Rossellini made *The Messiah* (1975) for the Marxists, and he was planning a life of Marx for the Catholics. Whereas De Sica used anecdotal storytelling, Rossellini offered elliptical fragments of a reality beyond the reach of any camera. In *Paisà*, he depicted Italy's experience of World War II in six discrete episodes that evoked—by both what they did and did not show—a time of infinite misery and horror, and a nation whose protean nature was beyond simple characterization. Early on, Rossellini had already found his course set for a cinema of stark sublimity.

Always restlessly searching for something beyond the given, Rossellini eventually enraged pretty much everyone who had at first hailed him. The critics who reduced Neorealism to constricted but familiar notions of style and ideology lambasted him for failing to follow their jejune intellectual prescriptions.

But Fellini, who was drawn into Rossellini's orbit early on, called working on *Paisà* the turning point of his life. Before that film, he had little interest in movies. Through watching Rossellini work, Fellini said, "I discovered for the first time that it was possible to make films with the same intimate, direct, immediate rapport as a writer writes or a painter paints."

Embedded in Rossellini's films are scenes that often seem as if they were plucked from documentary footage and dropped awkwardly into the fictional narrative—the bloody tuna harvest in *Stromboli* (1950), the sequence with actual monks in *Paisà*'s "Romagna" episode, or the one with real tour guides delivering their spiels on Pompeii and Naples to Ingrid Bergman in *Voyage in Italy*.

For the "Po Delta" episode in *Paisà*, the screenwriter's original idea was to find tall, Nordic-looking Italians to portray the partisans who fought alongside the Allies in the swampy terrains bordering the northern Italian river. Instead Rossellini chose to use actual Resistance fighters who reenacted one of their experiences. The screenwriter complained that these "heroes" resembled chicken farmers more than noble warriors.

In *Paisà*'s final moments, we see the *partigiani*, their hands bound with rope, tossed by the Germans into the river like bags of garbage, without even being accorded the dignity of first being executed. The film's ending seems to defy any effort to ennoble the vicissitudes of war and, in so doing, acquires a harsh majesty unlike any other war picture ever made. The realism of Neorealism here goes beyond fidelity to external reality. As Tag Gallagher puts it in his brilliant study of Rossellini, "Reality for him is not the world of objects but the world of feelings which brute reality reflects."

Fellini admired how Rossellini turned the chaotic circumstances endemic to filmmaking to his advantage, transforming the welter of energies, adversities, and contradictions into "an emotional value." Rossellini would deliberately pit rival screenwriters and researchers against one another, drawing on the dynamic vortices and unpredictable perspectives uncovered through their conflicts. He used similarly antithetical tactics to get what he wanted from actors. In *Stromboli* he had Italian actors speak lines in English that they didn't understand. To cue them to speak, he would pull strings tied to their toes.

George Sanders, the British actor who played Bergman's estranged husband in *Voyage in Italy,* was ignored and inconvenienced on the set until he threatened to commit suicide—a plan to which Rossellini readily gave his encouragement. It was all a calculated effort to inspire the quality of stupefied anger that animates every pore of Sanders's onscreen presence.

In *General Della Rovere* (1959), Rossellini returned to the German occupation of Italy. The great actor and director Vittorio De Sica plays a con man who pretends to be a partisan general in order to save his own skin. Rossellini wanted to drain some of the floridity from De Sica's performance. He requested two takes for the memorable scene in which the pseudo-general addresses his followers and sympathizers in prison. The first time, De Sica delivered his lines with impassioned oratorical flair. Rossellini praised him to the skies, then asked if he wouldn't mind doing it again for close-ups. Confident the first take would be used, De Sica rattled off the speech in a tired, uninflected manner—providing Rossellini with exactly the texture of alienated conviction he was looking for.

By the mid-1950s, Rossellini was box office poison in Italy and abroad. In the United States, *Open City*'s distributors had teased audiences with the line "Sexier than Hollywood ever dared to be!"—and disappointed nearly everyone. The Italian filmmaker was even denounced in the U.S. Senate for his affair with Ingrid Bergman.

As financing for new projects dwindled, Rossellini spent much of his time in Paris, lionized by the "new wave" film community. François Truffaut offered his services as an assistant to the Italian director and worked on projects for three years. Jean-Luc Godard would later point to Rossellini as the major influence on his approach to film. Eric Rohmer and Truffaut filled the pages of the *Cahiers du Cinéma*—the bible of the new wave—with reviews and inspired interpretations of Rossellini's work.

In later years Rossellini found himself at odds with many of the young cinephiles who talked about "pure cinema." At a 1963 conference on cinema verité, he marked the divide he saw between himself and a new generation of purists, saying, "Film is a means of expression like a thousand others. I've given up film because I don't like it anymore. There doesn't exist a technique for grasping reality. Only a moral position can do so."

That moral imperative ultimately led Rossellini to abandon film for television, which he called "an evolution of the cinema." In the last fourteen years of his life, he spent much of his creative energy on a series of inquiries into history, whose didactic thrust was encapsulated in what he saw as his mission: "There is only a single question—how to awaken consciousness."

There was *Man's Struggle for His Survival* (1967–69), a twelve-part series for Italian TV. Also for Italian television Rossellini produced a series of meticulously researched reenactments of the lives of historical figures, including contemplative revolutionaries such as Socrates, Christ, the Apostles, St. Augustine, Descartes, and Pascal—as well as *The Rise of Louis XIV* and a three-part series on the Medici (1972) (see Essay 21). This fascination with contemplatives who changed the course of history was in no way frivolous. Although Rossellini the man may have charmed, cajoled, cadged, and conned his producers, financiers, and lovers, his work is the fruit of a profoundly contemplative mind with no patience for art divorced from ethical imperatives. "Once you become aware that something's wrong, you have to be prepared to break away from it and put it right," he said, distinguishing his art from the "postmodern" approach of directors like Antonioni.

For Roberto Rossellini the only "style" that mattered came from not striving for style; the only acceptable acting occurred when the actor wasn't trying to act; the only script was the one that happened by chance after the script was thrown away: pure *sprezzatura*. Yet amid this violence to his chosen medium, what erupts is a potent sublimity that embodies, with unmatched depth, the moral history of his fellow man.

—Thomas Matrullo

Forty-eight

An unlikely international bestseller: Lampedusa's *The Leopard*

Besides the author, no earthly lover would want to make love via a telescope.

—Giacomo Leopardi, commenting on his poem "To His Lady" (1823)

THE FOREMOST ITALIAN NOVEL of the twentieth century—some would say of all time—is *Il Gattopardo (The Leopard)*, written by a Sicilian nobleman, Giuseppe Tomasi, Prince of Lampedusa and Duke of Palma, whose family was said to stem from a sixth-century Byzantine emperor, and whose coat of arms featured a prancing leopard. Nicknamed by his cousins *il mostro* (The Monstrous Prodigy) for his staggering erudition, the tall and stout Lampedusa (1896–1957) never took a job, devoting himself to reading all the great literary works, and countless minor ones, of Italy, France, Britain, Germany, Russia, and Spain in the original languages but waiting until he was fifty-eight to begin writing his sole novel. Married but childless, he knew he was to be the last Prince of Lampedusa, just as the noble protagonist of his novel witnesses the death of his whole way of life and realizes he is the last of his line in any meaningful sense.

At least on the surface, *Il Gattopardo* employed a conventional narrative technique and was relatively devoid of action. By no means did it manifest a fashionably progressive worldview, and its Sicilian setting and aristocratic milieu were unfamiliar to the larger world. The author was a literary unknown, and his widow had a difficult time getting his book published even in its native land.

All these factors seemed to militate against even a local success, yet *Il Gattopardo* became the first Italian international bestseller, received enthusiastically in France, Britain, and the United States and translated twenty-three times in the first twenty years after publication. More than four decades after its appearance, it still sells in excess of 100,000 copies a year all over the world. In 1963 the book became the subject of one of

Luchino Visconti's best films, starring Burt Lancaster, Alain Delon, and Claudia Cardinale, and as recently as 2000 a film was made on Lampedusa's dealings with two young students of his, *Il manoscritto del principe* (The Prince's Manuscript).

The posthumous publication of *Il Gattopardo* in November of 1958 evoked a firestorm of controversy in Italy, where two hostile critical camps began "exalting the work as one of the most important, meaningful, and beautifully written in recent times," according to literary scholar Sergio Pacifici, "or condemning it for a variety of sins, usually as reactionary, fraudulent, structurally and stylistically archtraditional in an era of experimentation and openness." Nonetheless, the book sold almost 200,000 copies and sailed through fifty-two editions in Italy in little more than a year, winning the Strega Prize, the country's most prestigious award for fiction.

The world has the novelist Giorgio Bassani, author of *The Garden of the Finzi-Continis*, to thank for Lampedusa's book. He first recognized *Il Gattopardo* as a work of genius and secured its publication with the Milanese publisher Feltrinelli after both Mondadori and Einaudi rejected it, in both cases at the recommendation of the Sicilian novelist Elio Vittorini, whose leftist politics and literary trendiness blinded him to the book's essential humanity. Shortly before Bassani's crucial intervention, sixty-year-old Lampedusa died in Rome of lung cancer, in July of 1957, having been told that his immortal work was unpublishable.

In the end, the subtle characterizations, the bejeweled and pellucid style, the pathos of its theme of human transience and futility transcended all obstacles to the book's appeal across national boundaries. Lampedusa's aim was not so much to portray the end of an era in Sicily and the effect its attendant disruptions had on someone like the grandee Don Fabrizio Corbera, Prince of Salina (based on Lampedusa's great-grandfather), as to use those events to frame the existential loneliness and isolation of the human condition anywhere, anytime, especially in a person of refined sensibility and intellectual endowments.

The book opens in May of 1860, in the month of Garibaldi's epochal landing at the Sicilian port of Marsala, where the great Italian patriot initiated his conquest of southern Italy, wrenching it from the Bourbon dynasty and handing it over to Victor Emmanuel II of the House of Savoy (see Essay 42). These were the headiest days of the Risorgimento, when the entire peninsula would soon be unified in a modern nation state, including the backward South, which lagged far behind in social, economic, political, and intellectual development.

The book's key word, in Latin, occurs in its very first sentence, as Don Fabrizio's family recites the rosary: *"Nunc et in hora mortis nostrae"*—"Now and at the hour of our death." The Salina family, ensconced in a palace just outside Sicily's capital of Palermo, is not meditating on the Joyful or Glorious Mysteries of the rosary, but on the Sorrowful ones, which center on Christ's Passion. The daily rosary recital takes place in a room with a painted rococo ceiling celebrating far different kinds of passions—such as that of Perseus for the naked Andromeda. Also emblazoned on the ceiling is the family's blue heraldic crest depicting a rampant leopard, proudly upheld by the Olympian gods. It is with this sleek and dangerous feline that the novel's hero, Don Fabrizio, is constantly associated.

In the initial scene, we are introduced to the diminutive, hysterically jealous princess, Maria Stella. ("I've had seven children with her—*seven*—and never seen her navel," the prince ruminates. "Is that right?") There is the teenaged son, Francesco Paolo, the heir, whose only interests are horses and girls, and will remain so. There are three blue-eyed, school-age daughters and some nondescript younger children. We also meet the household priest, a likable but hidebound Jesuit, Padre Pirrone, and a thoroughly canine dog, Bendicò.

Don Fabrizio himself is a huge, arrogant paterfamilias built on a heroic scale. He is enormously strong and much too intelligent to be content. He's also a sensual man who keeps a mistress in town, and for whom the scent of a decaying rose in his garden conjures up the thigh of a dancer at the Opera.

But the prince is also "something rich and strange." Atop his palace is an observatory, from where he has discovered two asteroids. For these leisure-time pursuits, he was awarded a silver medal by the Sorbonne but is viewed with suspicion by his fellow aristocrats. Passionately devoted to astronomy (his "morphine," he calls it), he journeys nightly far from his narrow orbit into the immensity of space. Only there, in that relatively changeless world, does he feel completely at home. Lampedusa's distant relation and favorite Italian lyric poet Giacomo Leopardi (see Essay 41) had claimed in a note on "To His Lady" that his true love was *"la donna che non si trova"* ("the woman who cannot be found," except among the stars). Don Fabrizio escapes the nullity of the life around him by retreating to his telescope.

In many ways, the prince is a lost Odysseus—with his physical strength, ability to terrify when necessary, fondness for the ladies, verbal dexterity, long-suffering, instinct for survival, sharp nose for bullshit (including his own), and intellectual acumen—he, too, is *polutropos* (a man "of many turns" or stratagems) and *polumetis* (of many counsels)— but we see him wandering aimlessly in a much-shrunken world. He's the biggest frog in a pond being taken over by hungry cormorants and other birds of prey. With no head for business, he can only watch as his family's once regal fortune continues to hemorrhage.

In this wasteland, Fabrizio's nephew, the orphaned Tancredi, amuses the older man with his mordant aristocratic wit, mouthing the new patriotic platitudes with nasalized irony. Like Hamlet with Horatio, the fifty-year-old melancholy Sicilian wears only twenty-year-old Tancredi in his heart of hearts, preferring him to his own noisy brood. He finds it impossible to be bored in Tancredi's refined presence, although the young man teases him mercilessly, especially about his amorous adventures. Yet Tancredi's affection is conveyed even in how he addresses Fabrizio—*zione*—"dear big uncle."

Accommodating himself to the new order of things by donning a red shirt and fighting for the *garibaldini*, Tancredi utters the book's most famous line: "If we want everything to stay the same, everything has to change." By lending the allure of his name to the cause of liberation and national unity, the calculating young aristocrat helps stem the tide of popular resentment against his class. He thus goes off to the brief war to ensure that the new government will be another monarchy—that of the House of Savoy—instead of a republic as envisioned by radicals like Giuseppe Mazzini. Small wonder that cagey Tancredi eventually becomes a high-ranking diplomat, the Italian ambassador to the court of Vienna.

By no means is *Il Gattopardo* a tendentious tract extolling the good old days of the Bourbon monarchy of Naples and Sicily (the so-called Kingdom of the Two Sicilies). In a flashback to one of the prince's meetings with Ferdinand II (nicknamed "*Bomba*"), the late king is presented as a narrow-minded tyrant. The new Bourbon ruler, young Francis II, who is about to be swept away by the march of events, is dismissed by the prince as fitter for a seminary than a throne. But the man who will become the first king of a united Italy, Victor Emmanuel II, fares little better in Don Fabrizio's estimation. In setting up rigged plebiscites, Victor Emmanuel's operatives soon prove themselves to be just as corrupt as their predecessors.

If this perceived lack of enthusiasm for a united Italy offended many Italian readers, many Sicilians took umbrage at Don Fabrizio's deeply cynical colloquy about Sicily with Chevalley (a Piedmontese aristocrat who vainly tries to persuade the prince to accept an invitation to enter the new Italian Senate). Alternately, liberals saw Don Fabrizio's statements as a tirade against the notion of progress that ended up victimizing the victim. In Sicily, explains Don Fabrizio, the blazing sun mercilessly parches the land and enervates the inhabitants, whose collective death wish is expressed in their physical torpor, political indifference, exaggerated sensuality, and acts of mindless violence. Exhausted by 2,500 years of foreign rule, which always ends up the same despite superficial changes in the masters and governments, Sicilians hate activity of any sort and want only to be left alone to sleep before falling into the lap of death. Nor is there any need to try anything new: "Sicilians will never want to better themselves for the simple reason that they believe themselves to be perfect," he tells his astonished guest. In his own thoughts, he reflects that after an era of leopards and lions must come one of jackals and hyenas.

Here the political and the personal intersect. Don Fabrizio himself must arrange a marriage between a leopard and a jackal. His impoverished princely nephew Tancredi wants to marry the very wealthy Angelica, daughter of a beautiful but cretinous woman and of the toadlike Don Calogero Sedàra. The latter is an avaricious and corrupt politician of Italy's emerging bourgeoisie who snaps up the properties of noble bankrupts and newly confiscated Church lands.

Although Angelica is as lovely as an Andrea del Sarto Madonna, Tancredi will one day receive a pair of cuckold's horns from this granddaughter of '*Peppe 'Mmerda* (Joe Shit), a peasant who had been murdered by a *lupara* blast. In fact, Angelica is an aptly meretricious symbol of the progressive and materialistic age that is about to descend on Sicily—attractive enough on the surface, but hopelessly coarse, boring, and soulless.

Another problem is that Don Fabrizio's daughter Concetta—fiercely proud, good-looking, and intelligent—is in love with Tancredi. Her young cousin had reciprocated her feelings before doing something foolish. During a dinner party at the prince's palace, the very minimally wounded Tancredi—dazzled by Angelica's green-eyed and raven-haired beauty—tells war stories with great *sprezzatura*, "making it all seem like child's play and a matter of no consequence." When he regales the guests with a comrade's slightly salty remark in a nunnery they had occupied, Concetta feels a momentary revulsion at his crudeness and a violent hatred for her rival, who not only relishes the anecdote but brays delightedly when Tancredi follows up with a suggestive remark about Angelica herself. Angry and disappointed, Concetta rebukes him.

This contretemps leads to a scene the following day when Concetta, in true leopard fashion, exacts a little symbolic revenge on Tancredi, which convinces him that she no longer loves him (he is very much mistaken). Giving her up, he pursues and wins Angelica. Don Fabrizio, who knows his daughter's true feelings but, in any case, takes a dim view of romantic love—"fire and flames for one year, ashes for thirty"—agrees to serve as Tancredi's family representative in the negotiations for Angelica. With her wealth, reasons the prince, the dashing young aristocrat will be able to pursue his political ambitions with the new regime much more easily than he could with the declining fortunes of the Salinas.

In the book's climactic scene, a lavish ball set in November of 1862, Don Fabrizio is irritable and depressed. The women—a few of whom had been his mistresses—are now old and ugly. His friends are tedious. He'd much rather be in his observatory. While watching the dancers, especially the engaged couple, Tancredi and Angelica, Don Fabrizio sees only a danse macabre. He realizes that the golden pair (ironically named after a Tasso hero and an Ariosto heroine) don't have the slightest suspicion that their future may not correspond to their dreams. Always a little envious of Tancredi because of Angelica (a fragmentary chapter found in the author's notes describes the passion the prince conceives for the young beauty), Don Fabrizio now sees only pathos in "the mutual embrace of those bodies of theirs destined to die."

He experiences an epiphany in which he understands that compassion must be the chief emotion we feel for "those ephemeral beings who were trying to enjoy the slender ray of light accorded them between twin darknesses." He reflects on how we cannot decently be angry with creatures who must die. This is the ultimate insight of both the gentle Buddha and Christ, as well as of ferocious Achilles, who, at the end of the *Iliad*, feels pity for old King Priam, his suffering enemy. Life's supreme lesson learned, Don Fabrizio, who dances with fragrant Angelica once, is now ripe for death.

Although he lives another twenty years after the ball, the next time we see the prince he is dying. The septuagenarian has collapsed after a train trip to a medical specialist in Naples and must put up at a hotel in Palermo, too weak and sick to be brought to his nearby home.

His wife, Maria Stella, is dead. His son Paolo is dead (thrown from a horse). His friend, Padre Pirrone, is dead. His favorite son Giovanni has long ago fled the Salina household and moved to London. His young grandson is a twerp. The dying prince catalogs the happy moments of his life: two weeks before his wedding, six weeks after it; one half hour when his eldest son was born; many hours in his observatory; his love for Tancredi (who is now with him); some hunts with a peasant friend of his; various sexual transports; the moment he became aware of the beauty and noble character of his daughter Concetta; the honor he received at the Sorbonne; the sight of laughing, voluptuous women (including one spotted only yesterday at the train station in Catania). "Lived, truly lived, two years—three maximum," is his bottom line. "Pain and boredom? . . . seventy years."

In his delirium, a beautiful woman comes for him. Associated with the planet Venus, who always used to wait for him as he set out on his early morning hunting expeditions and whom he saw and longed for while walking home late on the night of the ball, she is far lovelier than Don Fabrizio had ever seen her. One of Lampedusa's favorite poets, John Keats, had confessed to being "half in love with easeful Death," and Tancredi had once accused his uncle of "courting death." Finally safe with his true love, the prince feels the roaring in his ears, like that of a raging sea growing steadily louder, cease altogether.

Lampedusa thus jumps from the period 1860–62 to 1883 and then to 1910 in the book's final two chapters, speeding up the clock to emphasize life's tragic brevity. Angelica, who is seventeen or so for most of the book, suddenly acquires "ripe breasts" in the penultimate chapter and appears as an old woman in the last one. As in the final chapter of Proust's monumental novel, we are stunned to see that all the characters have aged so rapidly or died.

In the stark conclusion of *Il Gattopardo*, set in 1910, Don Fabrizio's three old spinster daughters, including Concetta, have inherited his palace. Although their house is always full of priests, the reforming Church hierarchy cruelly deprives the pious and batty old women of scores of bogus relics and a "miraculous" painting in their private chapel. We learn a bit of the tawdry later history of Angelica and Tancredi (dead these past three years) and meet her former lover Tassoni (who of course had been a dear friend of her husband).

Only now, at age seventy or so, does Concetta, who still keeps her faded trousseau, finally discover that Tancredi had made up that fateful story about the nunnery just to show off for Angelica—and that he had been madly in love with Concetta at the time. In fact, she had seemed so beautiful to him, with her angry eyes and pouting lips, that he would have taken her in his arms in front of all the guests if he hadn't been too terrified of his *zione*. The next day, he had given up on her when he felt that she utterly despised him. All those years, Concetta had hated her father for betraying her by arranging Tancredi's marriage.

The last image in the book is that of the dog Bendicò, stuffed almost half a century earlier and now rotting away, flung out of the window at the self-lacerating Concetta's orders and landing in the courtyard's trash heap.

Lampedusa wrote little else: several early pieces of literary criticism; two short stories, "Joy and the Law" and the magical masterpiece "Lighea" (translated as "The Professor and the Siren"); a weak first chapter of a projected novel, *The Blind Kittens*; a brief memoir of the houses he had lived in as a youth; notes for courses in French and English literature that he gave to his adopted son and other young students. But *The Leopard*, an existentialist meditation in the guise of a conventional historical novel, is sure to remain a classic. In the words of Lampedusa's biographer, David Gilmour, "it ignored the fads of a literary generation and concentrated on perennial concerns."

In this sense, the book examines, in Robert Frost's phrase, "what to make of a diminished thing"—the accommodations we all have to make with life. Like Giacomo Leopardi, Don Fabrizio sloughs off one after another of life's illusions until he stands like Lear's "poor, bare, forked animal." Life's promises have proved mere ashes for both him and Concetta, but "while there's death, there's hope," he quips. In the end, the seemingly old-fashioned amateur author, the last Prince of Lampedusa, managed to invest his bare skeleton of a plot with an epic grandeur as timeless as Sicily itself.

Forty-nine

Ferrari—on the road to perfection

The demands of mass production are contrary to my temperament, for I am mainly interested in promoting new developments. I should like to put something new into my cars every morning—an inclination that terrifies my staff. Were my wishes in this respect to be indulged, there would be no production of standard models at all, but only a succession of prototypes.

—Enzo Ferrari

FOR DECADES, the name Ferrari has been synonymous with power, speed, and style—a car few can afford but most can recognize. The status that owning a Ferrari confers can hardly be overestimated and stems from several factors: the car's rarity (only about 3,600 are built annually); its sleek, majestic beauty; its performance, to which eleven Formula 1 world championships can attest; and its premium value, both at original and resale prices. Ferrari's durability is clearly evident as well, since almost all of the 100,000 cars produced are still running.

What separates the Ferrari from other sports cars? Its primary focus has always been racing: The cars were sold mainly to support the Ferrari racing team and were easily translated into road models with few modifications. Indeed, Ferrari's racing accomplishments are legendary, with over 1,500 outright victories to its credit, many of them international titles.

The man behind the machine, Enzo Ferrari, was born in 1898 in Modena, later the site of his first manufacturing plant. By 1919 he was an accomplished race car driver and had worked on cars in his hometown and in World War I. In the following year he joined the ranks of Alfa Romeo as a test driver while continuing to compete in races. When a colleague of Enzo's, Antonio Ascari, convinced Alfa Romeo to produce a series of sports cars, the company started with the 20/30 ES Sports, a modified version of the racing model. The car soon attracted buyers, pioneering in the new sports car market.

In 1929 Enzo was appointed head of a racing and modification department, Scuderia Ferrari. Because *scuderia* means "racing stable," a prancing horse was chosen as a logo. Within five years Scuderia Ferrari was producing cars for both racing and the consumer market. But German companies like Mercedes-Benz began stealing the racing spotlight when Hitler started pumping money into the industry. As a result, Alfa Romeo decided to take control of the Scuderia from Enzo in 1938, and in the following year he left to start his own business. During World War II, when he was allowed to produce only military materials, Ferrari moved his workshop from Modena to the nearby village of Maranello in a futile effort to avoid bombings. After the war, he started making cars again.

His first model appeared in 1946/47 and was named the 125 S, after the 125-cc capacity of each of the car's twelve cylinders. Less than three months after the first test drive of its prototype by Enzo himself, the car won the Rome Grand Prix. In 1948 the 166 S promptly won its first race, Sicily's Targa Florio, and a month later it triumphed in the Mille Miglia, Italy's thousand-mile race from Brescia to Rome and back (which Ferraris were to win eight times from 1948 to 1957). With the success of these early racing models, the stage was set for decades of achievement on and off the track, and the cars were constantly modified to enhance their performance.

The Ferrari racing team addressed individual needs one by one, making adjustments in the chassis, drive train, and body, and achieving numerous breakthroughs in engine design. A striking characteristic of the early Ferrari engine was its size. Despite being a V-12, it had a volume of only 1.5 liters—extremely small even by today's standards. The tremendously powerful engine was thus relatively light, boasting power-to-weight ratios comparable to many modern automobiles. Packing the clout of twelve cylinders into such a small engine was a difficult task for designer Gioachino Colombo, but it gave the Ferrari team a competitive edge.

The use of "hairpin" valve springs, as opposed to coil springs, was another important innovation. Shaped like clothespin springs, they were placed across from each other on each side of the valve stem, allowing the cylinder head to move freely between the two springs without being attached to either. The springs also took up less room vertically, thus allowing the valve stems to be shorter and the valve lighter. The shape of the spring provided more resistance at the same pressure, enabling the engine to attain higher speeds. Yet in 1959, a decade after the hairpin valve springs were designed, manufacturing advances were made in coil springs, and Ferrari was flexible enough to revert to them.

In 1961 the Ferrari team also explored ways to utilize wasted energy via turbo engines. Exhaust was partially redirected through a turbine that fed more fuel and air into the engine, thus generating more power. Unfortunately, high development costs and racing regulations prevented Ferrari from implementing this concept until the 1980s.

A significant advance was the flat engine, which lowered the Ferrari's center of gravity, giving the car increased traction and braking ability. The first Ferrari racing car with this feature was driver Lorenzo Bandini's 512 F1 in 1964, which achieved moderate success. The innovation was later applied to road cars such as the 512 BB in 1976 and the Testarossa in 1984.

The Ferrari team also recognized the need to cool air before it enters the combustion chamber. Since cooler air is denser and heavier, more power can be delivered to the engine when it mixes with the fuel. For the same reason, water injection was introduced in the 126 CB and 126 C3 racing models in 1983, the year Ferrari won the Constructors' Formula 1 World Championship.

Suspension systems were also altered to provide better handling, and brakes were adjusted to increase stability. Among the drive train innovations was the five-speed gearbox, which took greater advantage of the engine's power. The gearbox was also moved close to the clutch, minimizing the inertia of the rotating parts that had to change their speed during shifting. The semiautomatic transmission allowed the driver to focus on aspects of racing other than shifting: By pressing a paddle, he could upshift or downshift while keeping both hands on the wheel.

The chassis was constantly modified as well, with close attention paid to aerodynamics, since reducing drag prevented horsepower wastage. Placing a fin in the back of the car helped stabilize it, much as fins keep a dart steady. Wings created a downforce, up to twice the weight of the car, holding it closer to the road and allowing for better handling. This concept, introduced by Mauro Forghieri in 1968 on the 312 F1, is still used in racing.

In 1969 Enzo Ferrari sold a 50 percent share of his company to Fiat but stayed on as president until 1977. The cars that bear his name have remained expensive, rare, and highly collectible, and their stunning looks and high resale value make them attractive investments. Auctions routinely draw six, sometimes seven, figures. In 1990 a 1963 GTO, one of only thirty-nine made, sold for a record $17 million. Who knows what price the F1-2000 driven by phenomenal Ferrari racing ace Michael Schumacher will fetch someday?

The Ferrari's mystique precedes it everywhere and garners flattering publicity. An unforgettable scene in the 1992 film *Scent of a Woman* features Al Pacino's blind character taking a red Mondial Cabriolet out for a spin on the streets of Manhattan. In 1993 Rodeo Drive in Beverly Hills was closed down to make way for a parade of more than a hundred collectible Ferraris, along with the new 348 Spider convertible with its canvas roof. That same year New York's Museum of Modern Art opened the "Designed for Speed" exhibit, displaying three Ferraris. More than a thousand "F-cars" proudly gathered in Monterey in 1994 for a Ferrari owners' club meeting and assorted racing events. In September 2000, at a gala at the Italian Embassy in Washington, D.C., celebrating sixty years of Italian influence on the U.S. luxury auto market, eight vintage and current Ferraris, guarded by *carabinieri*, were on display.

Road models available in 2000/2001 included the 360 Modena, the 456M GT and GTA, and the 550 Maranello. The 360 Modena, named for the company's hometown and powered by a rear-mounted V-8 engine (visible through the rear window), utilizes its 400 hp at 8,500 rpm to go from 0 to 60 mph in 4.5 seconds. It can do 180 mph (at least). The 456M has a twelve-cylinder engine that delivers 436 hp at a top speed of over 186 mph. The 550 Maranello, also equipped with a V-12, promises 480 hp at 7,000 rpm, does 0 to 60 in 4.3 seconds, and tops out at almost 200 mph. (That's New York to Baltimore in 60 minutes.)

From its inception, the Ferrari has undergone constant evolution—with many successful design changes and many rendered obsolete—evincing an adaptability that has allowed it to thrive. Enzo Ferrari died in Modena at age ninety in 1988, but he lived to see the release of the F 40, the fastest Ferrari ever built. In 1997 the Ferrari company acquired Maserati, hoping to revive its splendor and compete with a reinvigorated Jaguar and Porsche. The company continues to forge ahead, profiting from the best financial position it has ever enjoyed.

Today's Italy is a land of harrowing highway speeds, where you're expected to move over for cars that can go faster than yours. But Italians have long been obsessed with automobiles and racing. As far back as 1909, Futurist poet Filippo Tommaso Marinetti proclaimed that "the world is the richer for a new beauty of speed, and our praise is for the man at the wheel." One likes to think that eleven-year-old Enzo Ferrari might have been listening.

—Dante D'Epiro

Fifty

La moda italiana: The art of apparel

The fashion wears out more apparel than the man.
—William Shakespeare, *Much Ado About Nothing* (c. 1598)

IN THE COURSE OF Martin Scorsese's documentary *Made in Milan* (1990), Giorgio Armani hacks the lining and padding from a man's traditional structured suit jacket and helps a male model put it on. In its new incarnation, the jacket fits him less like armor and more like gliding drapery. Fluidity—Armani's strike against the stultifying "Mao syndrome" that had characterized male clothing for decades—allowed men, in his words, "a more personal and real look."

His first menswear collection was recognized as a major transition in 1974, but its impact paled in comparison with the debut of his women's collection in the following year, which featured scaled-down versions of the same jackets he had made for men. Women were swelling the workforce, and Armani struck a resonant chord: "I realized women did not have a way of dressing that was easy, modern, somewhat close to a man's style." Unique because it combined the feminist with the feminine, his women's line was considered radical. Twenty years later, the audacious Gianni Versace would deride Armani for dressing the mothers of Italy. Times change, but the Armani and Versace houses still bookend the Italian fashion industry.

Paris dominated women's fashion during the nineteenth and early twentieth centuries, and wealthy European men, including Italian aristocrats, bought their suits on London's Savile Row. The Italians, however, were making steady gains as producers of fine textiles. The Cerruti company, founded in 1881 by three brothers, soon became renowned for its wools, which were sold to some of Europe's most elite design houses. Like many other Italian textile groups, Cerruti eventually began manufacturing men's suits, and by the early 1950s Italy had more tailors than

Britain and France combined. In 1952 the house of Brioni presented the first-ever runway show of men's clothing.

Leather goods were another early focus of the Italian fashion industry. After its millinery business failed in 1906, the Gucci family, led by Guccio Gucci, opened a saddlery and leather-goods shop in Florence, producing luggage inspired by the trunks and hatboxes Guccio had toted for wealthy guests while working as a bellboy at the Savoy in London. Fine moccasins and loafers were added to the line and would soon be recognizable throughout the world with Gucci's back-to-back G insignia. Guccio's son Aldo opened a store on the Via Condotti in Rome just a year before the start of World War II.

During the war Guccio kept the family enterprise afloat by producing boots for the Italian army. When the war ended, the Rome store was flooded by American soldiers looking for gifts to take home, and the small leather goods and bamboo-handled purses that traveled stateside with the GIs primed the pump for the Gucci store that Aldo opened in Manhattan in the early 1950s.

A leather shortage during the war forced Gucci and the innovative footwear designer Salvatore Ferragamo, who eventually produced more than twenty thousand shoe styles, to look to other materials for their small luxury goods. For both designers, necessity was the mother of innovations such as Gucci's signature red and green canvas luggage and Ferragamo's footwear constructed of cork, hemp, cellophane, lace, nylon, and, reputedly, snail shells. Other wartime designers saved material by manufacturing short, tight-fitting dresses and, in the case of Ermenegildo Zegna, by producing men's jackets that were meant to be torn down, turned inside out, and restitched when the fabric wore out on one side.

The Second World War marked the final stages of Elsa Schiaparelli's illustrious career. A philosopher by training, this Roman native spent her youth in Boston and New York and achieved a loyal following as a designer of "hard chic" in Paris during the 1930s. Her career began when a store buyer inquired about a sweater she had knit for herself—a black number incorporating a *trompe l'oeil* white bow tie—and placed numerous orders for it.

Until her last show in 1954 Schiaparelli created sleek, sophisticated, and fabulously witty clothing. Her fabric and accessory designers included the likes of Jean Cocteau and the artist Christian Bérard. Her most memorable collaborations, however, were with Salvador Dalí, who helped design the famous upturned shoe hat, which, as its name suggests, looked like a giant high heel turned upside down. With its heel spiking up and forward and the toe arching down over the wearer's forehead, the hat—amusing but not quite comic or grotesque—was available in black or Schiaparelli's signature color, shocking pink. Dalí also inspired her "drawer" suit, decorated with pockets made to look like furniture drawers. The wearer looks ready for the office, but whether as a crisp, tailored career woman or a walking file cabinet depends on your point of view.

Schiaparelli's other innovations include dyeing zippers to match a garment's color, especially pink, and making them integral aspects of the design rather than hiding them in a seam. Theme collections, now a fashion-world staple, are said to have been introduced by Schiaparelli in 1937 with musical motifs. For the 1938 circus collection, she commissioned cast-metal buttons made in the shapes of acrobats that tumbled down the front of a (pink) silk jacket.

In 1951, after decades on the periphery of the fashion world, exporting fabrics, accessories, and the likes of Schiaparelli, Italy scored decisively on the international scene. In an event that *Life* magazine called a bold threat to the dominance of Paris and that is now viewed as the birth of contemporary Italian clothing design, aristocrat and businessman Giovanni Battista Giorgini invited ten Roman and Milanese designers—and buyers from many American department stores—to a group show at his home, the Villa Torregiani in Florence. The event marked the beginning of the "Made in Italy" craze and was so successful that it was moved the following year to the White Room at the Pitti Palace, principal residence of the Medici family from about 1550.

One of the first Italian designers to emerge on the international stage at this time was no stranger to palaces imbued with the Medici legacy. Emilio Pucci, Marchese di Barsento, once claimed he was the first member of his family in a thousand years to work for a living. The Palazzo Pucci in Florence, now a monument to the marchese's career, has been inhabited by his family for centuries. In 1482 Lorenzo the Magnificent gave Giannozzo Pucci four Botticellis, one of which still hangs in the living room of Emilio's widow. The Medici pope Leo X made a Pucci a cardinal, the first of three in the family.

Despite his august lineage, the former member of the Italian Olympic ski squad began his career humbly in Oregon by designing the ski team uniform for Reed College, where he studied in the 1930s. After serving in the Italian Air Force in World War II (he is rumored to have sunk a British Red Cross ship), he lived as a wealthy playboy at resorts from

Switzerland to the Amalfi Coast. He is credited with inventing stretch pants with stirrups for skiing and with coining the turtleneck-under-a-shirt look. When photos of him in his own ski clothes appeared in American fashion magazines, he was asked to produce a line of women's sportswear for several large stores, notably Lord & Taylor.

The key to Pucci's success was his intimate knowledge of the women he squired across the world's playgrounds. "Because he loved women and knew their bodies, he understood what they needed as they moved from Capri to L.A. to Acapulco. Women looked pretty, and the dresses were sexy," explained a friend and former fashion editor to *Vanity Fair* magazine. The Pucci line included his famous ankle-kissing Capri pants, resort dresses, and silk blouses, all in bright colors and wildly imaginative, instantly recognizable prints that anticipated the psychedelic era. The designer's devotees included Marilyn Monroe, who is said to have been interred in a Pucci. Now-defunct Braniff Airlines hired the designer to paint its jets—and dress its flight attendants—in green, blue, and orange. At NASA's behest, Pucci designed the flight insignia for Apollo 15. He was the first designer to sign his garments on the outside, a now tiresomely ubiquitous practice.

The momentum initiated by the fashion exhibitions at the Pitti Palace accelerated during the 1960s. All things Italian—especially men's suits—spoke an international language of modernity and hipness, and London tailors were finding themselves emulating the clothes of the Roman *sarti*, as worn by stars like Marcello Mastroianni.

The designer known as Valentino, fresh from apprenticeships in Paris, first displayed his line at the Pitti Palace in 1962, leading to heavy buys at the high-end American store I. Magnin. The year 1968 was another watershed for the man nicknamed "Le Chic": The success of his so-called White Collection (a departure from his lavish red signature color), featuring short lace dresses, filigree stockings, and flat shoes, was crowned when Jacqueline Kennedy selected one of these ensembles for her wedding to Aristotle Onassis. Valentino was swamped with orders from other wealthy customers for the same dress—an unheard-of happening in couture culture that may have presaged the retail changes of the next decade.

By the early 1970s the fashion competition among Rome, Florence, and Milan was more heated than that between France and Italy. In 1975 the prêt-à-porter (ready-to-wear) movement, initially championed by the French houses of Yves Saint Laurent and Christian Dior, revolutionized the industry by making more reasonably priced designer clothing available to a wider public. Italian houses, especially those based in Milan, have distinguished themselves in prêt-à-porter by making well-priced clothing that women want to wear—the possible exceptions being outlandish getups like those created by Versace and his protégé, Schiaparelli wannabe Franco Moschino, which nonetheless have considerable entertainment value and keep fashion magazines in business. Imperious Armani decreed, "High fashion for the wealthy and very rich still exists, but the rule is that the articles shown on the runway, with a few corrections and modifications, must be capable of becoming clothes for everyone."

After Gianni Versace's murder by a jilted hanger-on in Miami in 1997, Giorgio Armani tried to downplay the legendary rancor between the two designers. But the polar extremes they represented were exemplified in an anecdote Armani recounted for *Vanity Fair*. During an exchange on Rome's Spanish Steps one afternoon, Versace told the older man, "You dress elegant women. You dress sophisticated women. *Io vesto delle zoccole*. [I dress sluts.]"

Versace overstated his case. As a young adult, he had worked as a buyer and designer for his mother's dressmaking shop. After a stint as a freelance designer, he opened his own business in 1978 with his brother and a sister, Donatella, and subsequently designed costumes for La Scala's opera company and the Béjart Ballet. Best known for his brash, histrionic women's evening attire—epitomized by Elizabeth Hurley's notorious safety-pin gown—his collections also included more sedate day wear. Much of Versace's appeal stemmed from his use of bias-cut fabrics, sometimes even for trousers. Untailored lengths of cloth held by sashes or belts swathed or draped the wearer, evoking images from ancient Greek and Roman art or lush Renaissance tapestries. Camille Paglia insists that the designer's "gaudy, glittering, iridescent patterns" are reminiscent of the Baroque sculptor, painter, and architect Bernini (see Essay 36).

Described by *Vogue* as possessing "loose-limbed chic" and exemplifying a "muted seduction," the primarily beige and gray clothes created by Giorgio Armani grab fewer headlines than those of Versace and feature nothing of Dolce & Gabbana's "southern Italian sex-bomb look," but their appeal seems nearly universal. In the catalog for the Armani exhibit that opened at New York's Guggenheim Museum in October 2000, Susan Cross wrote that the designer's clothing, which ranges from serious black or beige suits to colorful, sheer beaded skirts, had "allowed women to escape the burden of being either/or."

Armani spent three years as a medical student, training that clarified for him the relationship between anatomy and design. He left medicine in the late 1950s to work as a window dresser at a forward-thinking department store chain and later became a successful suit designer for Cerruti. With architect Sergio Galeotti, Armani started a business and soon became famous for the deconstruction of the suit. As strong influences on his designs, Armani cites the films of Italian Neorealists such as Roberto Rossellini (see Essay 47) and also movie stars, particularly the sexually ambiguous Marlene Dietrich.

Armani came to worldwide attention in 1980, when he fashioned Richard Gere's sleek, uncluttered wardrobe for the Paul Schrader film *American Gigolo*. He has designed clothing for at least a hundred films since then, and he has an intensely loyal following in Hollywood among male and female actors of all shapes and sizes, who, said Judith Thurman in *The New Yorker*, look up to him as "the champion of the insecure, the newly hatched, the self-doubting and ingenuous." Armani reportedly handpicked an assertive manager for his San Francisco store because of his concerns about the many female dot.com executives in that city who wear running shoes with a dress.

This "last Italian Puritan" has stated that "flesh visible under chiffon blouses is a scandal!" but apparently has no qualms about fairly extreme décolletage in a woman's tuxedo—or about men sporting fringed silk scarves. But embarrass the wearer, never. Of the many Armani dresses she's worn, Sophia Loren says, "When I have to face an audience, God knows how many doubts I have, and when I wear his clothes, I have no more doubts." In her tribute to Armani at the Guggenheim exhibit, Italian architect Gae Aulenti noted that "his persuasive power emanates from a process of studied choice—of form, materials, fabrics, and colors appropriate for every situation."

So many shelves of books and sheaves of magazine pages are dedicated to the artistic achievements and commercial successes of Italian fashion, that no more than a selection can be mentioned here: Capucci and his geometric coats, Cavalli's rhinestone jeans, Laura Biagiotti and her cushy cashmeres, Krizia's lighthearted designs, Fendi's furs, the outlandish knitwear of Missoni, Prada's sophisticated mix of fabrics, and the architectural shapes of Gianfranco Ferré. And how exquisitely Italy's trove of jewelers, who trace their craft back to Ghiberti and Cellini, can enhance a fine dress or jacket with a brooch or pair of earrings.

But what lies ahead for this fertile Italian industry is unclear, with the forces of consolidation and globalization threatening its national identity. Armani, worth billions, is one of the few fashion megastars still in sole control of his own company. Donatella Versace is now head of her late brother's business, a role she never anticipated. An American, Tom Ford, has been the creative director at Gucci for years and now assumes the same position at Yves Saint Laurent with Gucci's acquisition of that house. Gucci, now incorporated in the Netherlands, itself barely escaped being swallowed by the French conglomerate LVMH (Moët Hennessy Louis Vuitton), which bought Pucci and had the bad taste to announce that it had gotten the Italian company cheap. Is it any surprise that France, whose achievements in the visual arts are second only to Italy's, would be its major rival in these endeavors?

The real surprise would be if a land like Italy, with its stunning natural beauty and incomparable legacy in painting, sculpture, and architecture, did not excel in fashion and design. Artists like Armani, Pucci, Valentino, and Versace have well understood how our sense of the beautiful helps forge and strengthen our emotional bonds to life and how our daily self-presentation can be a nuanced part of a much larger canvas, hence Armani's quest for the "personal and real."

Whether they have designed clothes, written poetry, composed operas, built public squares, painted for popes, hewn marble, or sailed the fathomless seas, many Italians of genius have placed a premium on achieving an appearance of effortless mastery, or *sprezzatura*, that is attained only by costly, concentrated effort and unremitting labor. "In the end," says Giorgio Armani, "the most difficult thing to do is the simplest thing."

SUGGESTED READING

Only titles in English, or bilingual texts, are listed. Many of the works of art mentioned in this book may be viewed at the Web Gallery of Art: http://www.kfki.hu/~arthp/index1.html.

1: Rome gives the world a calendar—twice

Boorstin, Daniel J. *The Discoverers*. New York: Vintage Books, 1985, pp. 4–19, 596–603.

Duncan, David Ewing. *Calendar: Humanity's Epic Struggle to Determine a True and Accurate Year*. New York: Avon Books, 1998.

Gould, Stephen Jay. *Questioning the Millennium: A Rationalist's Guide to a Precisely Arbitrary Countdown*. New York: Harmony Books, 1997.

Ovid. *Ovid's Fasti: Roman Holidays*. Verse translation by Betty Rose Nagle. Bloomington, Ind.: Indiana University Press, 1995.

WEB SITE:

www.calendarzone.com/

2: The Roman Republic and our own

Grant, Michael. *The World of Rome*. New York: Mentor Books, 1960.

Hamilton, Alexander, James Madison, and John Jay. *The Federalist Papers*. Edited by Clinton Rossiter. New York: Mentor Books, 1999.

Lewis, Naphtali, and Meyer Reinhold, eds. *Roman Civilization. Sourcebook I: The Republic*. New York: Harper and Row, Publishers, 1966; 1951.

Livy. *The Early History of Rome,* books I–V of *The History of Rome from Its Foundation*. Translated by Aubrey de Sélincourt. New York: Penguin Books, 1971; 1960.

Polybius. *The Rise of the Roman Empire*. Translated by Ian Scott-Kilvert. New York: Penguin Books, 1979.

Rostovtzeff, M. *Rome*. Translated by J. D. Duff. Edited by Elias J. Bickerman. London: Oxford University Press, 1960; 1928.

Syme, Ronald. *The Roman Revolution*. New York: Oxford University Press, 1987; 1939.

3: Julius Caesar and the imperial purple

Appian. *The Civil Wars*. Translated by John Carter. New York: Penguin Books, 1996, pp. 69–153.

Barzini, Luigi. "Julius Caesar." In *From Caesar to the Mafia: Sketches of Italian Life*. New York: The Library Press, 1971, pp. 3–29.

Caesar. *The Civil War together with the Alexandrian War, the African War, and the Spanish War by Other Hands*. Translated by Jane F. Mitchell. New York: Penguin Books, 1967.

————. *The Conquest of Gaul*. Translated by S. A. Handford. Revised by Jane F. Gardner. New York: Penguin Books, 1982.

Gelzer, Matthias. *Caesar: Politician and Statesman*. Translated by Peter Needham. Cambridge, Mass.: Harvard University Press, 1968.

Meier, Christian. *Caesar*. Translated by David McLintock. New York: Basic Books, 1982.

Plutarch. *Fall of the Roman Republic: Six Lives by Plutarch*. Translated by Rex Warner. New York: Penguin Books, 1972.

Suetonius. "Julius Caesar." In *The Twelve Caesars*, translated by Robert Graves. New York: Penguin Books, 1957, pp. 9–49.

4: Catullus revolutionizes love poetry

Catullus. *The Poems of Catullus*. Verse translation by Guy Lee with facing Latin text. New York: Oxford University Press, 1990.

————. *The Poems of Catullus*. Verse translation by Peter Whigham. New York: Penguin USA, 1966.

Highet, Gilbert. *Poets in a Landscape*. London: Trafalgar Square, 1999; 1957.

Quinn, Kenneth. *The Catullan Revolution*. 2d rev. ed. Ann Arbor, Mich.: University of Michigan Press, 1971; 1959.

5: Master builders of the ancient world

De Camp, L. Sprague. *The Ancient Engineers*. New York: Ballantine Books, 1963.

Grant, Michael. *Art in the Roman Empire*. London: Routledge, 1995.

MacDonald, William L. *An Introductory Study*, vol. 1 of *The Architecture of the Roman Empire*. New Haven: Yale University Press, 1982.

Scarre, Chris, ed. *The Seventy Wonders of the Ancient World: The Great Monuments and How They Were Built*. London: Thames and Hudson, 1999.

Ward-Perkins, J. B. *Roman Imperial Architecture*. New Haven: Yale University Press, 1981.

Wheeler, Mortimer. *Roman Art and Architecture*. London: Thames and Hudson, 1996.

WEB SITE:

http://web.kyoto-inet.or.jp/org/orion/eng/hst/roma.htm/#pantheon

6: "Satire is wholly ours"

Hadas, Moses. *A History of Latin Literature*. New York: Columbia University Press, 1952, pp. 164–83, 278–301.

Horace. *The Complete Odes and Epodes with the Centennial Hymn*. Verse translation by W. G. Shepherd. New York: Penguin Books, 1983.

———. *The Complete Odes and Satires of Horace*. Verse translation by Sidney Alexander. Princeton, N.J.: Princeton University Press, 1999.

———. *The Complete Works of Horace*. Edited by Caspar J. Kraemer, Jr. New York: Modern Library, 1936.

———. *Horace's Satires and Epistles*. Verse translation by Jacob Fuchs. New York: W. W. Norton and Company, 1977.

Juvenal. *The Sixteen Satires*. Verse translation by Peter Green. New York: Penguin Books, 1967.

Lucilius. *Remains of Old Latin III: Lucilius; The Twelve Tables*. Rev. ed. Prose translation by E. H. Warmington with facing Latin text. Cambridge, Mass.: Harvard University Press, Loeb Classical Library, 1993; 1967.

Martial. *The Epigrams*. Verse translation of a selection by James Michie with facing Latin text. New York: Penguin Books, 1978.

———. *Selected Epigrams*. Verse translation by Rolfe Humphries. Bloomington, Ind.: Indiana University Press, 1963.

Persius. *The Satires of Persius*. Verse translation by W. S. Merwin. Bloomington, Ind.: Indiana University Press, 1961.

Petronius. *The Satyricon*. Translated by William Arrowsmith. New York: New American Library, 1959.

Petronius and Seneca. *The Satyricon. The Apocolocyntosis*. Translated by J. P. Sullivan. New York: Penguin Books, 1986.

7: Ovid's treasure hoard of myth and fable

Grant, Michael. *Myths of the Greeks and Romans*. New York: Mentor Books, 1986; 1962, pp. 328–56.

Hughes, Ted. *Tales from Ovid*. New York: Farrar, Straus and Giroux, 1997.

Lowell, Robert. "Ovid's *Metamorphoses*." In *Collected Prose*. New York: Farrar, Straus and Giroux, 1987, pp. 152–60.

Ovid. *The Metamorphoses*. Verse translation by Horace Gregory. New York: Viking Press, 1958.

———. *Metamorphoses*. Verse translation by Rolfe Humphries. Bloomington, Ind.: Indiana University Press, 1955.

———. *Metamorphoses*. 2 vols., 3d rev. ed. Edited by G. P. Goold. Prose translation by Frank Justus Miller with facing Latin text. Cambridge, Mass.: Harvard University Press, Loeb Classical Library, 1994; 1977.

8: The Roman legacy of law

Grant, Michael. *The World of Rome*. New York: Mentor Books, 1960, pp. 87–148.

Justinian. *The Digest of Roman Law: Theft, Rapine, Damage, and Insult*. Translated by C. F. Kolbert. New York: Penguin Books, 1979.

The Twelve Tables. *Remains of Old Latin III: Lucilius; The Twelve Tables*. Rev. ed. Translated by E. H. Warmington with facing Latin text. Cambridge, Mass.: Harvard University Press, Loeb Classical Library, 1993; 1967.

Wolff, Hans Julius. *Roman Law: An Historical Introduction*. Norman, Okla.: University of Oklahoma Press, 1951.

9: St. Benedict: Father of Western monasticism, preserver of the Roman heritage

Benedict, St. *The Rule of St. Benedict*. Edited by Timothy Fry. New York: Vintage Books, 1998.

———. *The Rule of St. Benedict*. Translated by Anthony C. Meisel and M. L. del Mastro. Garden City, N.Y.: Image Books, 1975.

Gregory the Great, Pope St. *Life and Miracles of St. Benedict*, book 2 of *The Dialogues*. Translated by Odo J. Zimmermann and Benedict R. Avery. Collegeville, Minn.: The Liturgical Press, n.d.

LaTourette, Kenneth Scott. *Beginnings to 1500*, vol. 1 of *A History of Christianity*. San Francisco: Harper San Francisco, 1975.

Norris, Kathleen. *The Cloister Walk*. New York: Riverhead Books, 1996.

Southern, Richard William. *Western Society and the Church in the Middle Ages*. New York: Viking Press, 1990.

WEB SITES:

The Abbey at Monte Cassino:
http://www.officine.it/montecassino/main_e.htm.
The Monastery of Christ in the Desert:
http://www.christdesert.org/pax.html.

10: Salerno and Bologna: The earliest medical school and university

Bettmann, Otto L. *A Pictorial History of Medicine*. Springfield, Ill.: Charles C. Thomas, 1956.

Cieślak-Golonka, Maria, and Bruno Morten. "The Women Scientists of Bologna." *American Scientist* 88 (January–February 2000): 68–73.

Garrison, Fielding H. *An Introduction to the History of Medicine*. 4th ed. Philadelphia: W. B. Saunders Company, 1929.

Green, Monica H. *The "Trotula": A Medieval Compendium of Women's Medicine*. Philadelphia: University of Pennsylvania Press, 2001.

Haskins, Charles Homer. "The Revival of Jurisprudence" and "The Beginnings of Universities." In *The Renaissance of the Twelfth Century*. Cambridge, Mass.: Harvard University Press, 1990; 1927, chapters 7 and 12.

———. *The Rise of Universities*. Ithaca, N.Y.: Cornell University Press, 1957; 1923.

Marti-Ibañez, Felix, ed. *The Epic of Medicine*. New York: Clarkson N. Potter, Inc., 1959.

Nutton, Vivian. "Medicine in Medieval Western Europe, 1000–1500." In *The Western Medical Tradition: 800 B.C. to A.D. 1800*, by Lawrence I. Conrad, Michael Neve, Vivian Nutton, Roy Porter, and Andrew Wear. Cambridge, England: Cambridge University Press, 1995, pp. 139–205.

Siraisi, Nancy G. *Medieval and Early Renaissance Medicine: An Introduction to Knowledge and Practice*. Chicago: University of Chicago Press, 1990.

11: St. Francis of Assisi, "alter Christus"

Bonaventure. *The Life of St. Francis of Assisi*. Edited by Cardinal Manning. Rockford, Ill.: TAN Books and Publishers, 1992.

Chesterton, G. K. *St. Francis of Assisi*. New York: Image Books, 1987; 1923.

Covington, Richard. "An Act of Faith and the Restorer's Art." *Smithsonian* 30 (November 1999): 76–85.

Green, Julien. *God's Fool: The Life and Times of Francis of Assisi*. Translated by Peter Heinegg. San Francisco: Harper and Row, 1985.

Moorman, John. *A History of the Franciscan Order from Its Origins to the Year 1517*. Chicago: Franciscan Press, 1988.

Southern, Richard William. *Western Society and the Church in the Middle Ages*. New York: Viking Press, 1990.

Ugolino di Monte Santa Maria. *The Little Flowers of St. Francis of Assisi*. New York: Vintage Books, 1998.

WEB SITES:

Frescoes by Giotto in the Upper Church at the Basilica of St. Francis in Assisi: http://gallery.euroweb.hu/html/g/giotto/assisi/upper.

Thomas of Celano, First and Second Lives of Saint Francis: http://www.fordham.edu/halsall/source/stfran-lives.html.

Treasury of Saint Francis: http://www.treasuryofstfrancis.com.

12: *"Stupor mundi"*: Emperor Frederick II, King of Sicily and Jerusalem

Abulafia, David. *Frederick II: A Medieval Emperor*. New York: Oxford University Press, 1988.

Harrison, Barbara Grizzuti. "Frederico Secundo." In *An Accidental Autobiography*. Boston: Houghton Mifflin Company, 1996, pp. 262–88.

Kay, George R., trans. *The Penguin Book of Italian Verse*. Prose translations with Italian texts. New York: Penguin Books, 1965, pp. 19–50.

Symonds, John Addington. *Renaissance in Italy: Italian Literature in Two Parts*. Part 1. New York: Capricorn Books, 1964; 1881, pp. 18–24.

13: St. Thomas Aquinas: Titan of theology

Aquinas, St. Thomas. *Introduction to Saint Thomas Aquinas* [selections from the *Summa theologica* and the *Summa contra gentiles*]. Edited by Anton C. Pegis. New York: Modern Library, 1948.

Boorstin, Daniel J. "The Way of Disputations: Universities." In *The Seekers: The Story of Man's Continuing Quest to Understand His World*. New York: Random House, 1998, pp. 81–90.

Durant, Will. "The Adventure of Reason: 1120–1308." In *The Age of Faith: A History of Medieval Civilization—Christian, Islamic, and Judaic—from Constantine to Dante:* A.D. *325–1300*. New York: Simon and Schuster, 1950, pp. 949–83.

Hyman, Arthur, and James J. Walsh, eds. *Philosophy in the Middle Ages: The Christian, Islamic, and Jewish Traditions.* 2d ed. Indianapolis: Hackett Publishing Company, 1983.

Noon, William T. *Joyce and Aquinas.* New Haven: Yale University Press, 1957.

WEB SITE:

Summa Theologica of St. Thomas Aquinas (complete searchable English text): http://www.newadvent.org/summa/

14: Dante's incomparable *Comedy*

Alighieri, Dante. *The Divine Comedy.* Verse translation by Allen Mandelbaum with facing Italian text. 3 vols. New York: Bantam Books, 1982.

———. *The Divine Comedy.* Prose translation by John D. Sinclair with facing Italian text. 3 vols. New York: Oxford University Press, 1969; 1939.

———. *The Divine Comedy.* Prose translation by Charles S. Singleton with facing Italian text. 3 vols. Princeton, N.J.: Princeton University Press, Bollingen Series LXXX, 1975.

———. *Inferno.* Verse translation by Robert and Jean Hollander with facing Italian text. New York: Doubleday, 2000.

———. *La Vita Nuova.* Translated by Dante Gabriel Rossetti. In *The Portable Dante,* edited by Paolo Milano. New York: Viking Press, 1947, pp. 545–618.

Auerbach, Erich. *Dante: Poet of the Secular World.* Translated by Ralph Manheim. Chicago: University of Chicago Press, 1961; 1929.

Barbi, Michele. *Life of Dante.* Translated by Paul G. Ruggiers. Berkeley: University of California Press, 1954; 1933.

Bergin, Thomas Goddard. *A Diversity of Dante.* New Brunswick, N.J.: Rutgers University Press, 1969.

Bloom, Harold. "The Strangeness of Dante: Ulysses and Beatrice." In *The Western Canon: The Books and School of the Ages.* New York: Harcourt Brace & Company, 1994, pp. 76–104.

Eliot, T. S. "Dante." In *Selected Prose of T. S. Eliot,* edited by Frank Kermode. New York: Harcourt Brace Jovanovich, 1977; 1929, pp. 205–30.

Freccero, John, ed. *Dante: A Collection of Critical Essays.* Englewood Cliffs, N.J.: Prentice-Hall, Inc., 1965.

Rossetti, Dante Gabriel. *Dante and His Circle, with the Italian Poets Preceding Him (1100–1200–1300): A Collection of Lyrics Edited and Translated in the Original Metres*. Boston: Roberts Brothers, 1887; 1861.

WEB SITE:

http://www.princeton.edu/dante/

15: Banks, bookkeeping, and the rise of commercial capitalism

de Roover, Raymond. *The Rise and Decline of the Medici Bank, 1397–1494*. New York: W. W. Norton & Company, 1966; 1963.

Lopez, Robert S. *The Commercial Revolution of the Middle Ages, 950–1350*. Cambridge, England: Cambridge University Press, 1976.

Lopez, Robert S., and Irving W. Raymond. *Medieval Trade in the Mediterranean World: Illustrative Documents Translated with Introductions and Notes*. New York: W. W. Norton & Company, 1969; 1955.

Miskimin, Harry A. *The Economy of Early Renaissance Europe, 1300–1460*. Cambridge, England: Cambridge University Press, 1975.

16: Petrarch: Creator of the modern lyric

Bishop, Morris. "Petrarch." In *The Italian Renaissance*, edited by J. H. Plumb. Boston: Houghton Mifflin Company, 1987; 1961, pp. 160–75.

Durant, Will. "The Age of Petrarch and Boccaccio: 1304–75." In *The Renaissance: A History of Civilization in Italy, 1304–1576 A.D.* New York: Simon and Schuster, 1953, pp. 3–48.

Kristeller, Paul Oskar. "Petrarch." In *Eight Philosophers of the Italian Renaissance*. Stanford, Calif.: Stanford University Press, 1964, pp. 1–18.

Petrarch. *The Canzoniere, or Rerum vulgarium fragmenta*. Verse translation by Mark Musa with facing Italian text. Indianapolis: Indiana University Press, 1999.

———. *Petrarch's Lyric Poems*. Translated by Robert M. Durling. Cambridge, Mass.: Harvard University Press, 1976.

Praz, Mario. "Petrarch in England." In *The Flaming Heart: Essays on Crashaw, Machiavelli, and Other Studies in the Relations between Italian and English Literature from Chaucer to T. S. Eliot*. New York: W. W. Norton and Company, 1973; 1958, pp. 264–86.

Robinson, James Harvey, and Henry Winchester Rolfe. *Petrarch: The First Modern Scholar and Man of Letters*. New York: Haskell House Publishers Ltd., 1970; 1898.

17: Boccaccio and the development of Western literary realism

Auerbach, Erich. "Frate Alberto." In *Mimesis: The Representation of Reality in Western Literature*, translated by Willard R. Trask. Princeton, N.J.: Princeton University Press, 1974; 1946, pp. 203–31.

Boccaccio, Giovanni. *The Decameron*. 2d ed. Translated by G. W. McWilliam. New York: Penguin, 1996.

———. *The Decameron*. Translated by Mark Musa and Peter Bondanella. New York: New American Library, 1989.

———. *Nymphs of Fiesole*. Verse translation by Joseph Tusiani. Madison, N.J.: Fairleigh Dickinson University Press, 1971.

Boorstin, Daniel J. "Escaping the Plague." In *The Creators*. New York: Random House, 1992, pp. 266–75.

Symonds, John Addington. *Renaissance in Italy: Italian Literature in Two Parts*. Part 1. New York: Capricorn Books, 1964; 1881, pp. 83–119.

WEB SITE:

Decameron Web site:
www.brown.edu/Departments/Italian_Studies/dweb/dweb.shtml

18: The mystic as activist: St. Catherine of Siena

Catherine of Siena. *The Letters of St. Catherine of Siena*. Translated by Suzanne Noffke. Binghamton, N.Y.: Center for Medieval and Early Renaissance Studies, State University of New York at Binghamton, 1988.

King, Margaret L. *Women of the Renaissance*. Chicago: University of Chicago Press, 1991.

LaTourette, Kenneth Scott. *Beginnings to 1500*, vol. 1 of *A History of Christianity*. San Francisco: Harper San Francisco, 1975.

Raymond of Capua. *The Life of St. Catherine of Siena*. Translated by George Lamb. New York: P. J. Kennedy & Sons, 1960.

WEB SITE:

The Dialogues of St. Catherine of Siena:
http://ccel.wheaton.edu/catherine/dialog/dialog.html

19: Inventors of the visual language of the Renaissance: Brunelleschi, Donatello, Masaccio

Freemantle, Richard. *Masaccio: The Complete Paintings by the Master of Perspective*. New York: Smithmark Publishers, 1998.

Grafton, Anthony. *Leon Battista Alberti: Master Builder of the Italian Renaissance*. New York: Hill and Wang, 2000.

Heydenreich, Ludwig H. *Architecture in Italy 1400–1500*. New Haven: Yale University Press, 1996.

Johnson, Paul. *The Renaissance: A Short History*. New York: Modern Library, 2000.

King, Ross. *Brunelleschi's Dome*. New York: Walker & Company, 2000.

Levey, Michael. *Florence: A Portrait*. Cambridge, Mass.: Harvard University Press, 1996.

Olson, Roberta J. M. *Italian Renaissance Sculpture*. London: Thames and Hudson, 1992.

Pope-Hennessy, John. *Italian Renaissance Sculpture*. 4th ed. London: Phaidon Press Limited, 1996.

Toman, Rolf, ed. *The Art of the Italian Renaissance: Architecture, Sculpture, Painting, Drawing*. Cologne, Germany: Könemann, 1995.

Vasari, Giorgio. *Lives of the Artists*. Vol. 1. Translated by George Bull. London: Penguin Books, 1987.

Wirtz, Rolf C. *Donatello*. Cologne, Germany: Könemann, 1998.

WEB SITE:

http://www.christusrex.org/www2/art/masaccio.htm

20: Lorenzo Ghiberti and the "Gates of Paradise"

Levey, Michael. *Florence: A Portrait*. Cambridge, Mass.: Harvard University Press, 1996.

Toman, Rolf, ed. *The Art of the Italian Renaissance: Architecture, Sculpture, Painting, Drawing*. Cologne, Germany: Könemann, 1995.

Vasari, Giorgio. "Life of Lorenzo Ghiberti." In *Lives of the Artists*. Vol. 1. Translated by George Bull. London: Penguin Books, 1987, pp. 105–23.

Welch, Evelyn. *Art and Society in Italy, 1350–1500*. New York: Oxford University Press, 1997.

21: Cosimo and Lorenzo de' Medici, grand patrons of art and learning

Hibbert, Christopher. *Florence: The Biography of a City*. London: Folio Society, 1997.

————. *The House of the Medici: Its Rise and Fall*. New York: Morrow Quill Paperbacks, 1980.

Hood, William. *Fra Angelico at San Marco*. New Haven: Yale University Press, 1993.

Kent, Dale. *Cosimo de' Medici and the Florentine Renaissance*. New Haven: Yale University Press, 2000.

Kristeller, Paul Oskar. "Ficino" and "Pico." In *Eight Philosophers of the Italian Renaissance*. Stanford, Calif.: Stanford University Press, 1964, pp. 37–71.

————. "The Platonic Academy of Florence." In *Renaissance Thought: Papers on Humanism and the Arts*. Vol. 2. New York: Harper Torchbooks, 1965, pp. 89–101.

Levey, Michael. *Florence: A Portrait*. Cambridge, Mass.: Harvard University Press, 1996.

Roeder, Ralph. "Lorenzo de' Medici." In *The Italian Renaissance*, edited by J. H. Plumb. Boston: Houghton Mifflin Company, 1961, pp. 207–21.

Schevill, Ferdinand. *The Age of the Medici and the Coming of Humanism*, vol. 2 of *Medieval and Renaissance Florence*. New York: Harper Torchbooks, 1961.

————. *The Medici*. New York: Harper Torchbooks, 1960; 1949.

Welch, Evelyn. *Art and Society in Italy, 1350–1500*. New York: Oxford University Press, 1997.

Young, G. F. *The Medici*. New York: Modern Library, 1930.

22: Sigismondo Malatesta: The condottiere with a vision

Grafton, Anthony. *Leon Battista Alberti: Master Builder of the Italian Renaissance*. New York: Hill and Wang, 2000.

Jones, P. J. *The Malatesta of Rimini and the Papal State: A Political History*. London: Cambridge University Press, 1974.

Pope-Hennessy, John. "Agostino di Duccio and the Tempio Malatestiano." In *An Introduction to Italian Sculpture*, vol. 2 of *Italian Renaissance Sculpture*. 4th ed. London: Phaidon Press Limited, 1996, pp. 243–55, 388–90.

Pound, Ezra. "Cantos VIII–XI" ["The Malatesta Cantos"]. In *The Cantos of Ezra Pound*. New York: New Directions, 1972, pp. 28–52.

Stokes, Adrian. *Stones of Rimini*. New York: Schocken Books, 1988; 1934.

WEB SITES:

A Photo Essay on Sigismondo Malatesta and the *Tempio Malatestiano*:
http://www.english.uiuc.edu/maps/poets/m_r/pound/tempio.htm
Web Gallery of Art: Agostino di Duccio:
http://www.kfki.hu/~arthp/html/d/duccio/agostino/index.html

23: Leonardo da Vinci: Renaissance man, eternal enigma

Bramly, Serge. *Leonardo: The Artist and the Man*. London: Penguin Books, 1994.

Clark, Kenneth. *Leonardo da Vinci*. London: Penguin Books, 1988.

Freud, Sigmund. *Leonardo da Vinci: A Study in Psychosexuality*. Translated by A. A. Brill. New York: Vintage Books, 1947.

Johnson, Paul. *The Renaissance: A Short History*. New York: Modern Library, 2000.

Marani, Pietro C. *Leonardo da Vinci: The Complete Paintings*. Translated by A. Lawrence Jenkens. New York: Harry N. Abrams, Inc., 2000.

Masters, Roger D. *Fortune Is a River: Leonardo da Vinci and Niccolò Machiavelli's Magnificent Dream to Change the Course of Florentine History*. New York: Plume Books, 1998.

Richter, Jean Paul, ed. *The Notebooks of Leonardo da Vinci*. 2 vols. New York: Dover Press, 1970.

Vezzosi, Alessandro. *Leonardo da Vinci: The Mind of the Renaissance*. New York: Harry N. Abrams, 1997.

24: A new world beckons: Columbus, Cabot, Vespucci, Verrazano

Boorstin, Daniel J. *The Discoverers*. New York: Vintage Books, 1985, pp. 115–254.

Columbus, Christopher. *The Four Voyages*. Translated by J. M. Cohen. London: Penguin Books, 1969.

Morison, Samuel Eliot. *The Great Explorers: The European Discovery of America*. New York: Oxford University Press, 1978.

Rubin, Nancy. *Isabella of Castile: The First Renaissance Queen*. New York: St. Martin's Press, 1991.

25: Machiavelli and the dawn of modern political science

Chabod, Federico. *Machiavelli and the Renaissance*. New York: Harper and Row, 1958.

Eliot, T. S. "Niccolo Machiavelli." In *For Lancelot Andrewes: Essays on Style and Order*. Garden City, N.Y.: Doubleday, Doran and Company, Inc., 1929.

Hale, J. R. *Machiavelli and Renaissance Italy*. New York: Collier Books, 1960.

Machiavelli, Niccolò. *The Discourses*. Edited by Bernard Crick. New York: Penguin Books USA, 1970.

———. *The History of Florence and Other Selections*. Edited by Myron P. Gilmore. New York: Washington Square Press, 1970.

———. *The Portable Machiavelli*. Edited and translated by Peter Bondanella and Mark Musa. New York: Viking Press, 1983.

———. *The Prince*. Translated by George Bull. New York: Penguin USA, 1961.

———. *The Prince*. Translated by Daniel Donno. New York: Bantam Classics, 1984.

Praz, Mario. "'The Politic Brain': Machiavelli and the Elizabethans." In *The Flaming Heart: Essays on Crashaw, Machiavelli, and Other Studies in the Relations between Italian and English Literature from Chaucer to T. S. Eliot*. New York: W. W. Norton and Company, 1973; 1958, pp. 90–145.

Roeder, Ralph. *The Man of the Renaissance: Four Lawgivers: Savonarola, Machiavelli, Castiglione, Aretino*. New York: Time Inc., 1966; 1933.

Ruffo-Fiore, Silvia. *Niccolò Machiavelli*. Boston: Twayne Publishers, 1982.

Viroli, Maurizio. *Niccolò's Smile: A Biography of Machiavelli*. Translated by Antony Shugaar. New York: Farrar, Straus and Giroux, 2000.

26: Michelangelo: Epitome of human artistry

Boorstin, Daniel J. "'Divine Michelangelo.'" In *The Creators*. New York: Random House, 1992, pp. 407–19.

Clark, Kenneth. *The Nude: A Study in Ideal Form*. Princeton, N.J.: Princeton University Press, 1956.

———. "The Young Michelangelo." In *The Italian Renaissance*, edited by J. H. Plumb. Boston: Houghton Mifflin Company, 1987; 1961, pp. 192–205.

Hartt, Frederick. *History of Italian Renaissance Art: Painting, Sculpture, Architecture*. 4th ed. Revised by David G. Wilkins. New York: Harry N. Abrams, Inc., Publishers, 1994.

———. *Michelangelo*. New York: Harry N. Abrams, Inc., Publishers, n.d. [1964].

Levey, Michael. *Florence: A Portrait*. Cambridge, Mass.: Harvard University Press, 1996.

Michelangelo. *The Complete Poems of Michelangelo*. Verse translation by John Frederick Nims. Chicago: University of Chicago Press, 1998.

———. *The Complete Poems of Michelangelo*. Verse translation by Joseph Tusiani. New York: Noonday Press, 1960.

———. *The Complete Poetry of Michelangelo*. Verse translation by Sidney Alexander. Athens, Ohio: Ohio University Press, 1993.

———. *The Sonnets of Michelangelo*. Verse translation by Elizabeth Jennings. Garden City, N.Y.: Doubleday and Company, 1970.

Murray, Linda. *Michelangelo: His Life, Work, and Times*. New York: Thames and Hudson, 1984.

Pater, Walter. "The Poetry of Michelangelo." In *The Renaissance*. New York: Mentor Books, 1959; 1873, pp. 59–73.

Vasari, Giorgio. "Life of Michelangelo Buonarroti." In *Lives of the Artists*. Vol. 1. Translated by George Bull. London: Penguin Books, 1987, pp. 325–442.

WEB SITES:

Exploring the Sistine Chapel Ceiling:
http://www.science.wayne.edu/~mcogan/Humanities/Sistine/index.html
1,200 Years of Italian Sculpture: The Renaissance Period:
http://www.thais.it/scultura/rinascim.htm

27: *Sprezzatura* and Castiglione's concept of the gentleman

Burke, Peter. *The Fortunes of the* Courtier: *The European Reception of Castiglione's* Cortegiano. University Park, Penn.: Pennsylvania State University Press, 1995.

Castiglione, Baldassare. *The Book of the Courtier*. Translated by George Bull. New York: Penguin Books, 1967.

———. *The Book of the Courtier*. Translated by Charles S. Singleton. New York: Anchor Books, 1959.

Norwich, John Julius, ed. *The Italians: History, Art, and the Genius of a People*. New York: Portland House, 1989, pp. 137–44.

Roeder, Ralph. *The Man of the Renaissance: Four Lawgivers: Savonarola, Machiavelli, Castiglione, Aretino*. New York: Time Inc., 1966; 1933, pp. 201–455.

28: Aretino: Self-publicist, pornographer, "secretary of the world"

Aretino, Pietro. *Aretino's Dialogues*. Translated by Raymond Rosenthal. New York: Ballantine Books, 1971.

————. *Selected Letters*. Translated by George Bull. New York: Penguin Books, 1976.

Roeder, Ralph. *The Man of the Renaissance: Four Lawgivers: Savonarola, Machiavelli, Castiglione, Aretino*. New York: Time Inc., 1966; 1933, pp. 457–502.

Rowland, Ingrid. "When in Rome . . ." *New York Review of Books* 47 (June 15, 2000): 36–40.

Symonds, John Addington. *Renaissance in Italy: Italian Literature in Two Parts*. Part 2. New York: Capricorn Books, 1964; 1881, pp. 149–57, 326–27, 336–75.

29: Giovanni Della Casa's *Galateo*: Etiquette book par excellence

Della Casa, Giovanni. *Galateo*. Translated by Konrad Eisenbichler. Asheville, N.C.: Pegasus Press, 1986.

Symonds, John Addington. *Renaissance in Italy: Italian Literature in Two Parts*. Part 2. New York: Capricorn Books, 1964; 1881, pp. 238–44.

30: Andrea Palladio and his "bible" of building

Alberti, Leon Battista. *The Ten Books of Architecture: The 1755 Leoni Edition*. New York: Dover Publications, Inc., 1986.

Jestaz, Bertrand. *Architecture of the Renaissance: From Brunelleschi to Palladio*. Translated by Caroline Beamish. New York: Harry N. Abrams, Inc., 1996.

Muraro, Michelangelo, and Paolo Marton. *Venetian Villas*. Translated by Peter Lauritzen, et al. Cologne, Germany: Könemann, 1986.

Murray, Peter. *The Architecture of the Italian Renaissance*. New York: Schocken Books, 1986.

Palladio, Andrea. *The Four Books of Architecture*. Translated by Isaac Ware. New York: Dover Publications, Inc., 1965.

Pevsner, Nikolaus. *An Outline of European Architecture*. Baltimore: Penguin Books, 1972.

Tavernor, Robert. *Palladio and Palladianism*. London: Thames and Hudson, 1991.

Vitruvius. *The Ten Books on Architecture*. Translated by Morris Hicky Morgan. New York: Dover Publications, Inc., 1960.

WEB SITE:

http://andrea.gsd.harvard.edu/palladio/bldgs97b.html

31: Catherine de' Medici: Godmother of French cuisine

Ballerini, Luigi. "Catherine de' Medici." *La Cucina Italiana* (May/June 1999): 90–91.

David, Elizabeth. *Italian Food*. New York: Penguin Books, 1999; 1954.

Della Cinqueterre, Berengario. *The Renaissance Cookbook: Historical Perspectives Through Cookery*. Crown Point, Ind.: Dunes Press, 1975.

Hale, William Harlan. *The Horizon Cookbook and Illustrated History of Eating and Drinking Through the Ages*. New York: American Heritage, 1968.

Knecht, R. J. *Catherine de' Medici*. New York: Longman, 1998.

Mennell, Stephen. *All Manners of Food: Eating and Taste in England and France from the Middle Ages to the Present*. New York: Basil Blackwell, Inc., 1985.

Roeder, Ralph. *Catherine de' Medici and the Lost Revolution*. New York: Viking Press, 1937.

Tannahill, Reay. *Food in History*. New York: Stein and Day, 1973.

Wheaton, Barbara Ketchum. *Savoring the Past: The French Kitchen and Table from 1300 to 1789*. Philadelphia: University of Pennsylvania Press, 1983.

Young, G. F. *The Medici*. New York: Modern Library, 1930.

32: Peri's *Euridice*: The birth of opera from the spirit of tragedy

Grout, Donald Jay, and Hermine Weigel Williams. *A Short History of Opera*. New York: Columbia University Press, 1988.

Parker, Roger, ed. *The Oxford History of Opera*. Oxford, England: Oxford University Press, 1996.

Price, Curtis, ed. *Music and Society: The Early Baroque Era from the Late 16th Century to the 1660s*. Englewood Cliffs, N.J.: Prentice Hall, 1994.

Saslow, James M. *The Medici Wedding of 1589: Florentine Festival as Theatrum Mundi*. New Haven: Yale University Press, 1996.

COMPACT DISCS:

Cavalieri, Malvezzi, Bardi. La Pellegrina: *Music for the Wedding of Ferdinando de' Medici and Christine de Lorraine, Princess of France, Florence, 1589*/Vivarte. Paul Van Nevel/Huelgas Ensemble.

Peri. *Euridice*/Pavane Records. Anibal E. Cetrangolo/La Compagnia dei Febi Armonici/Ensemble Albalonga.

———. *Il Zazzerino: Music of Jacopo Peri*/Harmonia Mundi. Ellen Hargis (soprano), Paul O'Dette (chitarrone), Andrew Lawrence-King (harp), Hille Perl (lirone).

33: Galileo frames the foundations of modern science

Biagioli, Mario. *Galileo, Courtier: The Practice of Science in the Culture of Absolutism.* Chicago: University of Chicago Press, 1994.

Drake, Stillman. *Galileo at Work: His Scientific Biography.* New York: Dover, 1978.

Galilei, Galileo. *Dialogue Concerning the Two Chief World Systems.* Translated by Stillman Drake. Berkeley: University of California Press, 1967.

———. *Dialogue Concerning Two New Sciences.* Translated by Henry Crew and Alfonso de Salvio. Buffalo, N.Y.: Prometheus Books, 1991.

———. *Discoveries and Opinions of Galileo.* Translated by Stillman Drake. New York: Anchor Books, 1957.

Gould, Stephen Jay. "The Sharp-Eyed Lynx, Outfoxed by Nature." In *The Lying Stones of Marrakech.* New York: Harmony Books, 2000, pp. 27–51.

Hawking, Stephen W. *A Brief History of Time.* New York: Bantam Books, 1998.

Kuhn, Thomas S. *The Structure of Scientific Revolutions.* 3d ed. Chicago: University of Chicago Press, 1996.

Popper, Karl R. *Conjectures and Refutations.* London: Routledge, 1992.

Sobel, Dava. *Galileo's Daughter: A Historical Memoir of Science, Faith, and Love.* New York: Walker & Company, 1999.

WEB SITE:

The Galileo Project: Rice University:
http://es.rice.edu:80/ES/humsoc/Galileo

34: Two sonorous gifts: The violin and the piano

Kolneder, Walter. *The Amadeus Book of the Violin: Construction, History, Music.* Portland, Ore.: Amadeus Press, 1998.

Loesser, Arthur. *Men, Women, and Pianos: A Social History.* New York: Simon and Schuster, 1954.

Siepmann, J. *The Piano.* London: David Campbell Publishers Ltd. and EMI Records, 1996.

WEB SITES:

How Does a Violin Work?:
http://www.phys.unsw.edu.au/~jw/violin.intro.html
The International Violinmakers School of Cremona:
http://www.graffiti.it/stradivari/welcome
The Way Famous String Instruments Went:
http://www.geocities.com/Vienna/1844

35: Claudio Monteverdi, father of modern music

Carse, Adam. *The History of Orchestration*. New York: Dover Publications, 1964.

Grout, Donald Jay, and Hermine Weigel Williams. *A Short History of Opera*. New York: Columbia University Press, 1988.

Parker, Roger, ed. *The Oxford History of Opera*. Oxford, England: Oxford University Press, 1996.

Price, Curtis, ed. *Music and Society: The Early Baroque Era from the Late 16th Century to the 1660s*. Englewood Cliffs, N.J.: Prentice Hall, 1994.

Schrade, Leo. *Monteverdi: Creator of Modern Music*. New York: W. W. Norton and Company, 1950.

COMPACT DISCS:

Monteverdi. *Altri Canti*. Harmonia Mundi. Les Arts Florissants/William Christie.

————. *Arie e Lamenti per Voce Sola*. Astrée Auvidis. Montserrat Figueras.

————. *Madrigals: Quarto libro dei madrigali, Quinto libro dei madrigali*. L'Oiseau-Lyre. The Consort of Musicke/Anthony Rooley.

————. *Madrigaux: Livre III*. Arion. Coeli et Terra/Métamorphoses/Maurice Bourbon.

————. *L'Orfeo*. EMI Classics. Chiaroscuro/London Baroque/The London Cornett and Sackbut Ensemble.

————. *Vespro della Beata Vergine*. Erato. Les Arts Florissants/William Christie.

36: The Baroque splendors of Bernini

Baldinucci, Filippo. *The Life of Bernini*. University Park, Penn.: Pennsylvania State University Press, 1966.

Hibbard, Howard. *Bernini*. London: Penguin Books, 1965.

Marder, T. A. *Bernini and the Art of Architecture*. New York: Abbeville Press, 1998.

Wittkower, Rudolf. *Bernini: The Sculptor of the Roman Baroque.* 4th ed. London: Phaidon Press, 1997.

37: Pioneers of modern anatomy: Eustachio, Fallopio, Malpighi, Morgagni, et al.

Boorstin, Daniel J. *The Discoverers.* New York: Vintage Books, 1985, pp. 376–83.

Clendering, Logan. *Source Book of Medical History.* New York: Dover Publications, 1960.

Conrad, Lawrence I., Michael Neve, Vivian Nutton, Roy Porter, and Andrew Wear. *The Western Medical Tradition: 800 B.C. to A.D. 1800.* Cambridge, England: Cambridge University Press, 1995.

Freedman, Meyer, and Gerald W. Friedland. *Medicine's 10 Greatest Discoveries.* New Haven: Yale University Press, 1998.

Garrison, Fielding H. *An Introduction to the History of Medicine.* 4th ed. Philadelphia: W. B. Saunders Company, 1929.

Siraisi, Nancy G. *Medieval and Early Renaissance Medicine: An Introduction to Knowledge and Practice.* Chicago: University of Chicago Press, 1990.

38: Founder of modern penology: Cesare Beccaria

Beccaria, Cesare. *On Crimes and Punishments.* Translated by Henry Paolucci. Englewood Cliffs, N.J.: Prentice Hall, 1963.

Voltaire. "Commentary on the Book *On Crimes and Punishments,* by a Provincial Lawyer." In *Voltaire: Political Writings,* edited by David Williams. New York: Cambridge University Press, 1994, pp. 244–79.

39: Trailblazers in electricity: Galvani and Volta

Dibner, Bern. *Galvani-Volta: A Controversy That Led to the Discovery of Useful Electricity.* Norwalk, Conn.: Burndy Library, 1952.

———. *Luigi Galvani.* Norwalk, Conn.: Burndy Library, 1971.

40: Venice: Rhapsody in stone, water, melody, and color

Aikema, Bernard, and Beverly Louise Brown, eds. *Renaissance Venice and the North: Crosscurrents in the Time of Bellini, Dürer, and Titian.* New York: Rizzoli, 1999.

Boccazzi-Varotto, Attilio. *Venice 360°.* New York: Random House, 1987.

Harrison, Barbara Grizzuti. "Venice: 'Mirror of Water.'" In *Italian Days*. New York: Atlantic Monthly Press, 1989, pp. 89–117.

Hartt, Frederick. *History of Italian Renaissance Art: Painting, Sculpture, Architecture.* 4th ed. Revised by David G. Wilkins. New York: Harry N. Abrams, Inc., Publishers, 1994, pp. 378–471, 582–630.

Hibbert, Christopher. *Venice: The Biography of a City.* London: The Folio Society, 1988.

Muraro, Michelangelo, and Paolo Marton. *Venetian Villas.* Translated by Peter Lauritzen, et al. Cologne, Germany: Könemann, 1986.

Nepi, Giovanna Scirè. *Treasures of Venetian Painting: The Gallerie dell'Accademia.* New York: The Vendome Press, 1991.

Norwich, John Julius. *A History of Venice.* New York: Vintage Books, 1982.

Steer, John. *A Concise History of Venetian Painting.* London: Thames and Hudson, 1970.

Villehardouin, Geoffroy de. *The Conquest of Constantinople.* In Jean de Joinville and Geoffroy de Villehardouin, *Chronicles of the Crusades.* Translated by M. R. B. Shaw. New York: Penguin Books, 1963.

Zuffi, Stefano. *Titian.* Translated by Sylvia Tombesi-Walton. London: Dorling Kindersley, 1998.

41: Europe's premier poet of pessimism: Giacomo Leopardi

Leopardi, Giacomo. *The Canti with a Selection of His Prose.* Translated by J. G. Nichols. Manchester, England: Carcanet Press, 1998.

————. *Operette Morali: Essays and Dialogues.* Translated by Giovanni Cecchetti with facing Italian text. Berkeley, Calif.: University of California Press, 1982.

————. *Selected Poems.* Verse translation by Eamon Grennan. Princeton, N.J.: Princeton University Press, 1997.

Origo, Iris. *Leopardi: A Study in Solitude.* N.p.: Books & Co. / Helen Marx Books, 1999; 1953.

Parks, Tim. "In Love with Leopardi." *New York Review of Books* 47 (March 23, 2000): 38–41.

42: Giuseppe Garibaldi: A united Italy emerges

Albrecht-Carrié, René. "Italy Becomes a National State." In *Italy from Napoleon to Mussolini.* New York: Columbia University Press, 1950, pp. 25–47.

Davis, John A. "Italy 1796–1870: The Age of the Risorgimento." In *The Oxford History of Italy*, edited by George Holmes. Oxford, England: Oxford University Press, 1997, pp. 177–209.

Mack Smith, Denis. *Garibaldi: A Great Life in Brief*. New York: Alfred A. Knopf, 1968; 1956.

———. *Italy: A Modern History*. Rev. ed. Ann Arbor, Mich.: University of Michigan Press, 1969.

———. *The Making of Italy, 1796–1866*. 2d ed. New York: Holmes and Meier Publishers, Inc., 1988.

43: The last "Renaissance" prince—D'Annunzio at Fiume

Albrecht-Carrié, René. *Italy from Napoleon to Mussolini*. New York: Columbia University Press, 1950, pp. 83–86, 95–98, 107–47.

Glenny, Misha. *The Balkans: Nationalism, War, and the Great Powers, 1804–1999*. New York: Viking, 1999, pp. 369–77.

Ledeen, Michael A. *The First Duce: D'Annunzio at Fiume*. Baltimore: The Johns Hopkins University Press, 1977.

Mack Smith, Denis. *Italy: A Modern History*. Rev. ed. Ann Arbor, Mich.: University of Michigan Press, 1969.

Pacifici, Sergio. "Gabriele d'Annunzio: The Birth of Superman." In *From Capuana to Tozzi*, vol. 2 of *The Modern Italian Novel*. Carbondale, Ill.: Southern Illinois University Press, 1973, pp. 32–48.

WEB SITE:

Il Vittoriale degli Italiani (D'Annunzio's villa):
http://vittoriale.gsnet.it/inglese/HOME.htm.

44: *La Dottoressa*: Maria Montessori and a new era in early childhood education

Kramer, Rita. *Maria Montessori*. New York: G. P. Putnam's Sons, 1976.

Montessori, Maria. *The Absorbent Mind*. New York: Holt, Rinehart and Winston, 1967.

———. *The Montessori Method*. New York: Frederick A. Stokes Company, 1912.

Standing, E. M. *Maria Montessori: Her Life and Work*. New York: Plume/Penguin Books, 1984.

45: Marconi invents the radio

Gunston, David. *Guglielmo Marconi: Father of Radio*. London: Weidenfeld & Nicolson (Educational) Ltd., 1965.

Marconi, Degna. *My Father, Marconi*. Tonawanda, N.Y.: Guernica Editions, Inc., 1996.

46: Enrico Fermi: Father of the atomic age

Fermi, Laura. *Atoms in the Family: My Life with Enrico Fermi*. Chicago: University of Chicago Press, 1954.

Rhodes, Richard. "Enrico Fermi." *Time* 153 (March 29, 1999): 155–58.

Segrè, Emilio. *Enrico Fermi, Physicist*. Chicago: University of Chicago Press, 1970.

47: Roberto Rossellini: Neorealist cinema and beyond

Bondanella, Peter. *The Cinema of Federico Fellini*. Princeton, N.J.: Princeton University Press, 1992.

———. *Italian Cinema: From Neorealism to the Present*. New York: Ungar, 1985.

Brunette, Peter. *Roberto Rossellini*. Berkeley, Calif.: University of California Press, 1996.

Constantini, Costanzo. *Conversations with Fellini*. San Diego, Calif.: Harcourt Brace & Company, 1995.

Gallagher, Tag. *The Adventures of Roberto Rossellini*. New York: Da Capo Press, 1998.

Hillier, Jim, ed. *Cahiers du Cinéma: The 1950s: Neo-Realism, Hollywood, New Wave*. Cambridge, Mass.: Harvard University Press, 1986.

Rocchio, Vincent F. *Cinema of Anxiety: A Psychoanalysis of Italian Neorealism*. Austin, Tex.: University of Texas Press, 1999.

Rossellini, Robert. *My Method: Writing and Interviews*. New York: Marsilio Publishers, 1995.

Vermilye, Jerry. *Great Italian Films*. New York: Citadel Press, 1994.

48: An unlikely international bestseller: Lampedusa's *The Leopard*

Barzini, Luigi. "The Quest for Lampedusa." In *From Caesar to the Mafia*. New York: The Library Press, 1971, pp. 201–21.

Gilmour, David. *The Last Leopard: A Life of Giuseppe di Lampedusa*. New York: Pantheon Books, 1988.

Lampedusa, Giuseppe Tomasi di. *The Leopard*. Translated by Archibald Colquhoun. New York: Pantheon Books, 1991.

————. *The Leopard: With Two Stories and a Memory*. Translated by Archibald Colquhoun. New York: Everyman's Library, 1991.

————. *The Siren and Selected Writings*. Translated by Archibald Colquhoun. London: Harvill Press, 1997.

Pacifici, Sergio. "Giuseppe Tomasi di Lampedusa: The View from Within." In *From Pea to Moravia*, vol. 3 of *The Modern Italian Novel*. Carbondale, Ill.: Southern Illinois University Press, 1979, pp. 68–78.

49: Ferrari—on the road to perfection

Ferrari 1947–1997. New York: Rizzoli, 1997.

Reynolds, Bill. *Ferrari: The World's Most Exotic Sportscar*. New York: Crescent Books, 1993.

WEB SITE:

http://www.ferrarina.com.

50: *La moda italiana*: The art of apparel

Bachrach, Judy. "Armani in Full." *Vanity Fair* (October 2000): 360–98.

Celant, Germano, and Harold Koda. *Giorgio Armani*. New York: Guggenheim Museum, 2000.

Collins, Amy Fine. "Pucci's Jet-Set Revolution." *Vanity Fair* (October 2000): 378–93.

Fiori, Pamela. "Valentino." *Town and Country* (November 2000): 262–69.

Foley, Bridget. "Tom Pumps Up." *W* (July 2000): 88–95.

Forden, Sara Gay. *The House of Gucci: A Sensational Story of Murder, Madness, Glamour, and Greed*. New York: William Morrow, 2000.

Mayes, Luke. "Italian Dressing." *Cigar Aficionado* (September/October 1999).
http://www.cigaraficionado.com/Cigar/Aficionado/Archives/199910/fk1099.html.

Mendes, Valerie, and Amy de la Haye. *20th Century Fashion*. London: Thames and Hudson, 1999.

Thurman, Judith. "Man of the Cloth: Armani at the Guggenheim." *The New Yorker* (November 6, 2000): 100–3.

WEB SITES:

The Italian Academy for Advanced Studies in America at Columbia
University, Gianni Versace: History and Invention:
http://www.italianacademy.columbia.edu/lectures/gv-visul.htm
Made in Italy Online: Fashion and Design:
http://www.made-in-italy.com/fashion/fm.htm
ModaOnline Italia: http://www.modaonline.it/
Virtual Runway: http://www.virtualrunway.com/
Armani: http://www.giorgioarmani.com/giorgio_armani_docs/index.html
Cerruti: http://www.cerruti.net/
Dolce & Gabbana: http://www.dolcegabbana.it/
Ferragamo: http://www.salvatoreferragamo.it/
Gianfranco Ferré: http://www.gianfrancoferre.com/
Gucci: http://www.gucci.com/index_flash.html
Moschino: http://www.moschino.it/eng/home.html
Valentino: http://www.valentino.it/Upgrade.htm
Versace: http://www.versace.com/home.nsf

INDEX OF NAMES

ABOUT THE CONTRIBUTORS

DANTE D'EPIRO (Essays 39, 46, 49) graduated from Fordham University with a degree in psychology and lives in Westchester, New York.

RICHARD JACKSON (Essay 15) received his Ph.D. in economic history from Yale University. He lived in Italy for a year while researching a dissertation on medieval sea captains and sailors. Now a freelance writer on fiscal and economic policy, he lives in Alexandria, Virginia, with his wife, Perrine, and their son, Benjamin.

THOMAS MATRULLO (Essays 33 and 47) lived in Italy for a year before receiving a graduate degree in comparative literature from Yale University. He has worked in print and on-line media in Florida and now writes about technology, culture, and media for magazines and Internet publications.

NANCY WALSH (Essay 45) is New York bureau chief for the International Medical News Group. She lives in Ridgewood, New Jersey, with her husband, Peter D'Epiro.

Dante D'Epiro, Thomas Matrullo, and Nancy Walsh also contributed essays to *What Are the Seven Wonders of the World? and 100 Other Great Cultural Lists—Fully Explicated* (Anchor Books, 1998), coauthored by Peter D'Epiro and Mary Desmond Pinkowish.